Twin★Star Exorcists

ONMYOJI

6

STORY & ART
YOSHIAKI SUKENO

Character Introduction

Seigen Amawaka

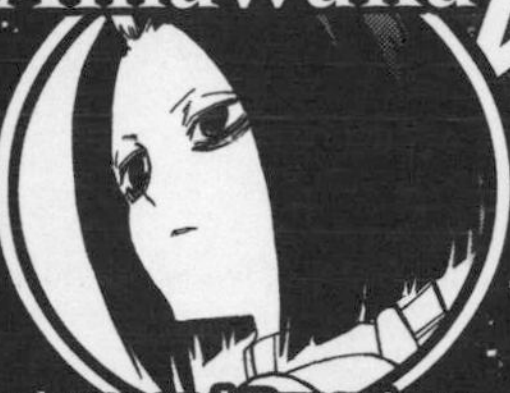

Rokuro and Ryogo's mentor. A former member of the Twelve Guardians, the strongest of the exorcists. He is also Mayura's father.

Mayura Otomi

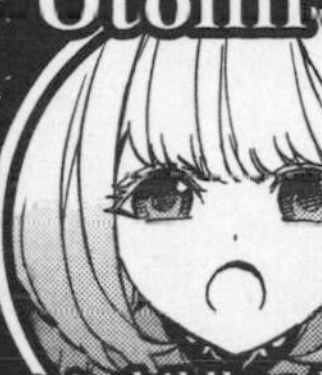

Rokuro's childhood friend, Zenkichi's granddaughter and Seigen's daughter. Does she have feelings for Rokuro...?

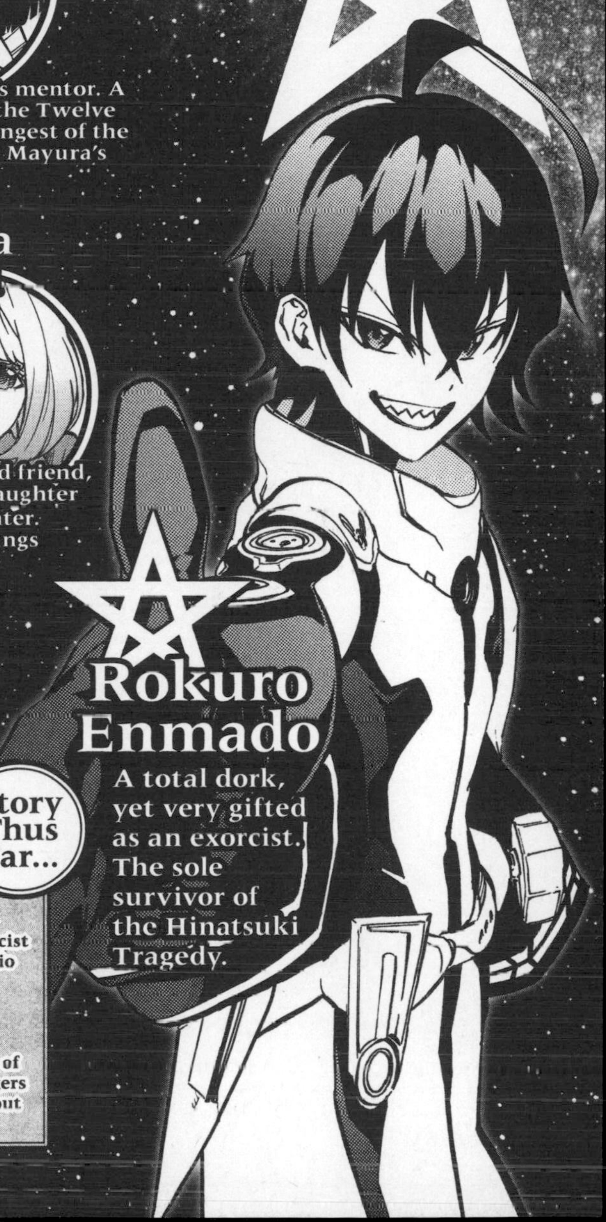

Rokuro Enmado

A total dork, yet very gifted as an exorcist. The sole survivor of the Hinatsuki Tragedy.

Story Thus Far...

Kegare are creatures from Magano, the underworld, who come to our world to spread chaos, fear and death. It is the mission of an exorcist to hunt, exorcise and purify them. Chief Exorcist Arima tells Rokuro and Benio that they are prophesied to become the Twin Star Exorcists, marry each other, and produce the Prophesied Child, the strongest exorcist of all. However, the two teenagers are far from enthusiastic about getting together...

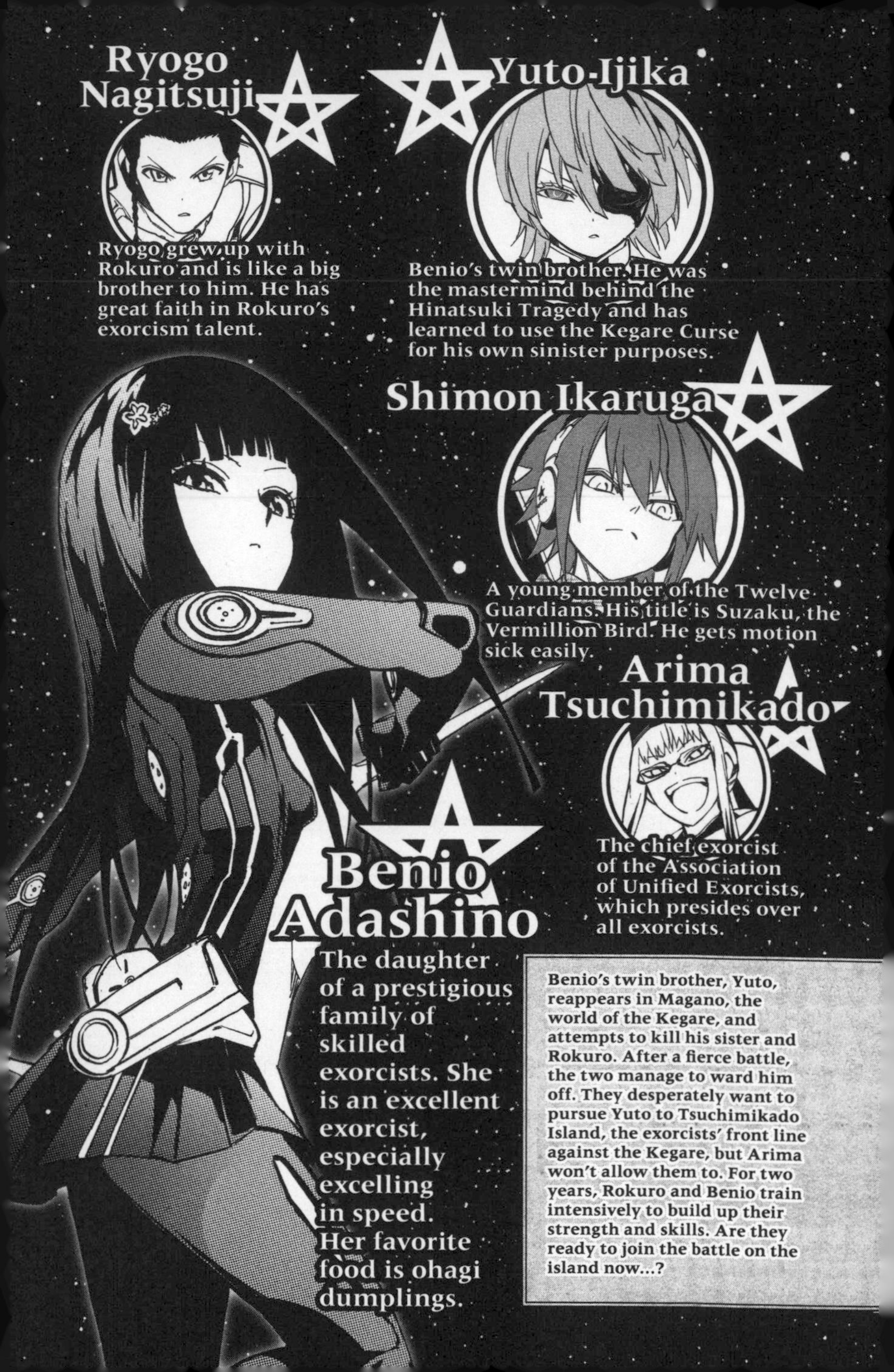
Ryogo Nagitsuji
Ryogo grew up with Rokuro and is like a big brother to him. He has great faith in Rokuro's exorcism talent.
Yuto Ijika
Benio's twin brother. He was the mastermind behind the Hinatsuki Tragedy and has learned to use the Kegare Curse for his own sinister purposes.
Shimon Ikaruga
A young member of the Twelve Guardians. His title is Suzaku, the Vermillion Bird. He gets motion sick easily.
Arima Tsuchimikado
The chief exorcist of the Association of Unified Exorcists, which presides over all exorcists.
Benio Adashino
The daughter of a prestigious family of skilled exorcists. She is an excellent exorcist, especially excelling in speed. Her favorite food is ohagi dumplings.
Benio's twin brother, Yuto, reappears in Magano, the world of the Kegare, and attempts to kill his sister and Rokuro. After a fierce battle, the two manage to ward him off. They desperately want to pursue Yuto to Tsuchimikado Island, the exorcists' front line against the Kegare, but Arima won't allow them to. For two years, Rokuro and Benio train intensively to build up their strength and skills. Are they ready to join the battle on the island now...?

Twin☆Star Exorcists

ONMYOJI

EXORCISMS

ONMYOJI have worked for the Imperial Court since the Heian era. In addition to exorcising evil spirits, as civil servants they performed a variety of roles, including advising nobles by foretelling the future, creating the calendar, observing the movements of the stars, measuring time...

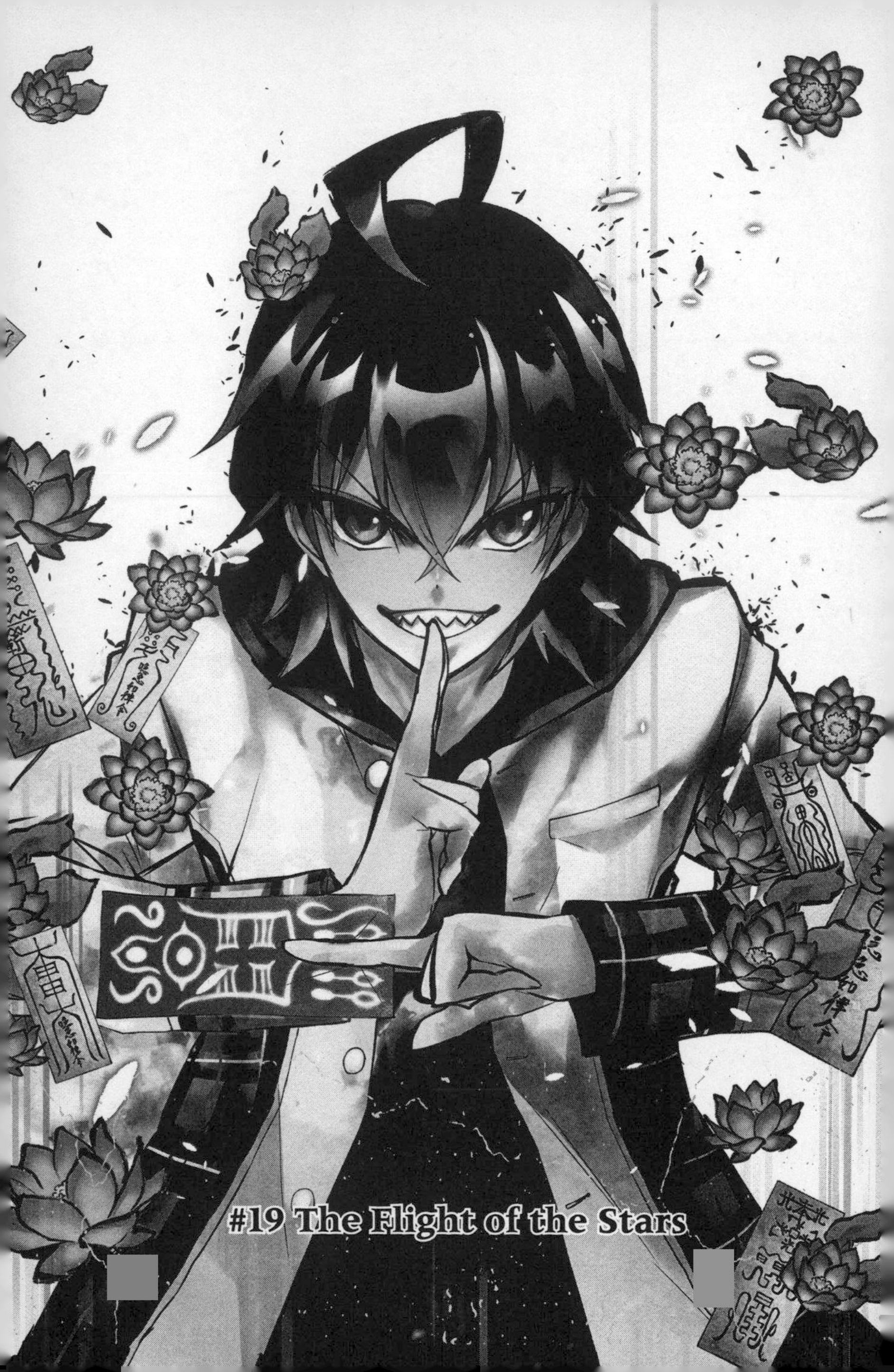
#19 The Flight of the Stars

Twin Star Exorcists

ONMYOJI

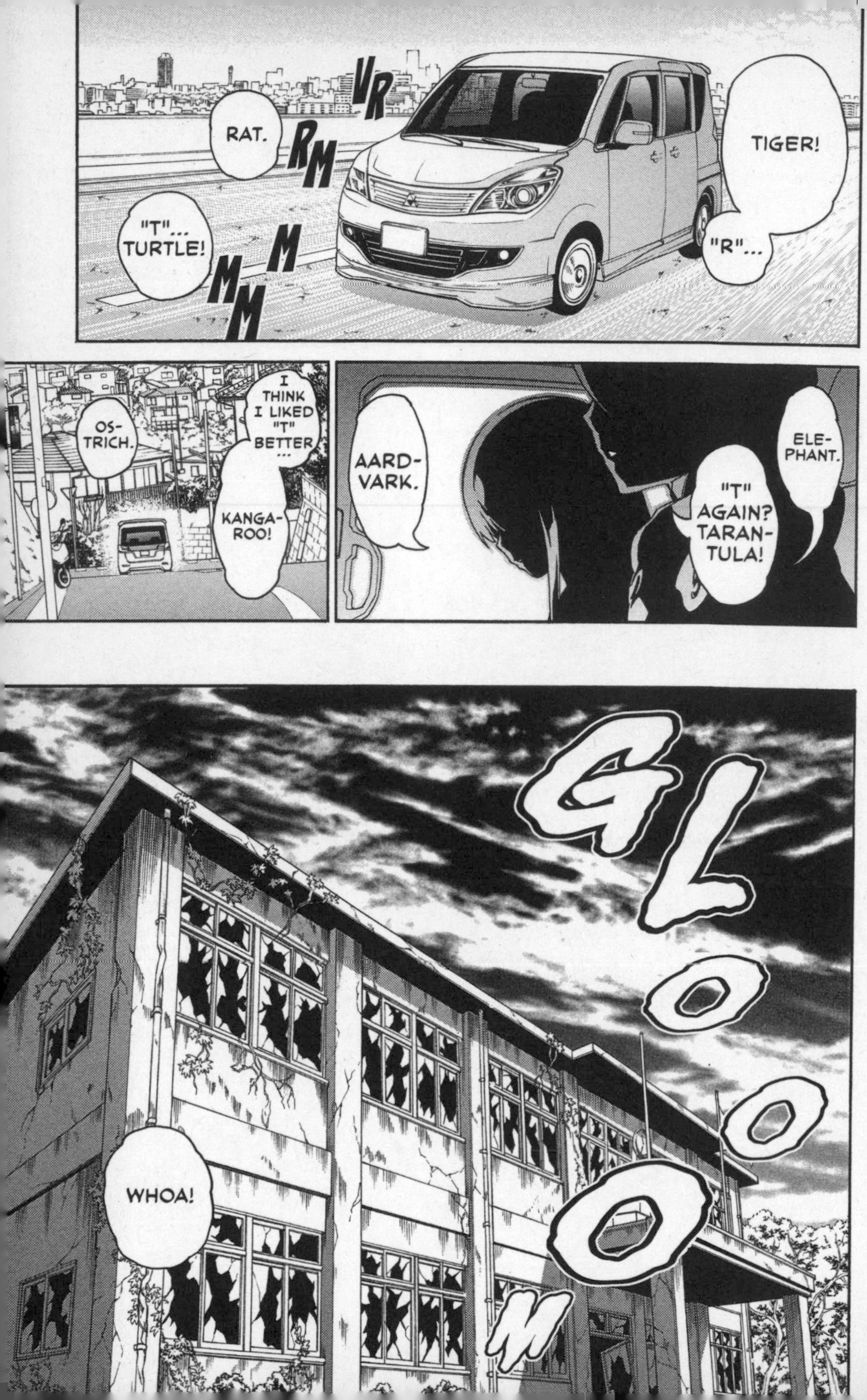
TIGER!
"R"...
RAT.
"T"... TURTLE!
VRRMMMMM
ELE-PHANT.
"T" AGAIN? TARAN-TULA!
AARD-VARK.
KANGA-ROO!
OS-TRICH.
I THINK I LIKED "T" BETTER...
GLOOOOM
WHOA!

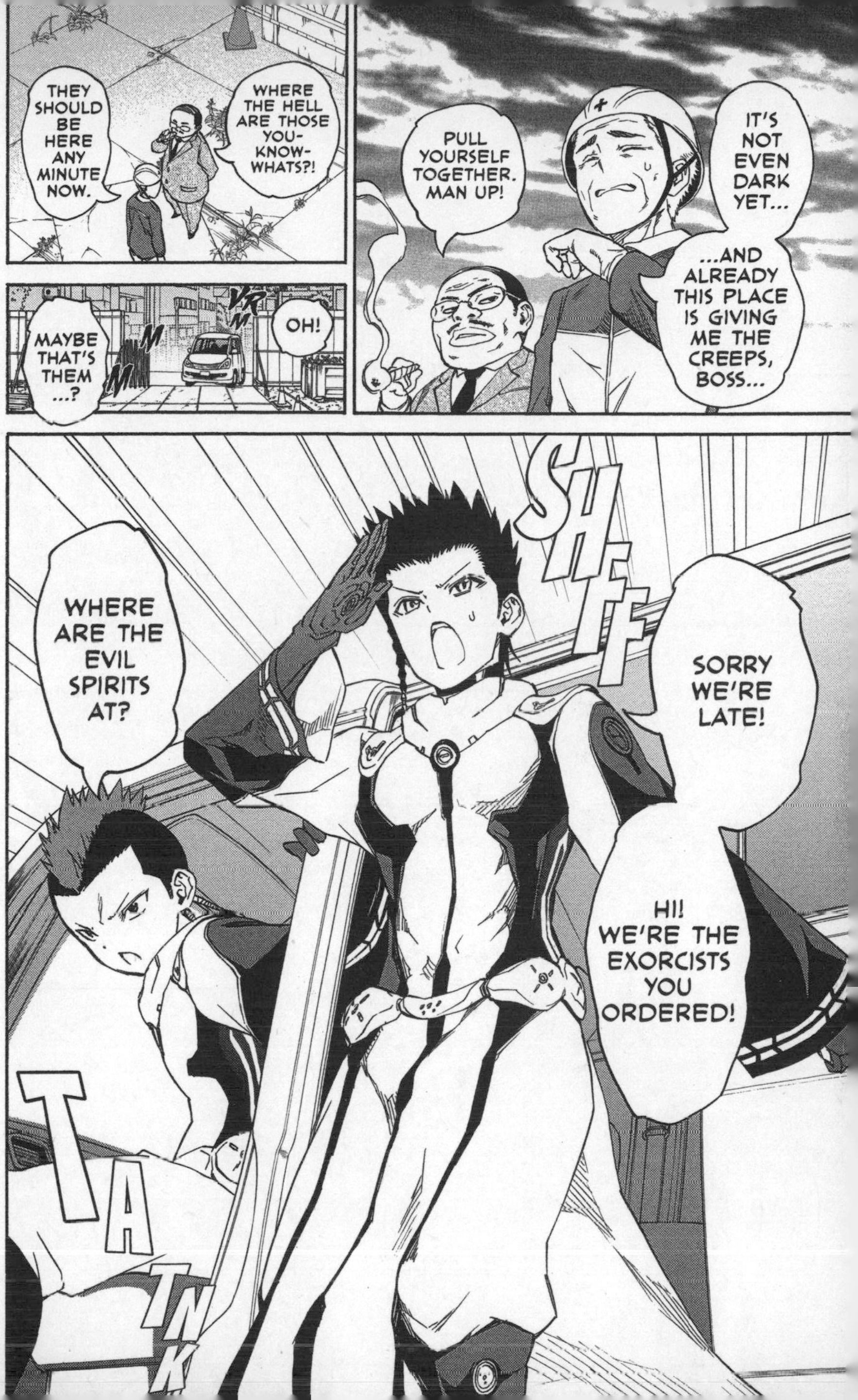
IT'S NOT EVEN DARK YET...
...AND ALREADY THIS PLACE IS GIVING ME THE CREEPS, BOSS...
PULL YOURSELF TOGETHER. MAN UP!
WHERE THE HELL ARE THOSE YOU-KNOW-WHATS?!
THEY SHOULD BE HERE ANY MINUTE NOW.
VRM
OH!
MMM
MAYBE THAT'S THEM ...?
SHFF
SORRY WE'RE LATE!
HI! WE'RE THE EXORCISTS YOU ORDERED!
WHERE ARE THE EVIL SPIRITS AT?
TA
TNK

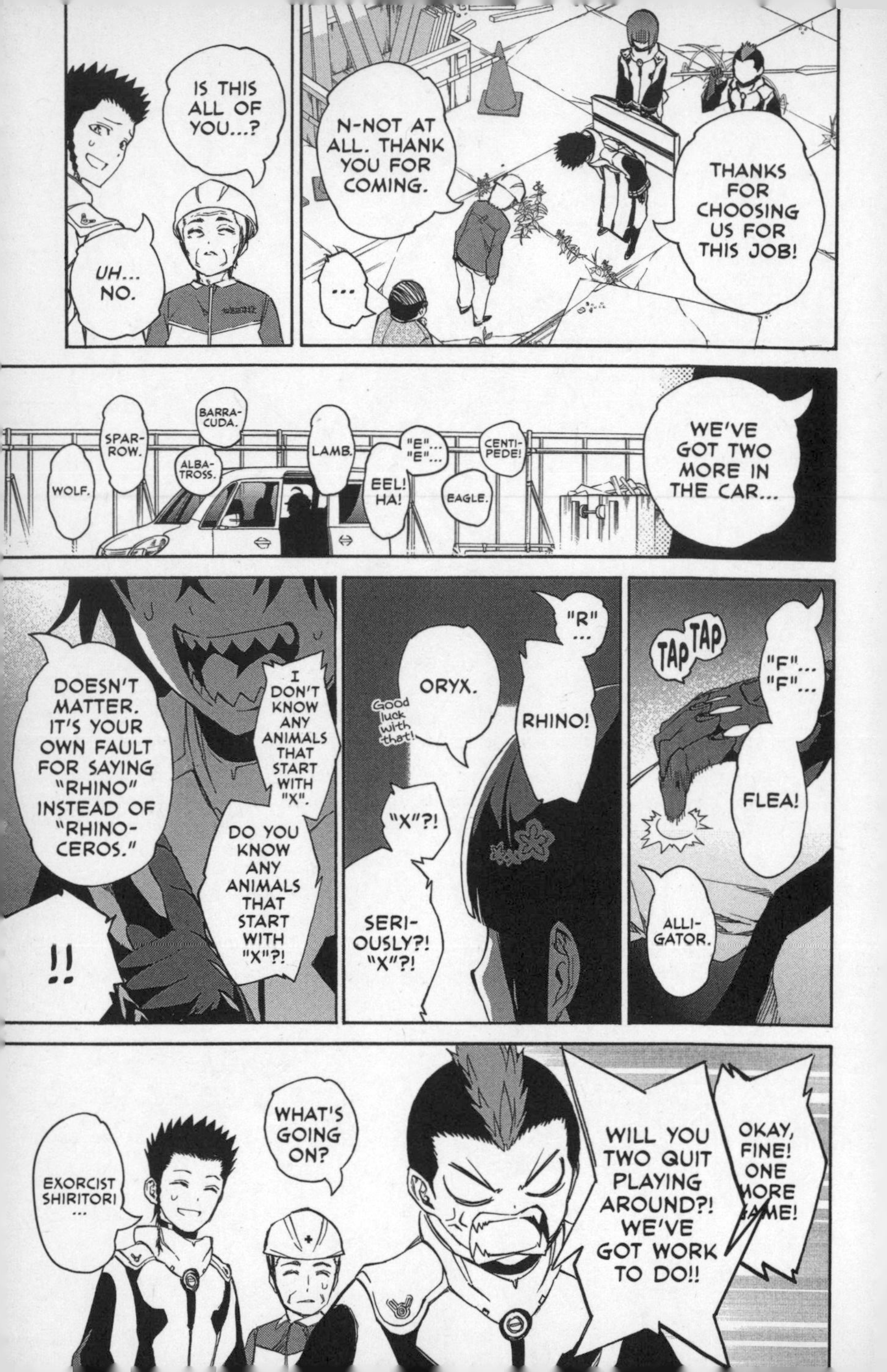
THANKS FOR CHOOSING US FOR THIS JOB!
N-NOT AT ALL. THANK YOU FOR COMING.
...
IS THIS ALL OF YOU...?
UH... NO.
WE'VE GOT TWO MORE IN THE CAR...
CENTI-PEDE!
"E"... "E"...
EAGLE.
EEL! HA!
LAMB.
BARRA-CUDA.
ALBA-TROSS.
SPAR-ROW.
WOLF.
TAP TAP
"F"... "F"...
FLEA!
ALLI-GATOR.
"R" ...
RHINO!
ORYX.
Good luck with that!
"X"?!
SERI-OUSLY?! "X"?!
I DON'T KNOW ANY ANIMALS THAT START WITH "X".
DOESN'T MATTER. IT'S YOUR OWN FAULT FOR SAYING "RHINO" INSTEAD OF "RHINO-CEROS."
DO YOU KNOW ANY ANIMALS THAT START WITH "X"?!
!!
OKAY, FINE! ONE MORE GAME!
WILL YOU TWO QUIT PLAYING AROUND?! WE'VE GOT WORK TO DO!!
WHAT'S GOING ON?
EXORCIST SHIRITORI ...

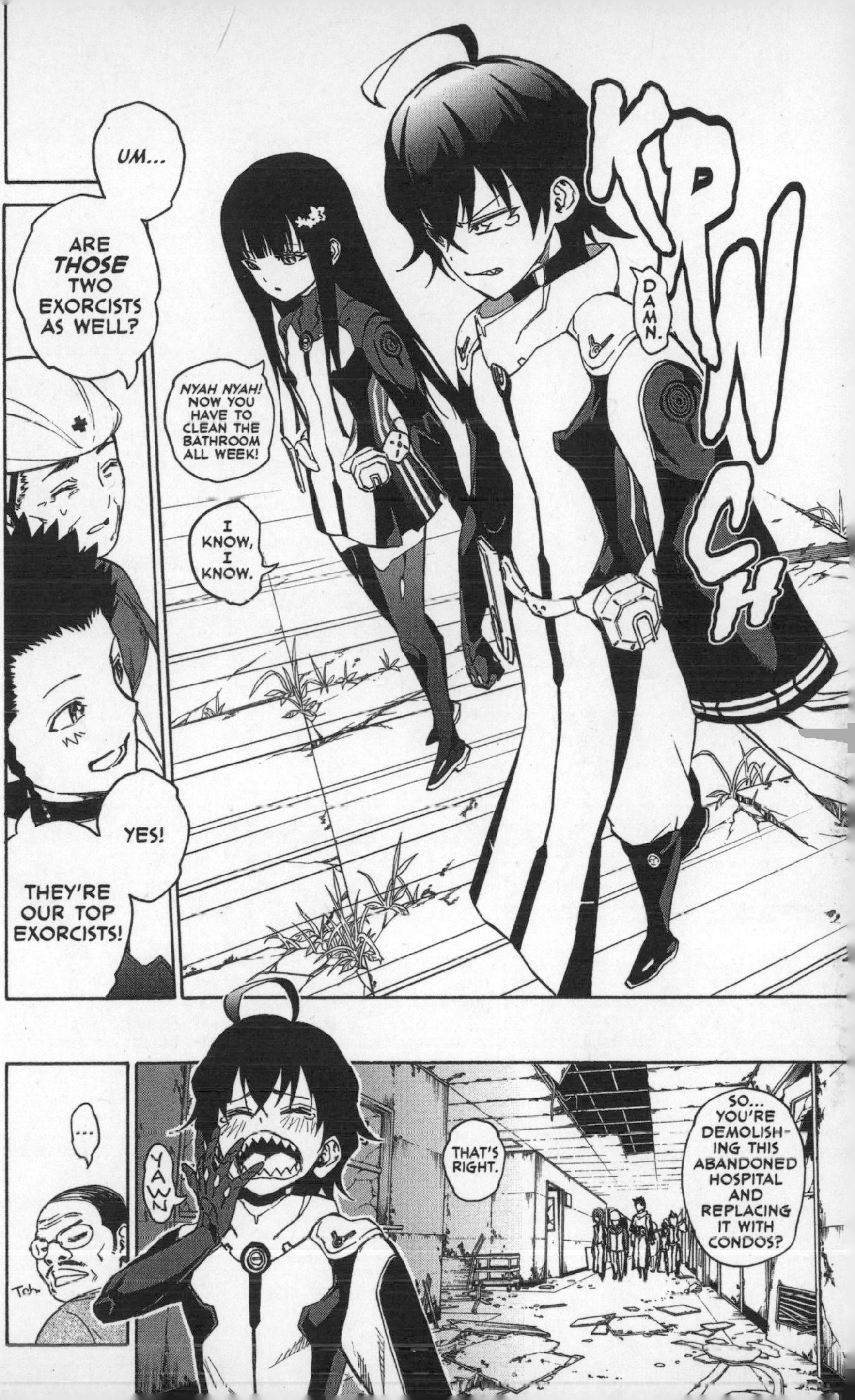
DAMN.
NYAH NYAH! NOW YOU HAVE TO CLEAN THE BATHROOM ALL WEEK!
I KNOW, I KNOW.
UM...
ARE *THOSE* TWO EXORCISTS AS WELL?
YES!
THEY'RE OUR TOP EXORCISTS!
SO... YOU'RE DEMOLISHING THIS ABANDONED HOSPITAL AND REPLACING IT WITH CONDOS?
THAT'S RIGHT.
YAWN
...
Tch

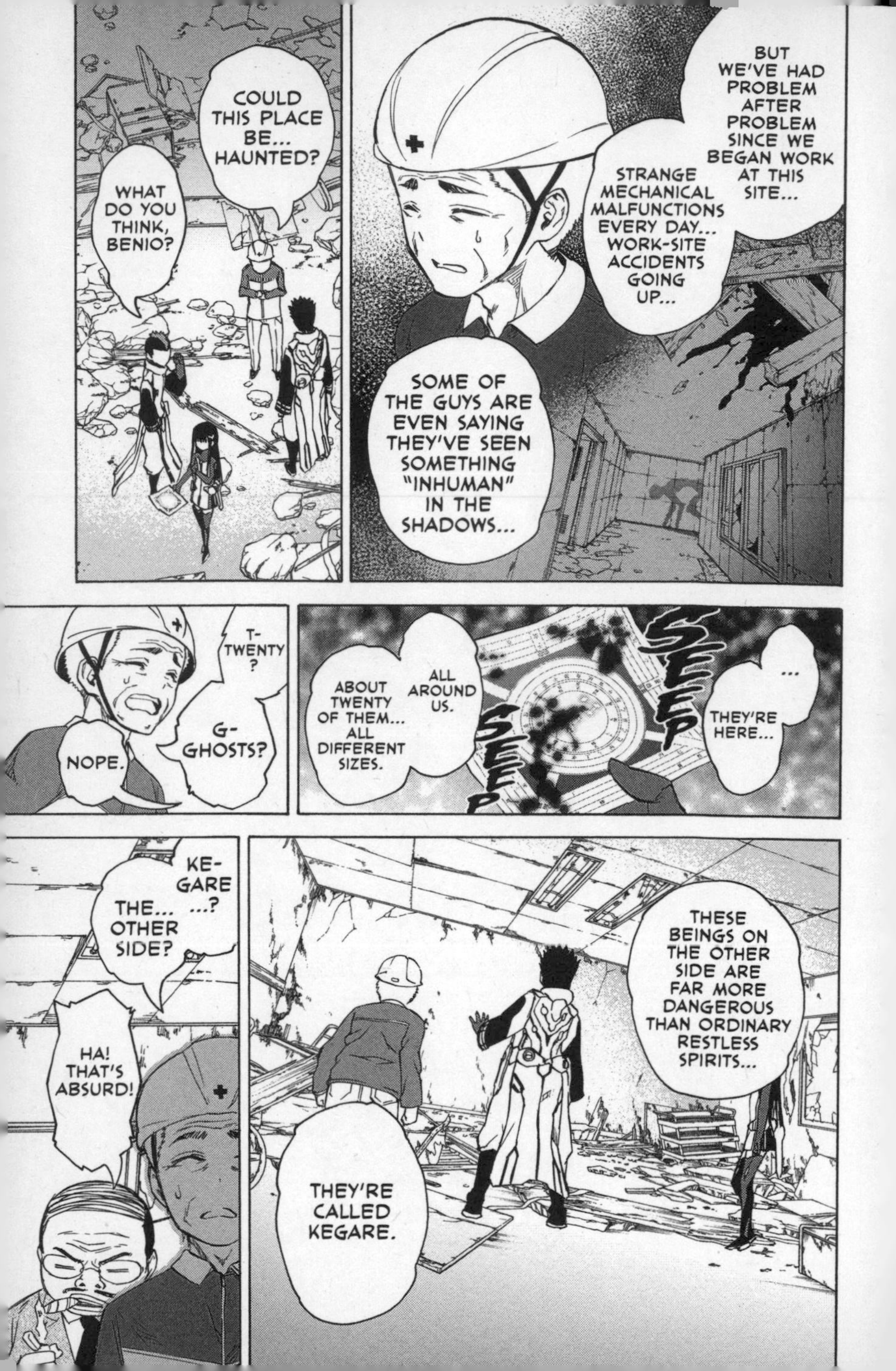
BUT WE'VE HAD PROBLEM AFTER PROBLEM SINCE WE BEGAN WORK AT THIS SITE...
STRANGE MECHANICAL MALFUNCTIONS EVERY DAY... WORK-SITE ACCIDENTS GOING UP...
SOME OF THE GUYS ARE EVEN SAYING THEY'VE SEEN SOMETHING "INHUMAN" IN THE SHADOWS...
COULD THIS PLACE BE... HAUNTED?
WHAT DO YOU THINK, BENIO?
SEEP
SEEP
...
THEY'RE HERE...
ALL AROUND US.
ABOUT TWENTY OF THEM... ALL DIFFERENT SIZES.
T-TWENTY?
G-GHOSTS?
NOPE.
THESE BEINGS ON THE OTHER SIDE ARE FAR MORE DANGEROUS THAN ORDINARY RESTLESS SPIRITS...
THEY'RE CALLED KEGARE.
KE-GARE...?
THE... OTHER SIDE?
HA! THAT'S ABSURD!

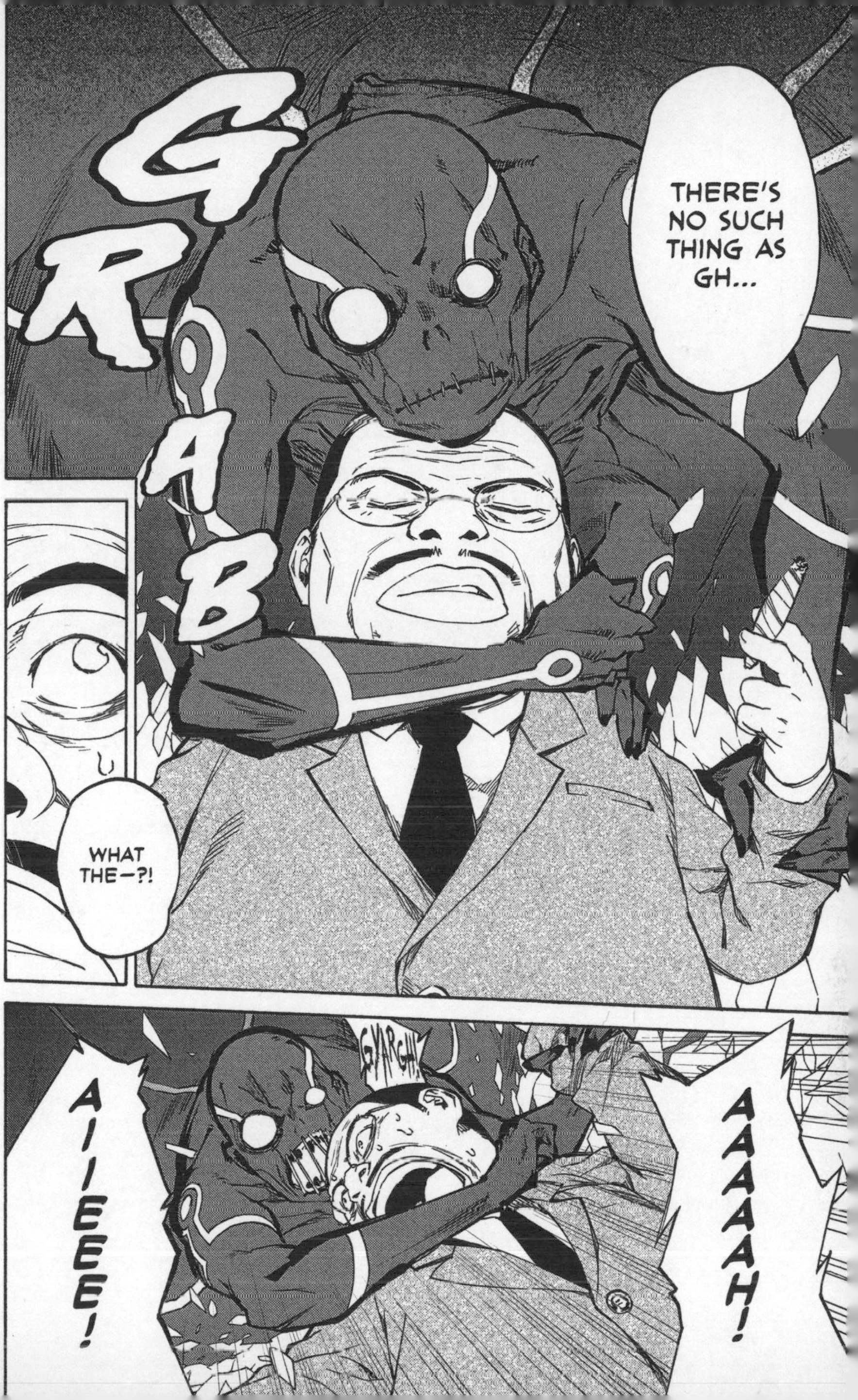
GRAB
THERE'S NO SUCH THING AS GH...
WHAT THE–?!
AAAAAH!
GYARGH!
AIIEEEE!

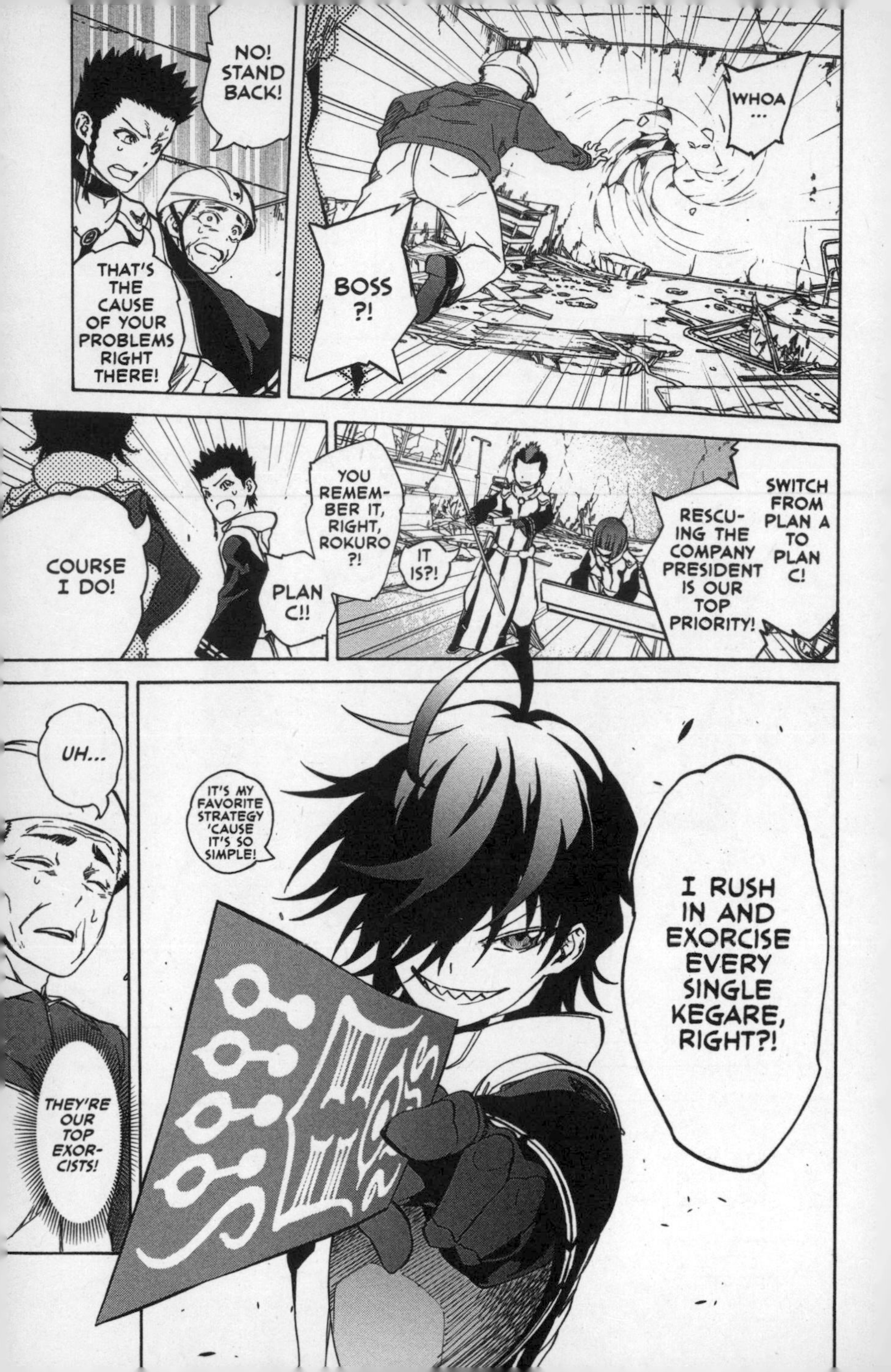
WHOA ...
BOSS ?!
NO! STAND BACK!
THAT'S THE CAUSE OF YOUR PROBLEMS RIGHT THERE!
SWITCH FROM PLAN A TO PLAN C!
RESCUING THE COMPANY PRESIDENT IS OUR TOP PRIORITY!
IT IS?!
YOU REMEMBER IT, RIGHT, ROKURO?!
PLAN C!!
COURSE I DO!
I RUSH IN AND EXORCISE EVERY SINGLE KEGARE, RIGHT?!
IT'S MY FAVORITE STRATEGY 'CAUSE IT'S SO SIMPLE!
UH...
THEY'RE OUR TOP EXORCISTS!

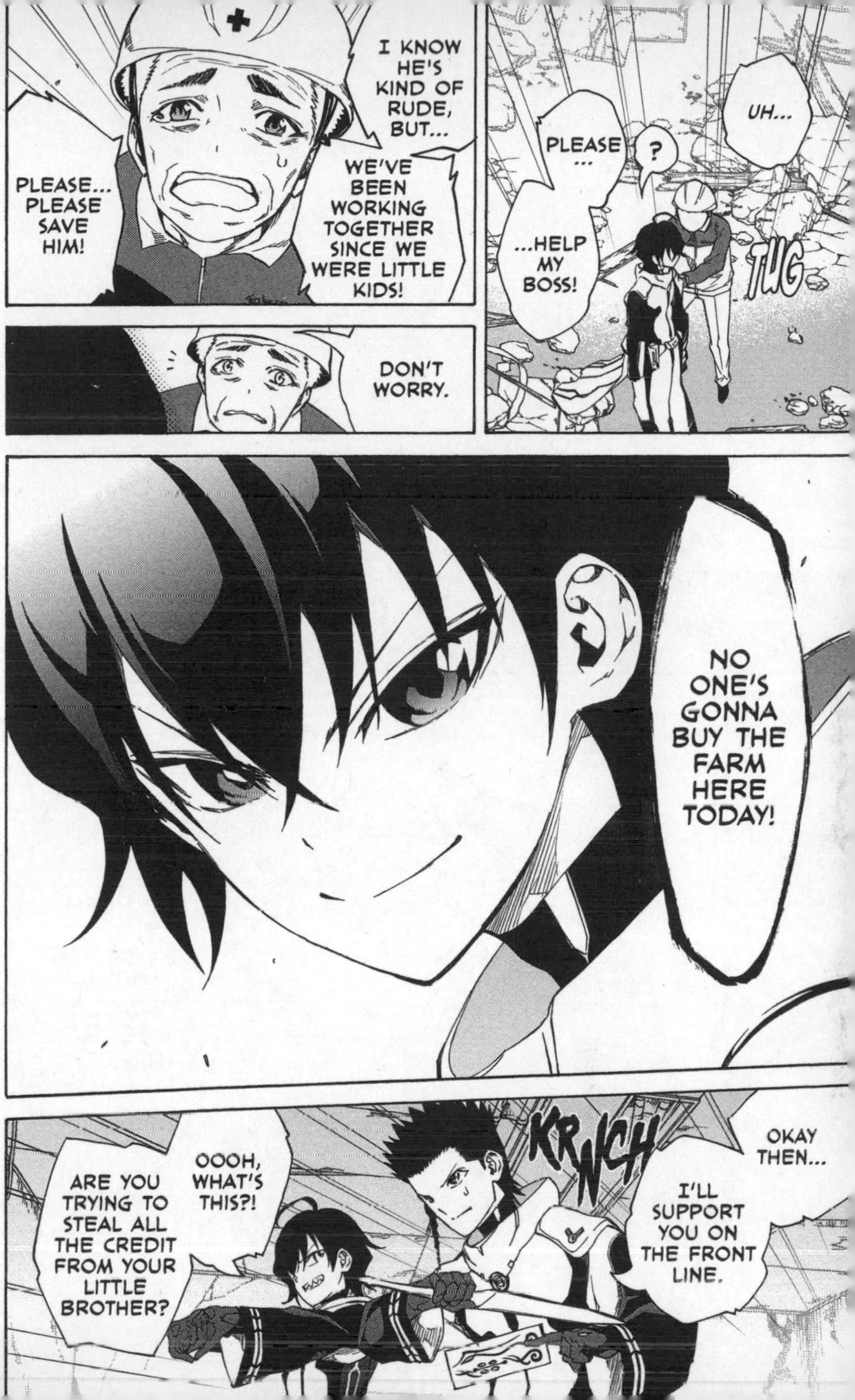
UH...
?
PLEASE ...
...HELP MY BOSS!
TUG
I KNOW HE'S KIND OF RUDE, BUT...
WE'VE BEEN WORKING TOGETHER SINCE WE WERE LITTLE KIDS!
PLEASE... PLEASE SAVE HIM!
DON'T WORRY.
NO ONE'S GONNA BUY THE FARM HERE TODAY!
OKAY THEN...
I'LL SUPPORT YOU ON THE FRONT LINE.
KRNCH
OOOH, WHAT'S THIS?!
ARE YOU TRYING TO STEAL ALL THE CREDIT FROM YOUR LITTLE BROTHER?

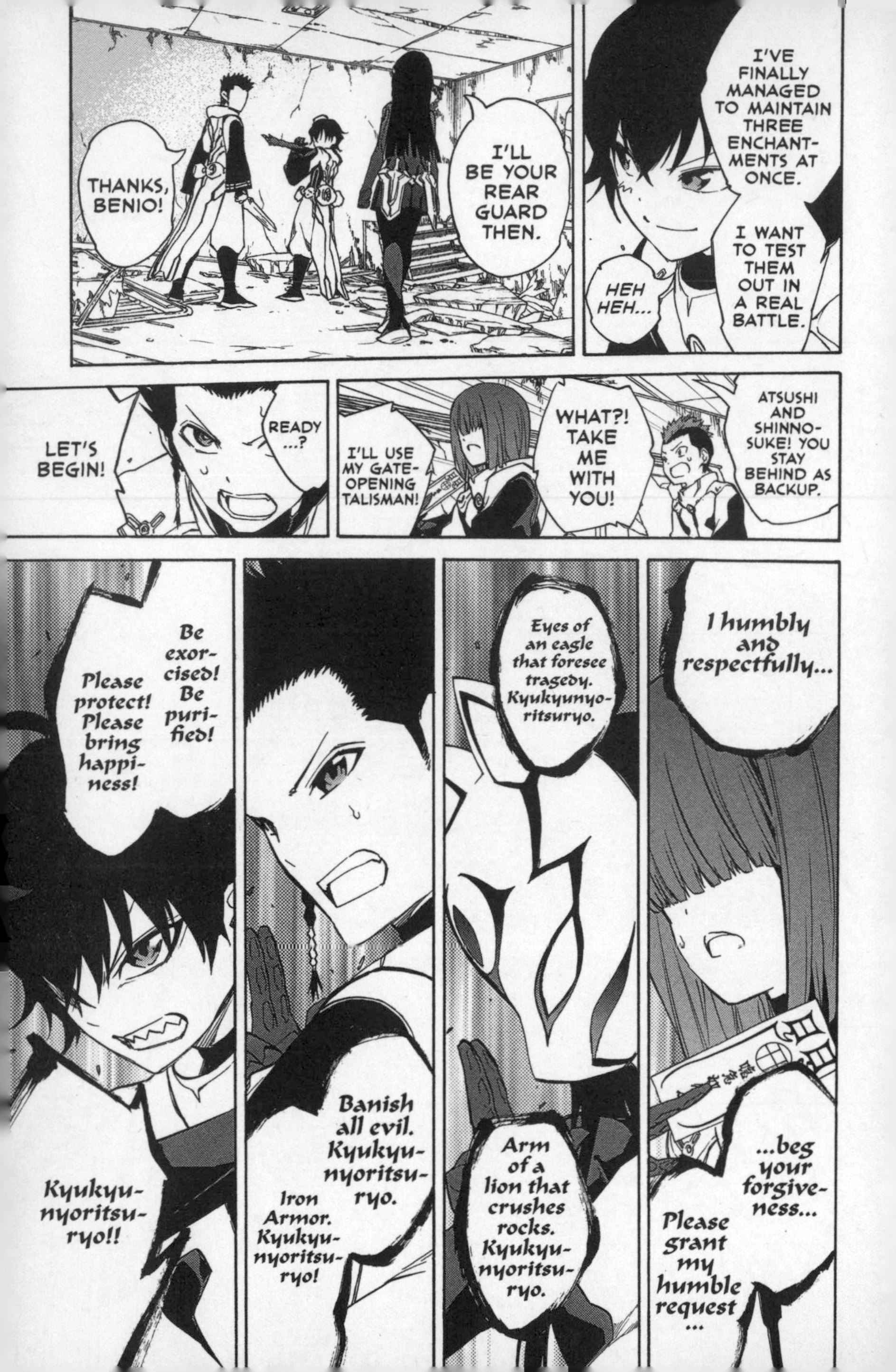
I'VE FINALLY MANAGED TO MAINTAIN THREE ENCHANTMENTS AT ONCE.
I WANT TO TEST THEM OUT IN A REAL BATTLE.
HEH HEH...
I'LL BE YOUR REAR GUARD THEN.
THANKS, BENIO!
ATSUSHI AND SHINNOSUKE! YOU STAY BEHIND AS BACKUP.
WHAT?! TAKE ME WITH YOU!
I'LL USE MY GATE-OPENING TALISMAN!
READY...?
LET'S BEGIN!
I humbly and respectfully...
...beg your forgiveness...
Please grant my humble request...
Eyes of an eagle that foresee tragedy. Kyukyunyoritsuryo.
Arm of a lion that crushes rocks. Kyukyunyoritsuryo.
Banish all evil. Kyukyunyoritsuryo.
Iron Armor. Kyukyunyoritsuryo!
Be exorcised! Be purified!
Please protect! Please bring happiness!
Kyukyunyoritsuryo!!

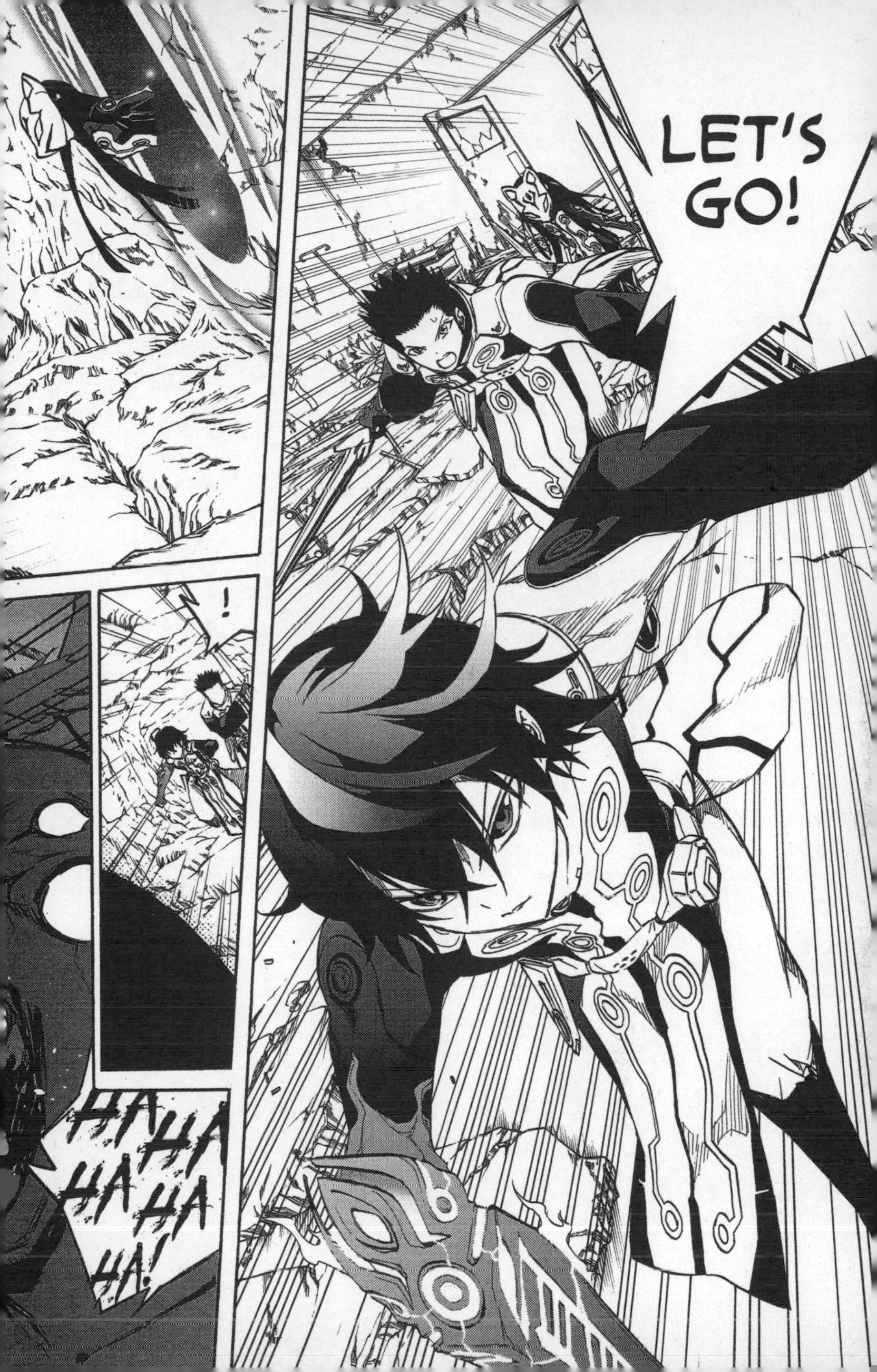
LET'S GO!
!
HA HA HA HA HA!

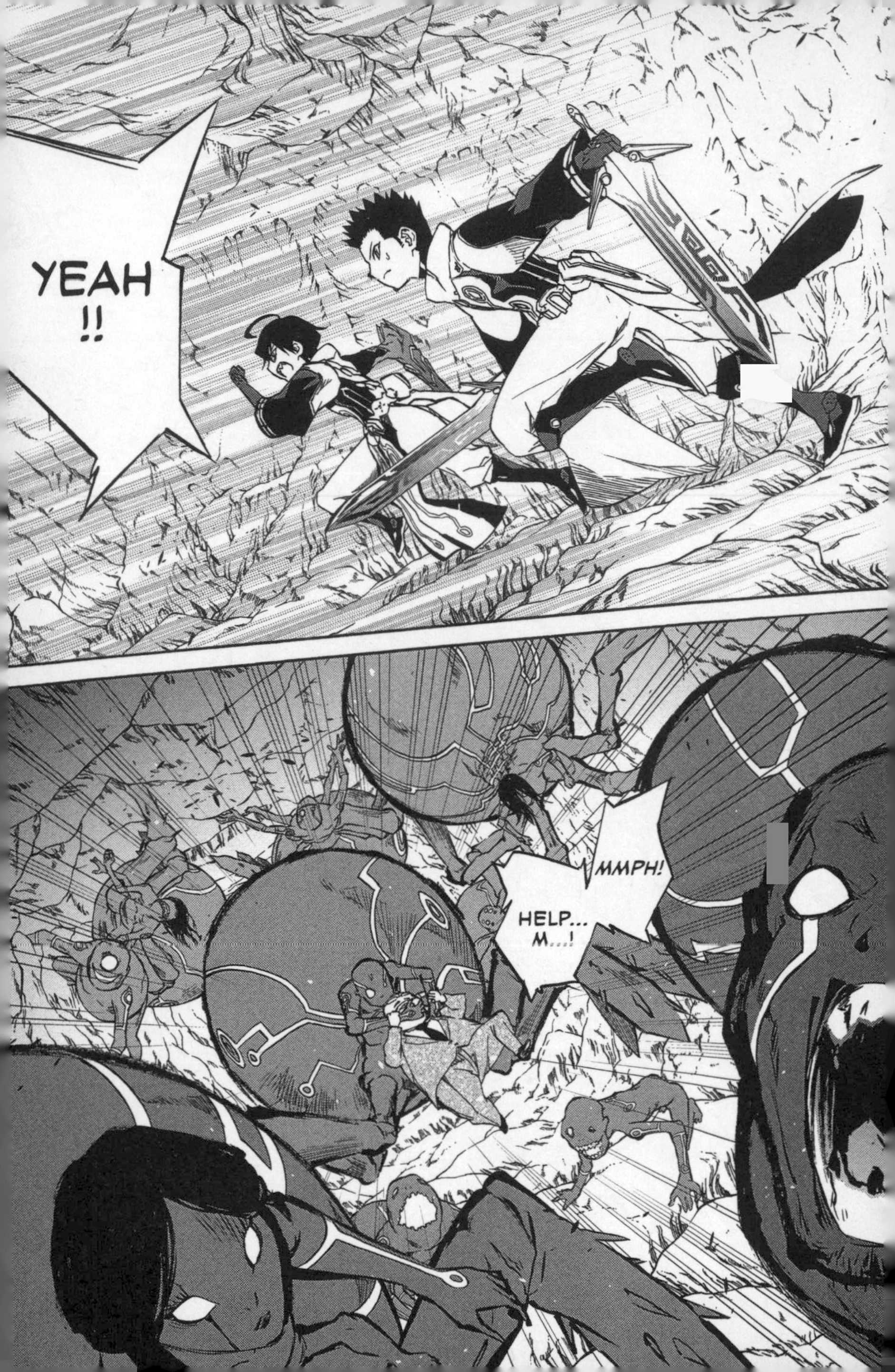
YEAH !!
MMPH!
HELP... M...!

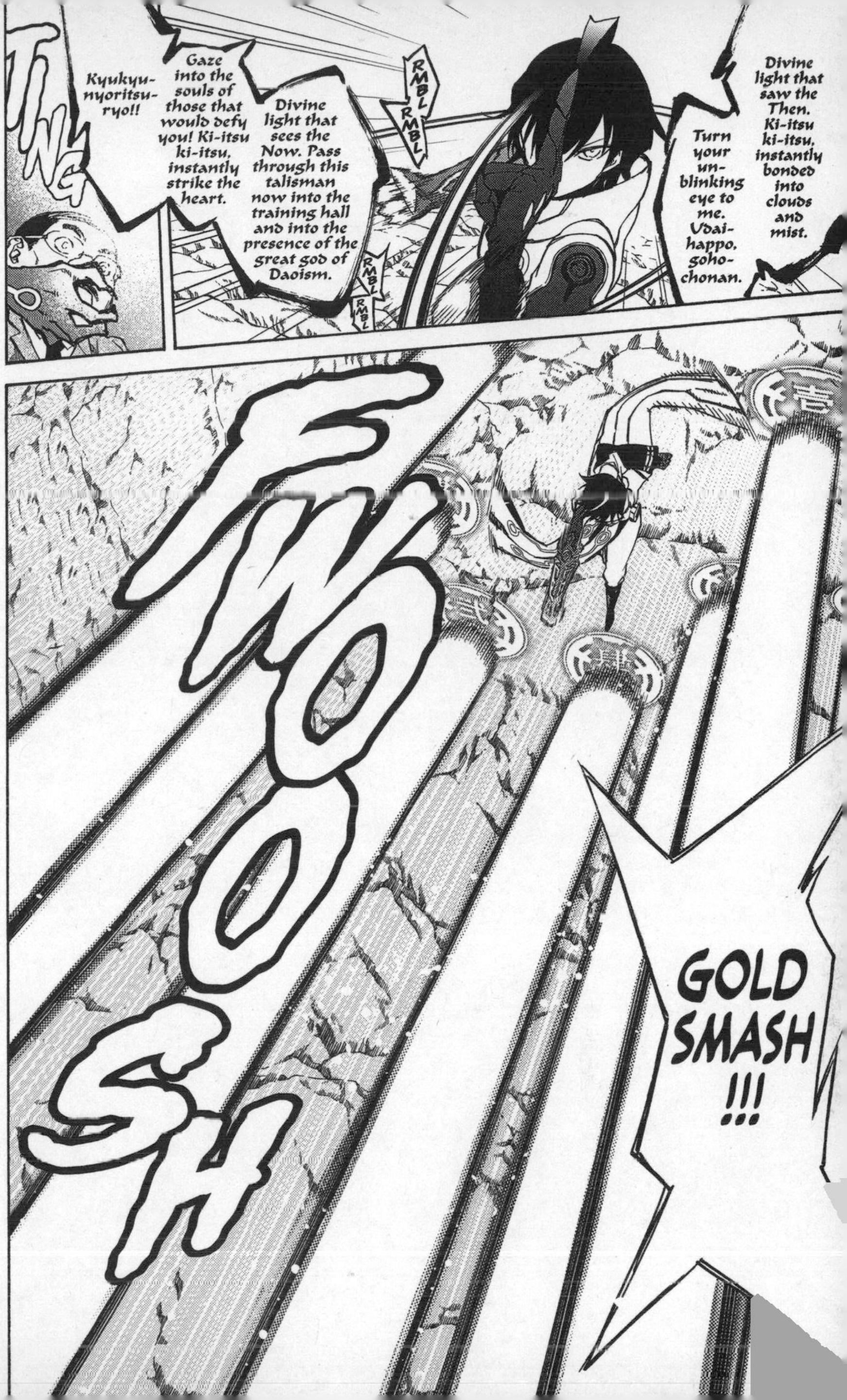
Divine light that saw the Then. Ki-itsu ki-itsu, instantly bonded into clouds and mist.
Turn your unblinking eye to me. Udai-happo, goho-chonan.
RMBL RMBL
RMBL RMBL
Divine light that sees the Now. Pass through this talisman now into the training hall and into the presence of the great god of Daoism.
Gaze into the souls of those that would defy you! Ki-itsu ki-itsu, instantly strike the heart.
Kyukyu-nyoritsu-ryo!!
TING
GOLD SMASH!!!
FWOOOSH

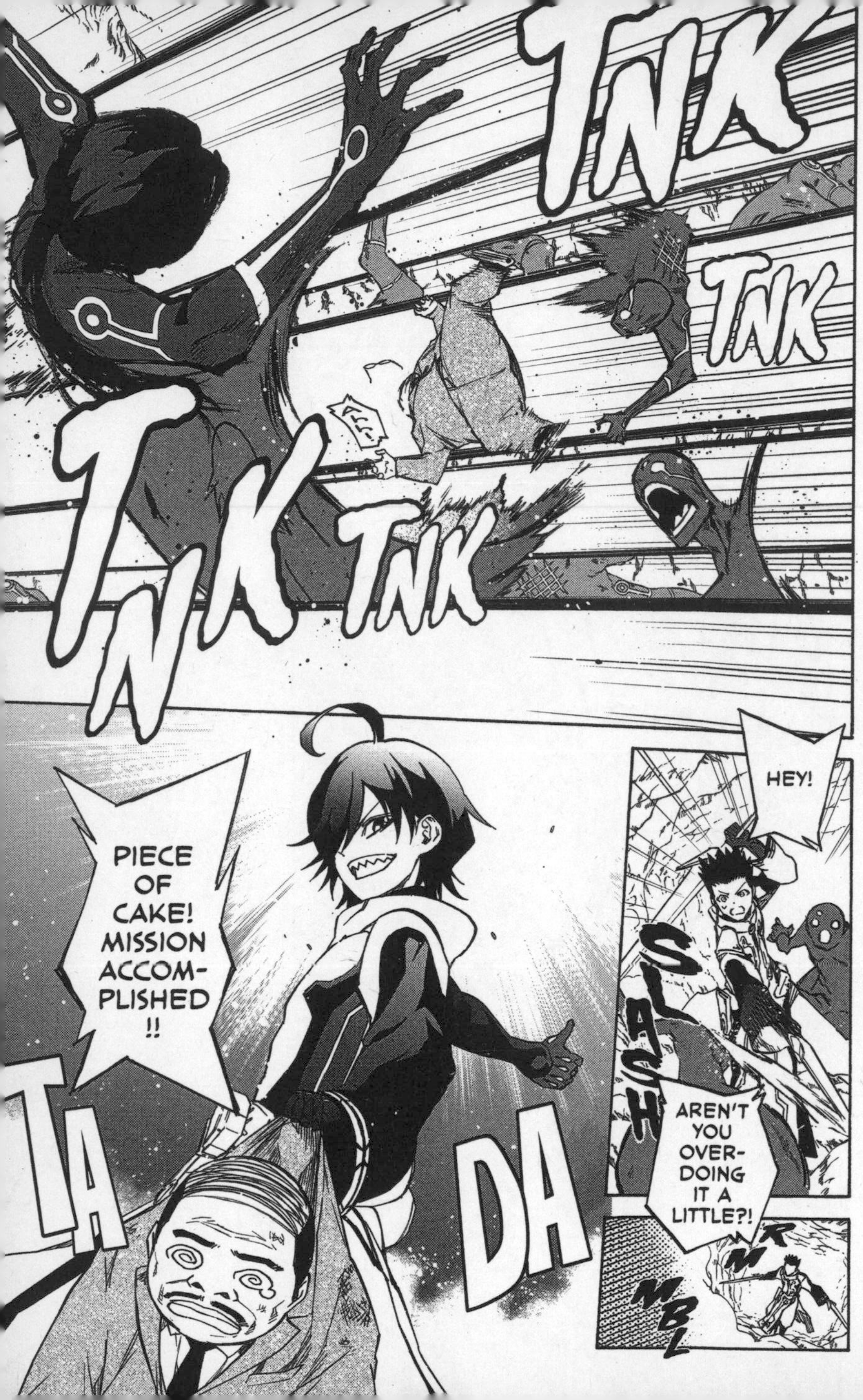
TNK
TNK
TNK
TNK
HEY!
SLASH
AREN'T YOU OVER-DOING IT A LITTLE?!
RMMBL
PIECE OF CAKE! MISSION ACCOM-PLISHED !!
TA
DA

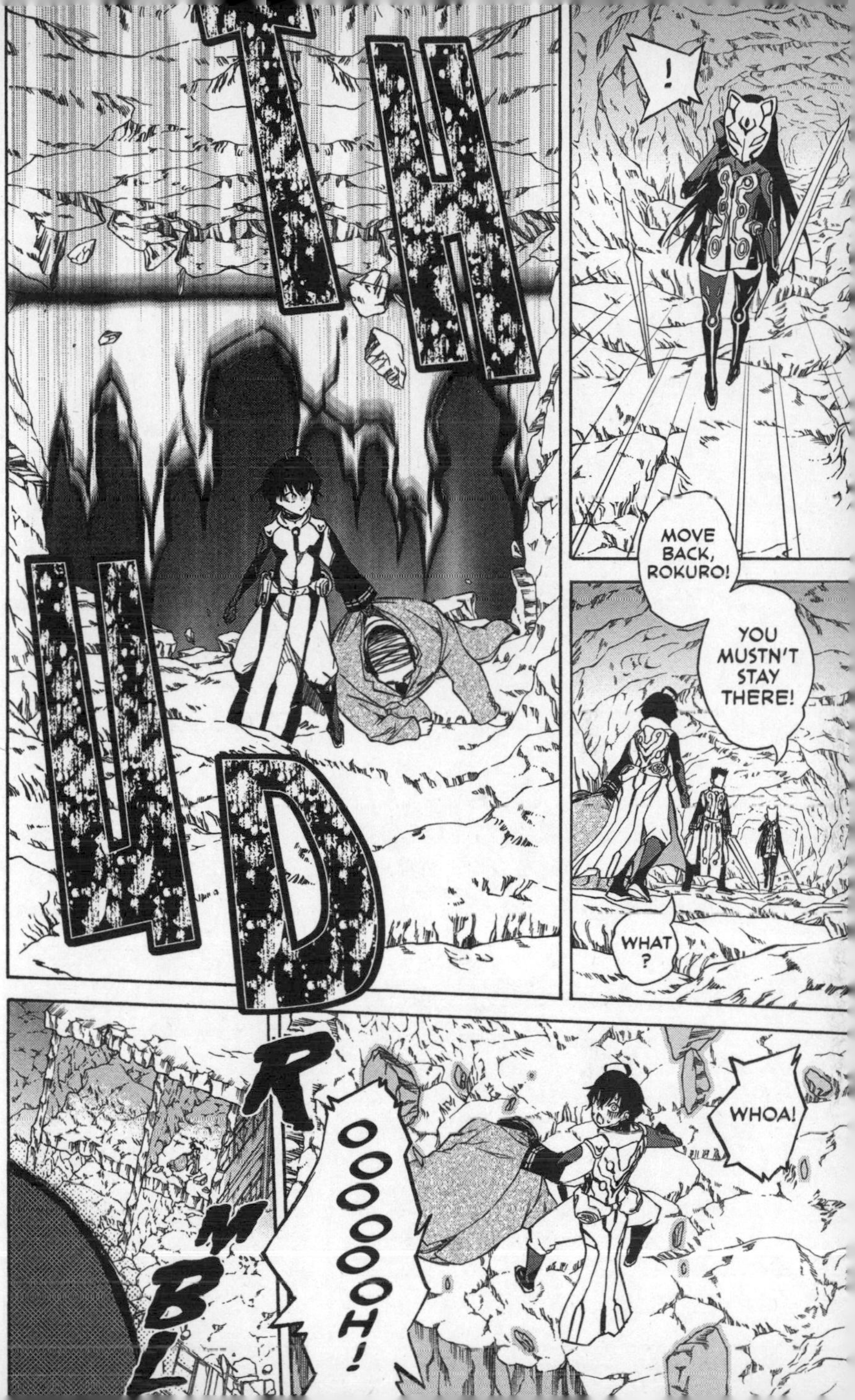
!
MOVE BACK, ROKURO!
YOU MUSTN'T STAY THERE!
WHAT?
THUD
WHOA!
OOOOOOOH!

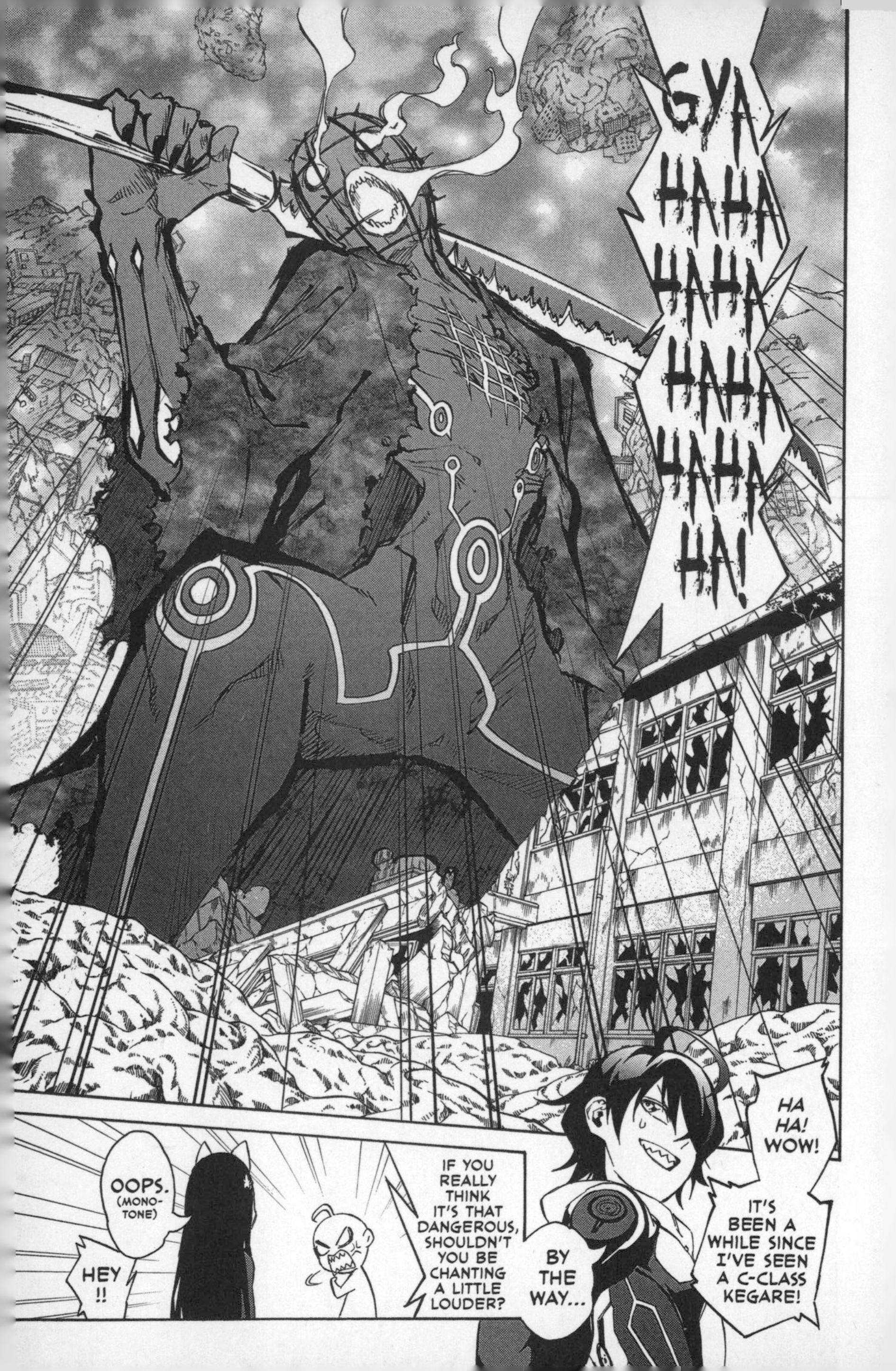
GYAHAHAHAHAHAHAHAHAHAHAHAHA!
HA HA! WOW!
IT'S BEEN A WHILE SINCE I'VE SEEN A C-CLASS KEGARE!
BY THE WAY...
IF YOU REALLY THINK IT'S THAT DANGEROUS, SHOULDN'T YOU BE CHANTING A LITTLE LOUDER?
OOPS. (MONOTONE)
HEY !!

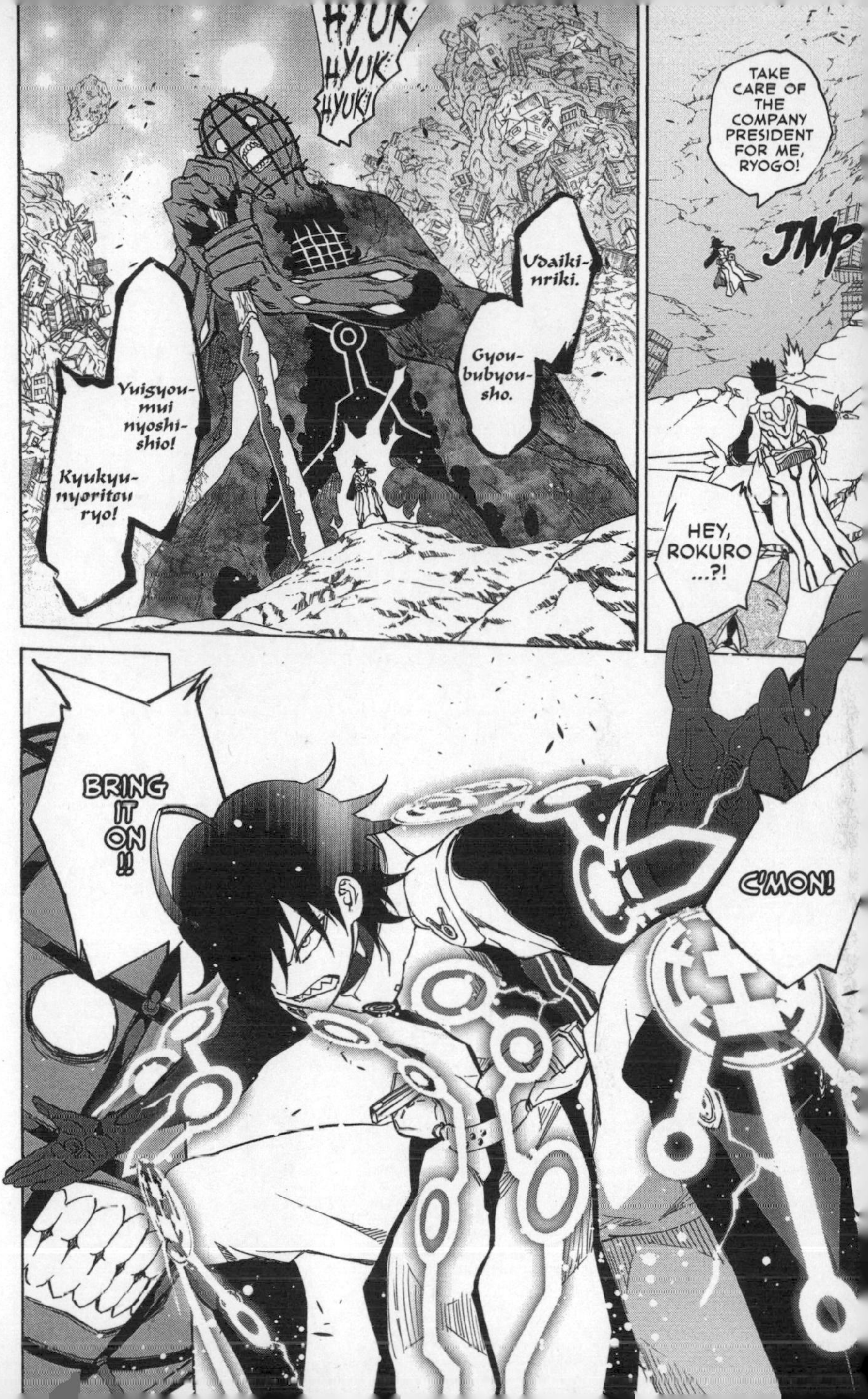
TAKE CARE OF THE COMPANY PRESIDENT FOR ME, RYOGO!
JMP
HEY, ROKURO ...?!
HYUK HYUK HYUK!
Udaiki-nriki.
Gyou-bubyou-sho.
Yuigyou-mui nyoshi-shio!
Kyukyu-nyoritsu ryo!
C'MON!
BRING IT ON!!

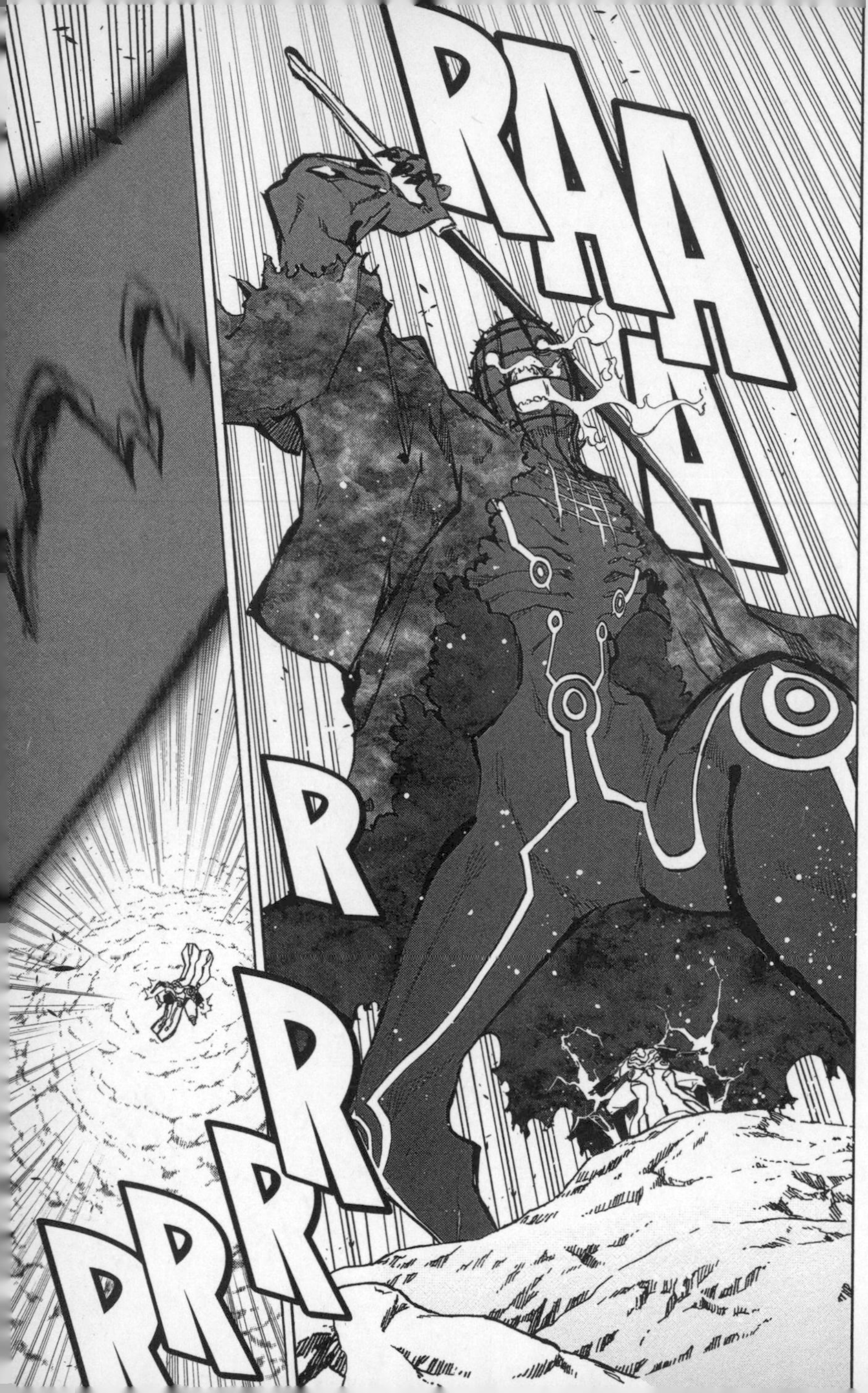
RAAAA
RRRRR

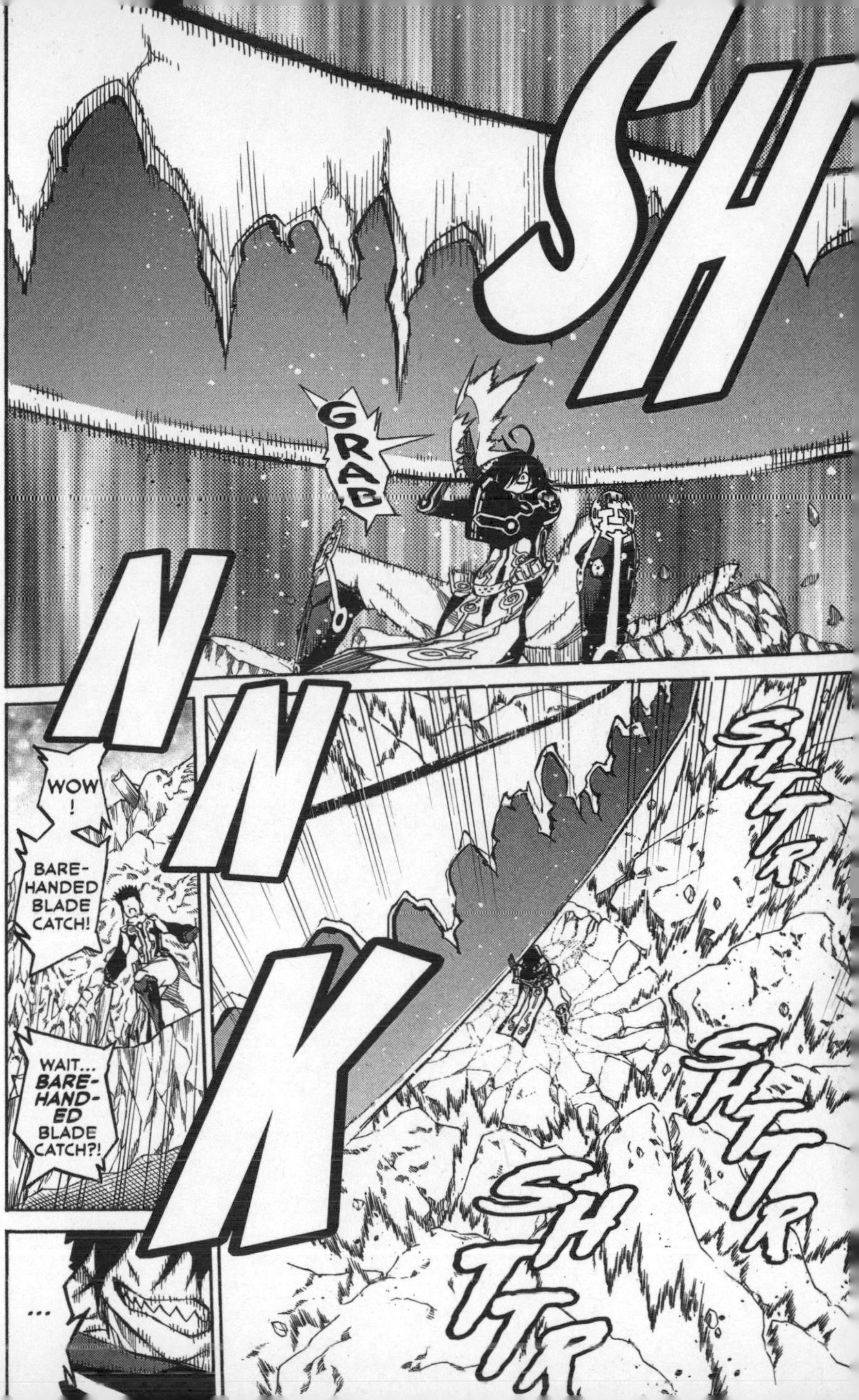
SH
GRAB
NNK
SHTR
SHTR
SHTR
SHTR
WOW!
BARE-HANDED BLADE CATCH!
WAIT... BARE-HANDED BLADE CATCH?!
...

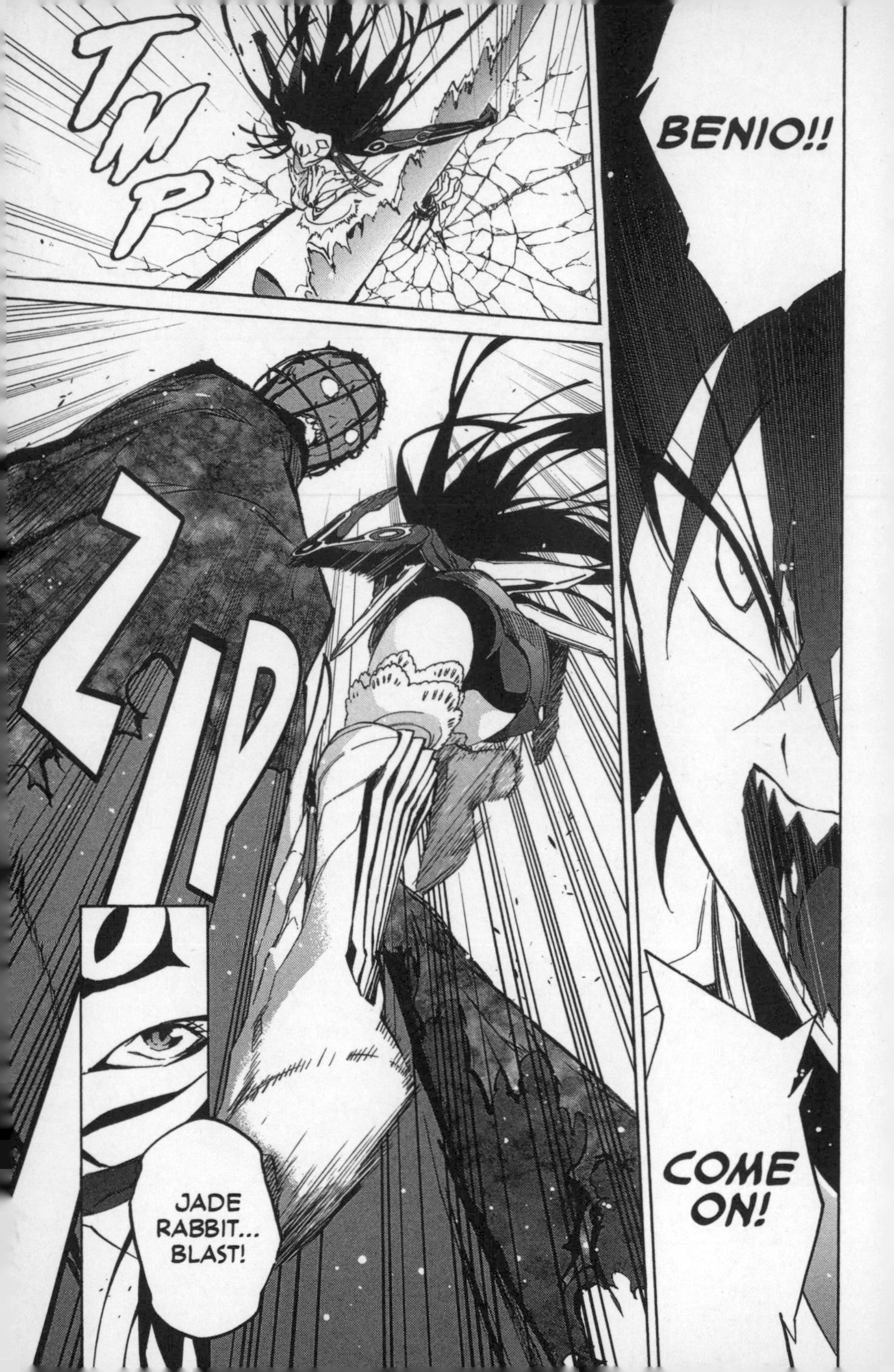
BENIO!!
COME ON!
TMP
ZIP
JADE RABBIT... BLAST!

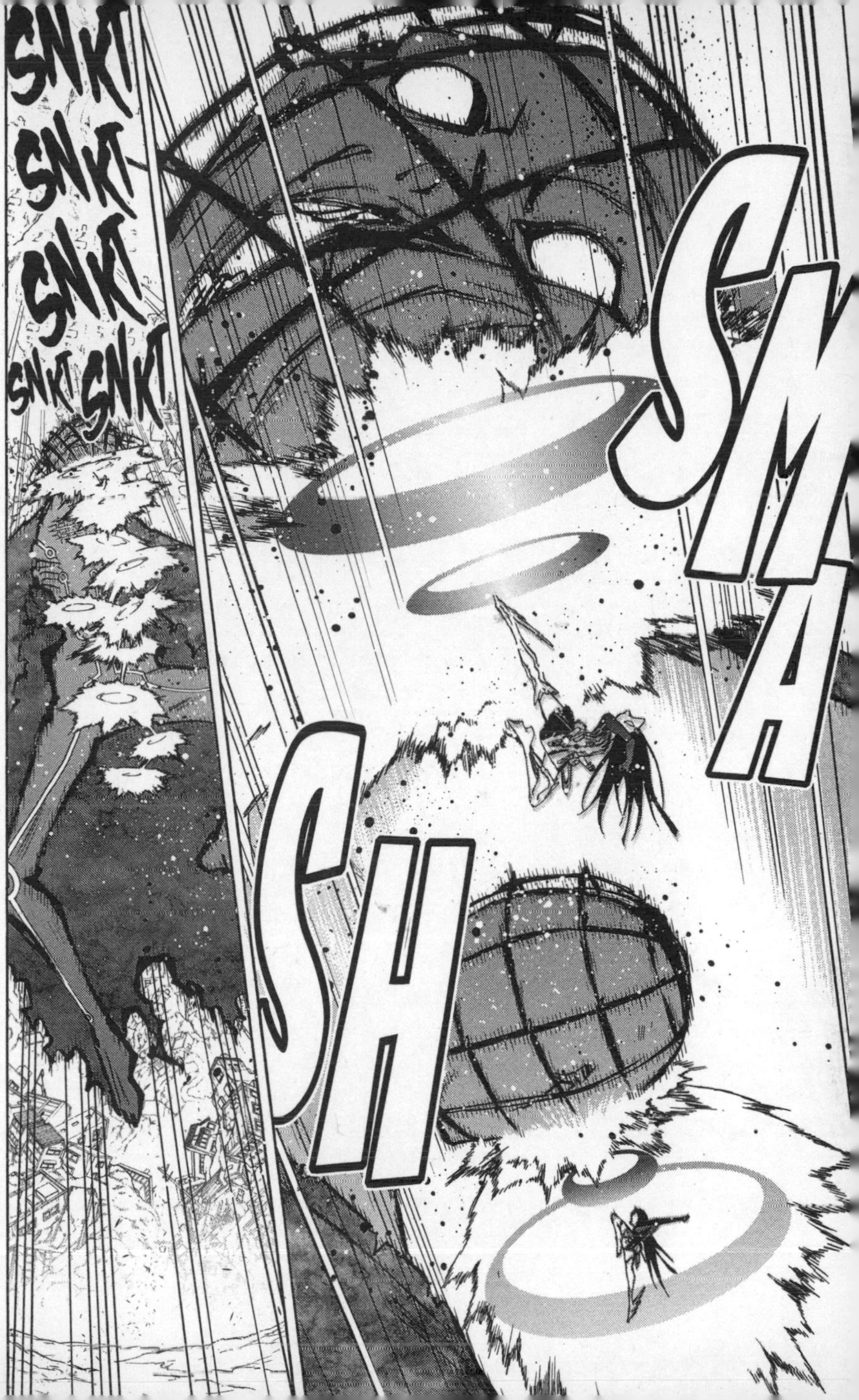
SMA
SH
SNKT
SNKT
SNKT
SNKT
SNKT

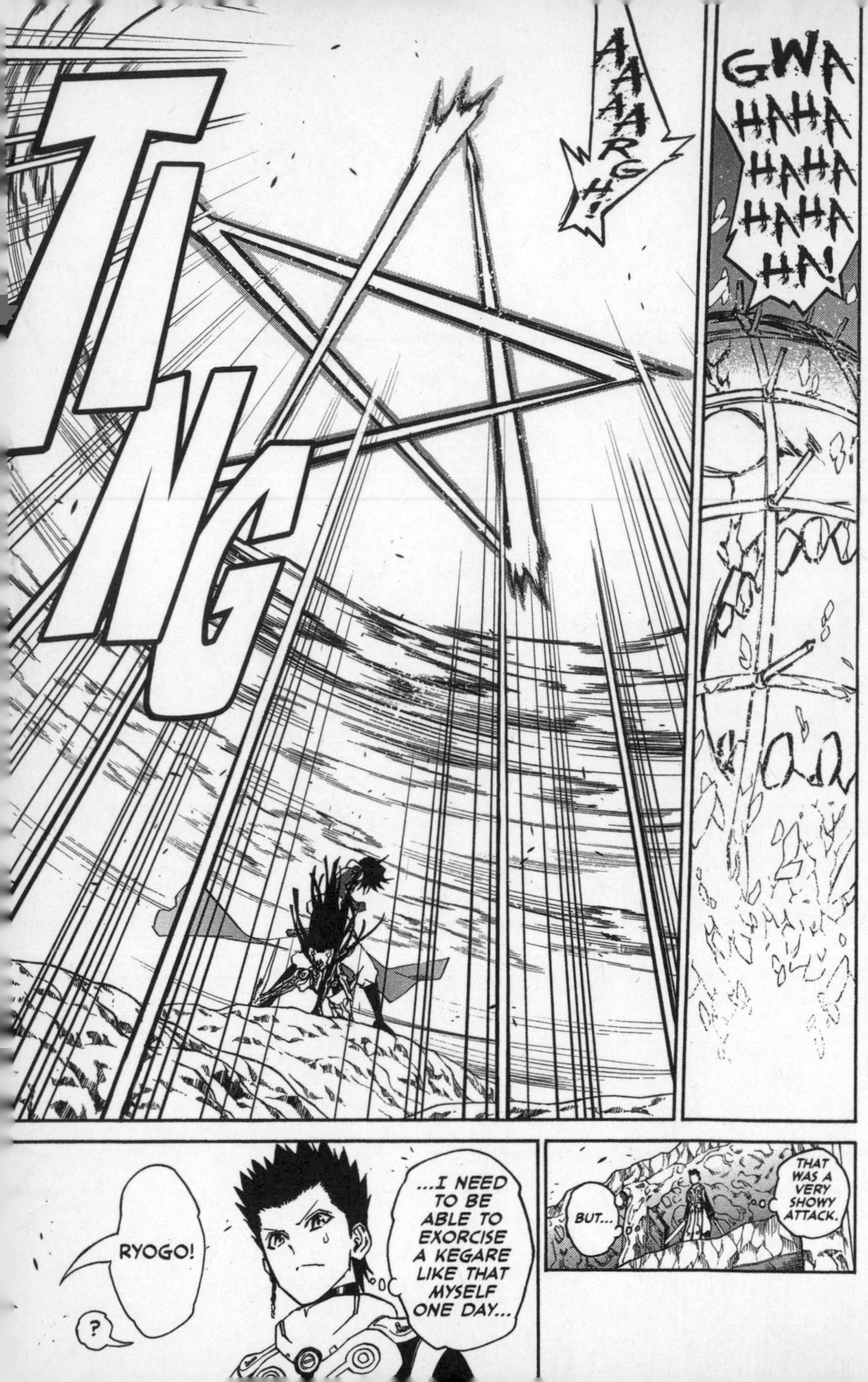
GWAHAHAHAHAHAHAHA!
AAAARGH!
TING
THAT WAS A VERY SHOWY ATTACK.
BUT...
...I NEED TO BE ABLE TO EXORCISE A KEGARE LIKE THAT MYSELF ONE DAY...
RYOGO!
?

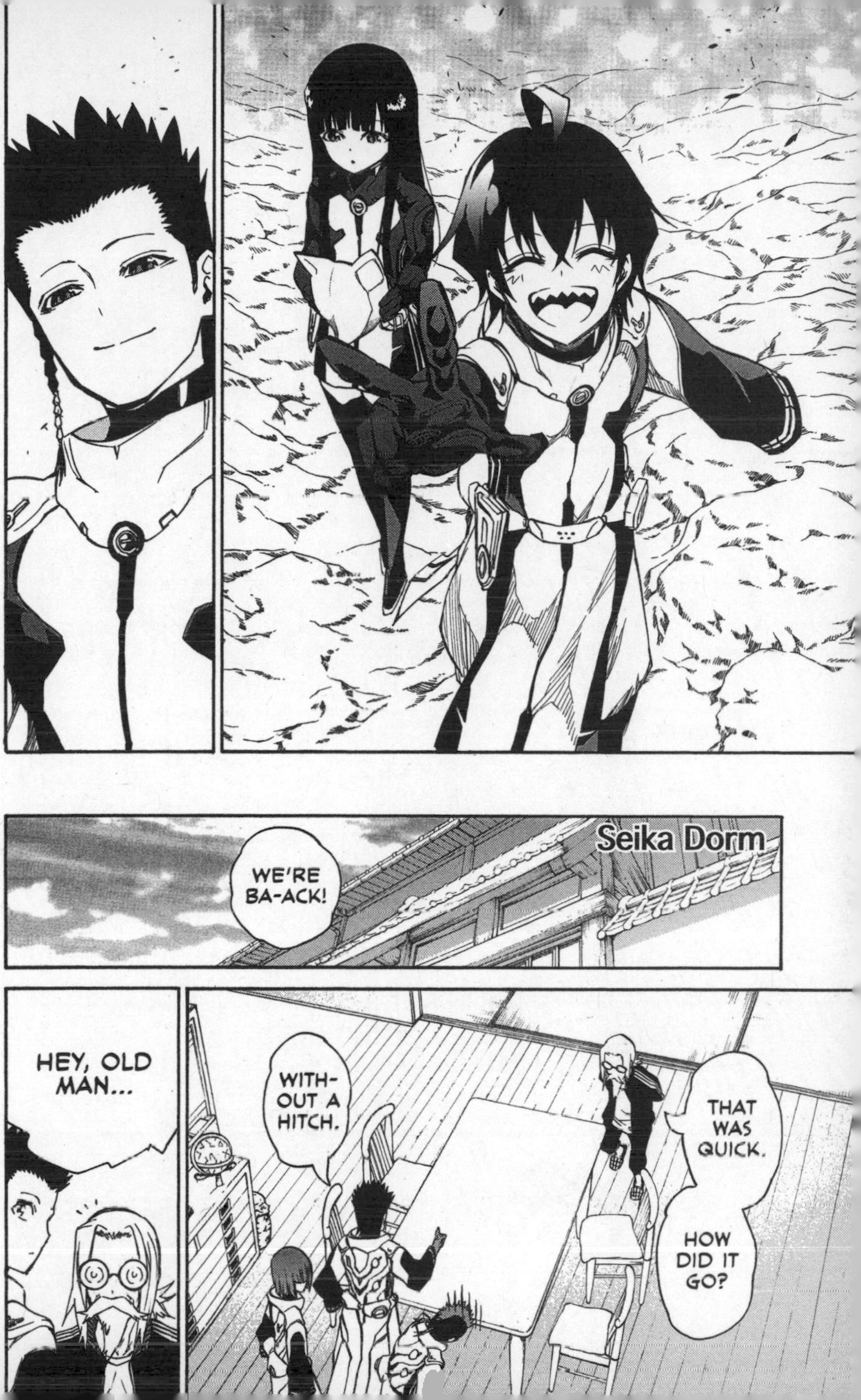
Seika Dorm
WE'RE BA-ACK!
THAT WAS QUICK.
HOW DID IT GO?
WITH-OUT A HITCH.
HEY, OLD MAN...

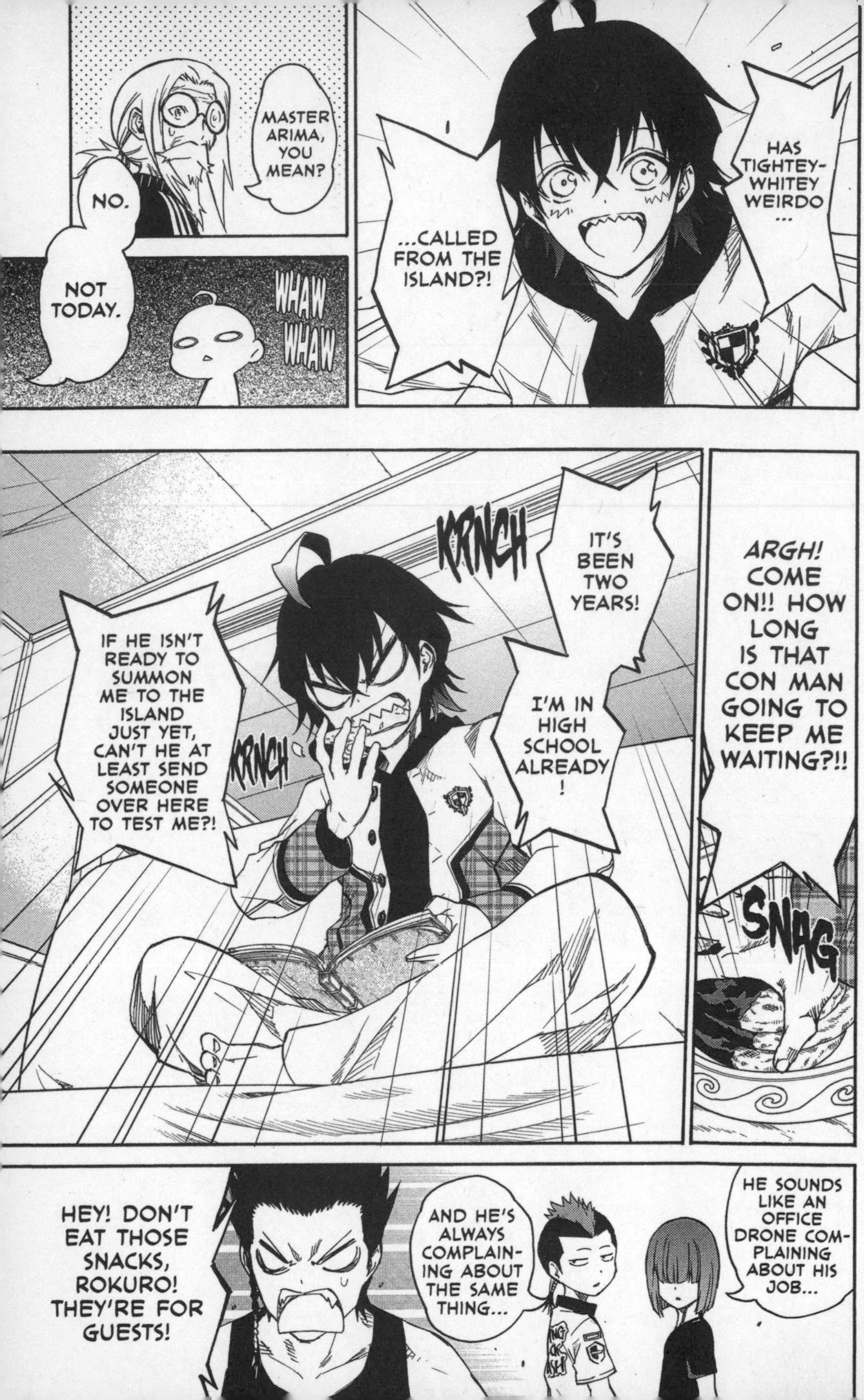
HAS TIGHTEY-WHITEY WEIRDO...
...CALLED FROM THE ISLAND?!
MASTER ARIMA, YOU MEAN?
NO.
NOT TODAY.
WHAW WHAW
ARGH! COME ON!! HOW LONG IS THAT CON MAN GOING TO KEEP ME WAITING?!!
SNAG
KRNCH
IT'S BEEN TWO YEARS!
I'M IN HIGH SCHOOL ALREADY!
IF HE ISN'T READY TO SUMMON ME TO THE ISLAND JUST YET, CAN'T HE AT LEAST SEND SOMEONE OVER HERE TO TEST ME?!
KRNCH
HE SOUNDS LIKE AN OFFICE DRONE COMPLAINING ABOUT HIS JOB...
AND HE'S ALWAYS COMPLAINING ABOUT THE SAME THING...
HEY! DON'T EAT THOSE SNACKS, ROKURO! THEY'RE FOR GUESTS!

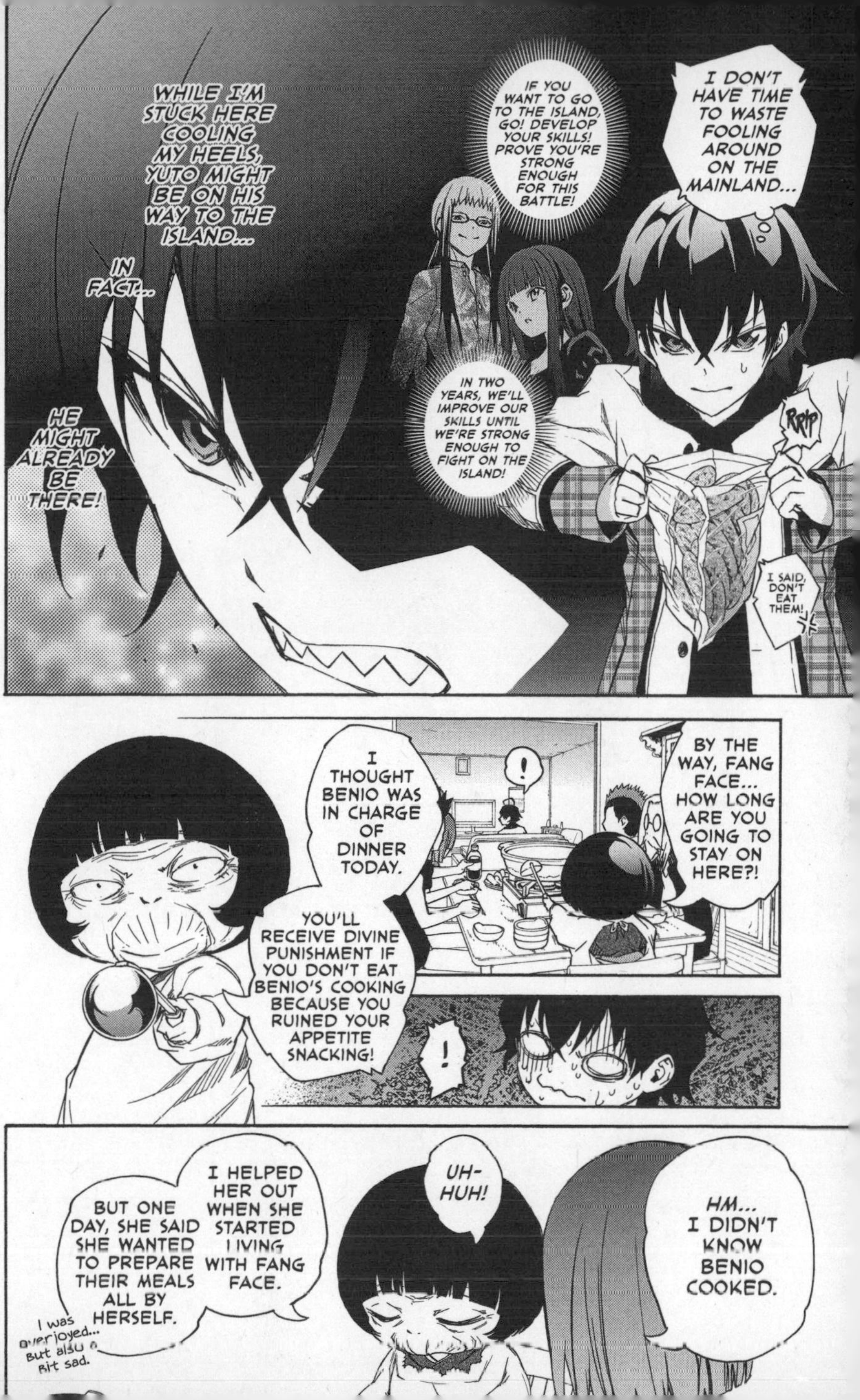
I DON'T HAVE TIME TO WASTE FOOLING AROUND ON THE MAINLAND...
IF YOU WANT TO GO TO THE ISLAND, GO! DEVELOP YOUR SKILLS! PROVE YOU'RE STRONG ENOUGH FOR THIS BATTLE!
IN TWO YEARS, WE'LL IMPROVE OUR SKILLS UNTIL WE'RE STRONG ENOUGH TO FIGHT ON THE ISLAND!
RRIP
I SAID, DON'T EAT THEM!
WHILE I'M STUCK HERE COOLING MY HEELS, YUTO MIGHT BE ON HIS WAY TO THE ISLAND...
IN FACT...
HE MIGHT ALREADY BE THERE!
BY THE WAY, FANG FACE... HOW LONG ARE YOU GOING TO STAY ON HERE?!
!
!
I THOUGHT BENIO WAS IN CHARGE OF DINNER TODAY.
YOU'LL RECEIVE DIVINE PUNISHMENT IF YOU DON'T EAT BENIO'S COOKING BECAUSE YOU RUINED YOUR APPETITE SNACKING!
HM... I DIDN'T KNOW BENIO COOKED.
UH-HUH!
I HELPED HER OUT WHEN SHE STARTED LIVING WITH FANG FACE.
BUT ONE DAY, SHE SAID SHE WANTED TO PREPARE THEIR MEALS ALL BY HERSELF.
I was overjoyed... But also a Bit sad.

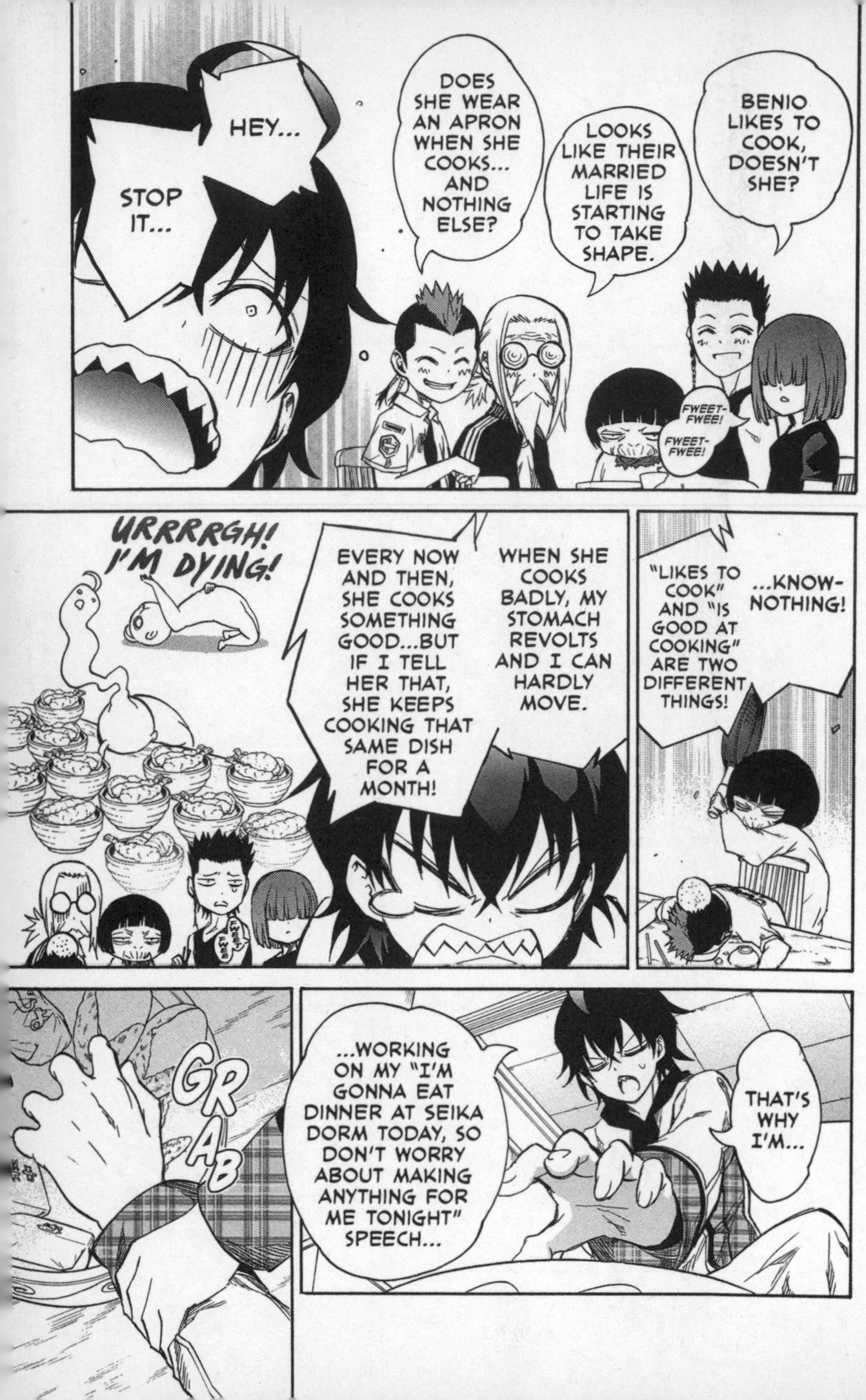
BENIO LIKES TO COOK, DOESN'T SHE?
LOOKS LIKE THEIR MARRIED LIFE IS STARTING TO TAKE SHAPE.
DOES SHE WEAR AN APRON WHEN SHE COOKS... AND NOTHING ELSE?
HEY...
STOP IT...
FWEET-FWEE!
FWEET-FWEE!
...KNOW-NOTHING!
"LIKES TO COOK" AND "IS GOOD AT COOKING" ARE TWO DIFFERENT THINGS!
WHEN SHE COOKS BADLY, MY STOMACH REVOLTS AND I CAN HARDLY MOVE.
EVERY NOW AND THEN, SHE COOKS SOMETHING GOOD...BUT IF I TELL HER THAT, SHE KEEPS COOKING THAT SAME DISH FOR A MONTH!
URRRRGH! I'M DYING!
FWEET-FWEE
THAT'S WHY I'M...
...WORKING ON MY "I'M GONNA EAT DINNER AT SEIKA DORM TODAY, SO DON'T WORRY ABOUT MAKING ANYTHING FOR ME TONIGHT" SPEECH...
GRAB

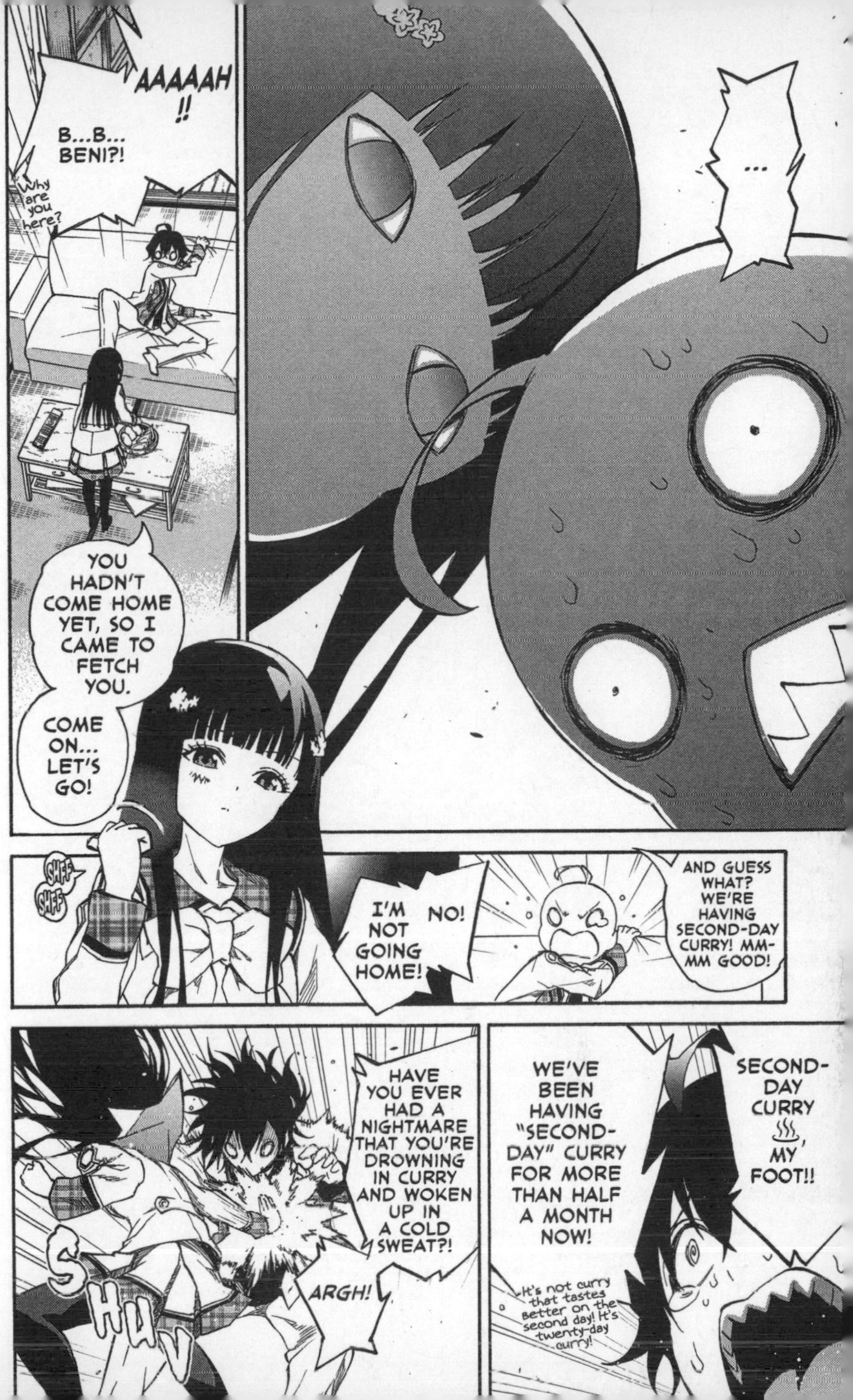
...
AAAAAH!!
B...B... BENI?!
Why are you here?
YOU HADN'T COME HOME YET, SO I CAME TO FETCH YOU.
COME ON... LET'S GO!
AND GUESS WHAT? WE'RE HAVING SECOND-DAY CURRY! MM-MM GOOD!
NO!
I'M NOT GOING HOME!
SHFF SHFF
SECOND-DAY CURRY, MY FOOT!!
WE'VE BEEN HAVING "SECOND-DAY" CURRY FOR MORE THAN HALF A MONTH NOW!
It's not curry that tastes better on the second day! It's twenty-day curry!
HAVE YOU EVER HAD A NIGHTMARE THAT YOU'RE DROWNING IN CURRY AND WOKEN UP IN A COLD SWEAT?!
ARGH!
SHUV

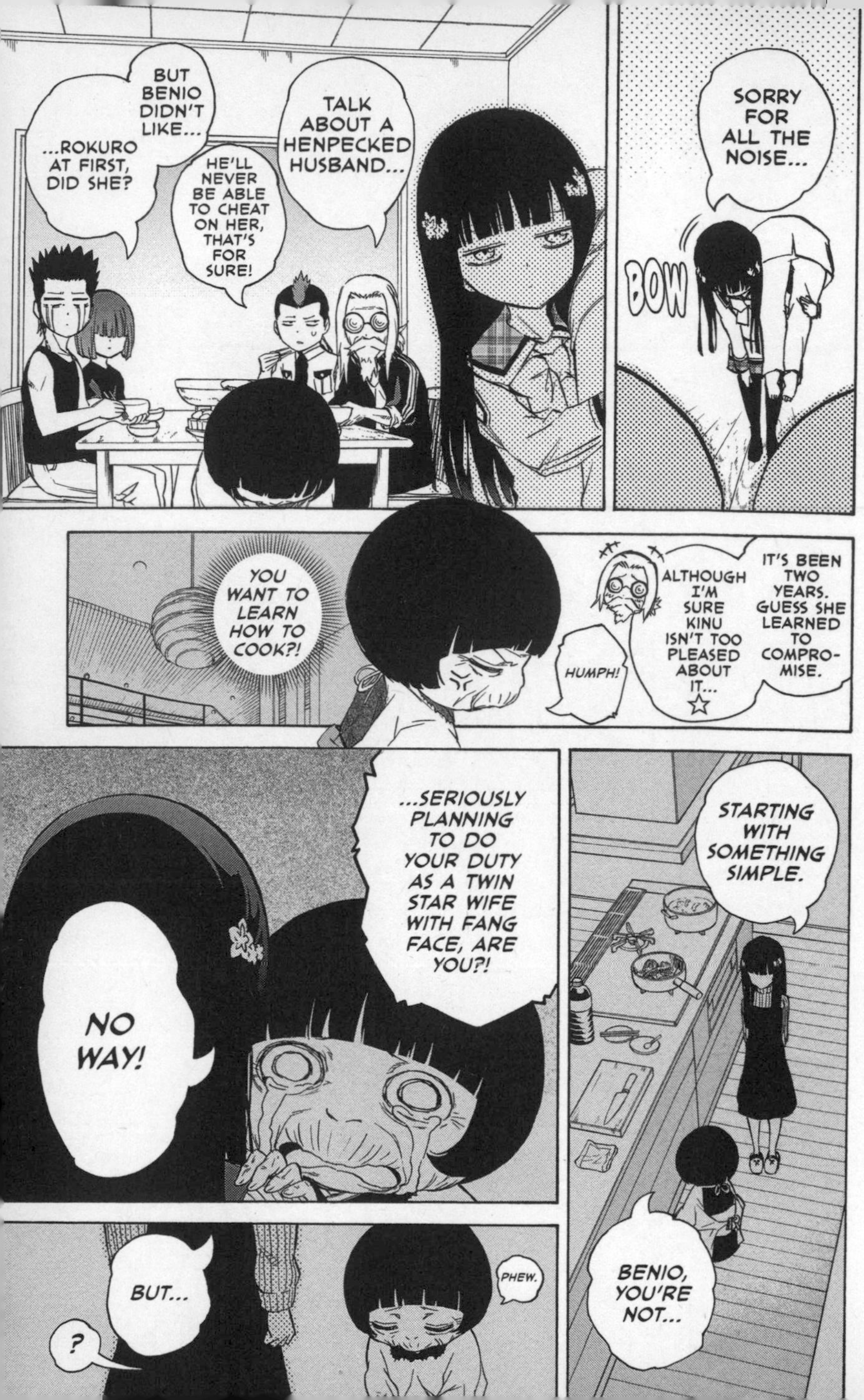
SORRY FOR ALL THE NOISE...
BOW
TALK ABOUT A HENPECKED HUSBAND...
HE'LL NEVER BE ABLE TO CHEAT ON HER, THAT'S FOR SURE!
BUT BENIO DIDN'T LIKE...
...ROKURO AT FIRST, DID SHE?
IT'S BEEN TWO YEARS. GUESS SHE LEARNED TO COMPROMISE.
ALTHOUGH I'M SURE KINU ISN'T TOO PLEASED ABOUT IT... ☆
HUMPH!
YOU WANT TO LEARN HOW TO COOK?!
STARTING WITH SOMETHING SIMPLE.
BENIO, YOU'RE NOT...
...SERIOUSLY PLANNING TO DO YOUR DUTY AS A TWIN STAR WIFE WITH FANG FACE, ARE YOU?!
NO WAY!
PHEW.
BUT...
?

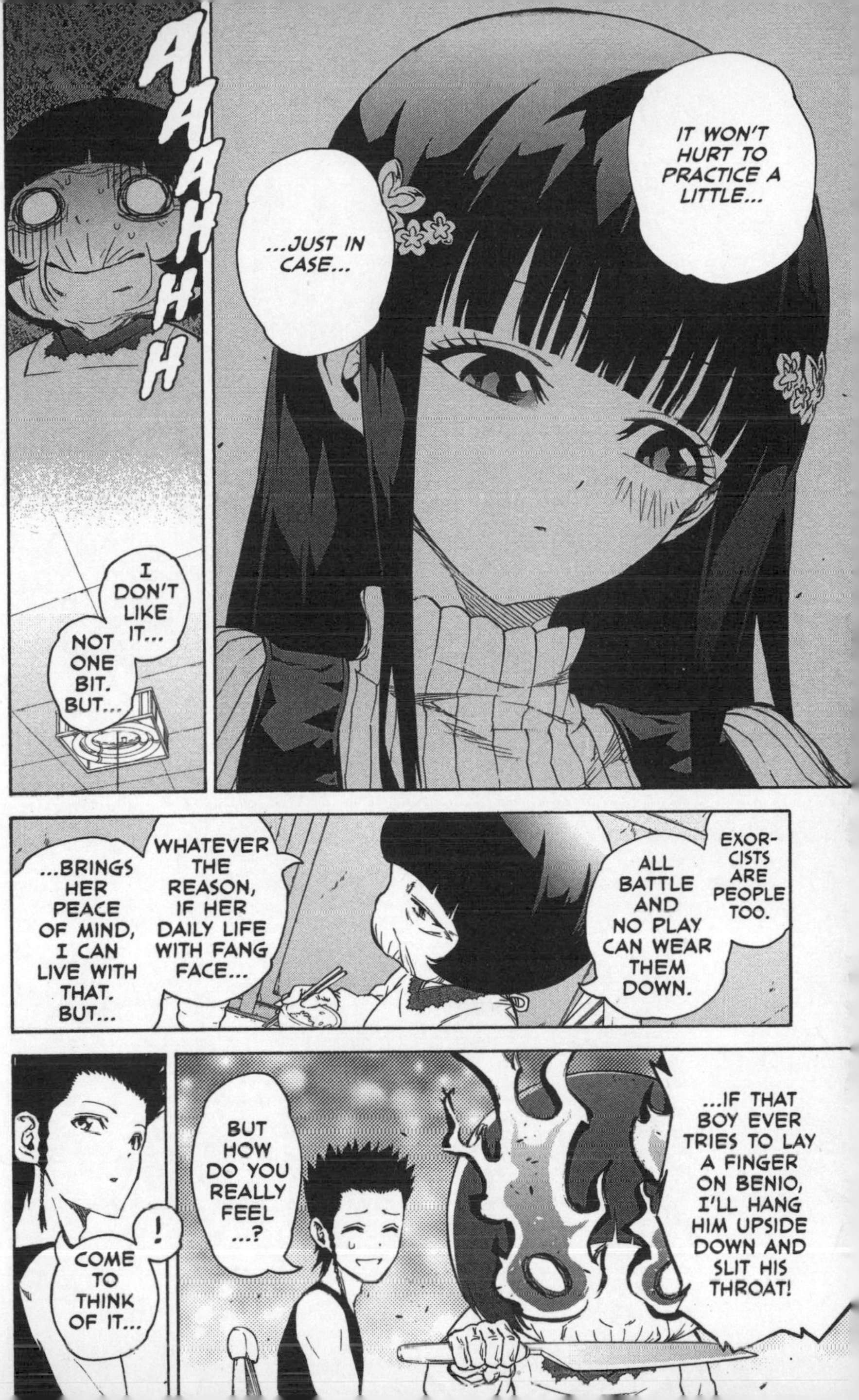
IT WON'T HURT TO PRACTICE A LITTLE...
...JUST IN CASE...
AAAAHHHH
I DON'T LIKE IT...
NOT ONE BIT. BUT...
EXOR-CISTS ARE PEOPLE TOO.
ALL BATTLE AND NO PLAY CAN WEAR THEM DOWN.
WHATEVER THE REASON, IF HER DAILY LIFE WITH FANG FACE...
...BRINGS HER PEACE OF MIND, I CAN LIVE WITH THAT. BUT...
...IF THAT BOY EVER TRIES TO LAY A FINGER ON BENIO, I'LL HANG HIM UPSIDE DOWN AND SLIT HIS THROAT!
BUT HOW DO YOU REALLY FEEL ...?
!
COME TO THINK OF IT...

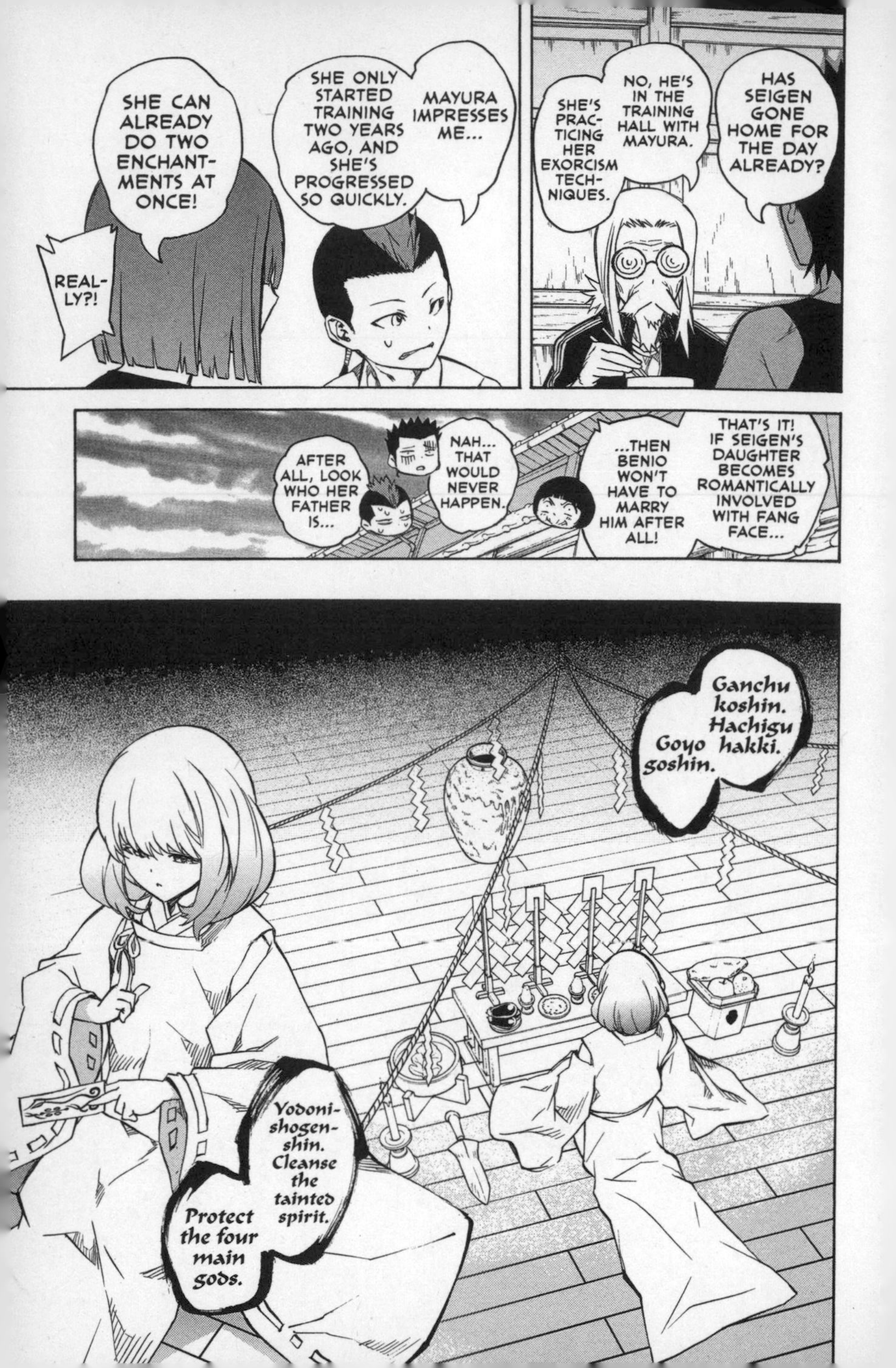
HAS SEIGEN GONE HOME FOR THE DAY ALREADY?
NO, HE'S IN THE TRAINING HALL WITH MAYURA.
SHE'S PRACTICING HER EXORCISM TECHNIQUES.
MAYURA IMPRESSES ME...
SHE ONLY STARTED TRAINING TWO YEARS AGO, AND SHE'S PROGRESSED SO QUICKLY.
SHE CAN ALREADY DO TWO ENCHANTMENTS AT ONCE!
REALLY?!
THAT'S IT! IF SEIGEN'S DAUGHTER BECOMES ROMANTICALLY INVOLVED WITH FANG FACE...
...THEN BENIO WON'T HAVE TO MARRY HIM AFTER ALL!
NAH... THAT WOULD NEVER HAPPEN.
AFTER ALL, LOOK WHO HER FATHER IS...
Ganchu koshin. Hachigu hakki. Goyo goshin.
Yodonishogenshin. Cleanse the tainted spirit.
Protect the four main gods.

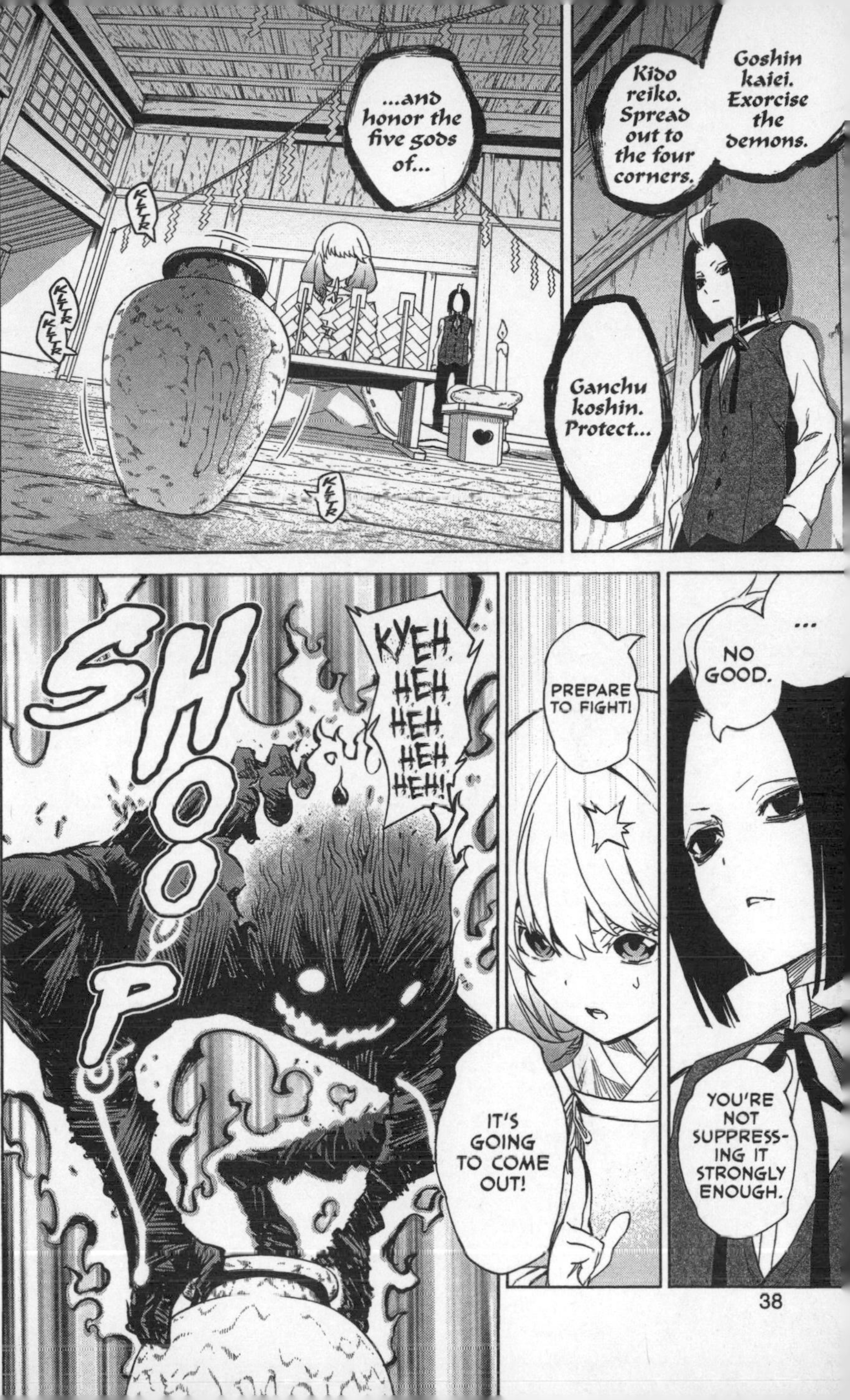
Goshin kaiei. Exorcise the demons.
Kido reiko. Spread out to the four corners.
Ganchu koshin. Protect...
...and honor the five gods of...
KETR
KETR KETR
KETR
...
NO GOOD.
YOU'RE NOT SUPPRESSING IT STRONGLY ENOUGH.
PREPARE TO FIGHT!
IT'S GOING TO COME OUT!
KYEH HEH HEH HEH HEH!
SHOOOP

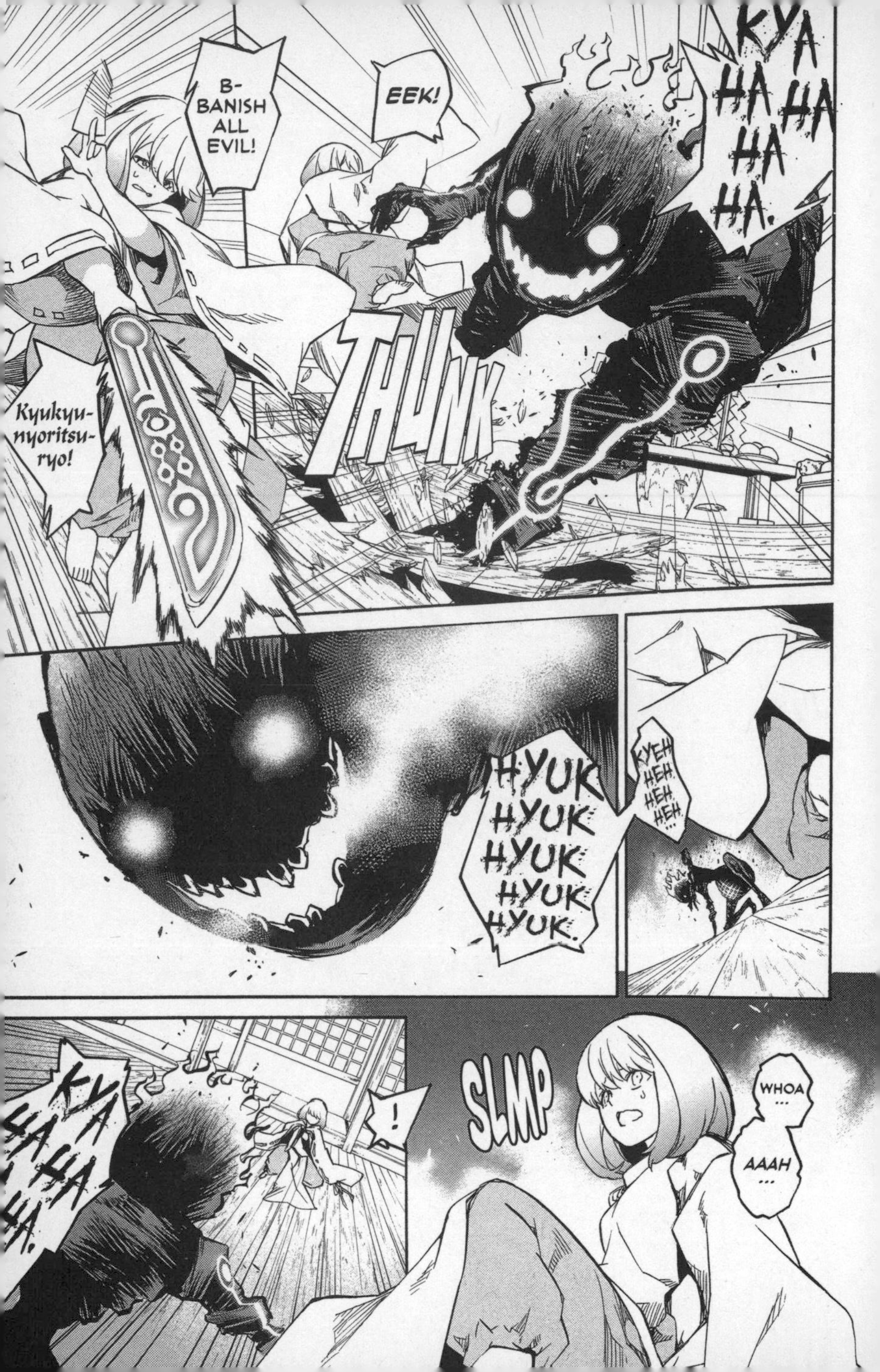
KYA HA HA HA HA HA.
EEK!
B-BANISH ALL EVIL!
THUNK
Kyukyu-nyoritsu-ryo!
KYEH HEH HEH HEH...
HYUK HYUK HYUK HYUK HYUK.
WHOA...
AAAH...
SLMP
!
KYA HA HA HA HA.

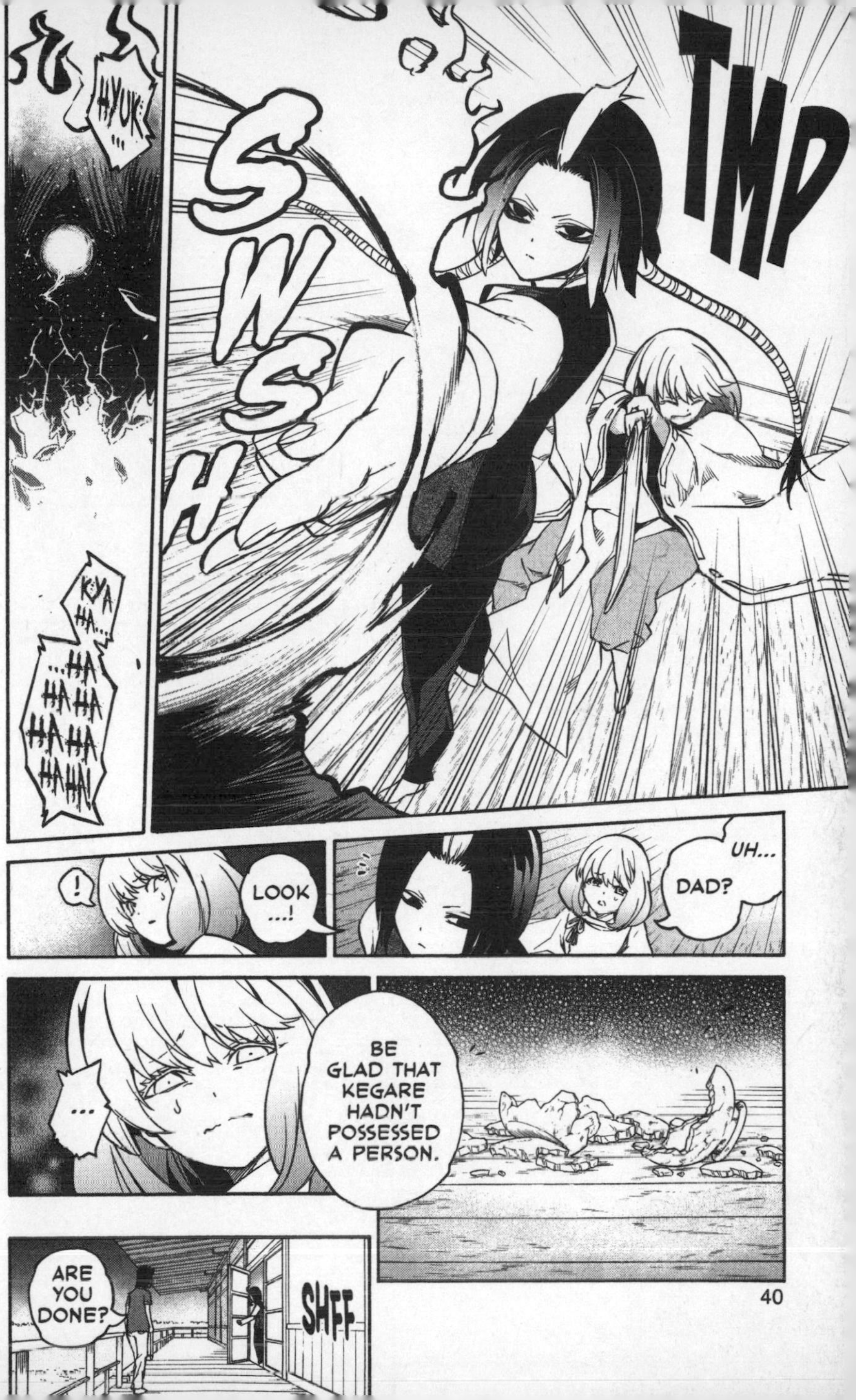
TMP
SWSH
HYUK...
KYA HA...
...HA HA HA HA HA HA HAH!
UH... DAD?
!
LOOK...!
BE GLAD THAT KEGARE HADN'T POSSESSED A PERSON.
...
SHFF
ARE YOU DONE?

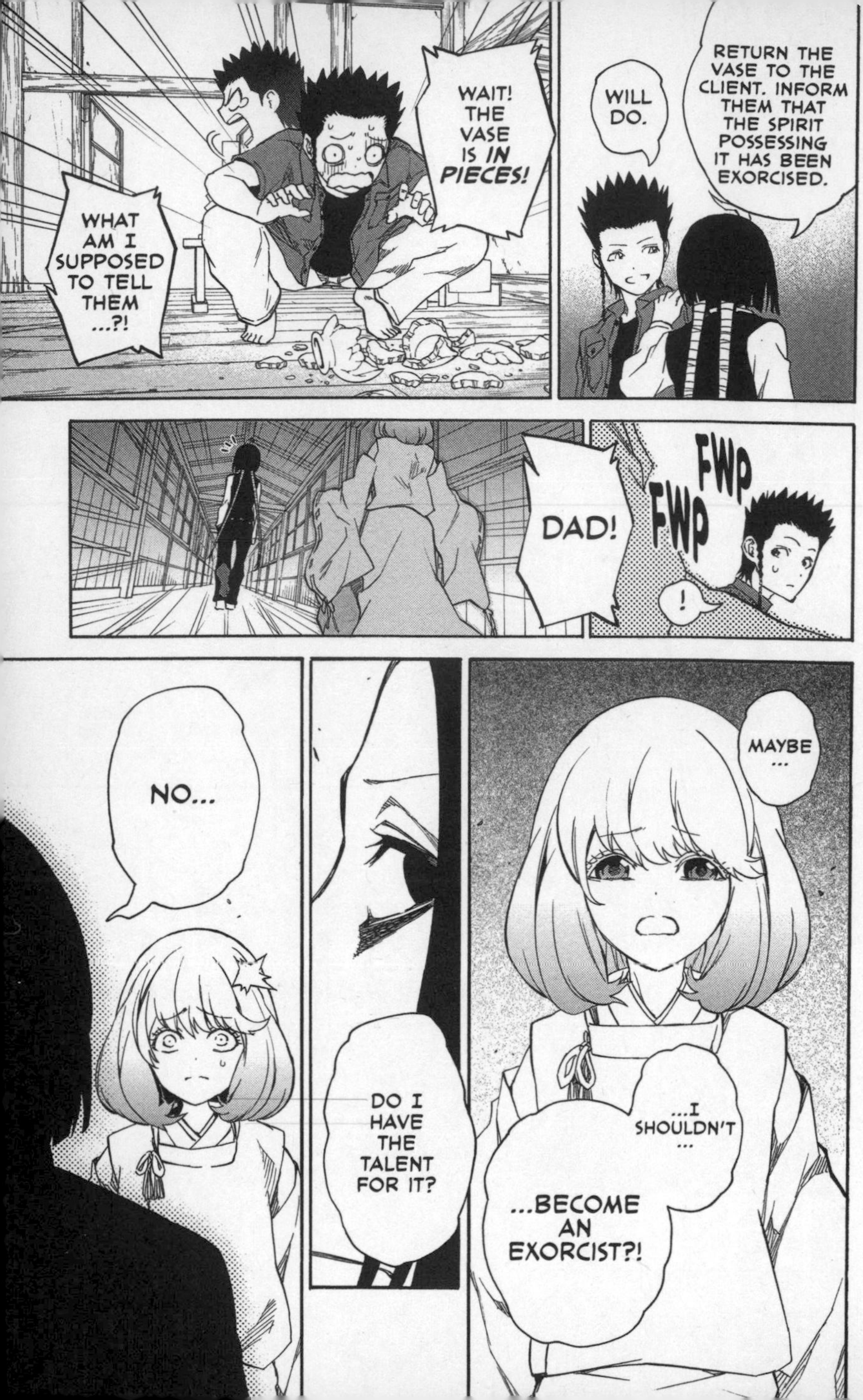
RETURN THE VASE TO THE CLIENT. INFORM THEM THAT THE SPIRIT POSSESSING IT HAS BEEN EXORCISED.
WILL DO.
WAIT! THE VASE IS *IN PIECES!*
WHAT AM I SUPPOSED TO TELL THEM ...?!
FWP
FWP
!
DAD!
MAYBE ...
...I SHOULDN'T ...
...BECOME AN EXORCIST?!
DO I HAVE THE TALENT FOR IT?
NO...

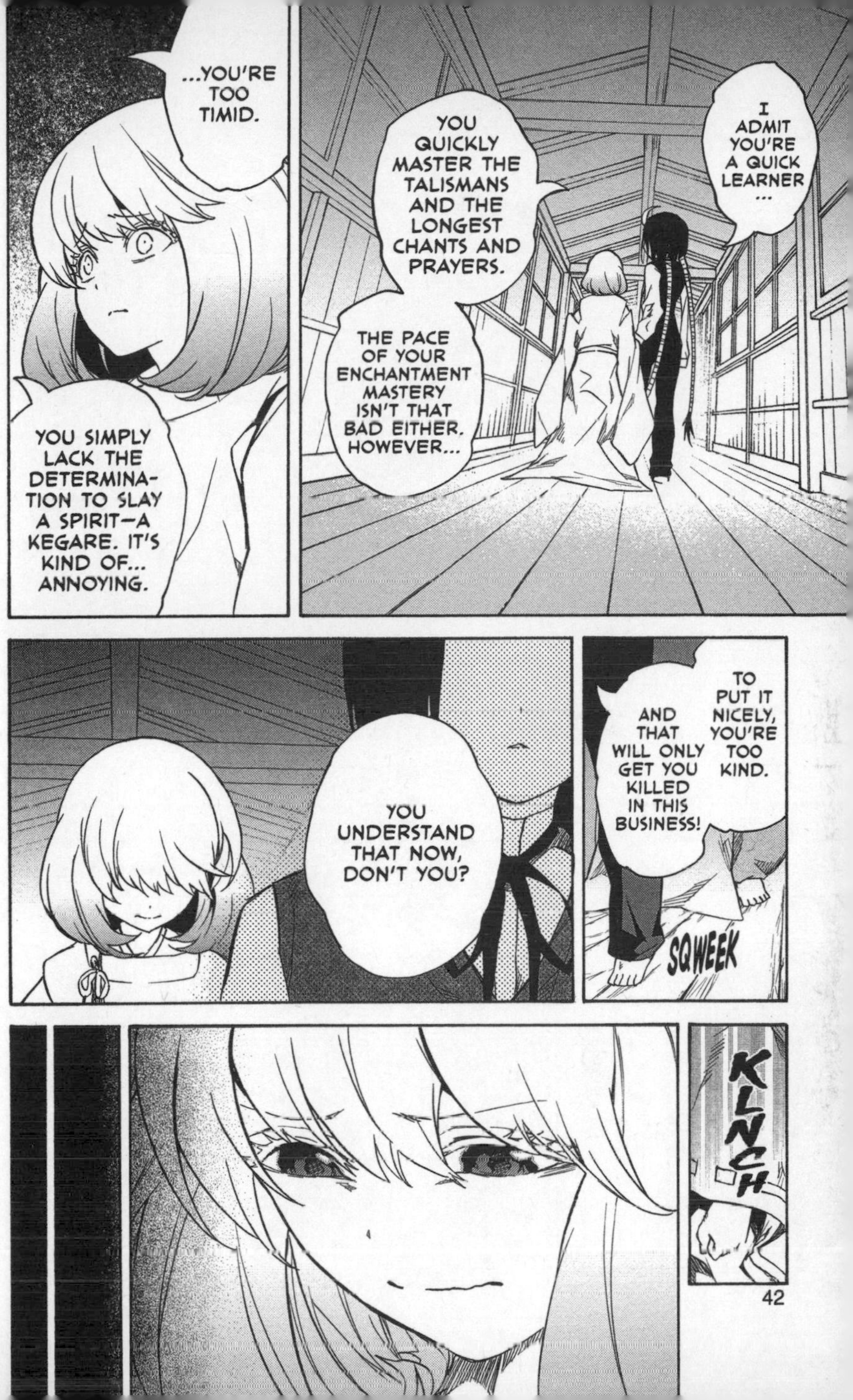
I ADMIT YOU'RE A QUICK LEARNER...
YOU QUICKLY MASTER THE TALISMANS AND THE LONGEST CHANTS AND PRAYERS.
THE PACE OF YOUR ENCHANTMENT MASTERY ISN'T THAT BAD EITHER. HOWEVER...
...YOU'RE TOO TIMID.
YOU SIMPLY LACK THE DETERMINATION TO SLAY A SPIRIT—A KEGARE. IT'S KIND OF... ANNOYING.
TO PUT IT NICELY, YOU'RE TOO KIND.
AND THAT WILL ONLY GET YOU KILLED IN THIS BUSINESS!
SQWEEK
YOU UNDERSTAND THAT NOW, DON'T YOU?
KLNCH

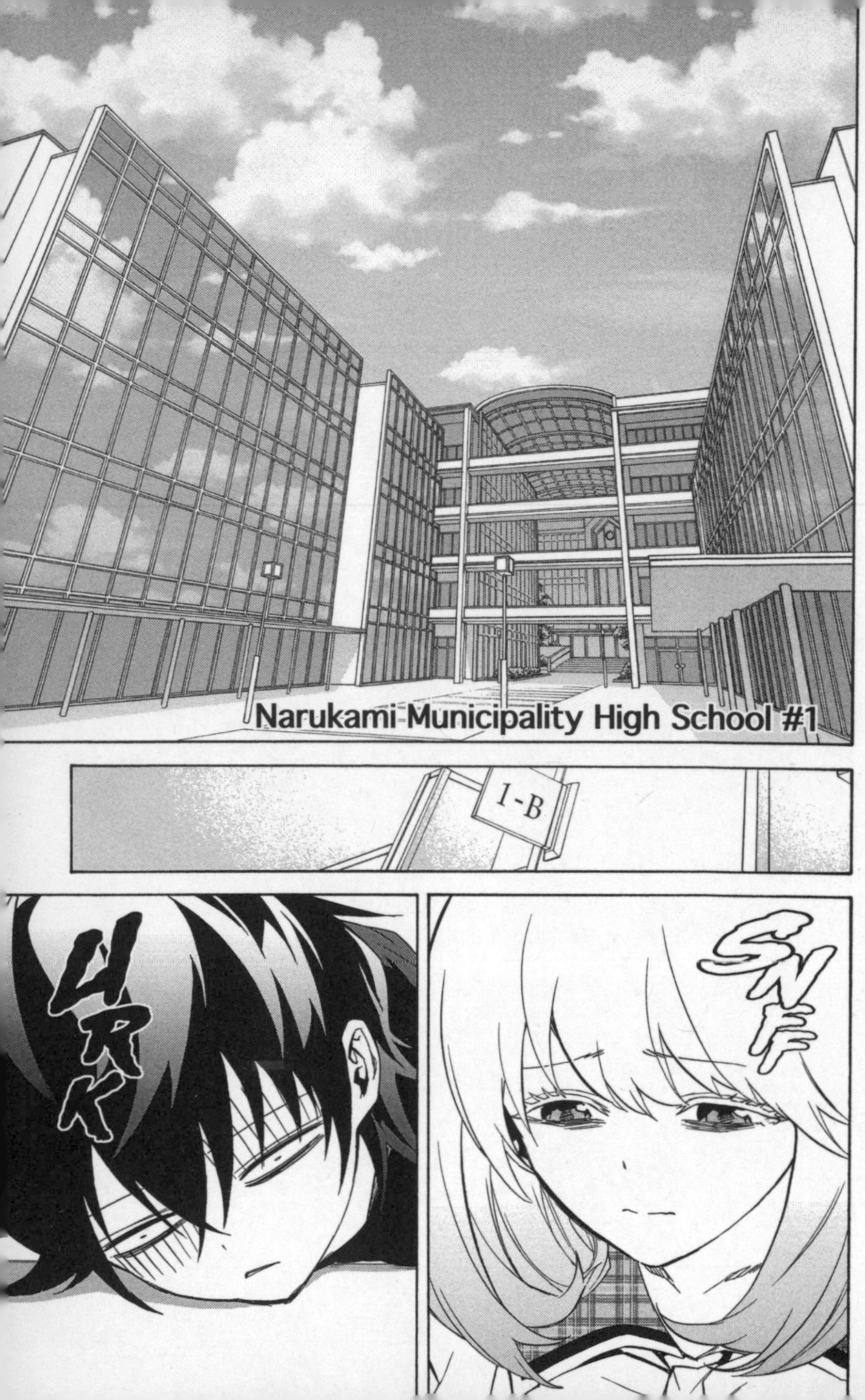
Narukami Municipality High School #1
1-B
SNFF
URK

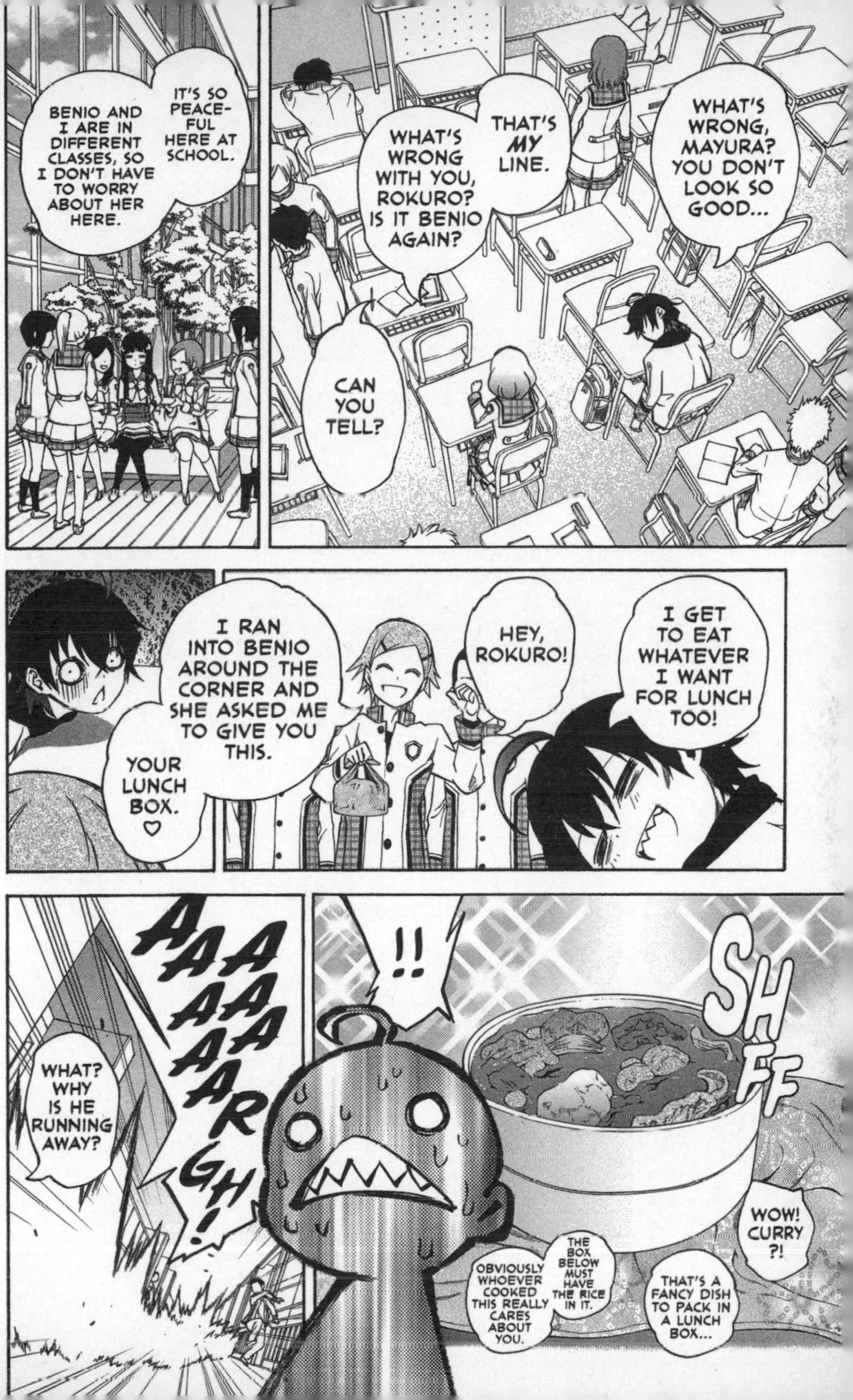
WHAT'S WRONG, MAYURA? YOU DON'T LOOK SO GOOD...
THAT'S MY LINE.
WHAT'S WRONG WITH YOU, ROKURO? IS IT BENIO AGAIN?
CAN YOU TELL?
IT'S SO PEACE-FUL HERE AT SCHOOL.
BENIO AND I ARE IN DIFFERENT CLASSES, SO I DON'T HAVE TO WORRY ABOUT HER HERE.
I GET TO EAT WHATEVER I WANT FOR LUNCH TOO!
HEY, ROKURO!
I RAN INTO BENIO AROUND THE CORNER AND SHE ASKED ME TO GIVE YOU THIS.
YOUR LUNCH BOX. ♡
SHFF
!!
WOW! CURRY?!
THAT'S A FANCY DISH TO PACK IN A LUNCH BOX...
THE BOX BELOW MUST HAVE THE RICE IN IT.
OBVIOUSLY WHOEVER COOKED THIS REALLY CARES ABOUT YOU.
AAAAAAAAARGH!
WHAT? WHY IS HE RUNNING AWAY?

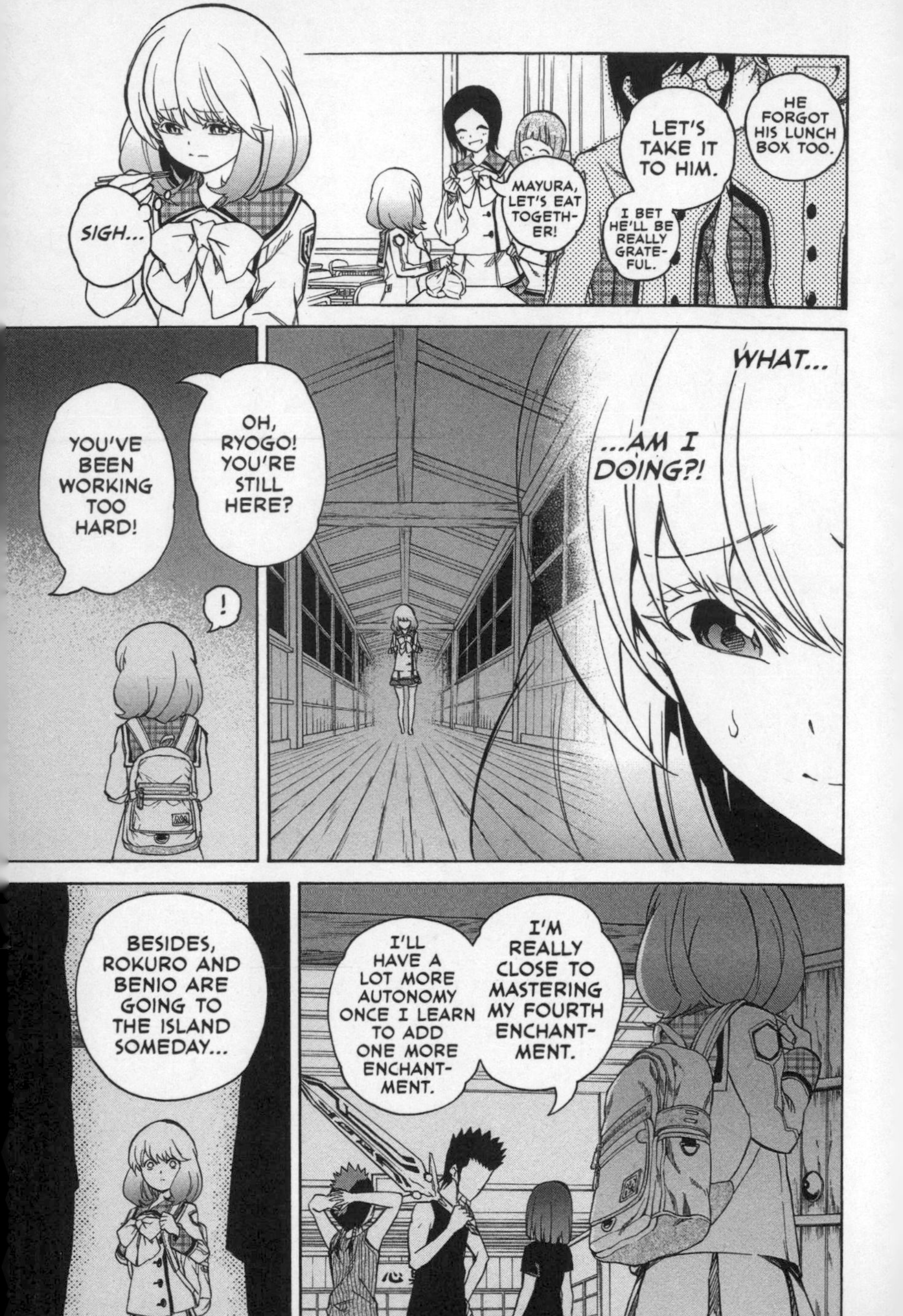
HE FORGOT HIS LUNCH BOX TOO.
LET'S TAKE IT TO HIM.
I BET HE'LL BE REALLY GRATEFUL.
MAYURA, LET'S EAT TOGETHER!
SIGH...
WHAT...
...AM I DOING?!
OH, RYOGO! YOU'RE STILL HERE?
YOU'VE BEEN WORKING TOO HARD!
!
I'M REALLY CLOSE TO MASTERING MY FOURTH ENCHANTMENT.
I'LL HAVE A LOT MORE AUTONOMY ONCE I LEARN TO ADD ONE MORE ENCHANTMENT.
BESIDES, ROKURO AND BENIO ARE GOING TO THE ISLAND SOMEDAY...

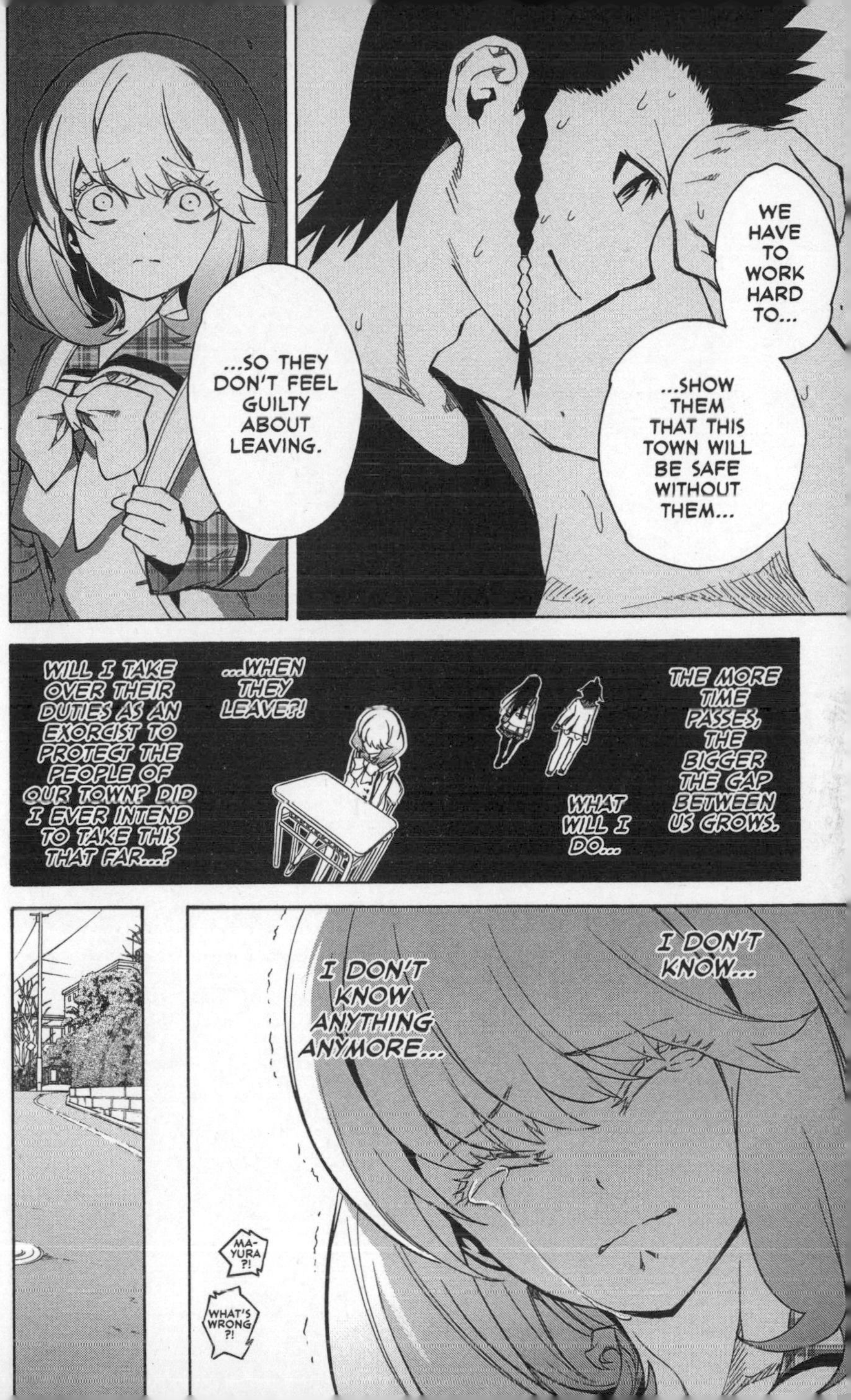
WE HAVE TO WORK HARD TO...
...SHOW THEM THAT THIS TOWN WILL BE SAFE WITHOUT THEM...
...SO THEY DON'T FEEL GUILTY ABOUT LEAVING.
THE MORE TIME PASSES, THE BIGGER THE GAP BETWEEN US GROWS.
WHAT WILL I DO...
...WHEN THEY LEAVE?!
WILL I TAKE OVER THEIR DUTIES AS AN EXORCIST TO PROTECT THE PEOPLE OF OUR TOWN? DID I EVER INTEND TO TAKE THIS THAT FAR...?
I DON'T KNOW...
I DON'T KNOW ANYTHING ANYMORE...
MA-YURA?!
WHAT'S WRONG?!

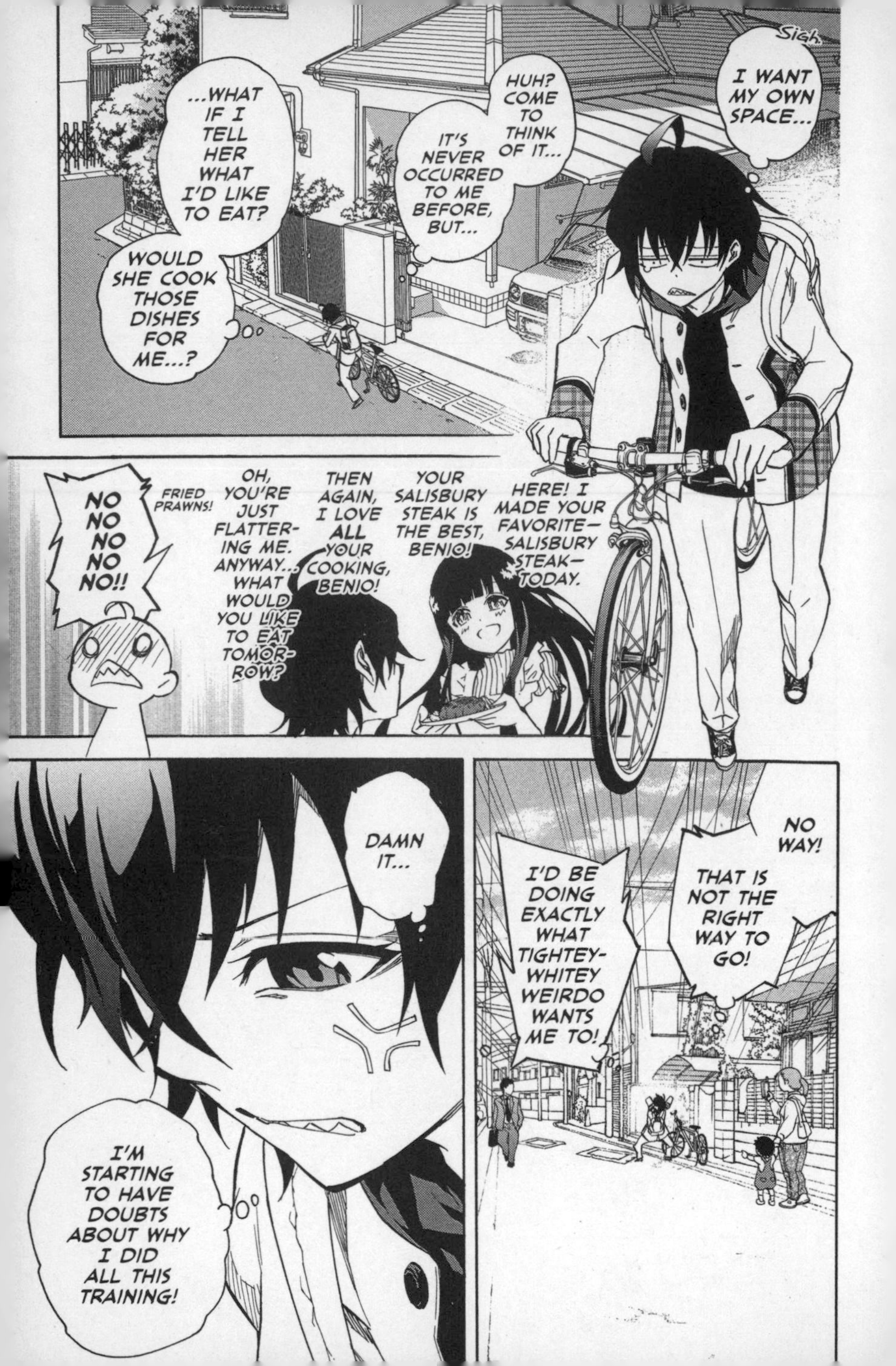
Sigh.
I WANT MY OWN SPACE...
HUH? COME TO THINK OF IT...
IT'S NEVER OCCURRED TO ME BEFORE, BUT...
...WHAT IF I TELL HER WHAT I'D LIKE TO EAT?
WOULD SHE COOK THOSE DISHES FOR ME...?
HERE! I MADE YOUR FAVORITE—SALISBURY STEAK—TODAY.
YOUR SALISBURY STEAK IS THE BEST, BENIO!
THEN AGAIN, I LOVE ALL YOUR COOKING, BENIO!
OH, YOU'RE JUST FLATTERING ME. ANYWAY... WHAT WOULD YOU LIKE TO EAT TOMORROW?
FRIED PRAWNS!
NO NO NO NO NO!!
NO WAY!
THAT IS NOT THE RIGHT WAY TO GO!
I'D BE DOING EXACTLY WHAT TIGHTEY-WHITEY WEIRDO WANTS ME TO!
DAMN IT...
I'M STARTING TO HAVE DOUBTS ABOUT WHY I DID ALL THIS TRAINING!

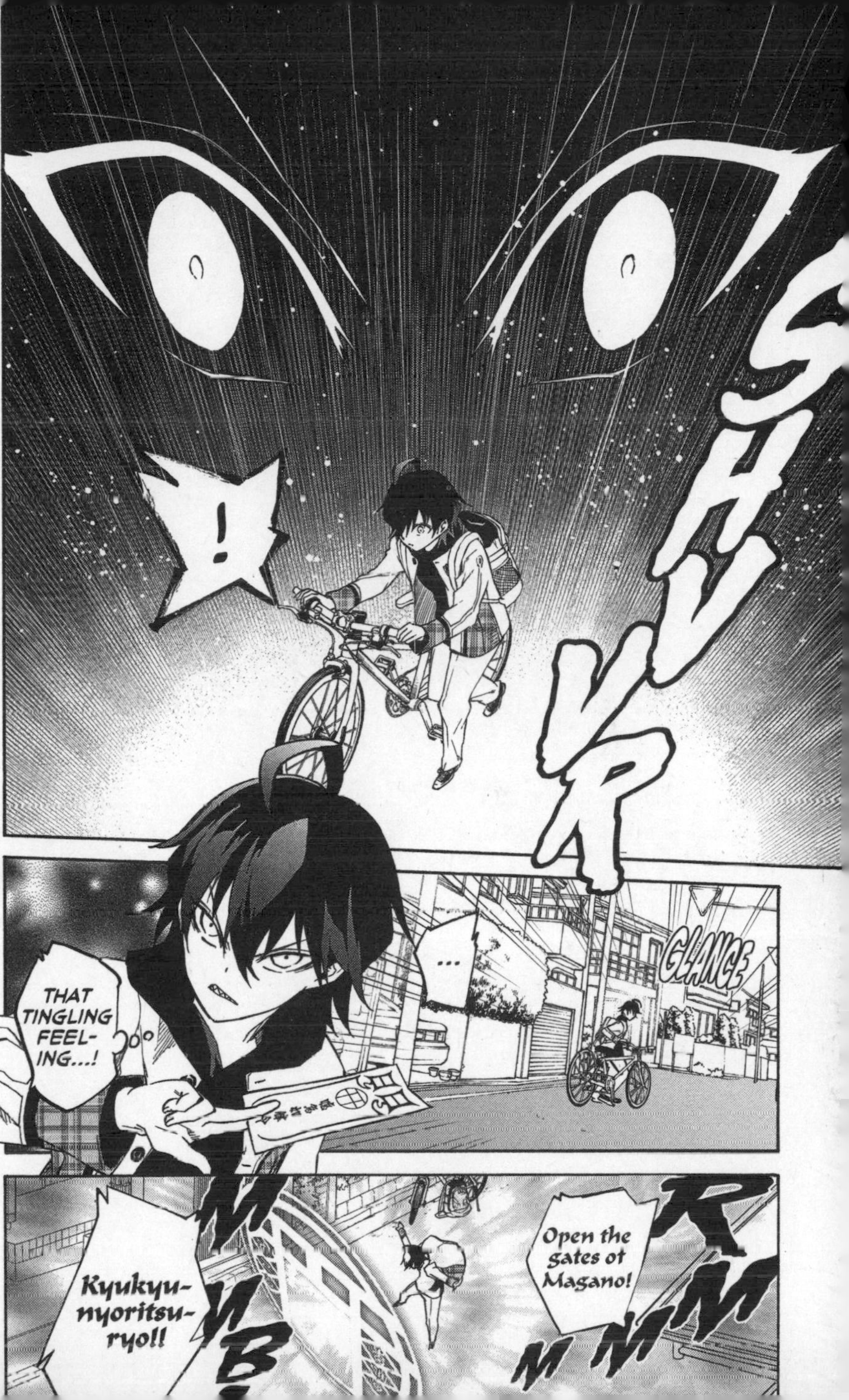

SHVVR
!
GLANCE
...
THAT TINGLING FEEL-ING...!
Open the gates of Magano!
Kyukyu-nyoritsu-ryo!!

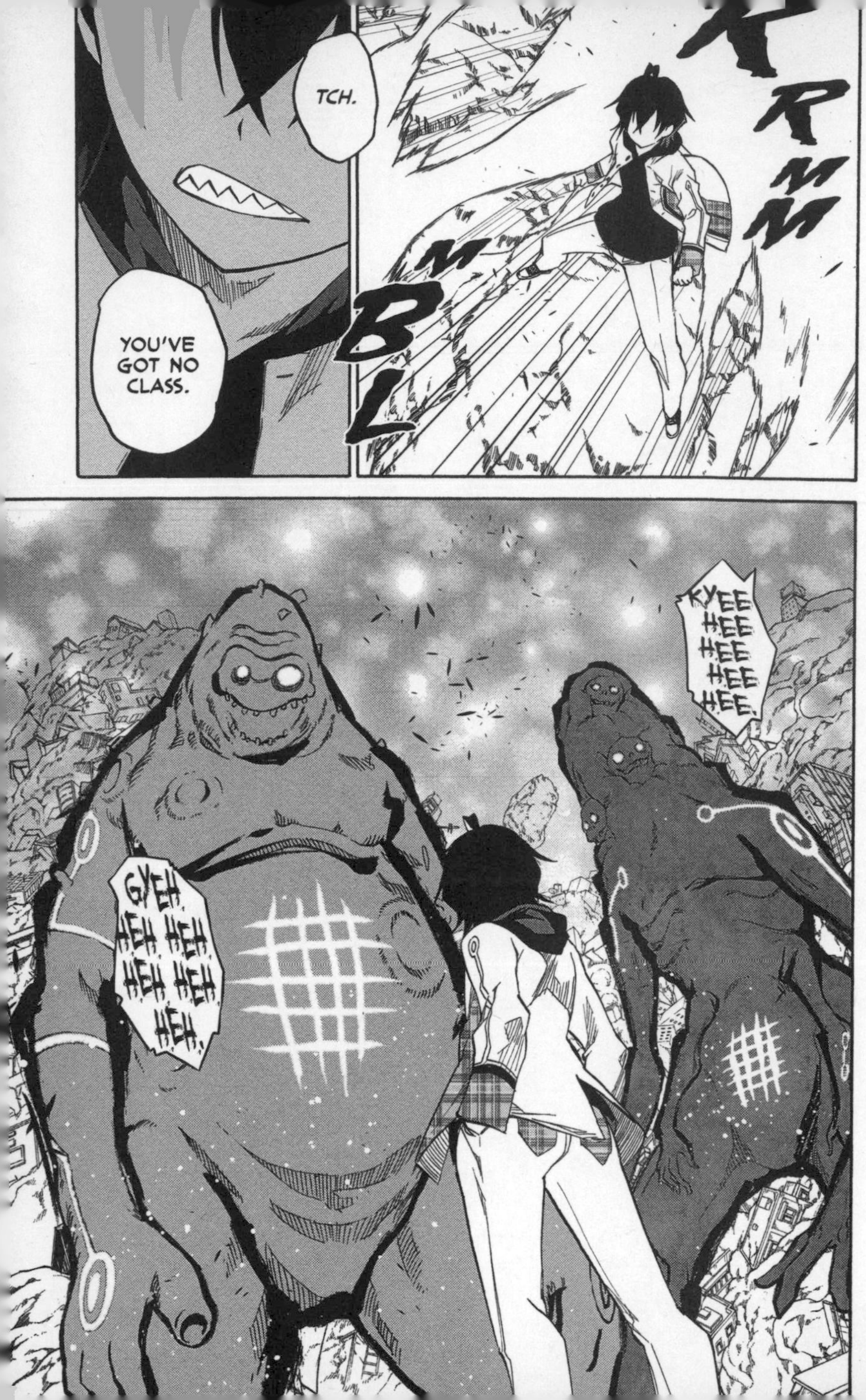
KRMMMBL
TCH.
YOU'VE GOT NO CLASS.
KYEE HEE HEE HEE HEE.
GYEH HEH HEH HEH HEH HEH.

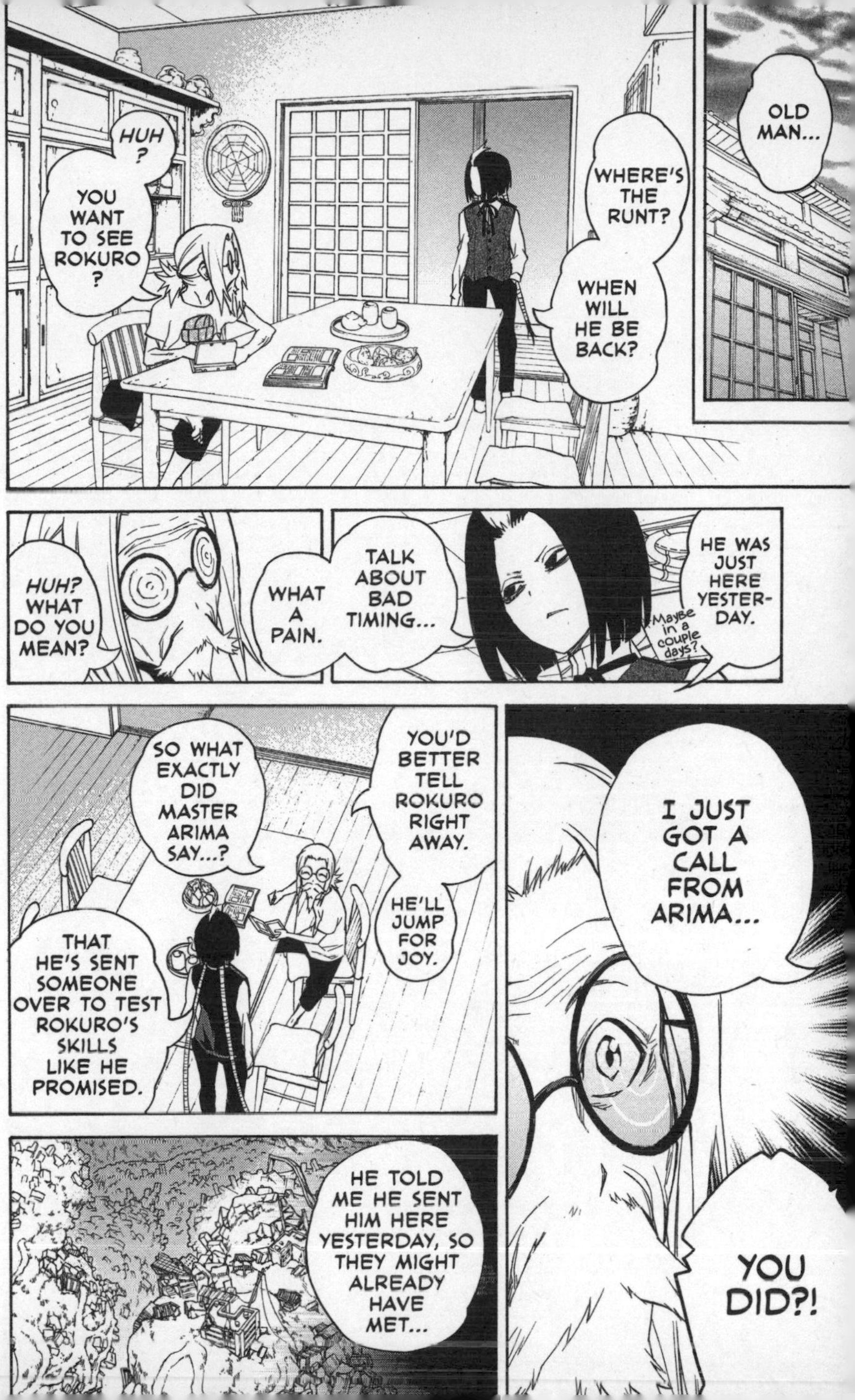
OLD MAN...
WHERE'S THE RUNT?
WHEN WILL HE BE BACK?
HUH?
YOU WANT TO SEE ROKURO?
HE WAS JUST HERE YESTERDAY.
Maybe in a couple days?
TALK ABOUT BAD TIMING...
WHAT A PAIN.
HUH? WHAT DO YOU MEAN?
I JUST GOT A CALL FROM ARIMA...
YOU DID?!
YOU'D BETTER TELL ROKURO RIGHT AWAY.
HE'LL JUMP FOR JOY.
SO WHAT EXACTLY DID MASTER ARIMA SAY...?
THAT HE'S SENT SOMEONE OVER TO TEST ROKURO'S SKILLS LIKE HE PROMISED.
HE TOLD ME HE SENT HIM HERE YESTERDAY, SO THEY MIGHT ALREADY HAVE MET...

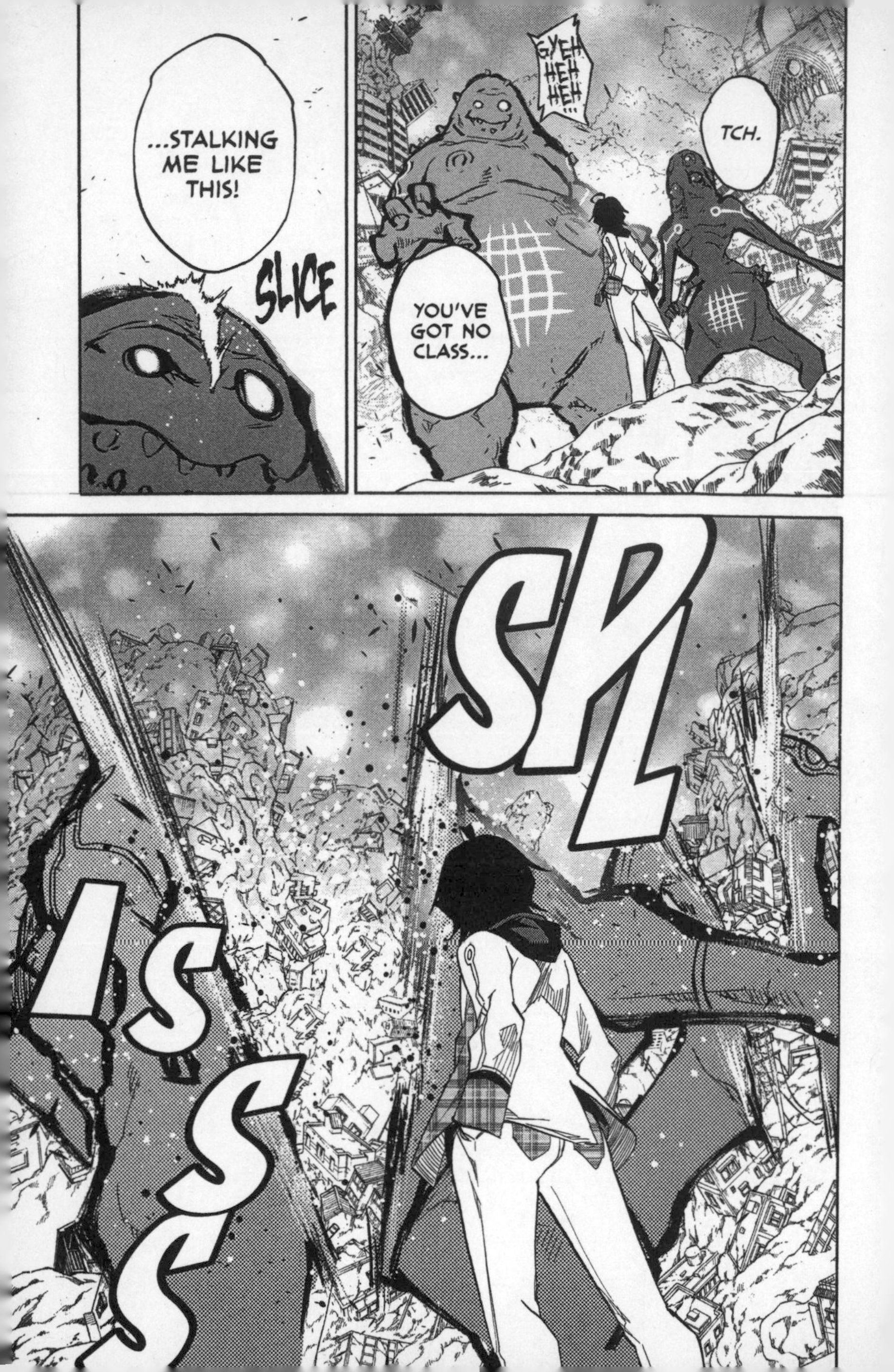
GYEH HEH HEH...
TCH.
YOU'VE GOT NO CLASS...
...STALKING ME LIKE THIS!
SLICE
SPLISSS

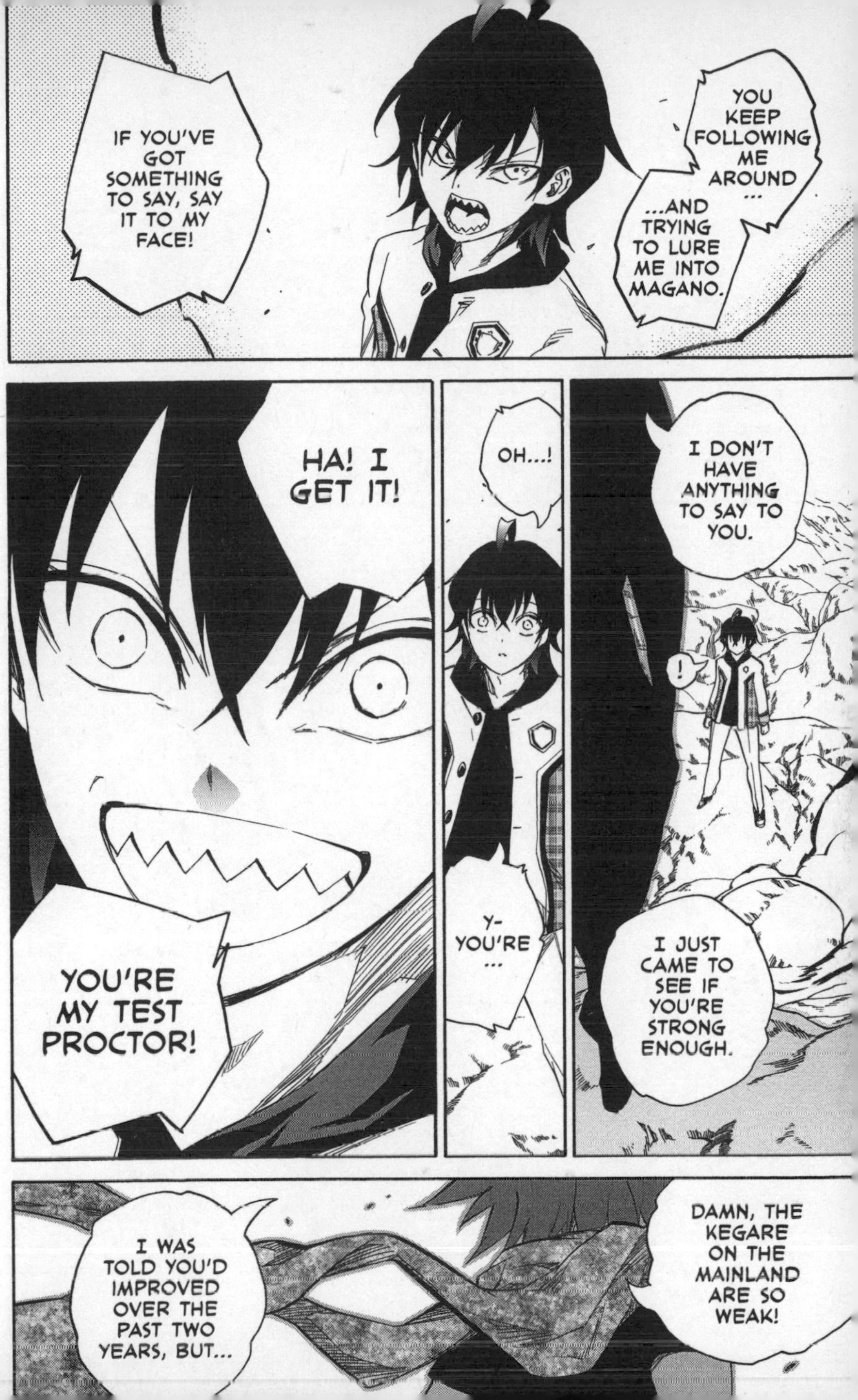
YOU KEEP FOLLOWING ME AROUND...
...AND TRYING TO LURE ME INTO MAGANO.
IF YOU'VE GOT SOMETHING TO SAY, SAY IT TO MY FACE!
I DON'T HAVE ANYTHING TO SAY TO YOU.
!
I JUST CAME TO SEE IF YOU'RE STRONG ENOUGH.
OH...!
Y-YOU'RE...
HA! I GET IT!
YOU'RE MY TEST PROCTOR!
DAMN, THE KEGARE ON THE MAINLAND ARE SO WEAK!
I WAS TOLD YOU'D IMPROVED OVER THE PAST TWO YEARS, BUT...

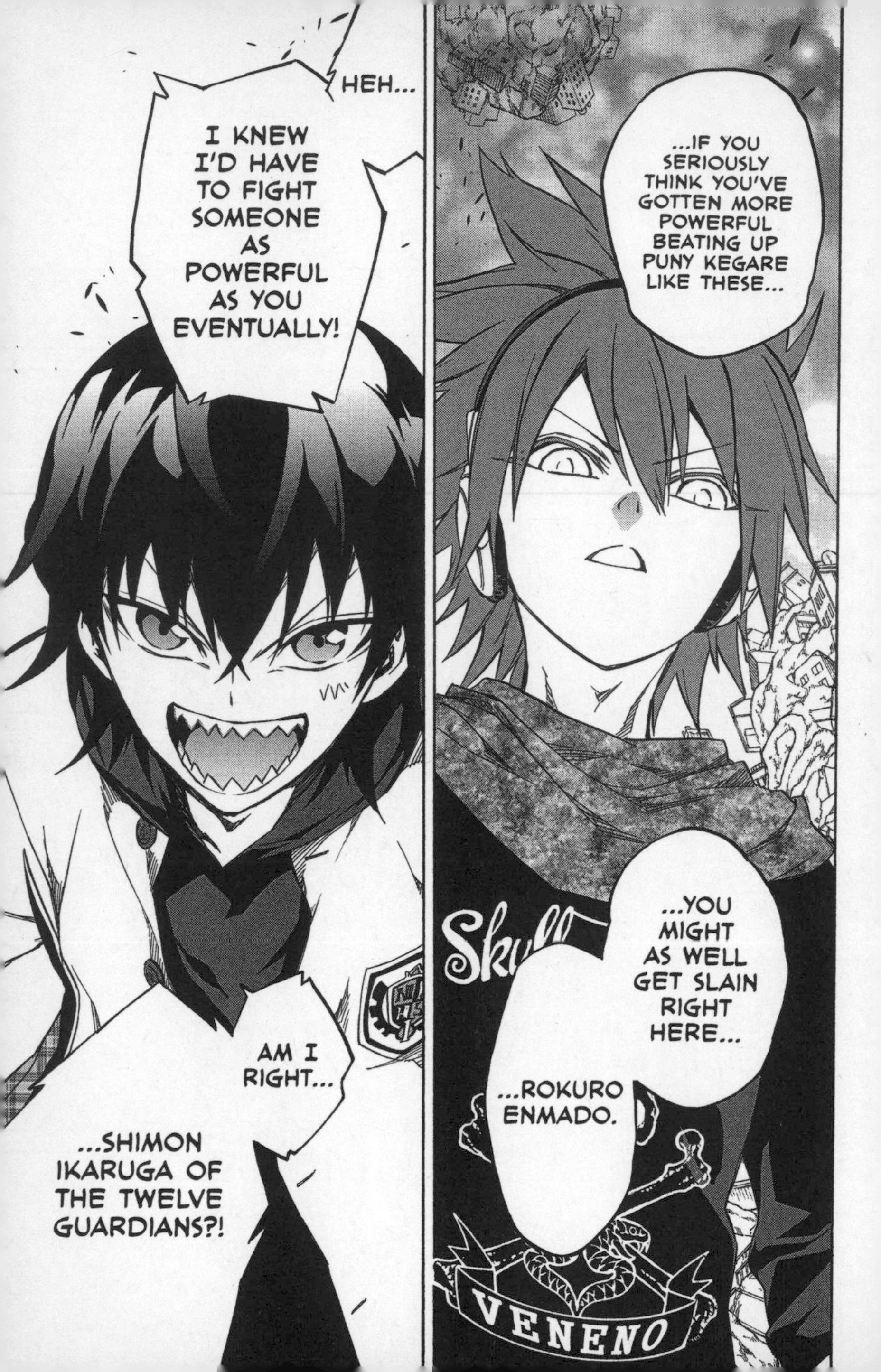
...IF YOU SERIOUSLY THINK YOU'VE GOTTEN MORE POWERFUL BEATING UP PUNY KEGARE LIKE THESE...
...YOU MIGHT AS WELL GET SLAIN RIGHT HERE...
...ROKURO ENMADO.
VENENO
HEH...
I KNEW I'D HAVE TO FIGHT SOMEONE AS POWERFUL AS YOU EVENTUALLY!
AM I RIGHT...
...SHIMON IKARUGA OF THE TWELVE GUARDIANS?!

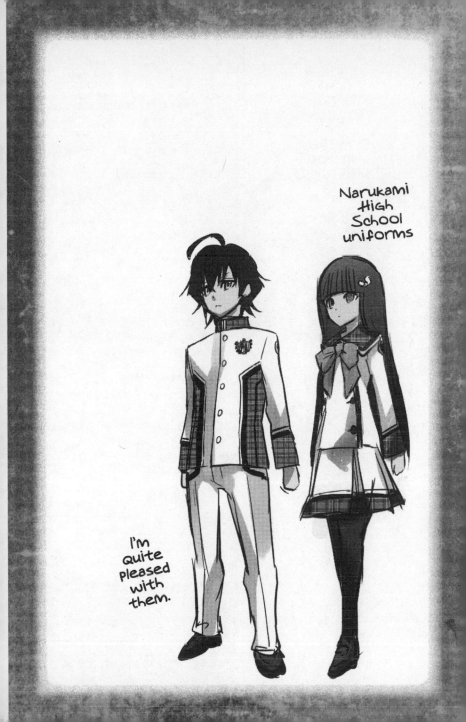

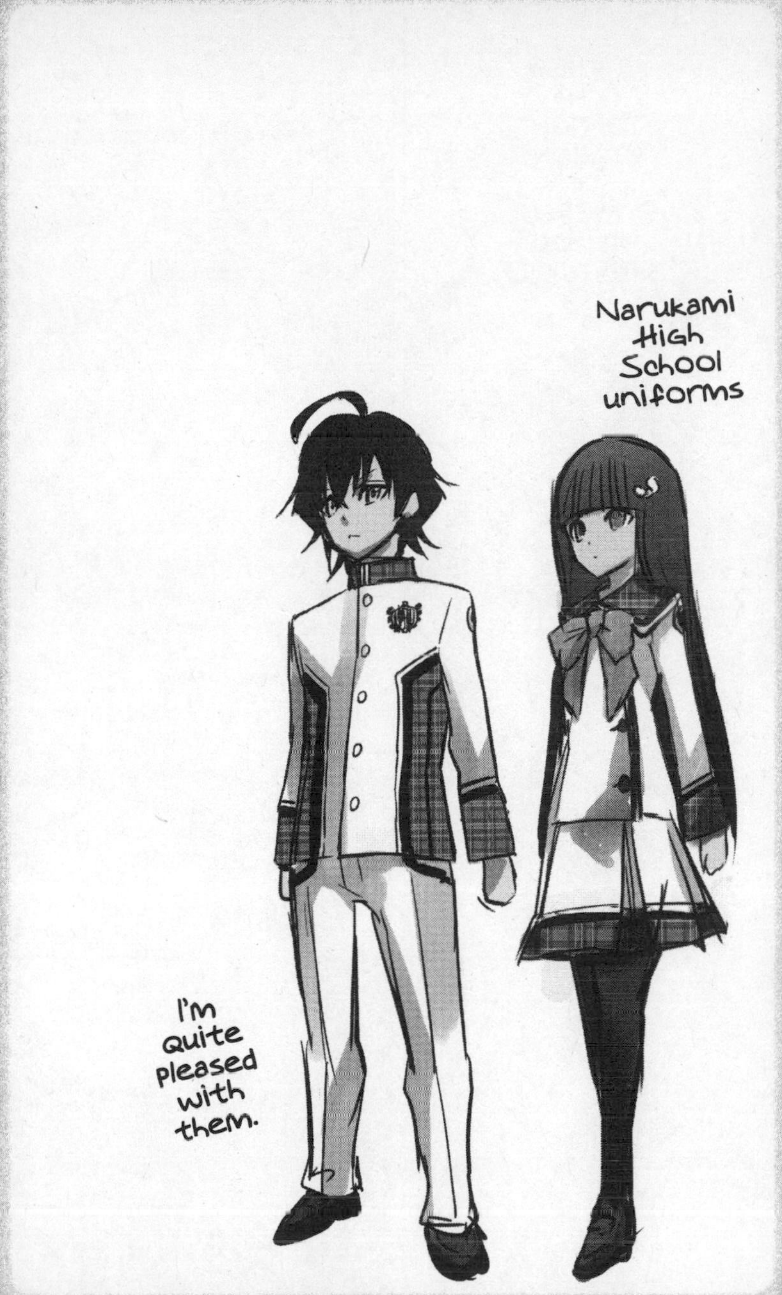
Narukami High School uniforms
I'm quite pleased with them.

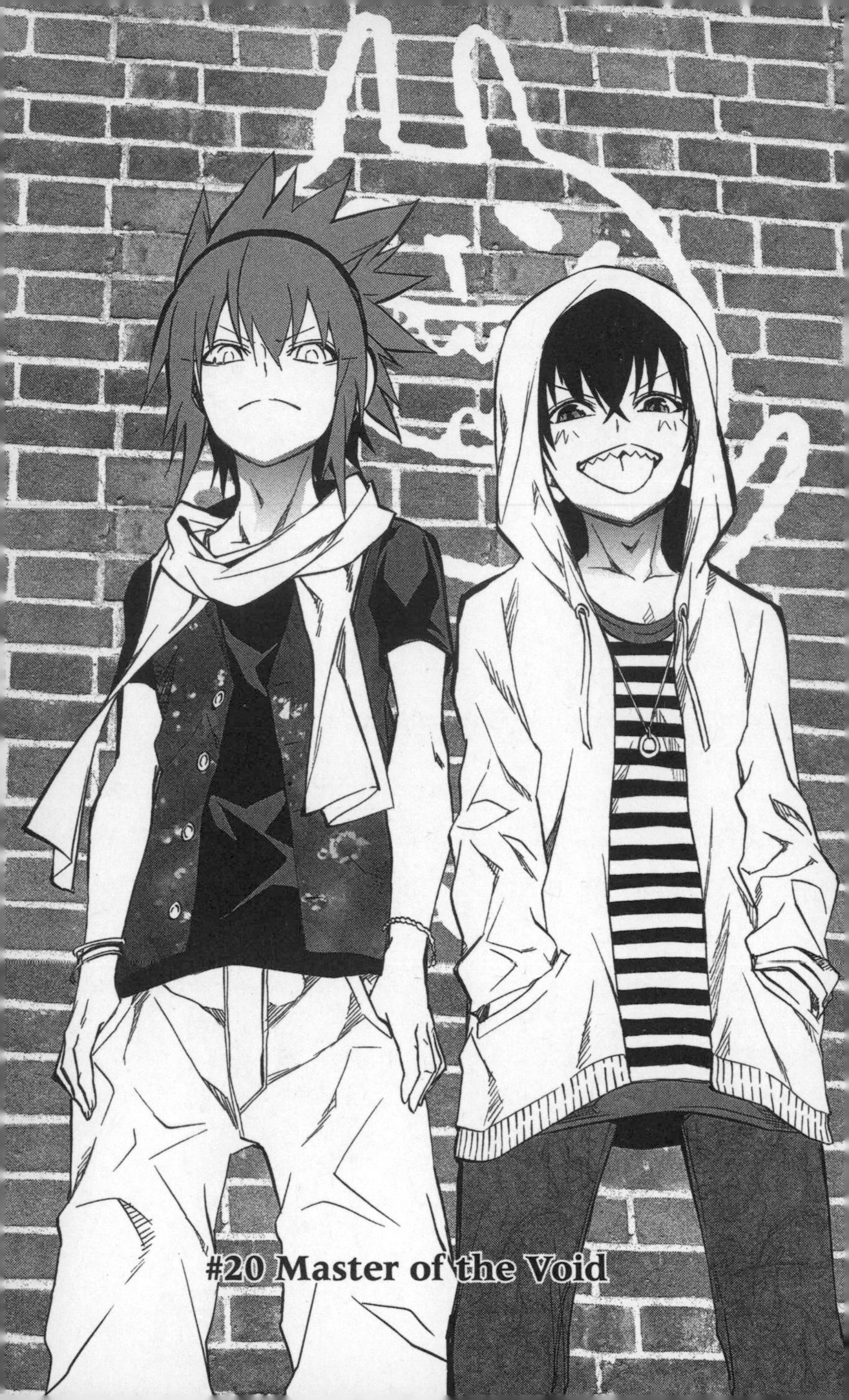

#20 Master of the Void

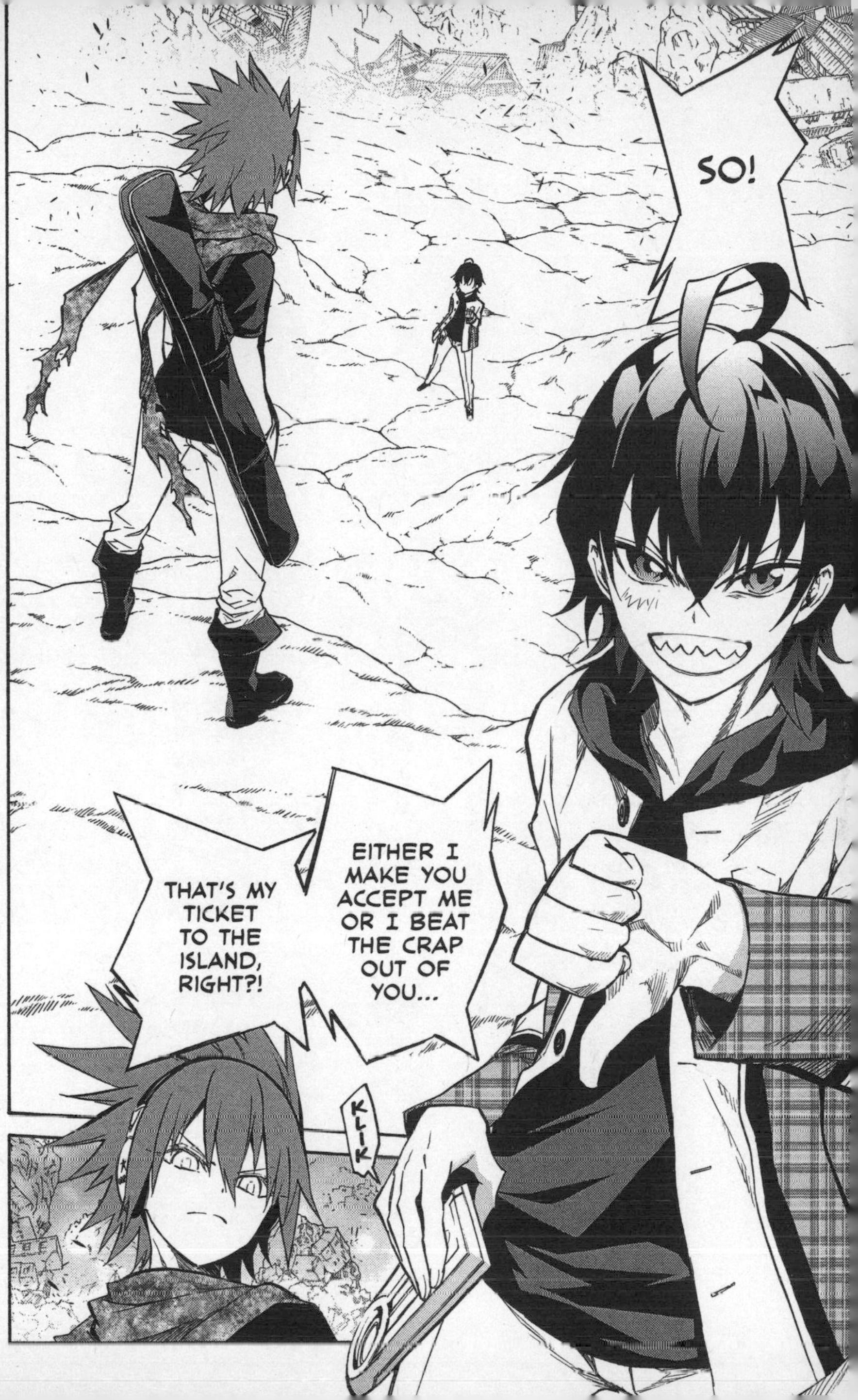
SO!
EITHER I MAKE YOU ACCEPT ME OR I BEAT THE CRAP OUT OF YOU...
THAT'S MY TICKET TO THE ISLAND, RIGHT?!
KLIK

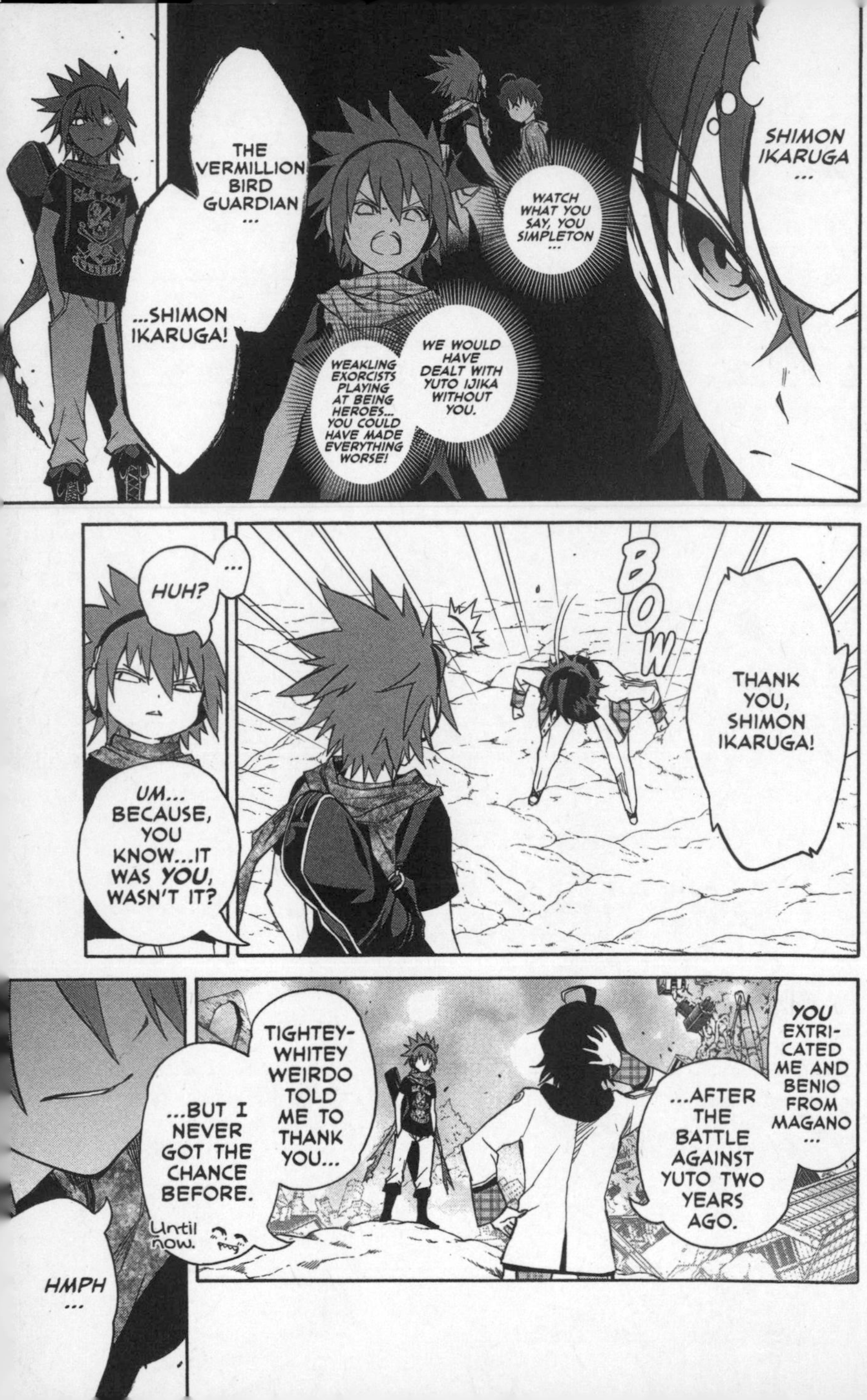
SHIMON IKARUGA ...
WATCH WHAT YOU SAY, YOU SIMPLETON ...
WE WOULD HAVE DEALT WITH YUTO IJIKA WITHOUT YOU.
WEAKLING EXORCISTS PLAYING AT BEING HEROES... YOU COULD HAVE MADE EVERYTHING WORSE!
THE VERMILLION BIRD GUARDIAN ...
...SHIMON IKARUGA!
BOW
THANK YOU, SHIMON IKARUGA!
...
HUH?
UM... BECAUSE, YOU KNOW...IT WAS *YOU*, WASN'T IT?
YOU EXTRICATED ME AND BENIO FROM MAGANO ...
...AFTER THE BATTLE AGAINST YUTO TWO YEARS AGO.
TIGHTEY-WHITEY WEIRDO TOLD ME TO THANK YOU...
...BUT I NEVER GOT THE CHANCE BEFORE.
Until now.
HMPH ...

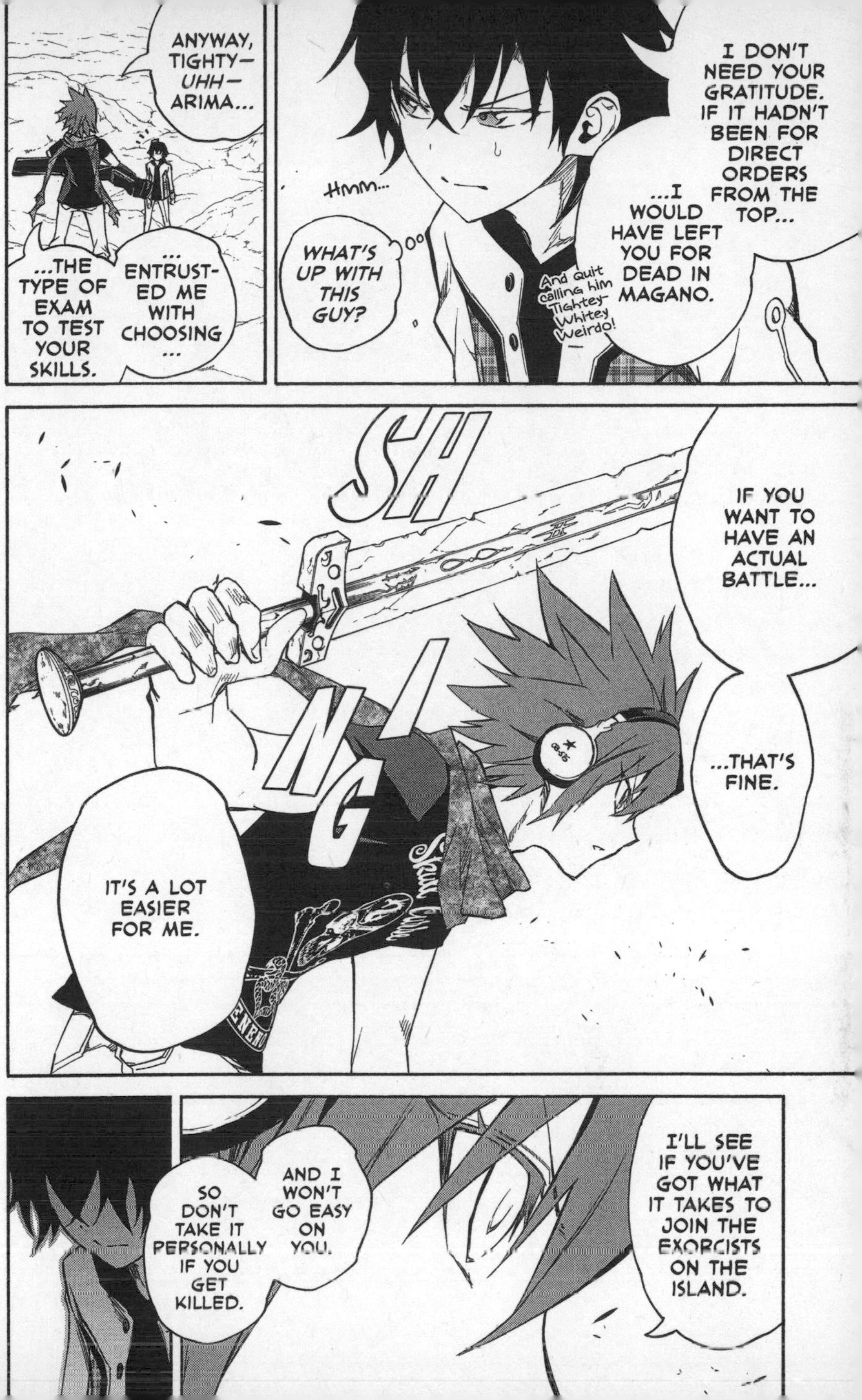
I DON'T NEED YOUR GRATITUDE. IF IT HADN'T BEEN FOR DIRECT ORDERS FROM THE TOP...
...I WOULD HAVE LEFT YOU FOR DEAD IN MAGANO.
And quit calling him Tightey-Whitey Weirdo!
Hmm...
WHAT'S UP WITH THIS GUY?
ANYWAY, TIGHTY—UHH—ARIMA...
...ENTRUST-ED ME WITH CHOOSING...
...THE TYPE OF EXAM TO TEST YOUR SKILLS.
IF YOU WANT TO HAVE AN ACTUAL BATTLE...
...THAT'S FINE.
SHING
IT'S A LOT EASIER FOR ME.
I'LL SEE IF YOU'VE GOT WHAT IT TAKES TO JOIN THE EXORCISTS ON THE ISLAND.
AND I WON'T GO EASY ON YOU.
SO DON'T TAKE IT PERSONALLY IF YOU GET KILLED.

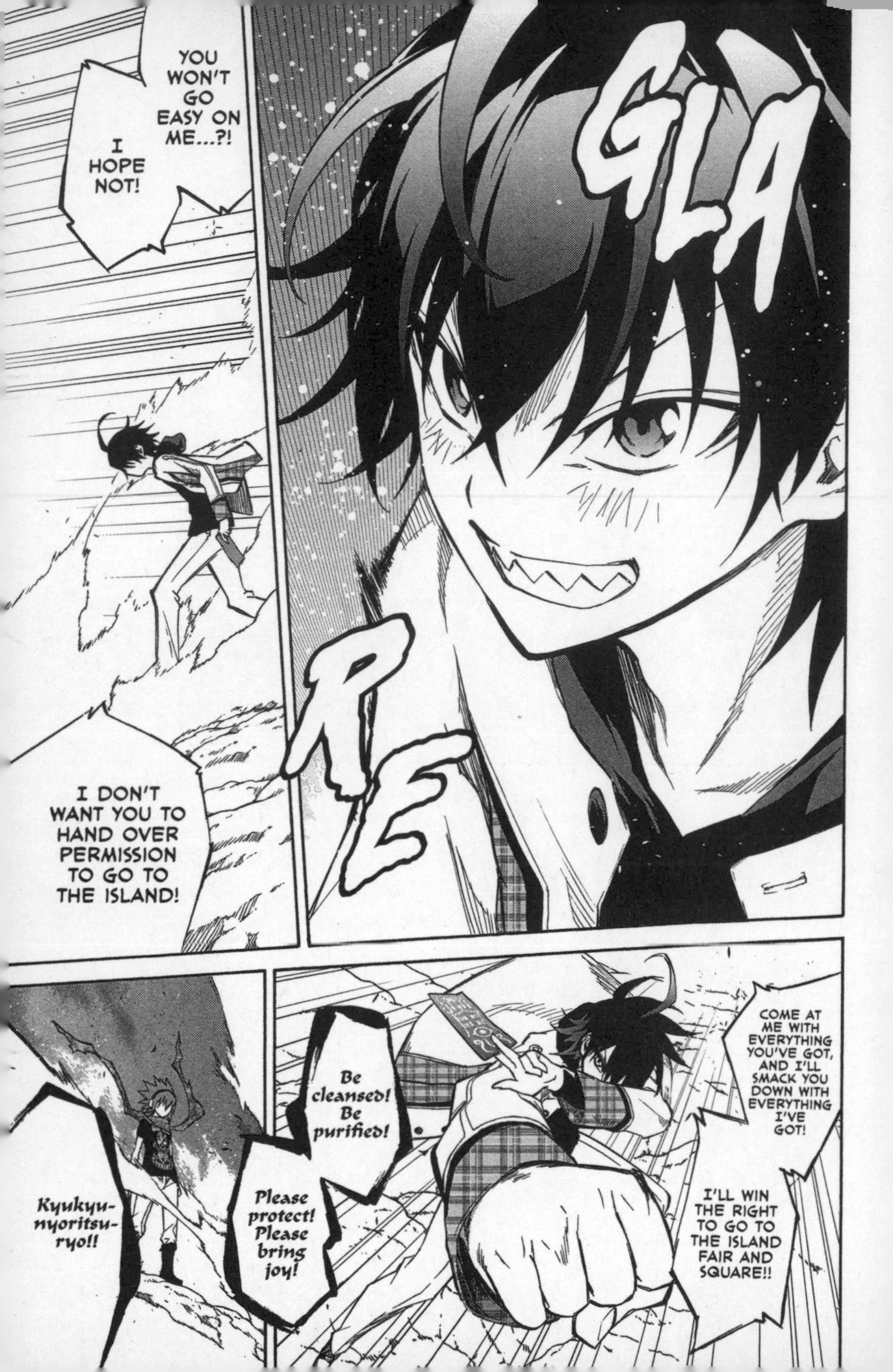
GLA
RE
YOU WON'T GO EASY ON ME...?!
I HOPE NOT!
I DON'T WANT YOU TO HAND OVER PERMISSION TO GO TO THE ISLAND!
COME AT ME WITH EVERYTHING YOU'VE GOT, AND I'LL SMACK YOU DOWN WITH EVERYTHING I'VE GOT!
I'LL WIN THE RIGHT TO GO TO THE ISLAND FAIR AND SQUARE!!
Be cleansed! Be purified!
Please protect! Please bring joy!
Kyukyu-nyoritsu-ryo!!

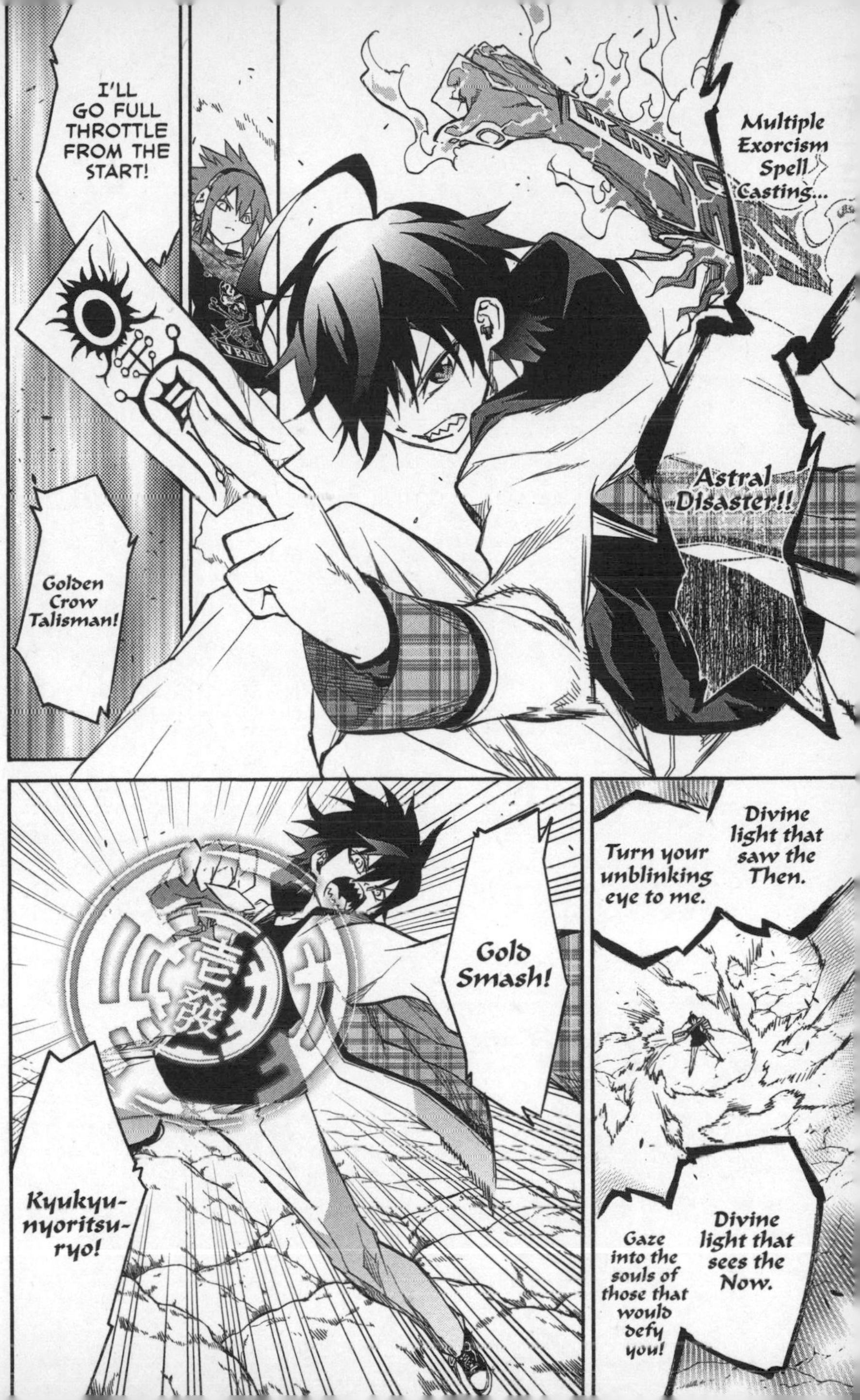
Multiple Exorcism Spell Casting...
Astral Disaster!!
I'LL GO FULL THROTTLE FROM THE START!
Golden Crow Talisman!
Divine light that saw the Then.
Turn your unblinking eye to me.
Divine light that sees the Now.
Gaze into the souls of those that would defy you!
Gold Smash!
Kyukyu-nyoritsu-ryo!

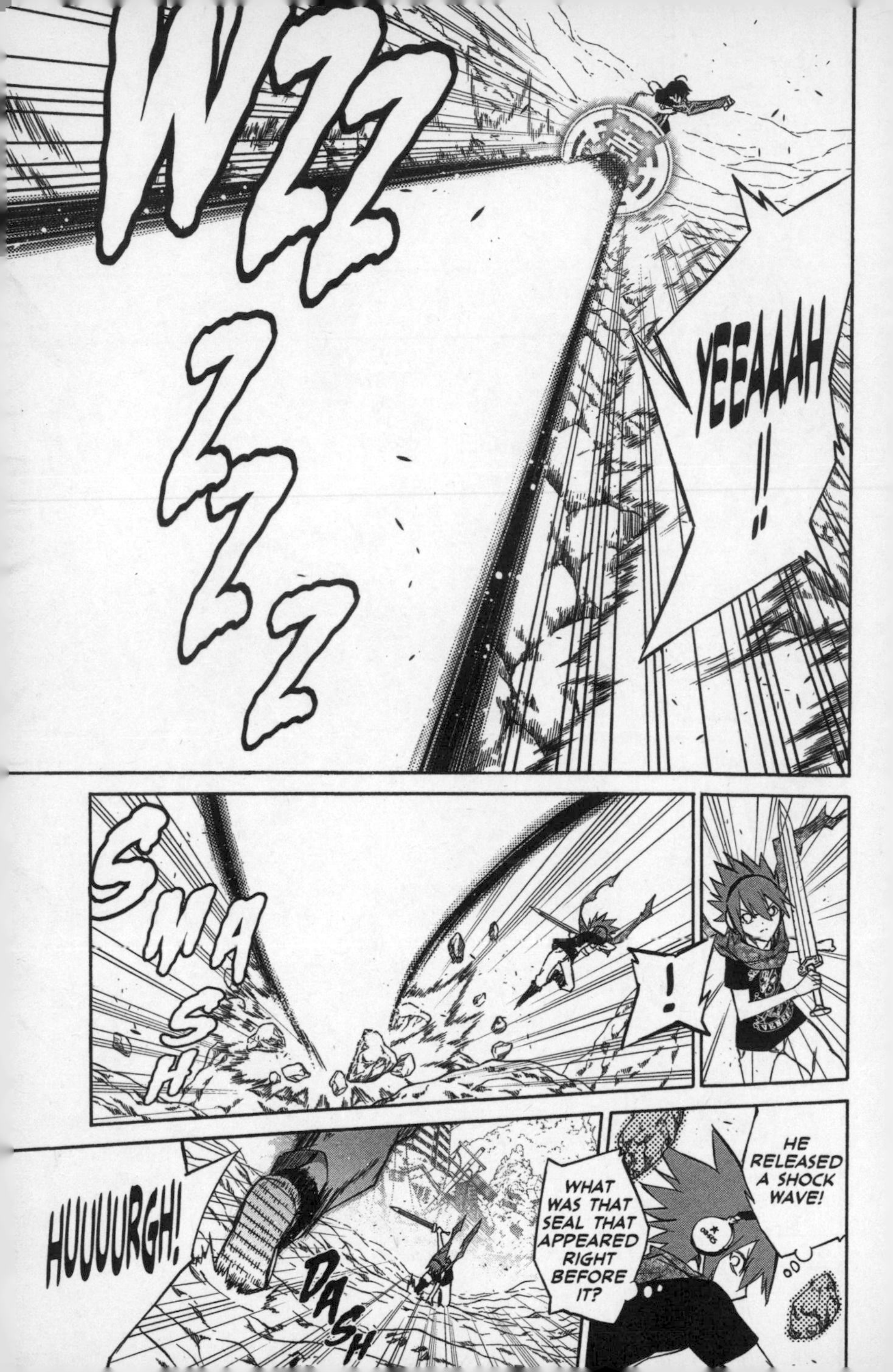
YEEAAAH!!
WZZZZZ
!
SMASH
HE RELEASED A SHOCK WAVE!
WHAT WAS THAT SEAL THAT APPEARED RIGHT BEFORE IT?
HUUUURGH!
DASH

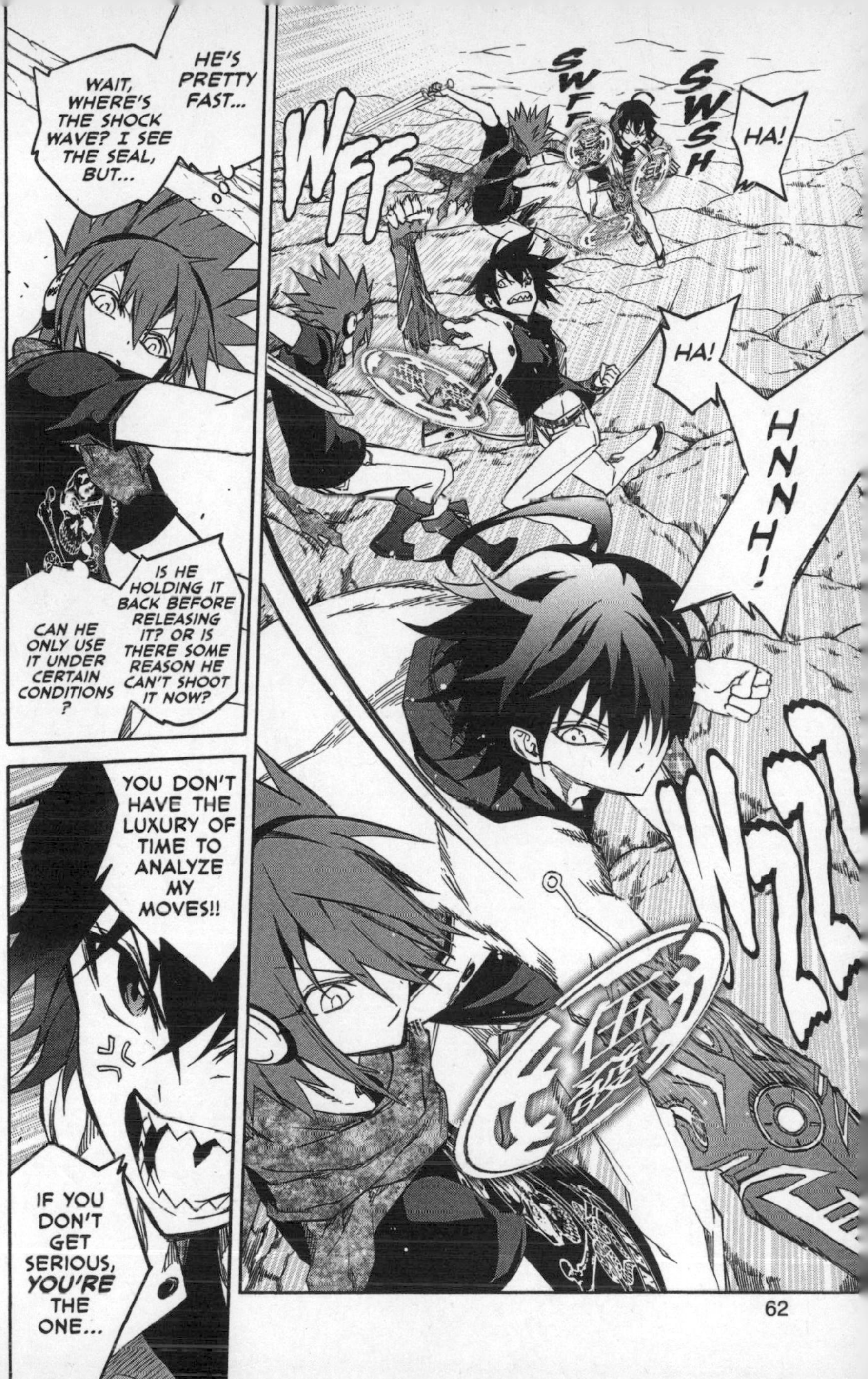
HA!
SWSH
SWFF
WFF
HA!
HNNH!
WZZ
HE'S PRETTY FAST...
WAIT, WHERE'S THE SHOCK WAVE? I SEE THE SEAL, BUT...
IS HE HOLDING IT BACK BEFORE RELEASING IT? OR IS THERE SOME REASON HE CAN'T SHOOT IT NOW?
CAN HE ONLY USE IT UNDER CERTAIN CONDITIONS?
YOU DON'T HAVE THE LUXURY OF TIME TO ANALYZE MY MOVES!!
IF YOU DON'T GET SERIOUS, *YOU'RE* THE ONE...

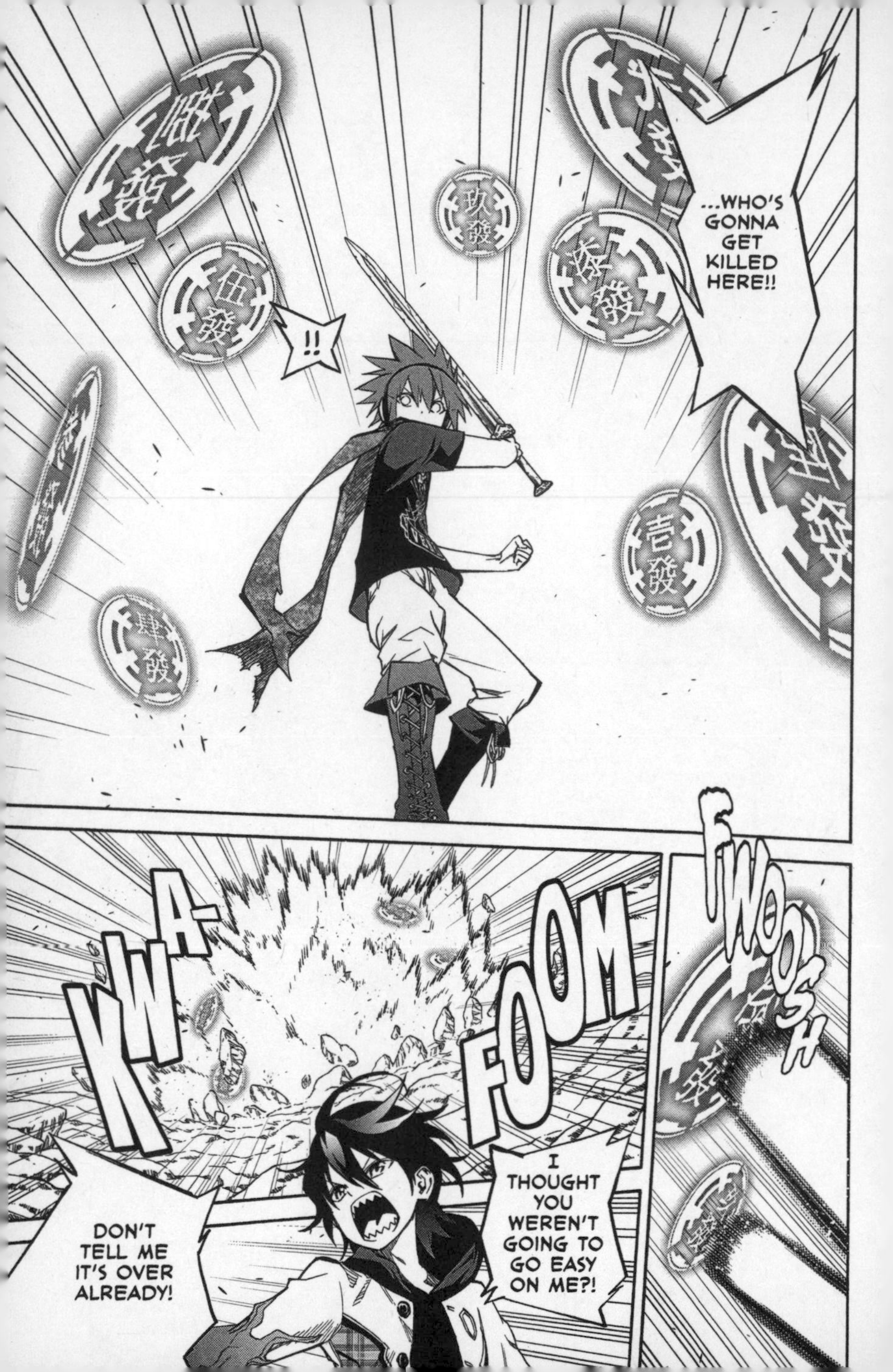
...WHO'S GONNA GET KILLED HERE!!
!!
FWOOSH
KWA-FOOM
I THOUGHT YOU WEREN'T GOING TO GO EASY ON ME?!
DON'T TELL ME IT'S OVER ALREADY!

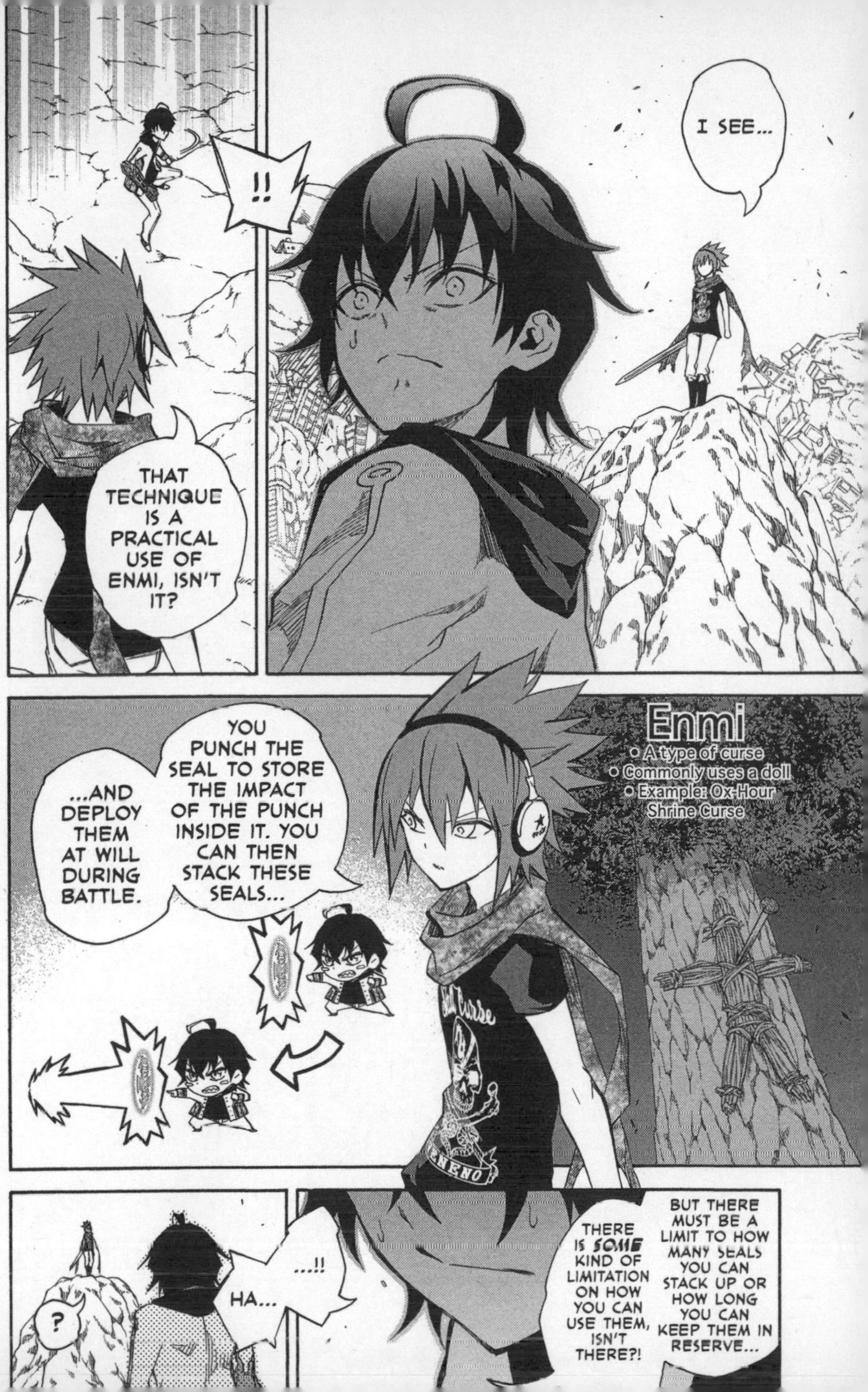
I SEE...
!!
THAT TECHNIQUE IS A PRACTICAL USE OF ENMI, ISN'T IT?
Enmi
• A type of curse
• Commonly uses a doll
• Example: Ox-Hour Shrine Curse
YOU PUNCH THE SEAL TO STORE THE IMPACT OF THE PUNCH INSIDE IT. YOU CAN THEN STACK THESE SEALS...
...AND DEPLOY THEM AT WILL DURING BATTLE.
BUT THERE MUST BE A LIMIT TO HOW MANY SEALS YOU CAN STACK UP OR HOW LONG YOU CAN KEEP THEM IN RESERVE...
THERE IS SOME KIND OF LIMITATION ON HOW YOU CAN USE THEM, ISN'T THERE?!
...!!
HA...
?

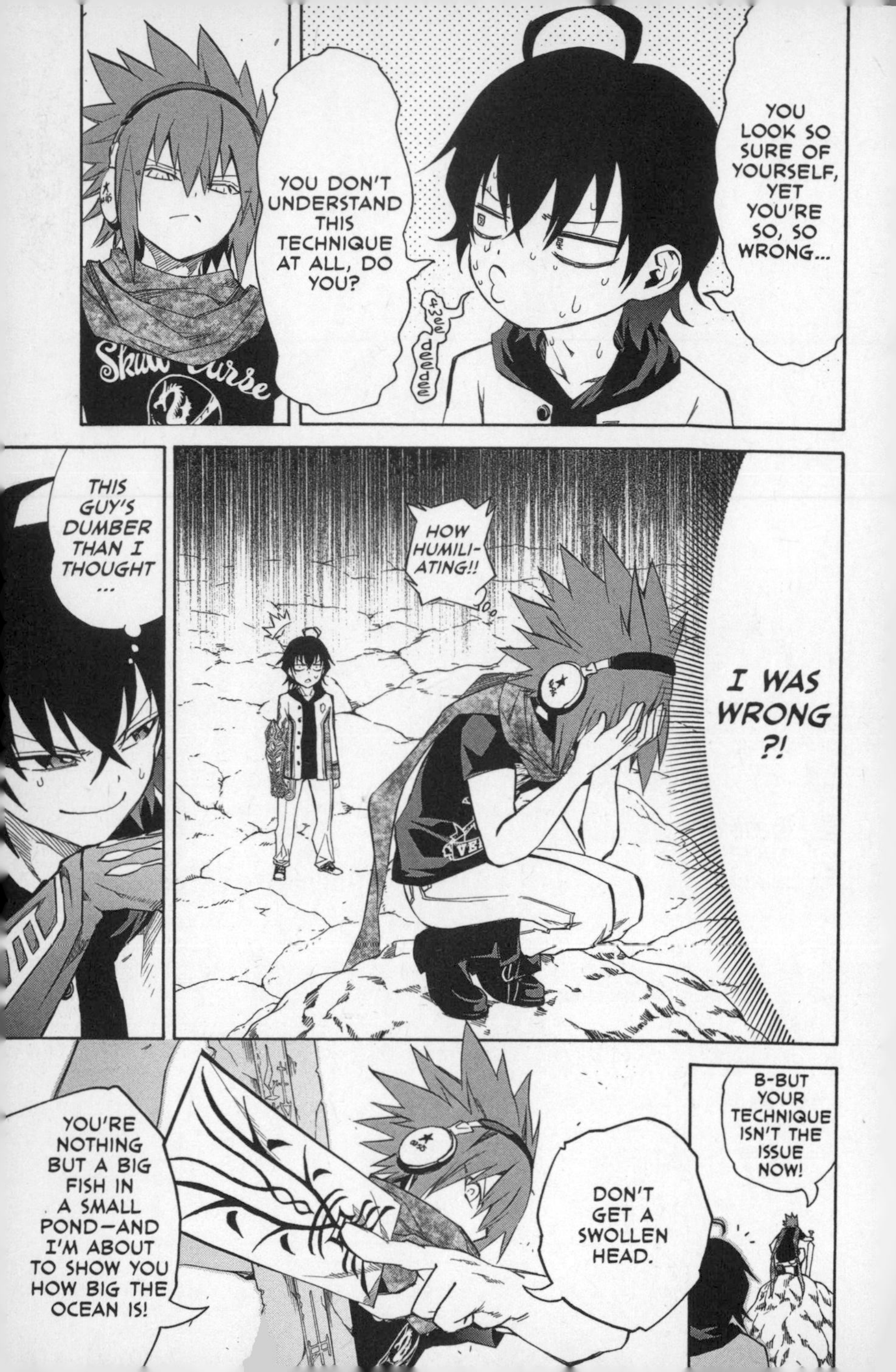
YOU LOOK SO SURE OF YOURSELF, YET YOU'RE SO, SO WRONG...
twee deedee
YOU DON'T UNDERSTAND THIS TECHNIQUE AT ALL, DO YOU?
I WAS WRONG ?!
HOW HUMILI-ATING!!
THIS GUY'S DUMBER THAN I THOUGHT ...
B-BUT YOUR TECHNIQUE ISN'T THE ISSUE NOW!
DON'T GET A SWOLLEN HEAD.
YOU'RE NOTHING BUT A BIG FISH IN A SMALL POND—AND I'M ABOUT TO SHOW YOU HOW BIG THE OCEAN IS!

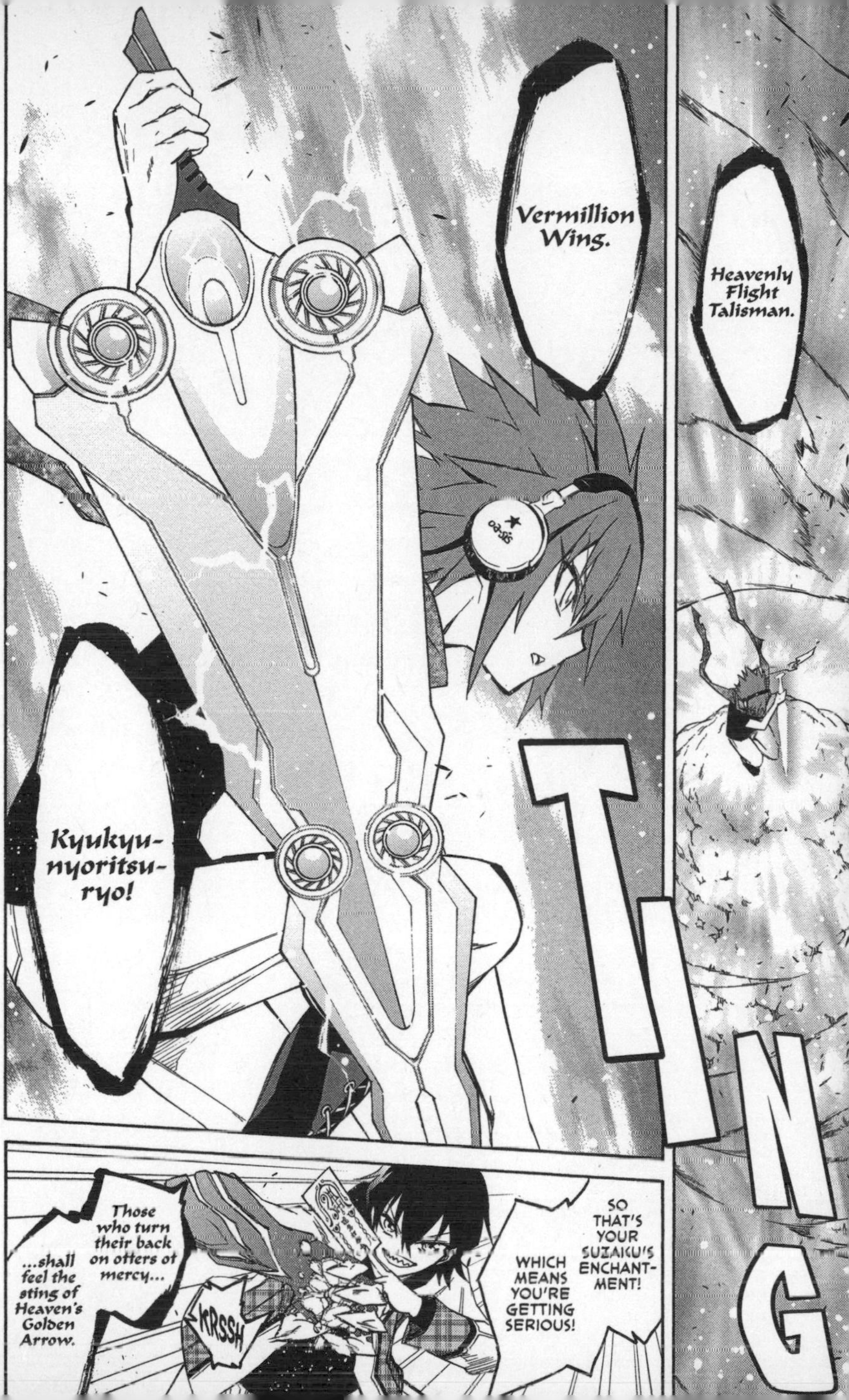
Heavenly Flight Talisman.
TING
Vermillion Wing.
Kyukyu-nyoritsu-ryo!
SO THAT'S YOUR SUZAKU'S ENCHANT-MENT!
WHICH MEANS YOU'RE GETTING SERIOUS!
Those who turn their back on offers of mercy...
...shall feel the sting of Heaven's Golden Arrow.
KRSSH

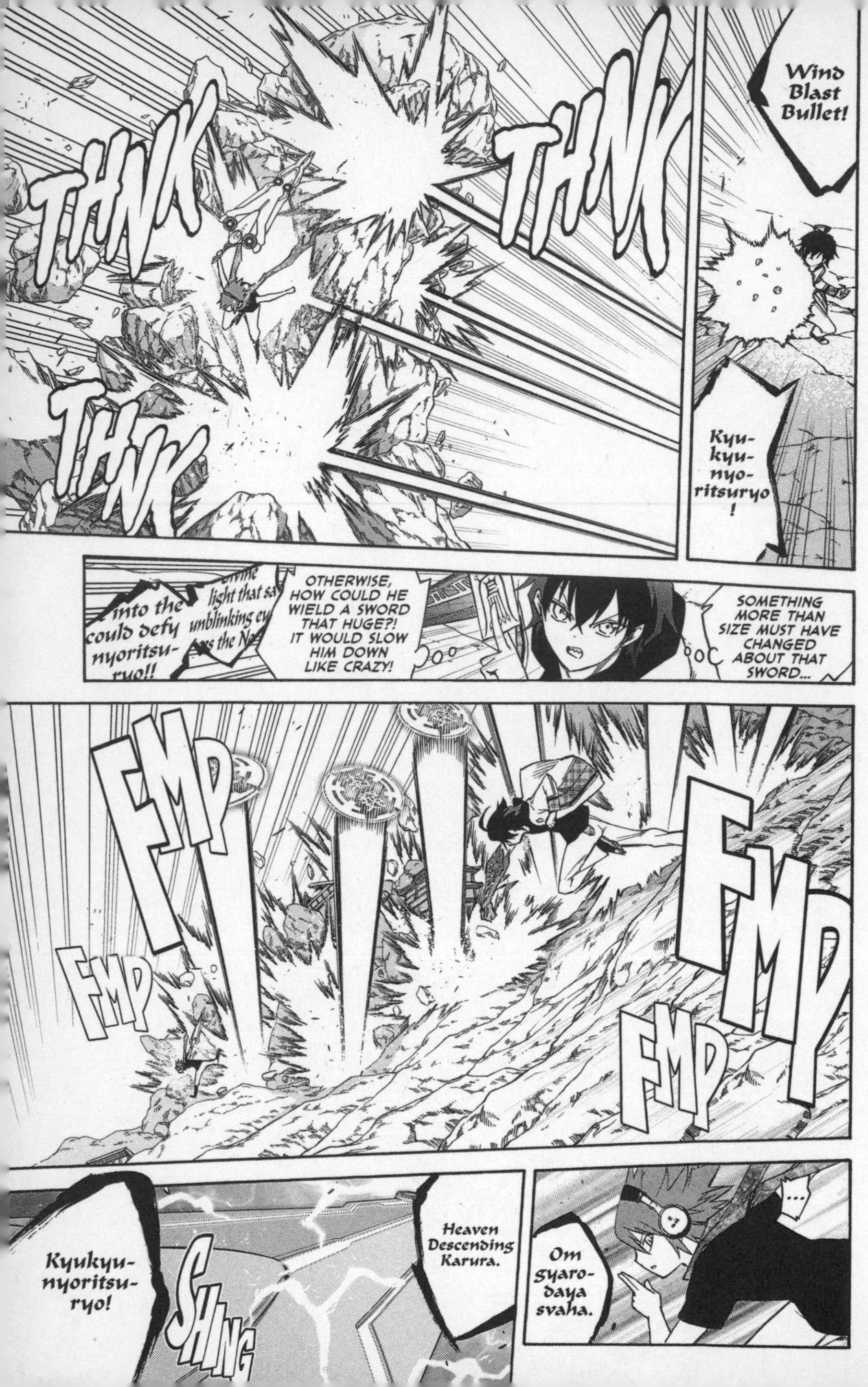
Wind Blast Bullet!
Kyu-kyu-nyo-ritsuryo!
THNK
THNK
THNK
SOMETHING MORE THAN SIZE MUST HAVE CHANGED ABOUT THAT SWORD...
OTHERWISE, HOW COULD HE WIELD A SWORD THAT HUGE?! IT WOULD SLOW HIM DOWN LIKE CRAZY!
into the could defy nyoritsu-ryo!!
FMP
FMP
FMP
FMP
...
Om gyaro-daya svaha.
Heaven Descending Karura.
Kyukyu-nyoritsu-ryo!
SHING

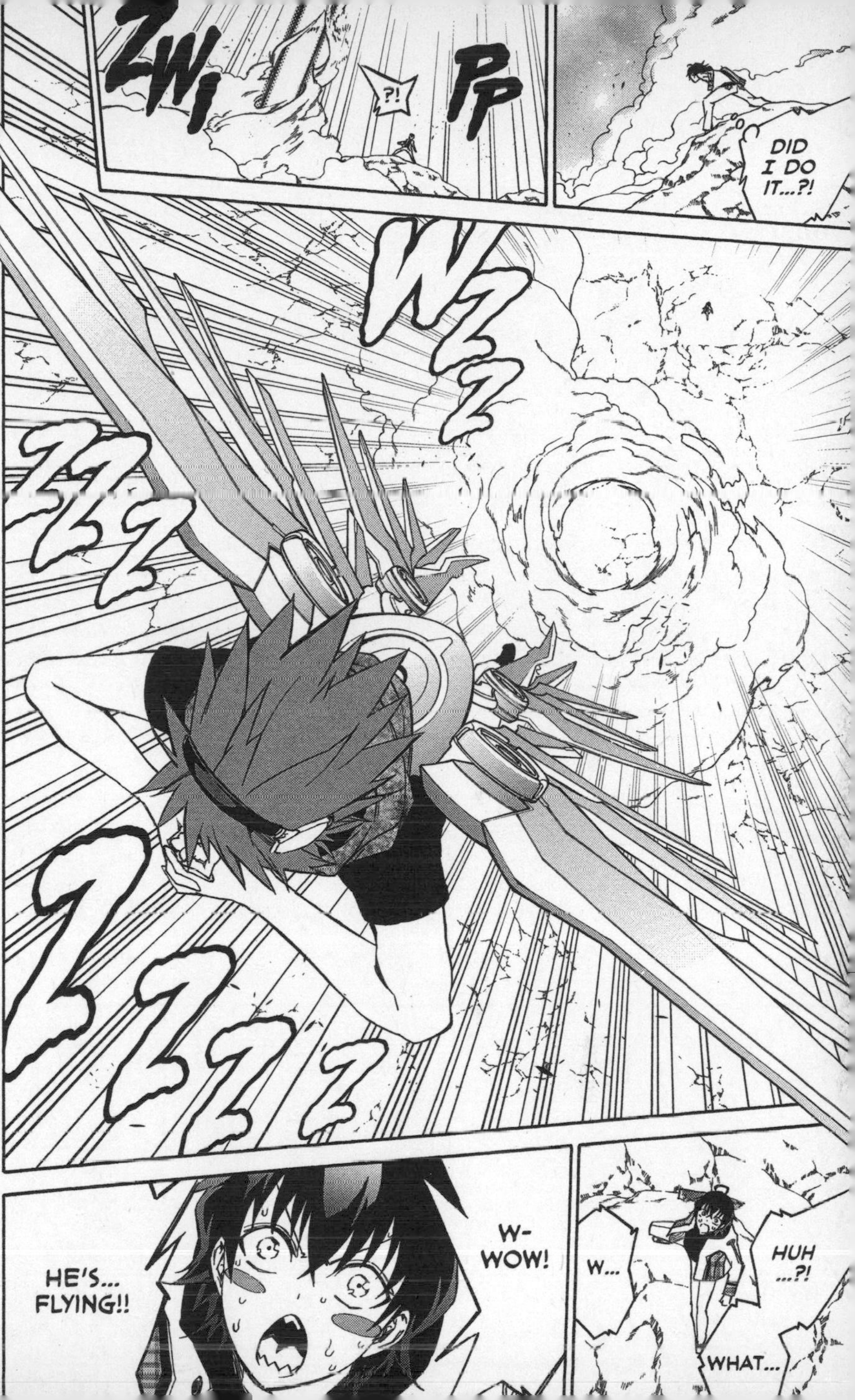
DID I DO IT...?!
ZWIPP
?!
WZZ
ZZZ
ZZZZZ
HUH ...?!
W...
WHAT...
W- WOW!
HE'S... FLYING!!

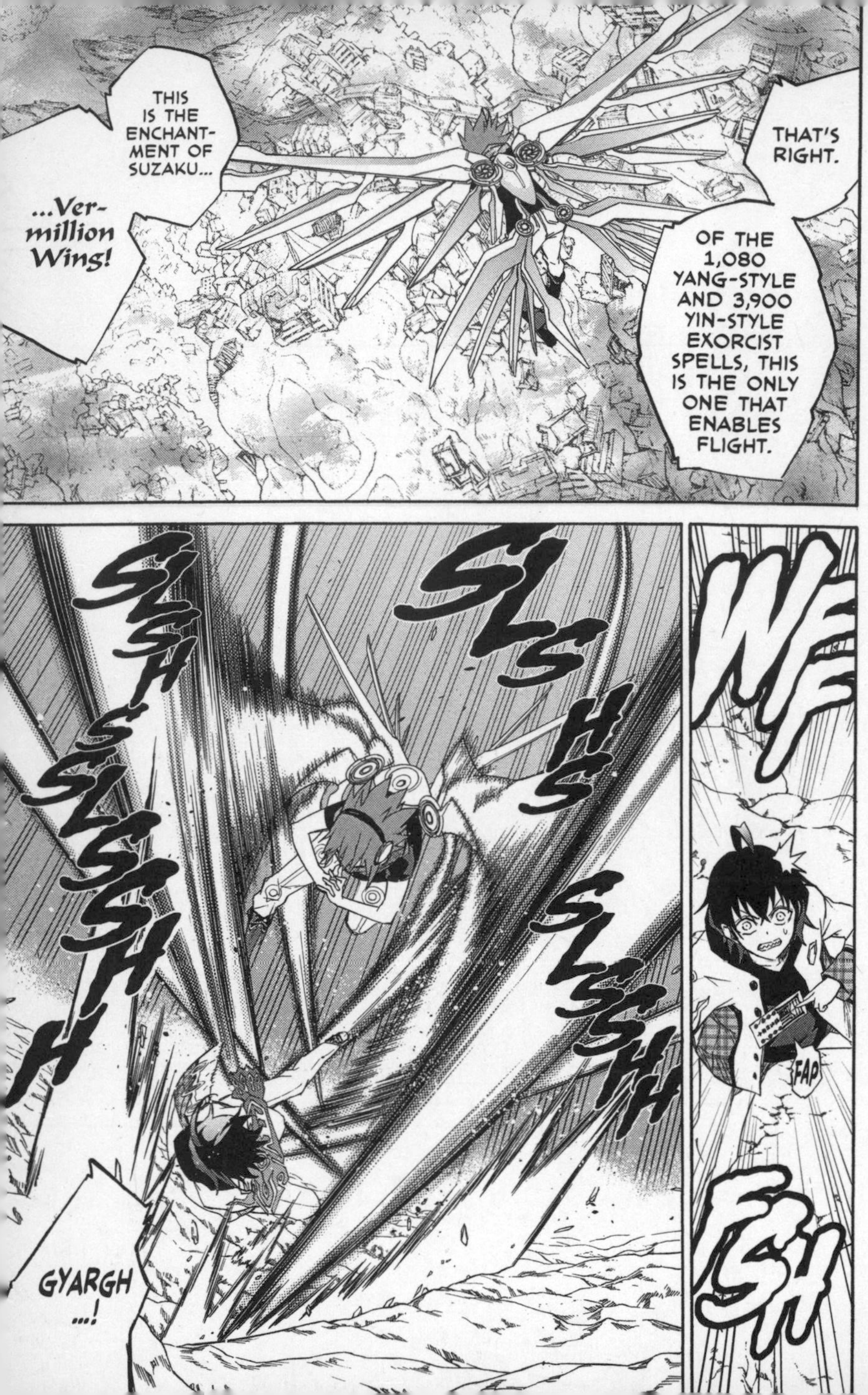

THIS IS THE ENCHANTMENT OF SUZAKU...
...Vermillion Wing!
THAT'S RIGHT.
OF THE 1,080 YANG-STYLE AND 3,900 YIN-STYLE EXORCIST SPELLS, THIS IS THE ONLY ONE THAT ENABLES FLIGHT.
WHF
FAP
FSH
SLSH
GYARGH ...!

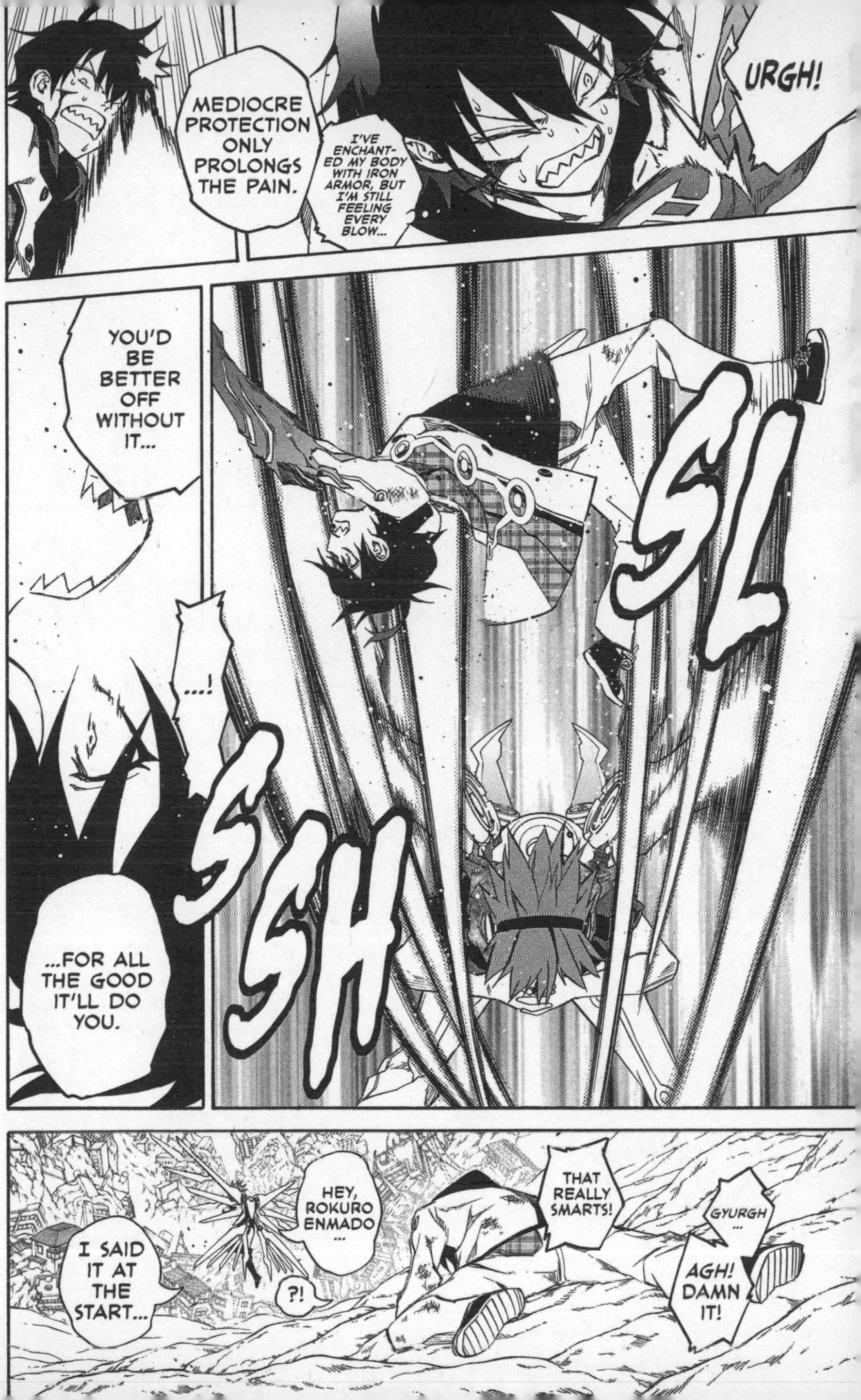
URGH!
I'VE ENCHANTED MY BODY WITH IRON ARMOR, BUT I'M STILL FEELING EVERY BLOW...
MEDIOCRE PROTECTION ONLY PROLONGS THE PAIN.
SL
SSH
YOU'D BE BETTER OFF WITHOUT IT...
...!
...FOR ALL THE GOOD IT'LL DO YOU.
AGH! DAMN IT!
GYURGH...
THAT REALLY SMARTS!
HEY, ROKURO ENMADO...
?!
I SAID IT AT THE START...

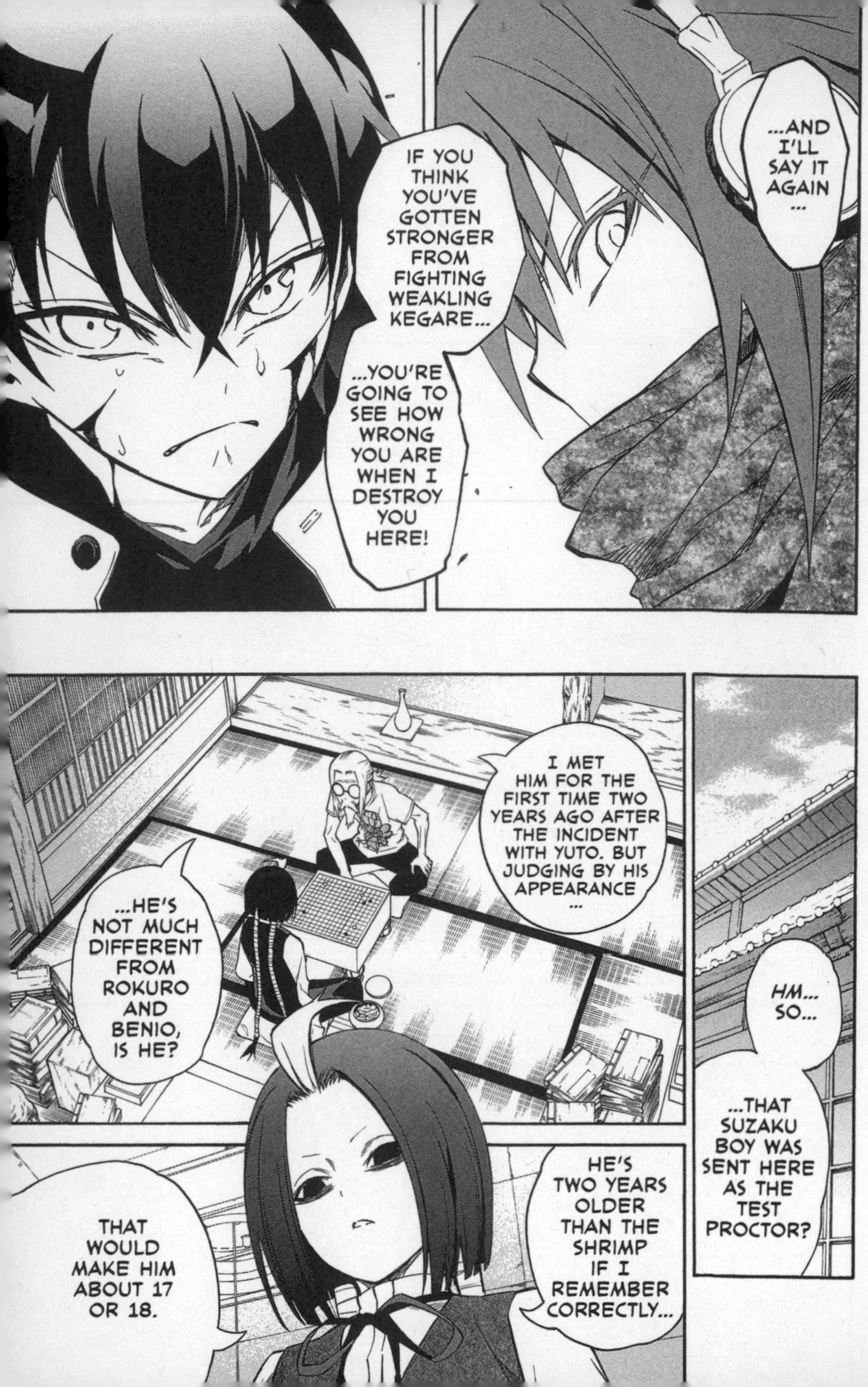

...AND I'LL SAY IT AGAIN...
IF YOU THINK YOU'VE GOTTEN STRONGER FROM FIGHTING WEAKLING KEGARE...
...YOU'RE GOING TO SEE HOW WRONG YOU ARE WHEN I DESTROY YOU HERE!
HM... SO...
...THAT SUZAKU BOY WAS SENT HERE AS THE TEST PROCTOR?
I MET HIM FOR THE FIRST TIME TWO YEARS AGO AFTER THE INCIDENT WITH YUTO. BUT JUDGING BY HIS APPEARANCE...
...HE'S NOT MUCH DIFFERENT FROM ROKURO AND BENIO, IS HE?
HE'S TWO YEARS OLDER THAN THE SHRIMP IF I REMEMBER CORRECTLY...
THAT WOULD MAKE HIM ABOUT 17 OR 18.

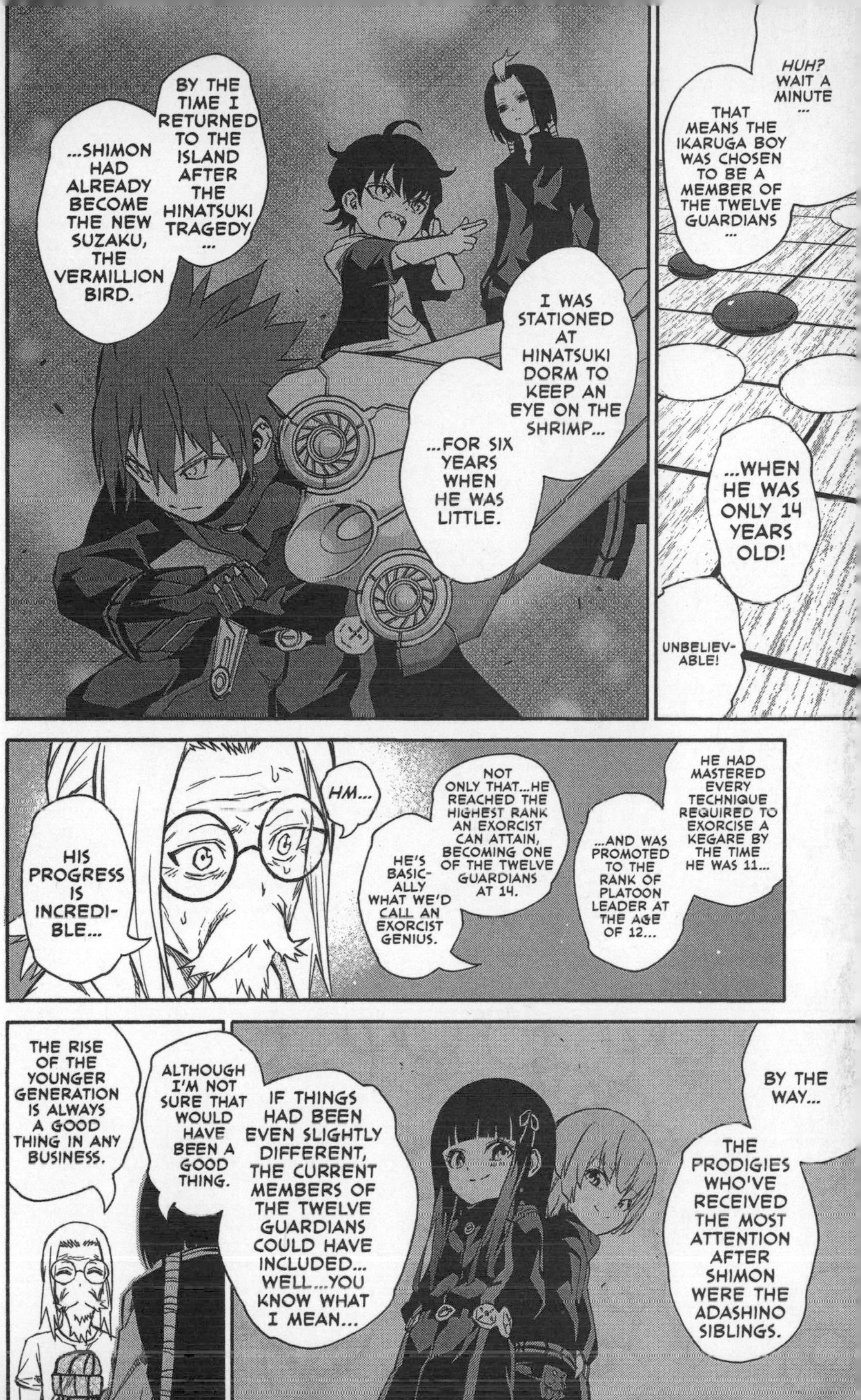
HUH? WAIT A MINUTE...
THAT MEANS THE IKARUGA BOY WAS CHOSEN TO BE A MEMBER OF THE TWELVE GUARDIANS...
...WHEN HE WAS ONLY 14 YEARS OLD!
UNBELIEV-ABLE!
I WAS STATIONED AT HINATSUKI DORM TO KEEP AN EYE ON THE SHRIMP...
...FOR SIX YEARS WHEN HE WAS LITTLE.
BY THE TIME I RETURNED TO THE ISLAND AFTER THE HINATSUKI TRAGEDY...
...SHIMON HAD ALREADY BECOME THE NEW SUZAKU, THE VERMILLION BIRD.
HE HAD MASTERED EVERY TECHNIQUE REQUIRED TO EXORCISE A KEGARE BY THE TIME HE WAS 11...
...AND WAS PROMOTED TO THE RANK OF PLATOON LEADER AT THE AGE OF 12...
NOT ONLY THAT...HE REACHED THE HIGHEST RANK AN EXORCIST CAN ATTAIN, BECOMING ONE OF THE TWELVE GUARDIANS AT 14.
HE'S BASIC-ALLY WHAT WE'D CALL AN EXORCIST GENIUS.
HM...
HIS PROGRESS IS INCREDI-BLE...
BY THE WAY...
THE PRODIGIES WHO'VE RECEIVED THE MOST ATTENTION AFTER SHIMON WERE THE ADASHINO SIBLINGS.
IF THINGS HAD BEEN EVEN SLIGHTLY DIFFERENT, THE CURRENT MEMBERS OF THE TWELVE GUARDIANS COULD HAVE INCLUDED... WELL...YOU KNOW WHAT I MEAN...
ALTHOUGH I'M NOT SURE THAT WOULD HAVE BEEN A GOOD THING.
THE RISE OF THE YOUNGER GENERATION IS ALWAYS A GOOD THING IN ANY BUSINESS.

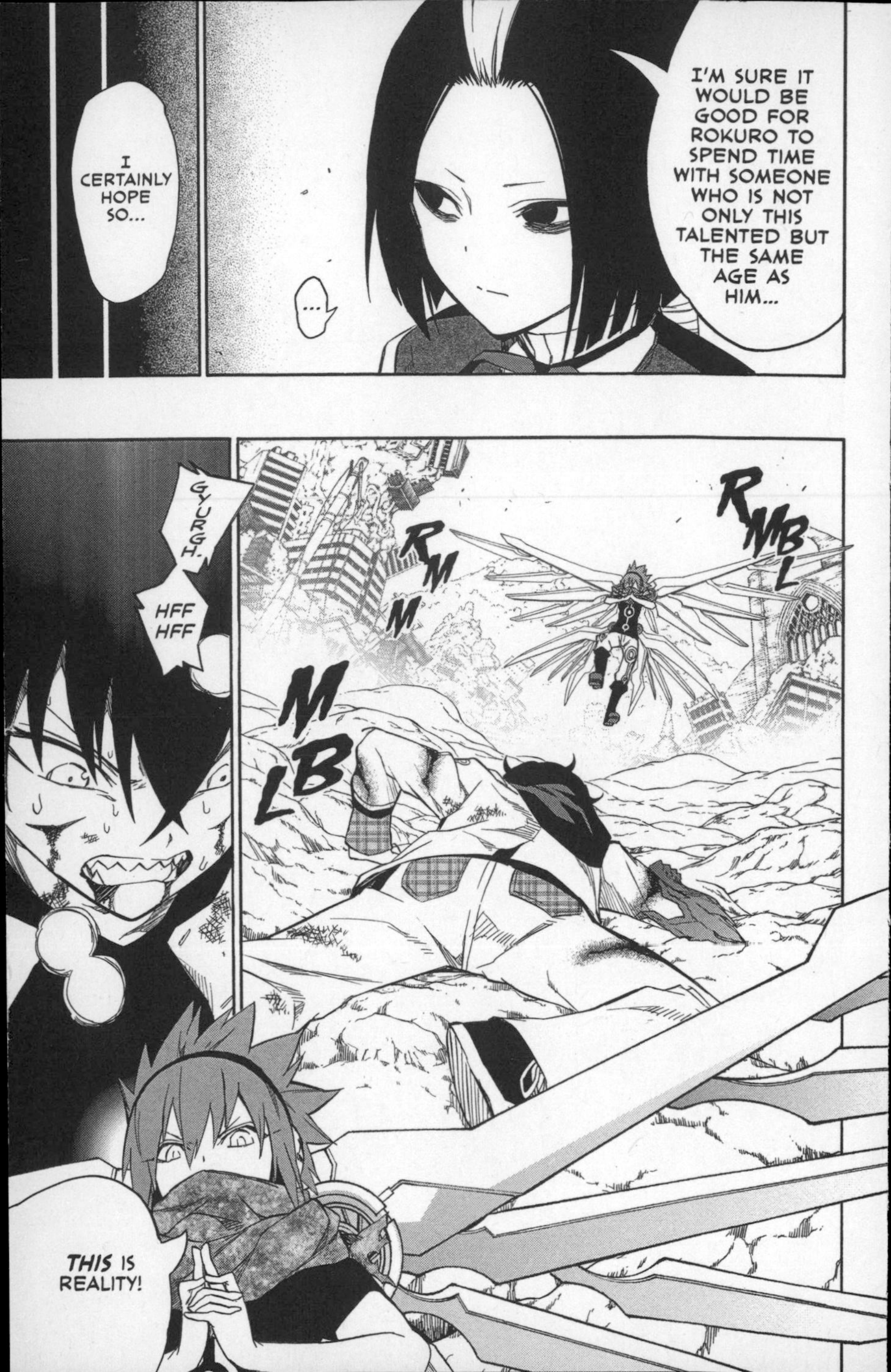
I'M SURE IT WOULD BE GOOD FOR ROKURO TO SPEND TIME WITH SOMEONE WHO IS NOT ONLY THIS TALENTED BUT THE SAME AGE AS HIM...
...
I CERTAINLY HOPE SO...
RMBL
RMM
MBL
GYURGH.
HFF HFF
THIS IS REALITY!

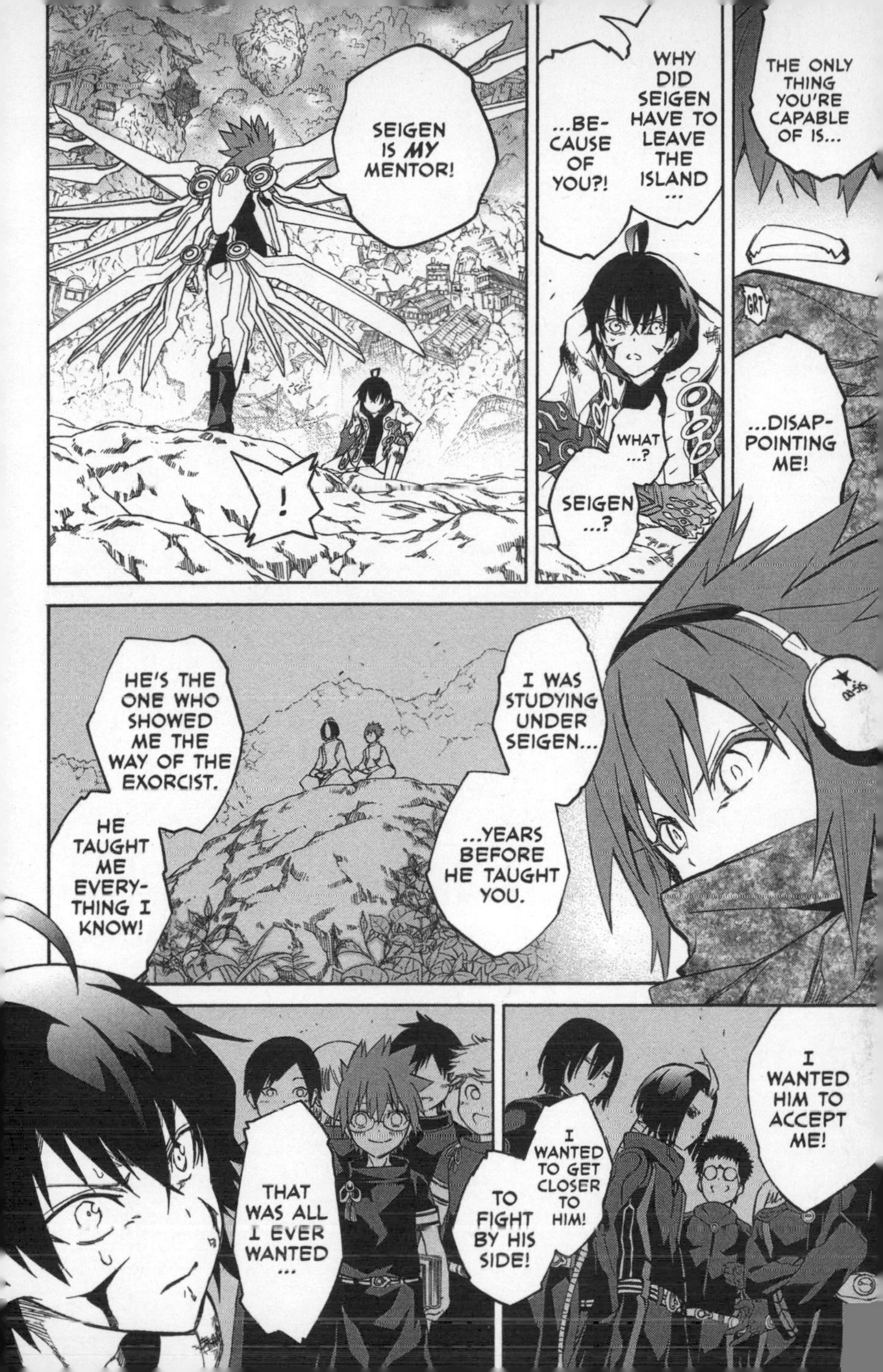
THE ONLY THING YOU'RE CAPABLE OF IS...
GRT
...DISAPPOINTING ME!
WHY DID SEIGEN HAVE TO LEAVE THE ISLAND...
...BECAUSE OF YOU?!
WHAT...?
SEIGEN...?
SEIGEN IS *MY* MENTOR!
!
I WAS STUDYING UNDER SEIGEN...
...YEARS BEFORE HE TAUGHT YOU.
HE'S THE ONE WHO SHOWED ME THE WAY OF THE EXORCIST.
HE TAUGHT ME EVERYTHING I KNOW!
I WANTED HIM TO ACCEPT ME!
I WANTED TO GET CLOSER TO HIM!
TO FIGHT BY HIS SIDE!
THAT WAS ALL I EVER WANTED...

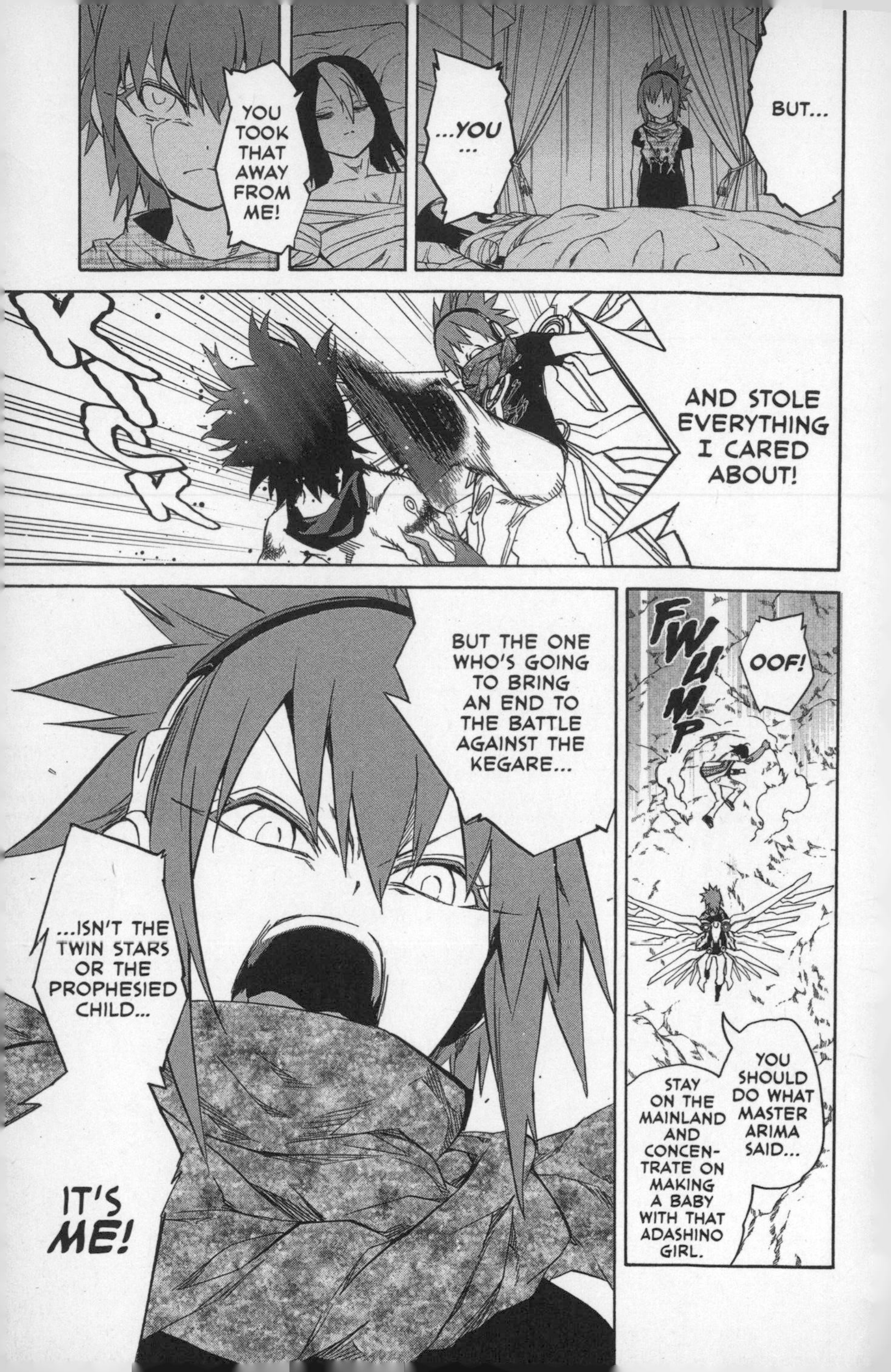
BUT...
...YOU ...
YOU TOOK THAT AWAY FROM ME!
AND STOLE EVERYTHING I CARED ABOUT!
FWUMP
OOF!
YOU SHOULD DO WHAT MASTER ARIMA SAID...
STAY ON THE MAINLAND AND CONCEN-TRATE ON MAKING A BABY WITH THAT ADASHINO GIRL.
BUT THE ONE WHO'S GOING TO BRING AN END TO THE BATTLE AGAINST THE KEGARE...
...ISN'T THE TWIN STARS OR THE PROPHESIED CHILD...
IT'S ME!

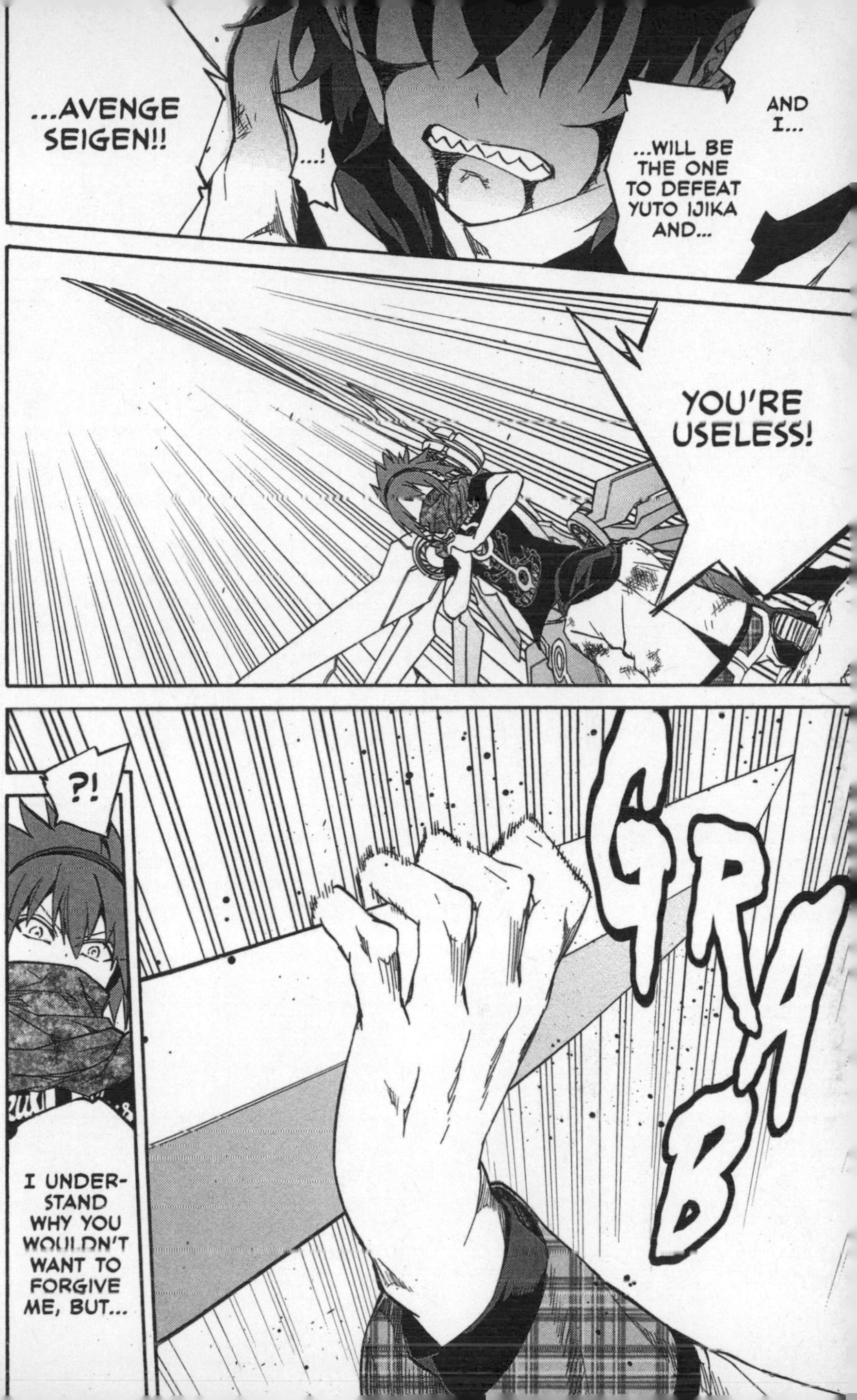
AND I...
...WILL BE THE ONE TO DEFEAT YUTO IJIKA AND...
...!
...AVENGE SEIGEN!!
YOU'RE USELESS!
GRAB
?!
I UNDER-STAND WHY YOU WOULDN'T WANT TO FORGIVE ME, BUT...

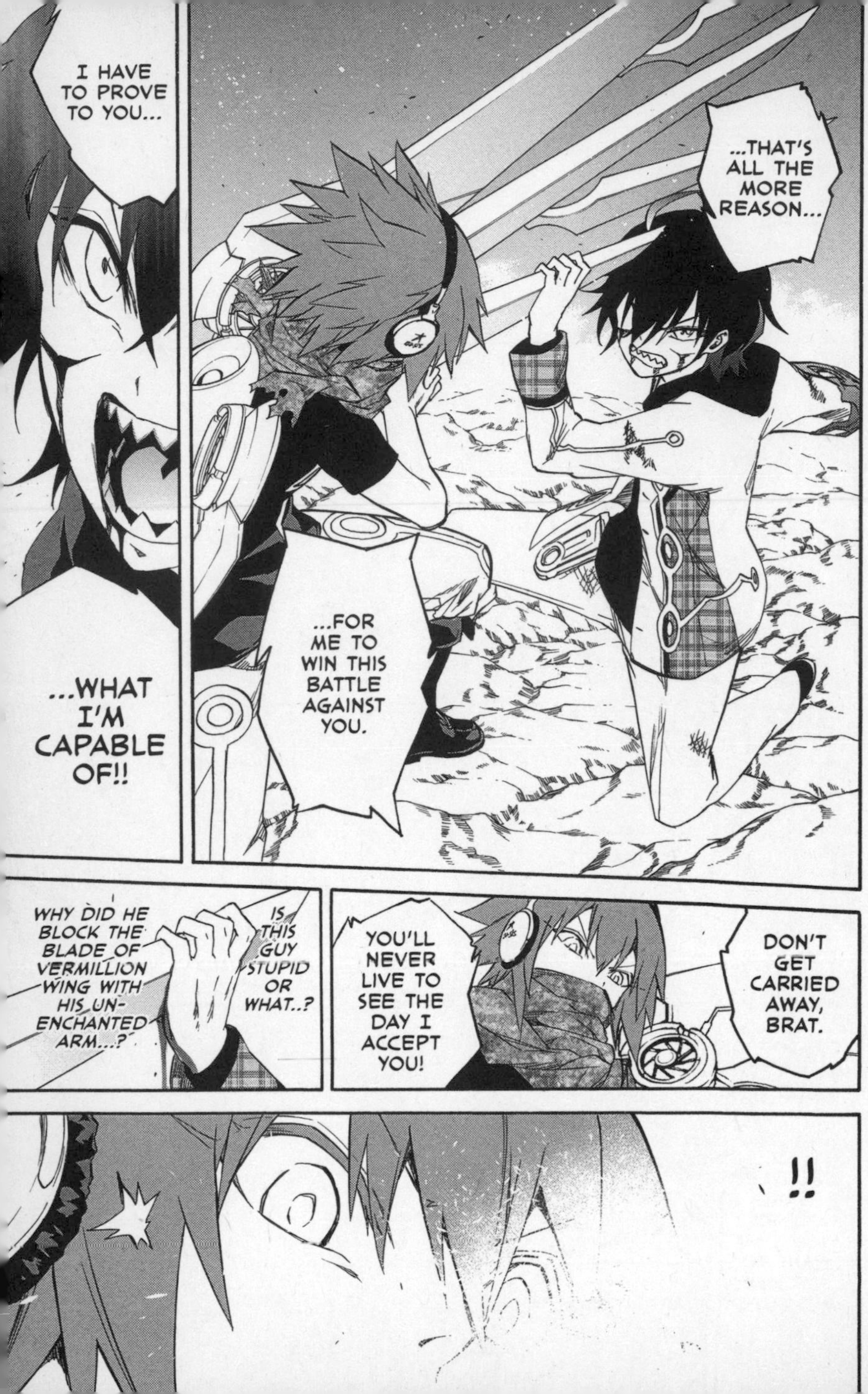
...THAT'S ALL THE MORE REASON...
...FOR ME TO WIN THIS BATTLE AGAINST YOU.
I HAVE TO PROVE TO YOU...
...WHAT I'M CAPABLE OF!!
DON'T GET CARRIED AWAY, BRAT.
YOU'LL NEVER LIVE TO SEE THE DAY I ACCEPT YOU!
IS THIS GUY STUPID OR WHAT..?
WHY DID HE BLOCK THE BLADE OF VERMILLION WING WITH HIS UN-ENCHANTED ARM...?
!!

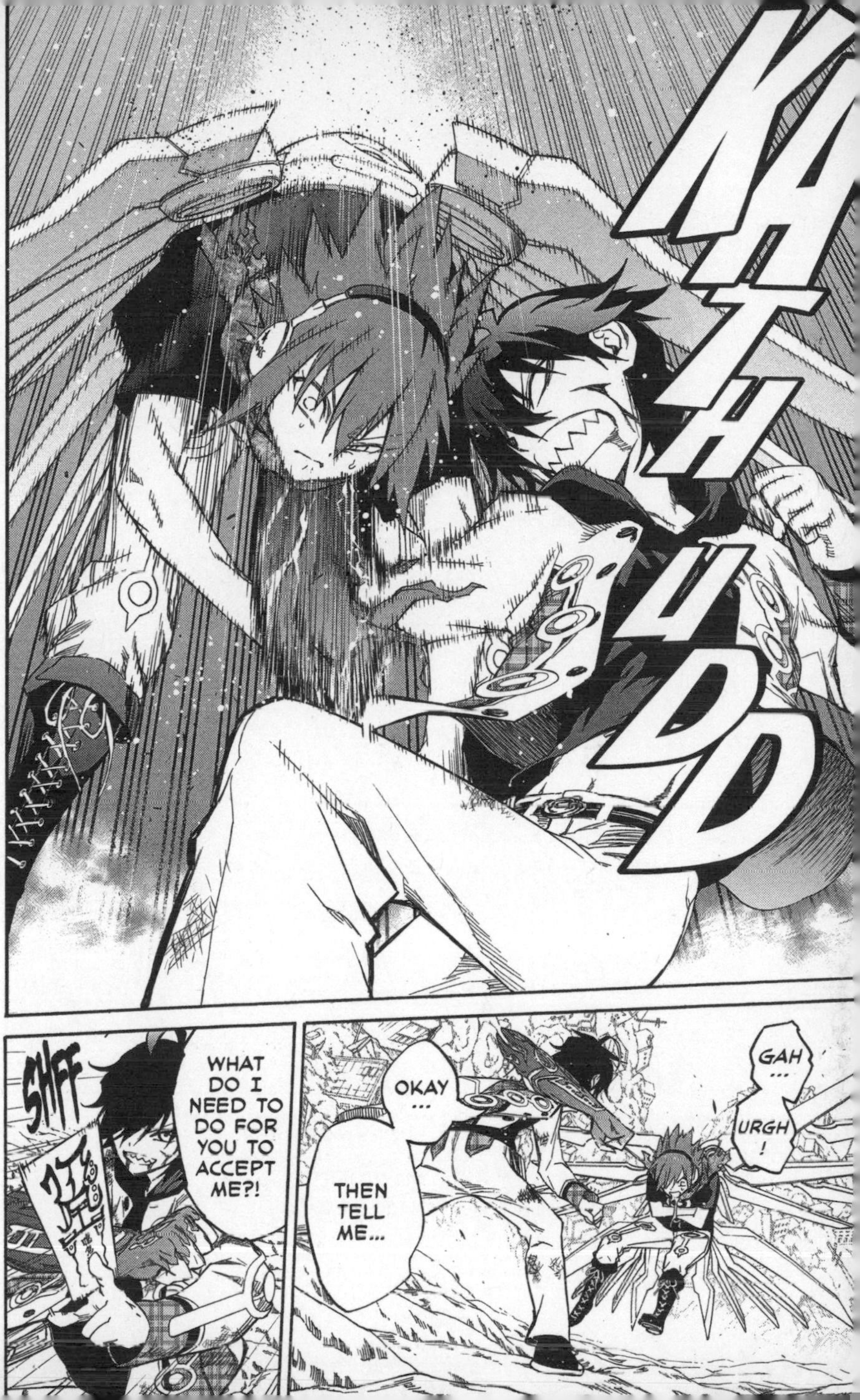
KATHUDD
GAH ...
URGH !
OKAY ...
THEN TELL ME...
WHAT DO I NEED TO DO FOR YOU TO ACCEPT ME?!
SHFF

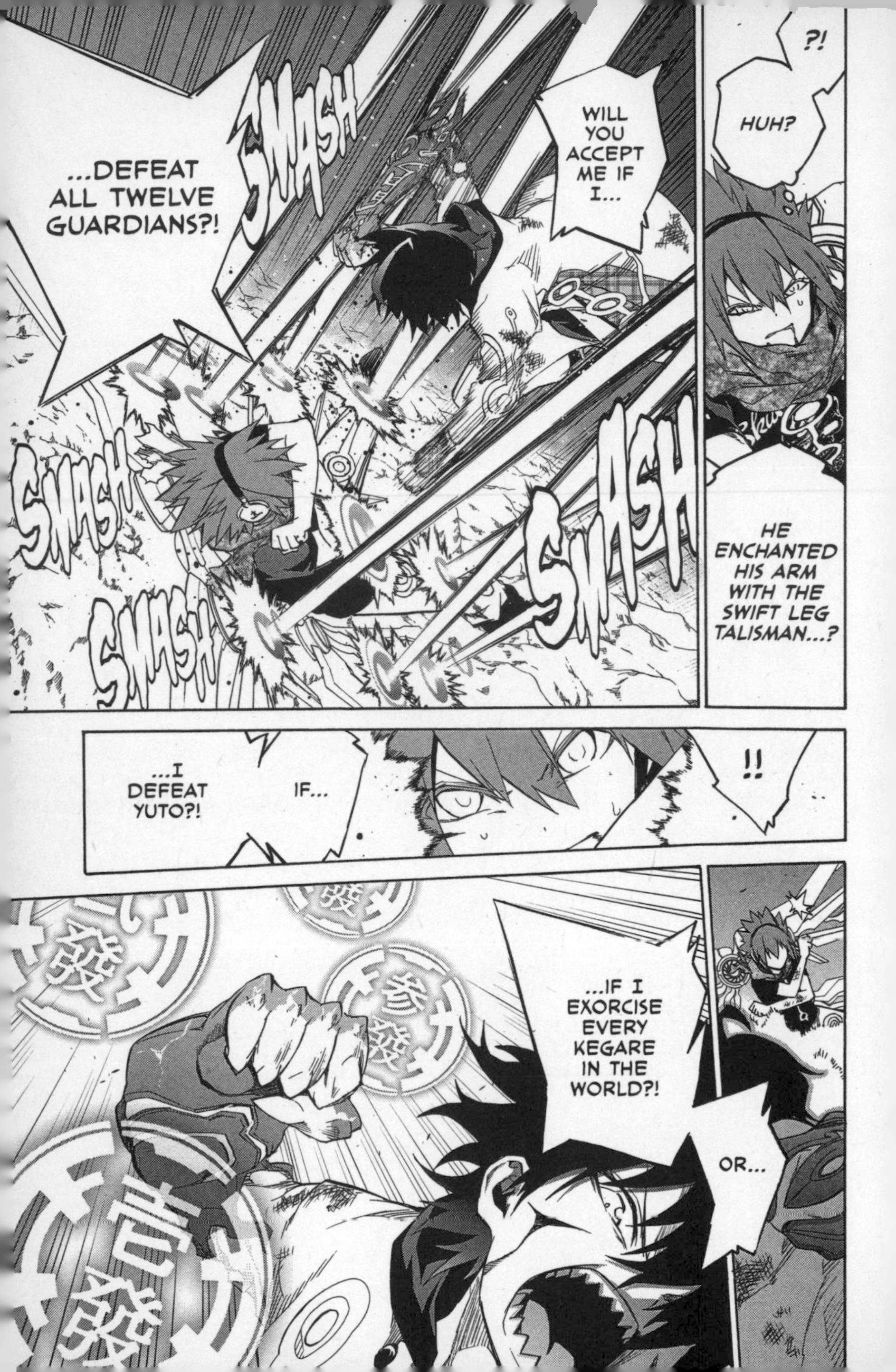
?!
HUH?
HE ENCHANTED HIS ARM WITH THE SWIFT LEG TALISMAN...?
WILL YOU ACCEPT ME IF I...
...DEFEAT ALL TWELVE GUARDIANS?!
SMASH
SMASH
SMASH
SMASH
!!
IF...
...I DEFEAT YUTO?!
...IF I EXORCISE EVERY KEGARE IN THE WORLD?!
OR...

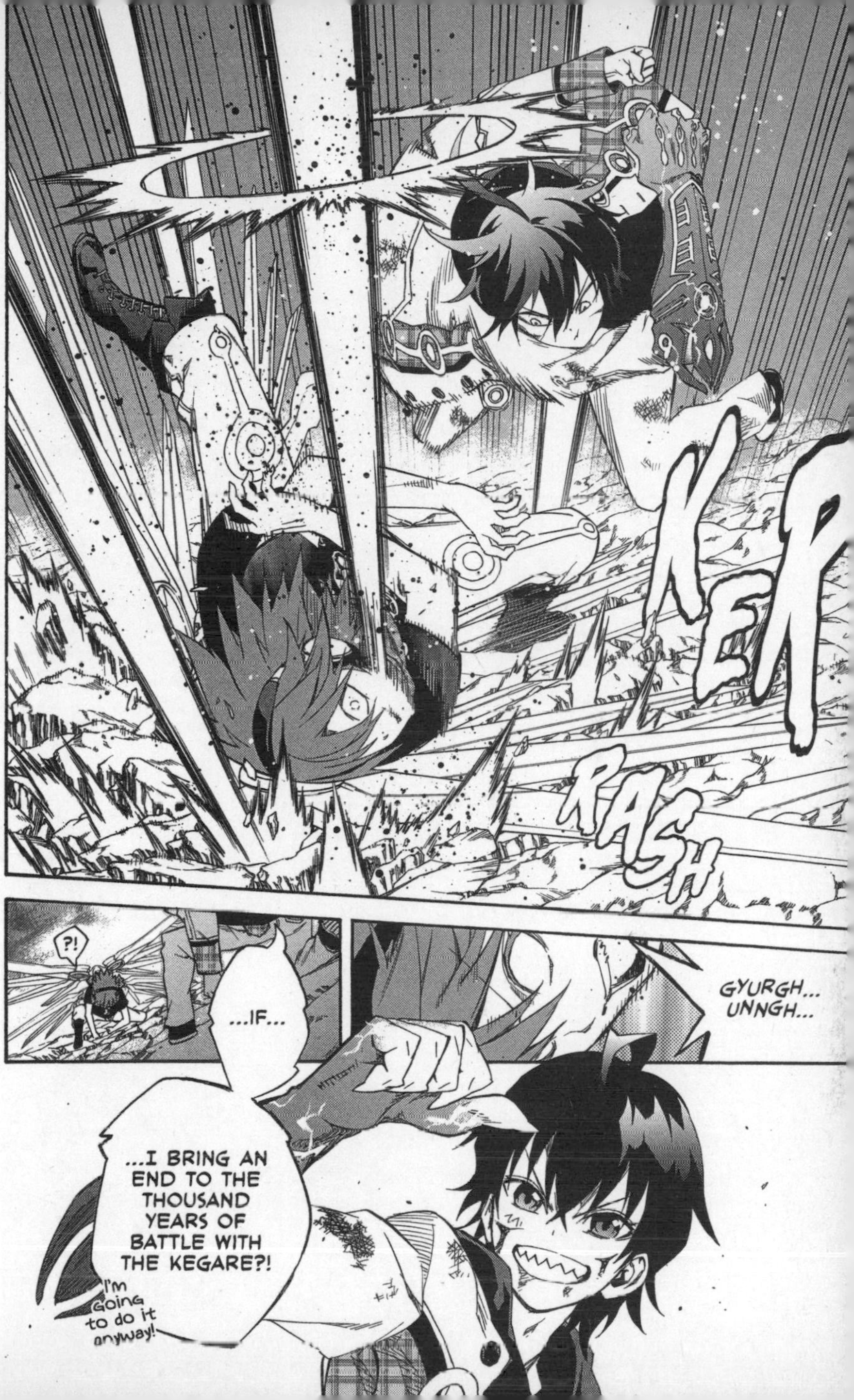
KERRASH
GYURGH... UNNGH...
?!
...IF...
...I BRING AN END TO THE THOUSAND YEARS OF BATTLE WITH THE KEGARE?!
I'm going to do it anyway!

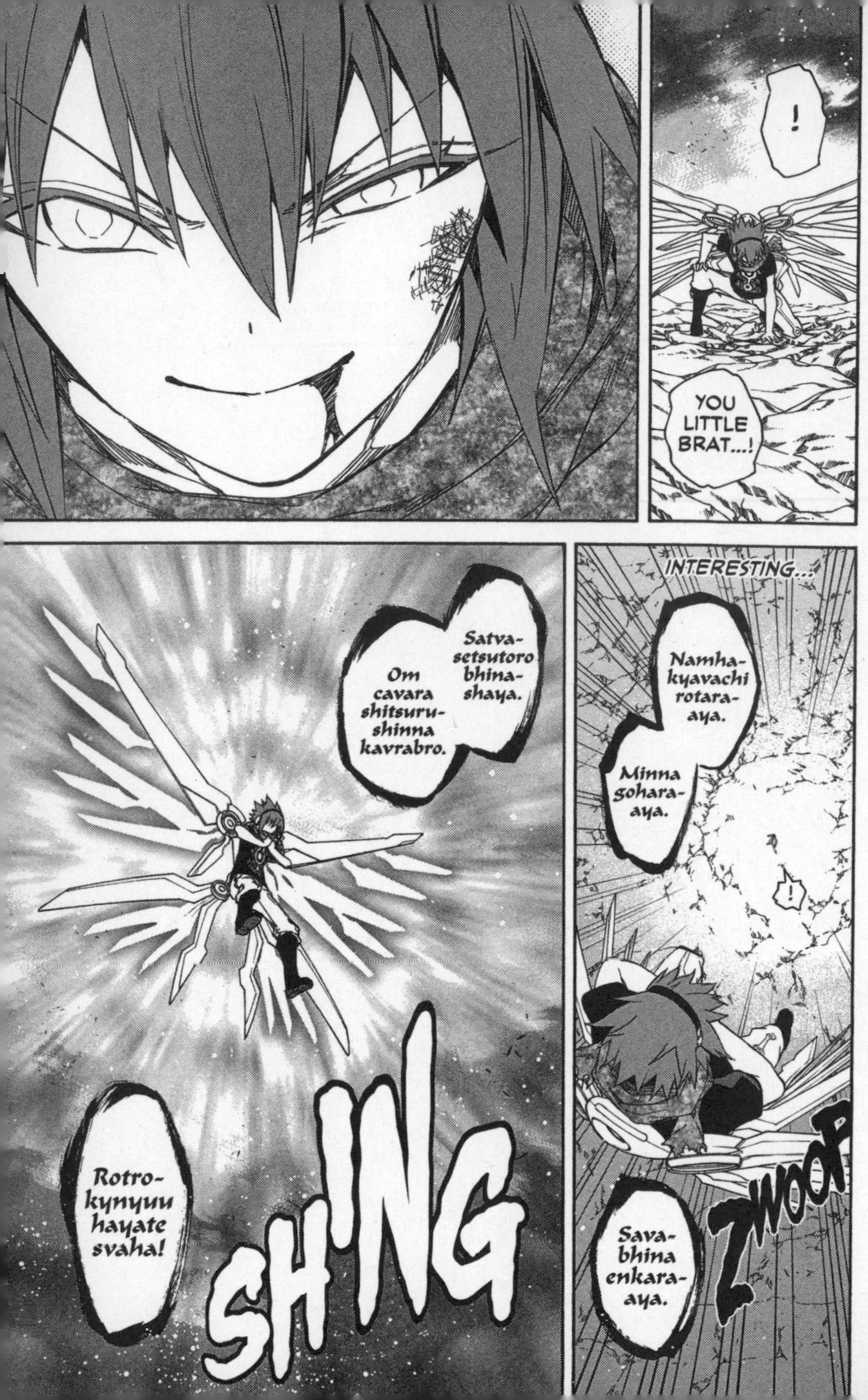
!
YOU LITTLE BRAT...!
INTERESTING...
Namha-kyavachi rotara-aya.
Minna gohara-aya.
!
Sava-bhina enkara-aya.
ZWOOP
Satva-setsutoro bhina-shaya.
Om cavara shitsuru-shinna kavrabro.
Rotro-kynyuu hayate svaha!
SHING

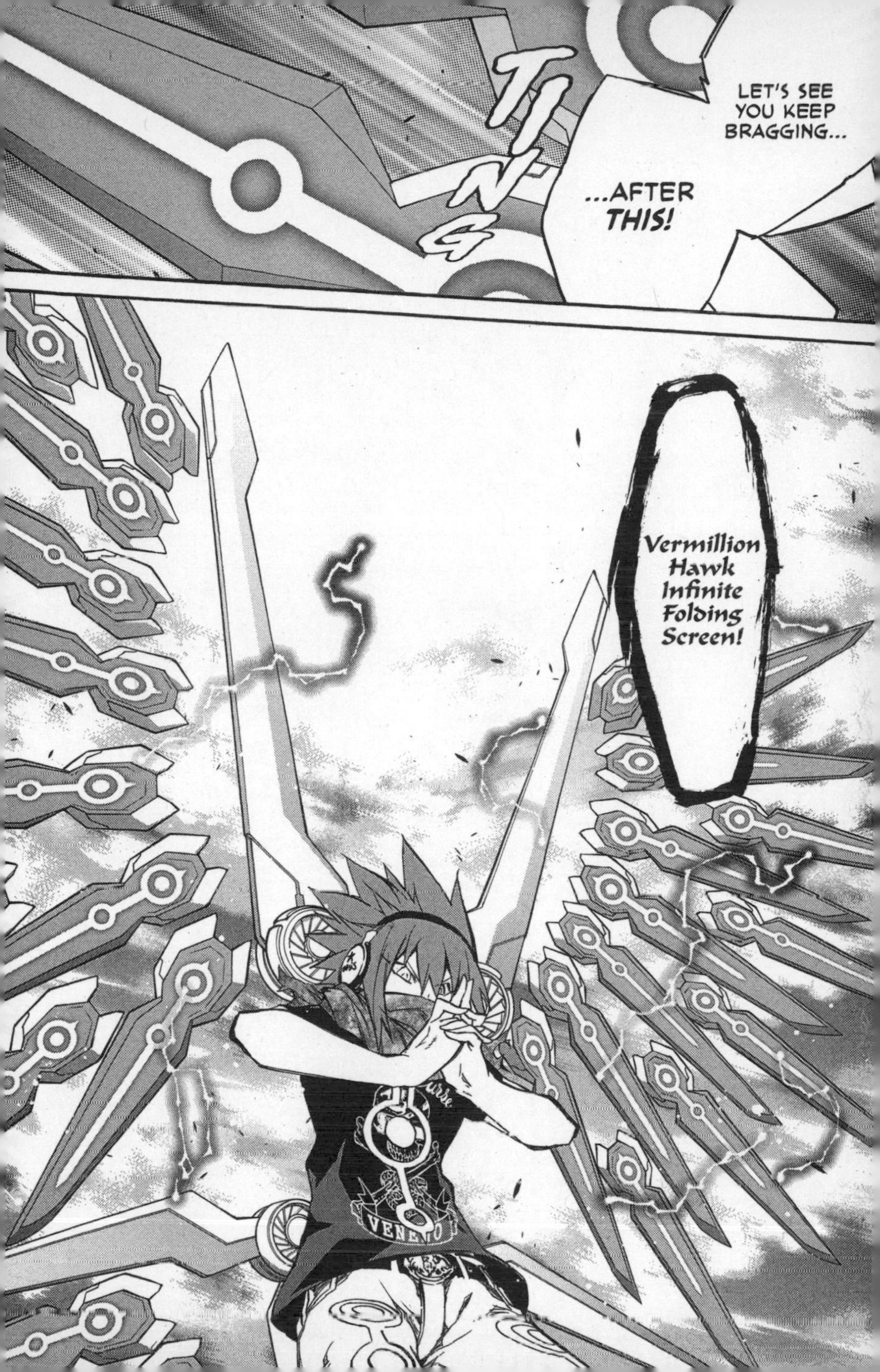
LET'S SEE YOU KEEP BRAGGING...
...AFTER THIS!
TING
Vermillion Hawk Infinite Folding Screen!
VENENO

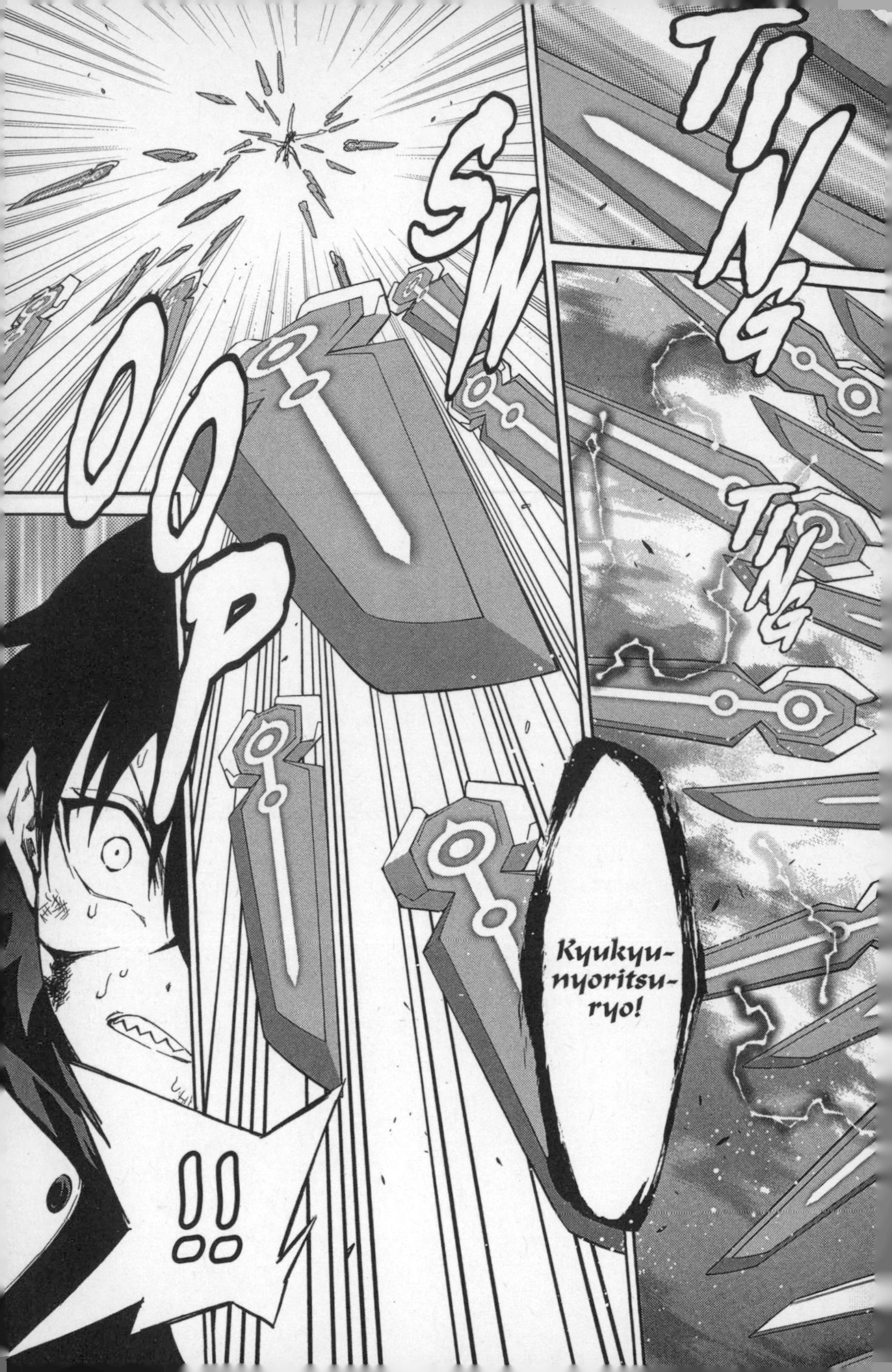
TING
TING
SN
Kyukyu-nyoritsu-ryo!
OOP
!!

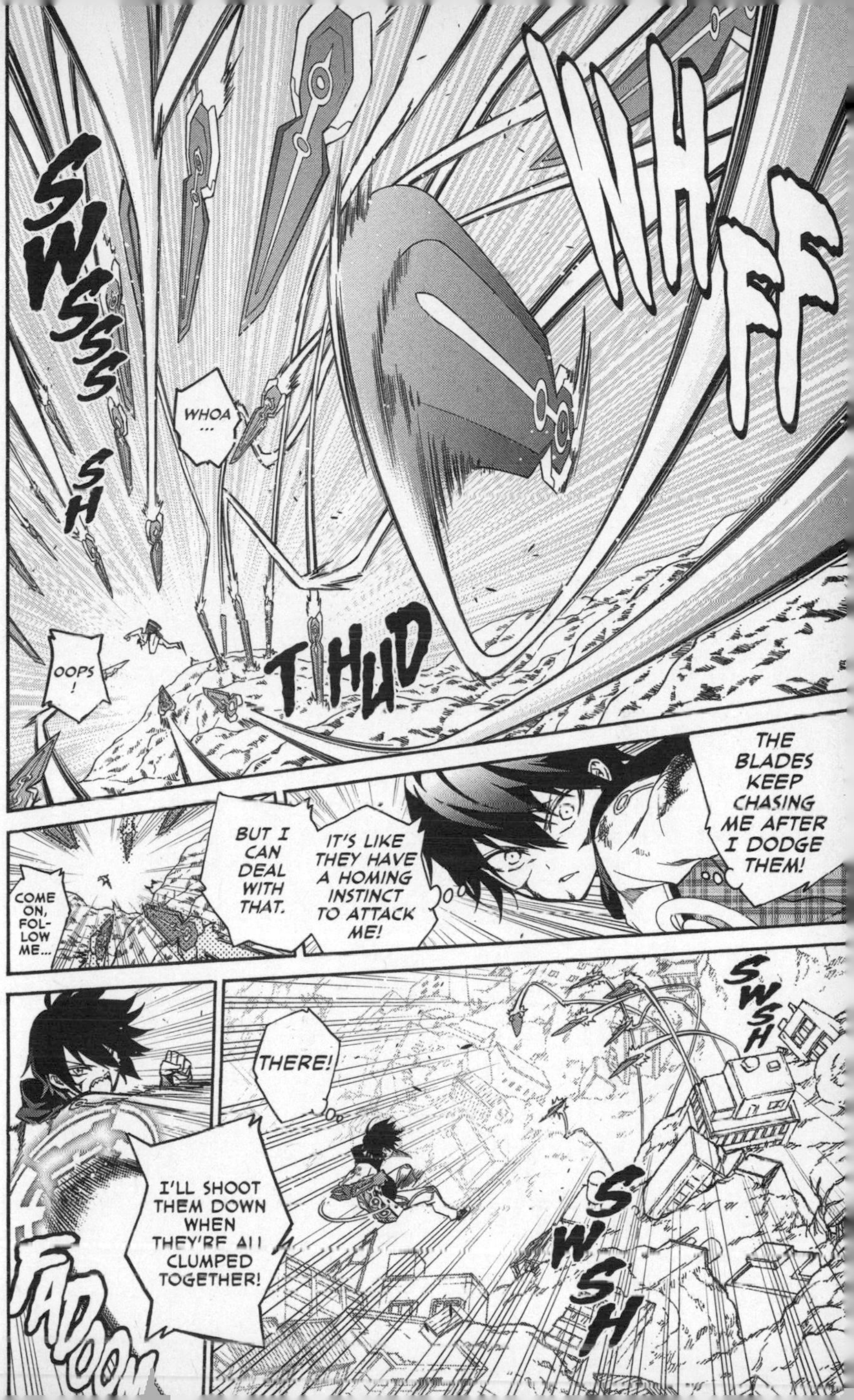
WHAFF
SWSSS
WHOA...
SH
THUD
OOPS!
THE BLADES KEEP CHASING ME AFTER I DODGE THEM!
IT'S LIKE THEY HAVE A HOMING INSTINCT TO ATTACK ME!
BUT I CAN DEAL WITH THAT.
COME ON, FOL-LOW ME...
SWSH
THERE!
SWSH
I'LL SHOOT THEM DOWN WHEN THEY'RE ALL CLUMPED TOGETHER!
FADOOM

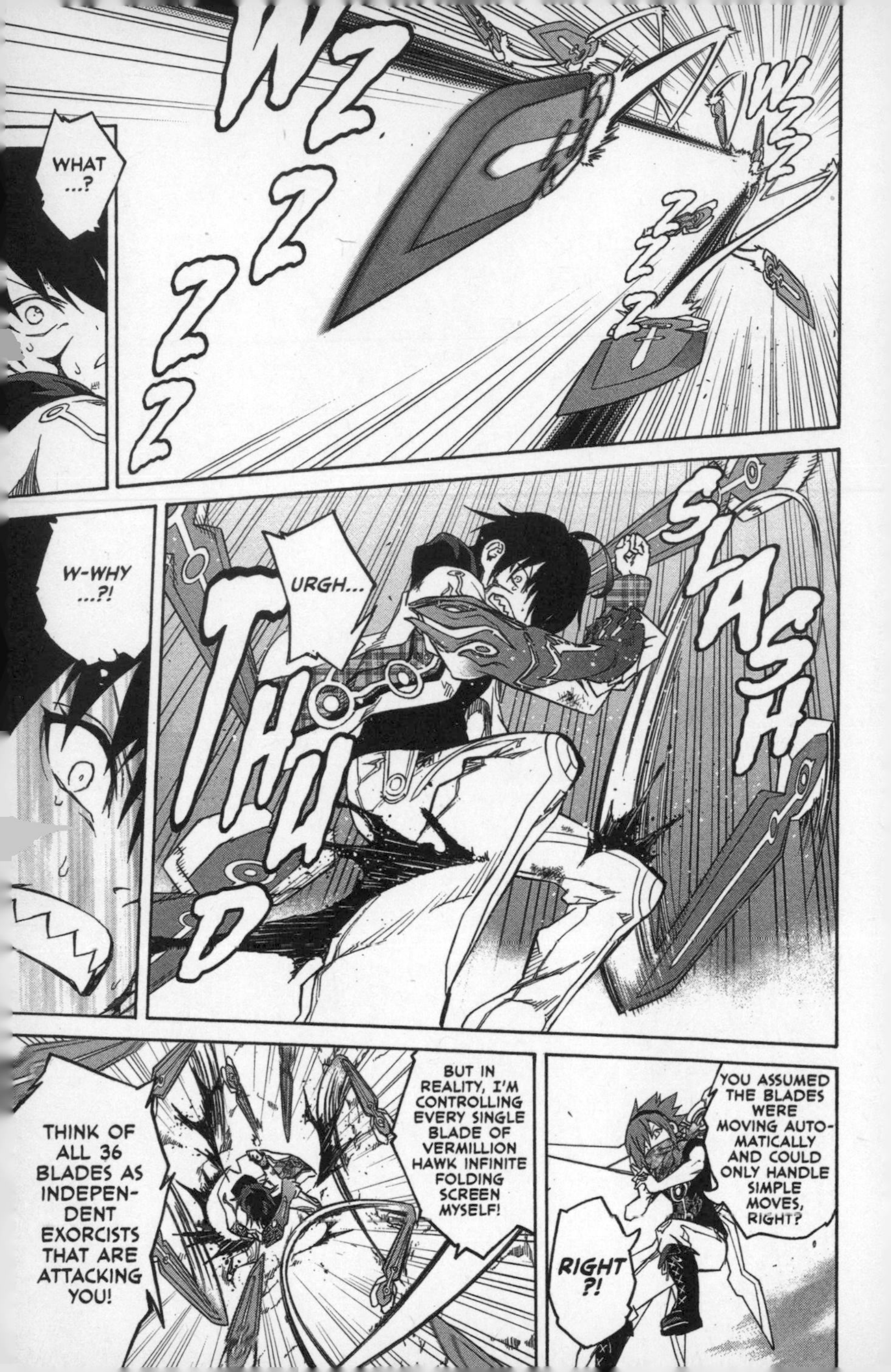
WZZ
ZZZ
WZZZZ
WHAT ...?
SLASH
URGH...
THUD
W-WHY ...?!
YOU ASSUMED THE BLADES WERE MOVING AUTO-MATICALLY AND COULD ONLY HANDLE SIMPLE MOVES, RIGHT?
RIGHT ?!
BUT IN REALITY, I'M CONTROLLING EVERY SINGLE BLADE OF VERMILLION HAWK INFINITE FOLDING SCREEN MYSELF!
THINK OF ALL 36 BLADES AS INDEPEN-DENT EXORCISTS THAT ARE ATTACKING YOU!

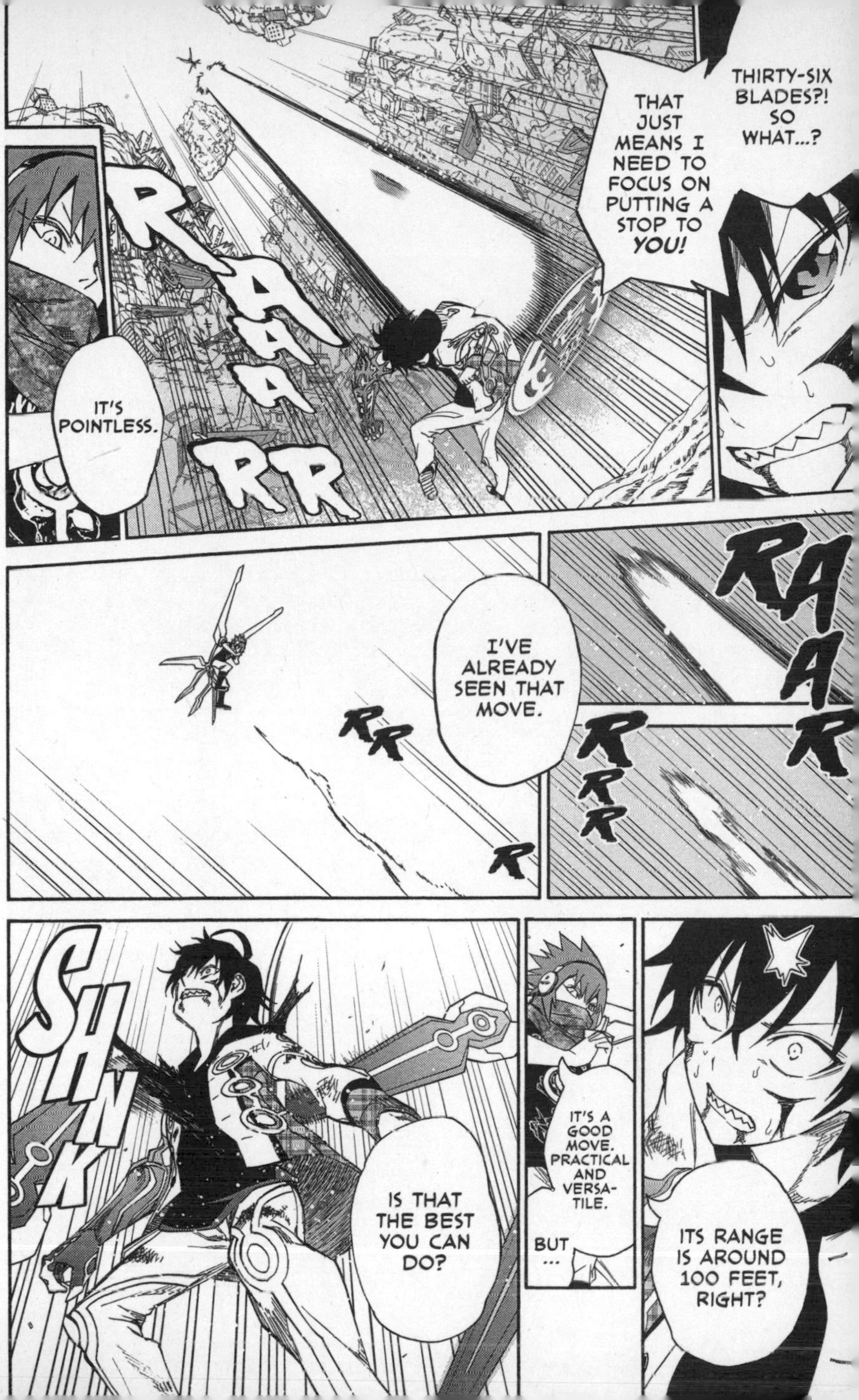
THIRTY-SIX BLADES?! SO WHAT...?
THAT JUST MEANS I NEED TO FOCUS ON PUTTING A STOP TO *YOU!*
RAAARR
IT'S POINTLESS.
RAAR
RRR
I'VE ALREADY SEEN THAT MOVE.
RR
R
ITS RANGE IS AROUND 100 FEET, RIGHT?
IT'S A GOOD MOVE. PRACTICAL AND VERSA-TILE.
BUT...
SHNK
IS THAT THE BEST YOU CAN DO?

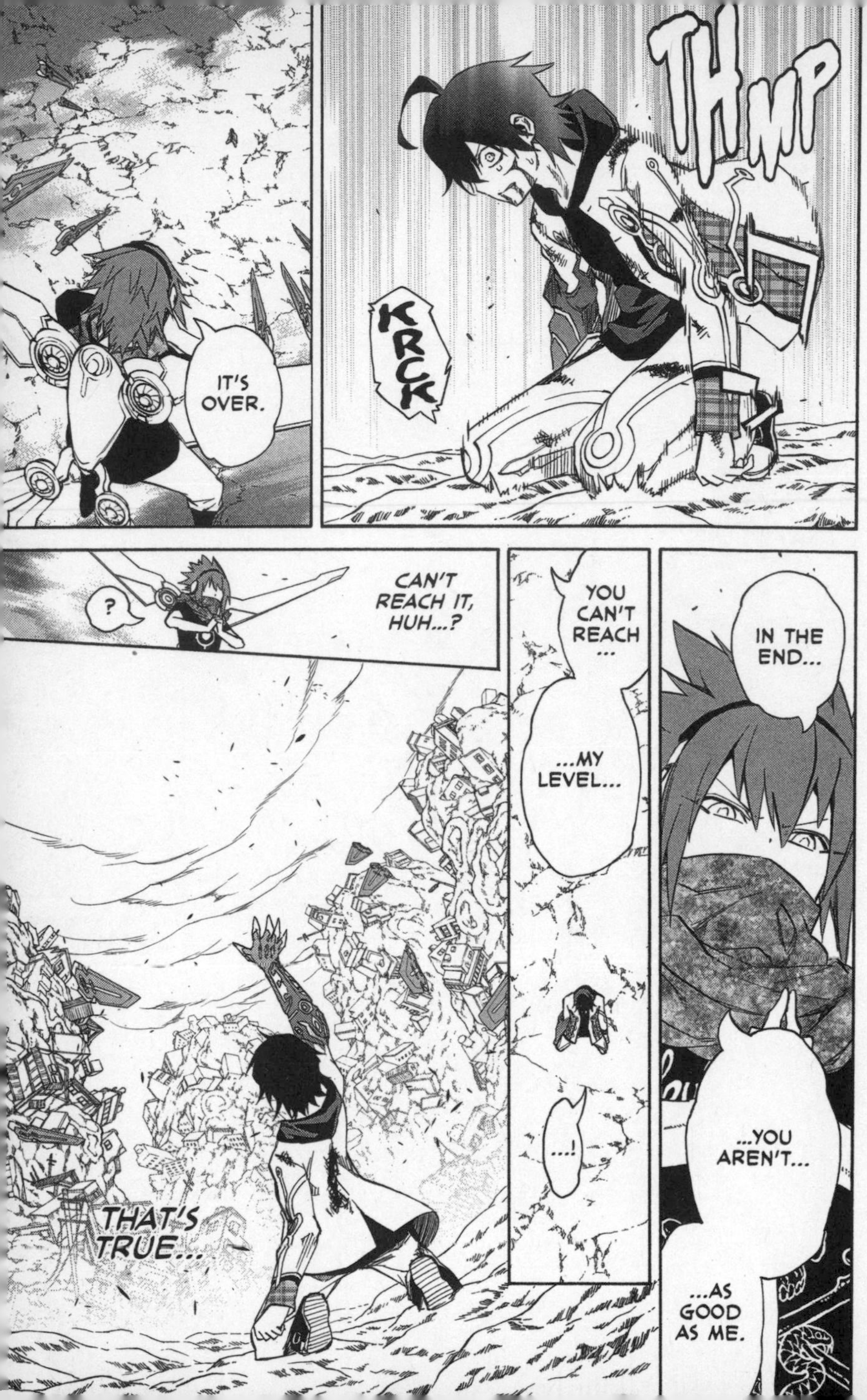
THMP
KRCK
IT'S OVER.
IN THE END...
...YOU AREN'T...
...AS GOOD AS ME.
YOU CAN'T REACH ...
...MY LEVEL...
...!
?
CAN'T REACH IT, HUH...?
THAT'S TRUE...

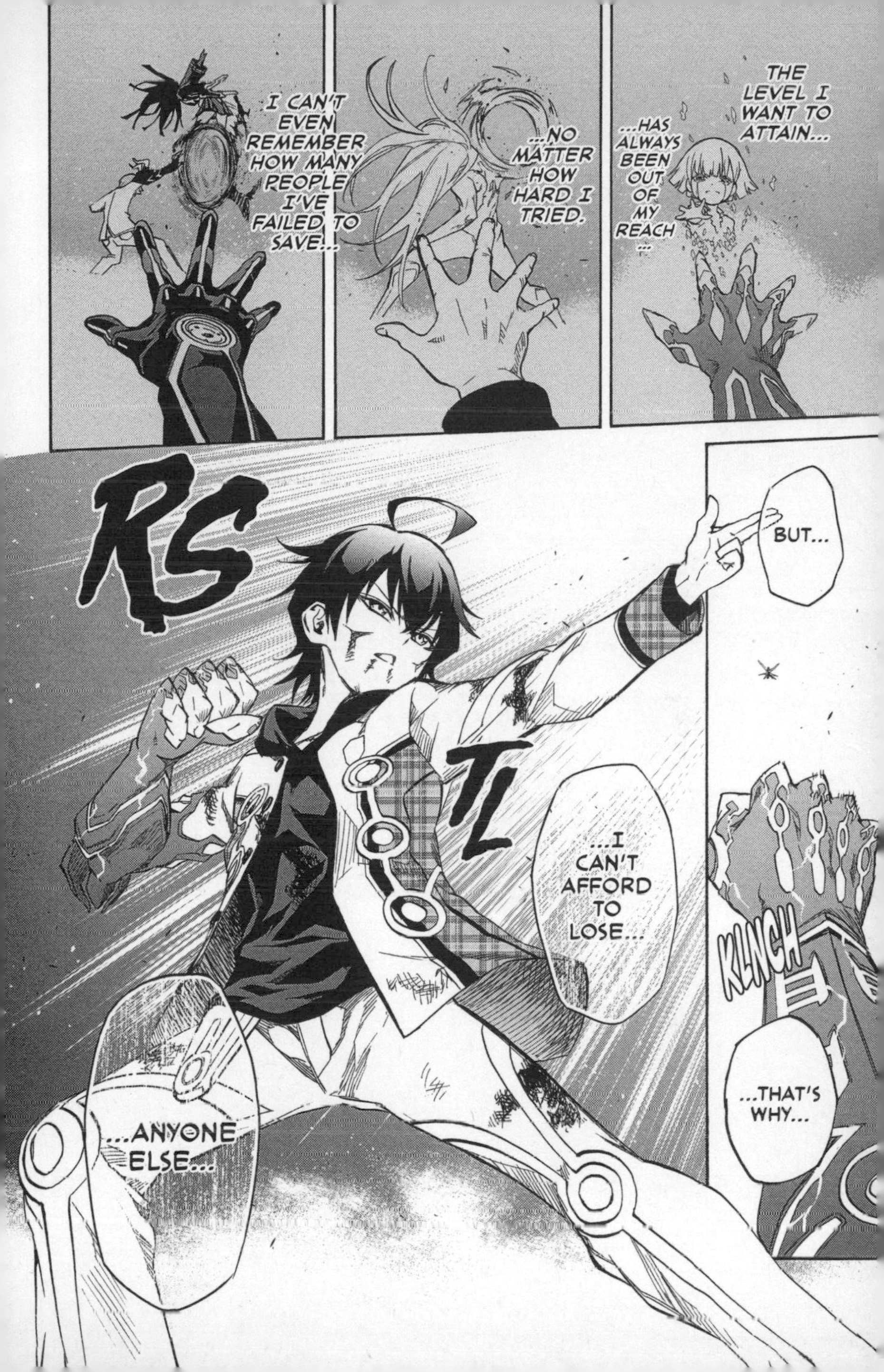
THE LEVEL I WANT TO ATTAIN...
...HAS ALWAYS BEEN OUT OF MY REACH...
...NO MATTER HOW HARD I TRIED.
I CAN'T EVEN REMEMBER HOW MANY PEOPLE I'VE FAILED TO SAVE...
BUT...
KLINCH
...THAT'S WHY...
RS
TL
...I CAN'T AFFORD TO LOSE...
...ANYONE ELSE...

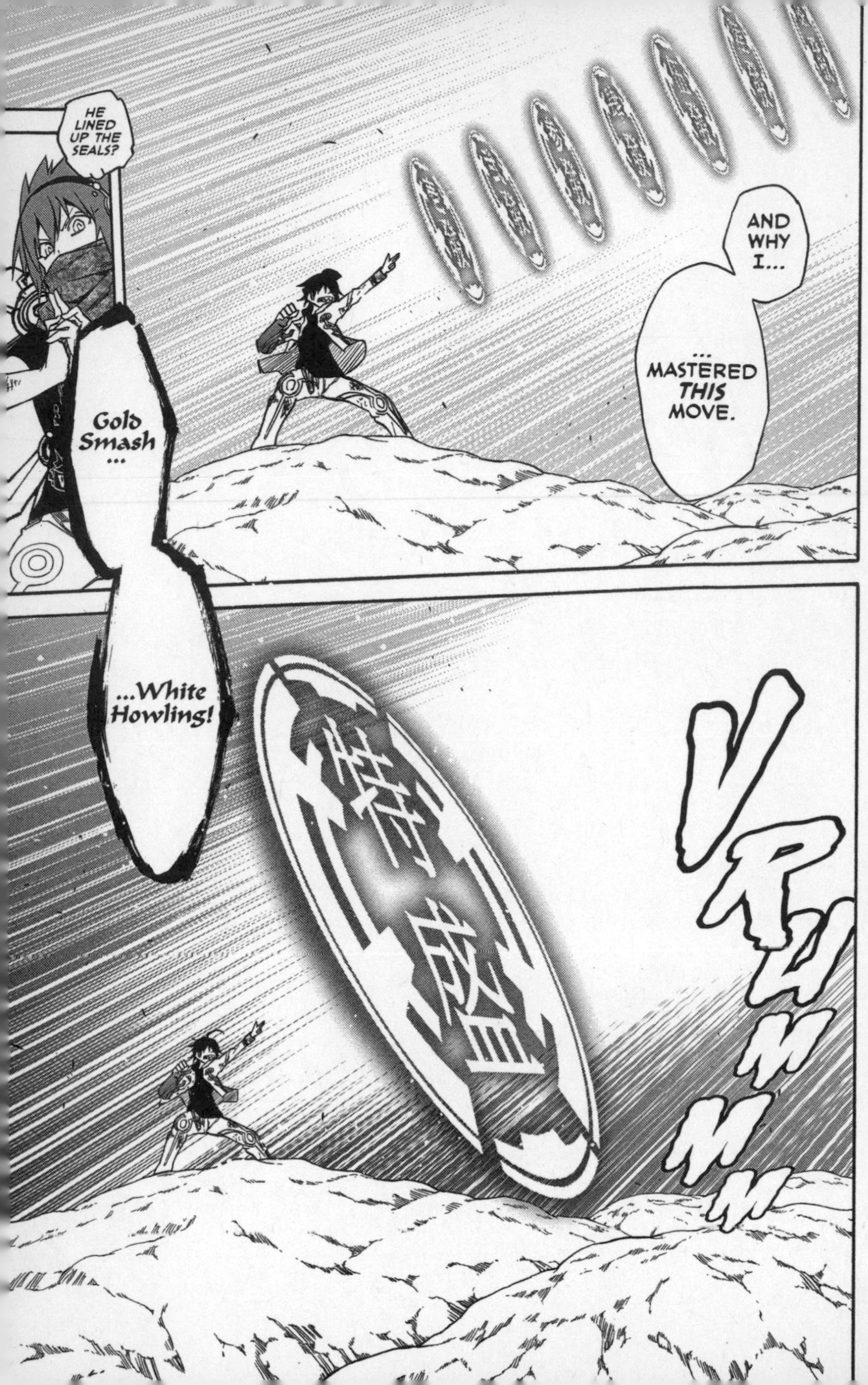
AND WHY I...
...MASTERED THIS MOVE.
HE LINED UP THE SEALS?
Gold Smash...
...White Howling!
VRUMMMM

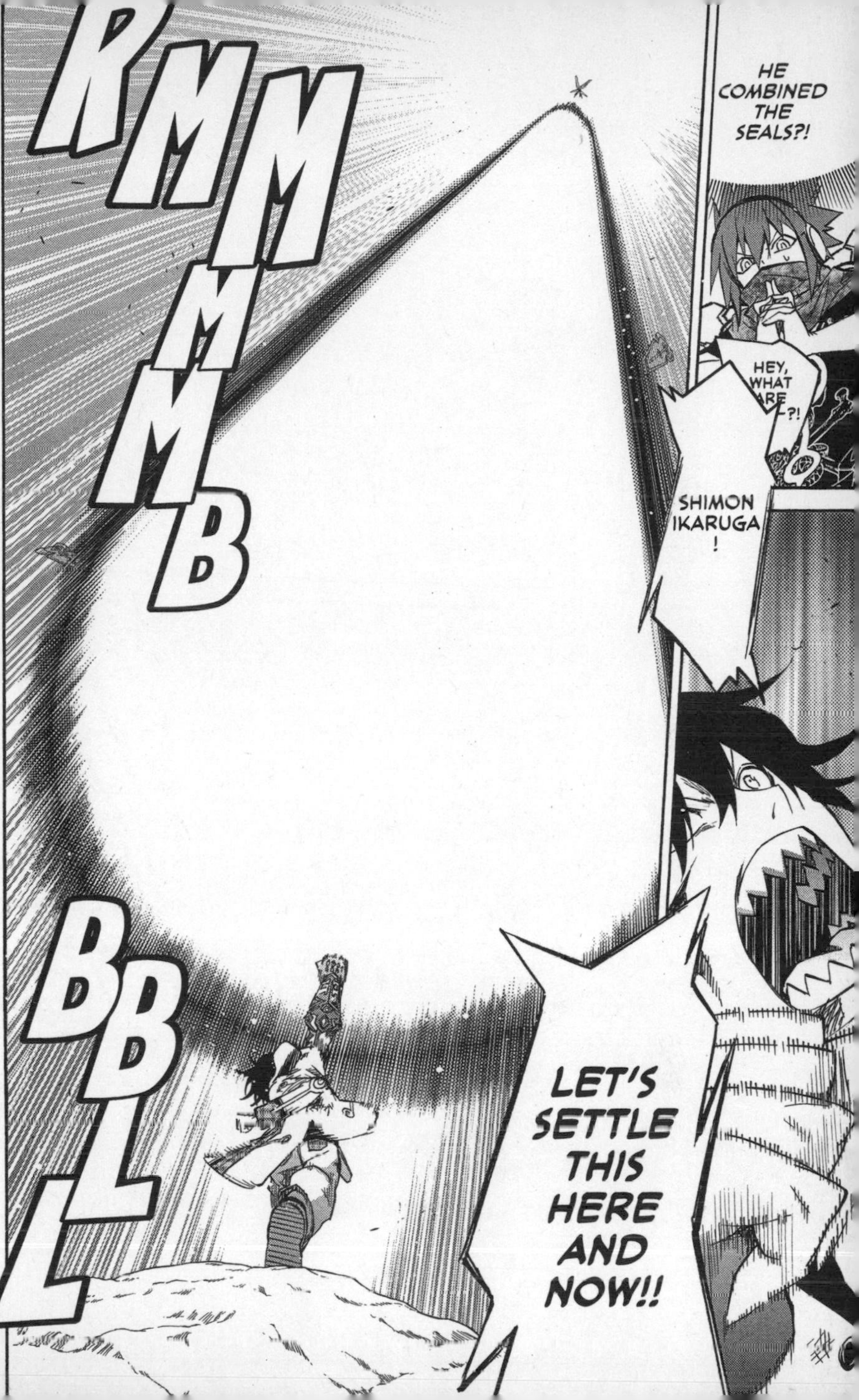
HE COMBINED THE SEALS?!
HEY, WHAT ARE ?!
SHIMON IKARUGA!
LET'S SETTLE THIS HERE AND NOW!!
RMMMMB
BBLL

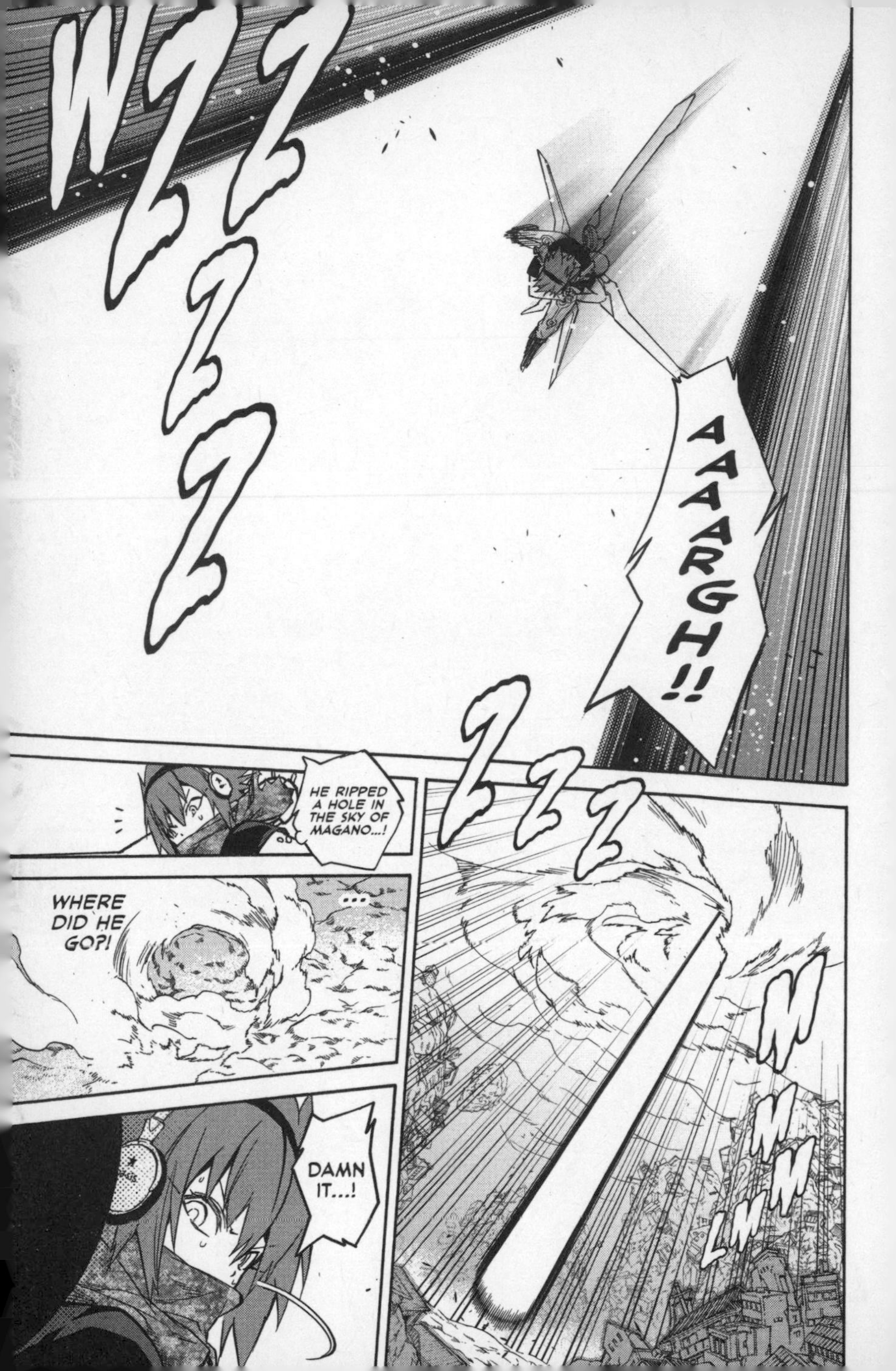
AAAARGH!!
WZZZZZZ
ZZZ
HE RIPPED A HOLE IN THE SKY OF MAGANO...!
WHERE DID HE GO?!
...
DAMN IT...!

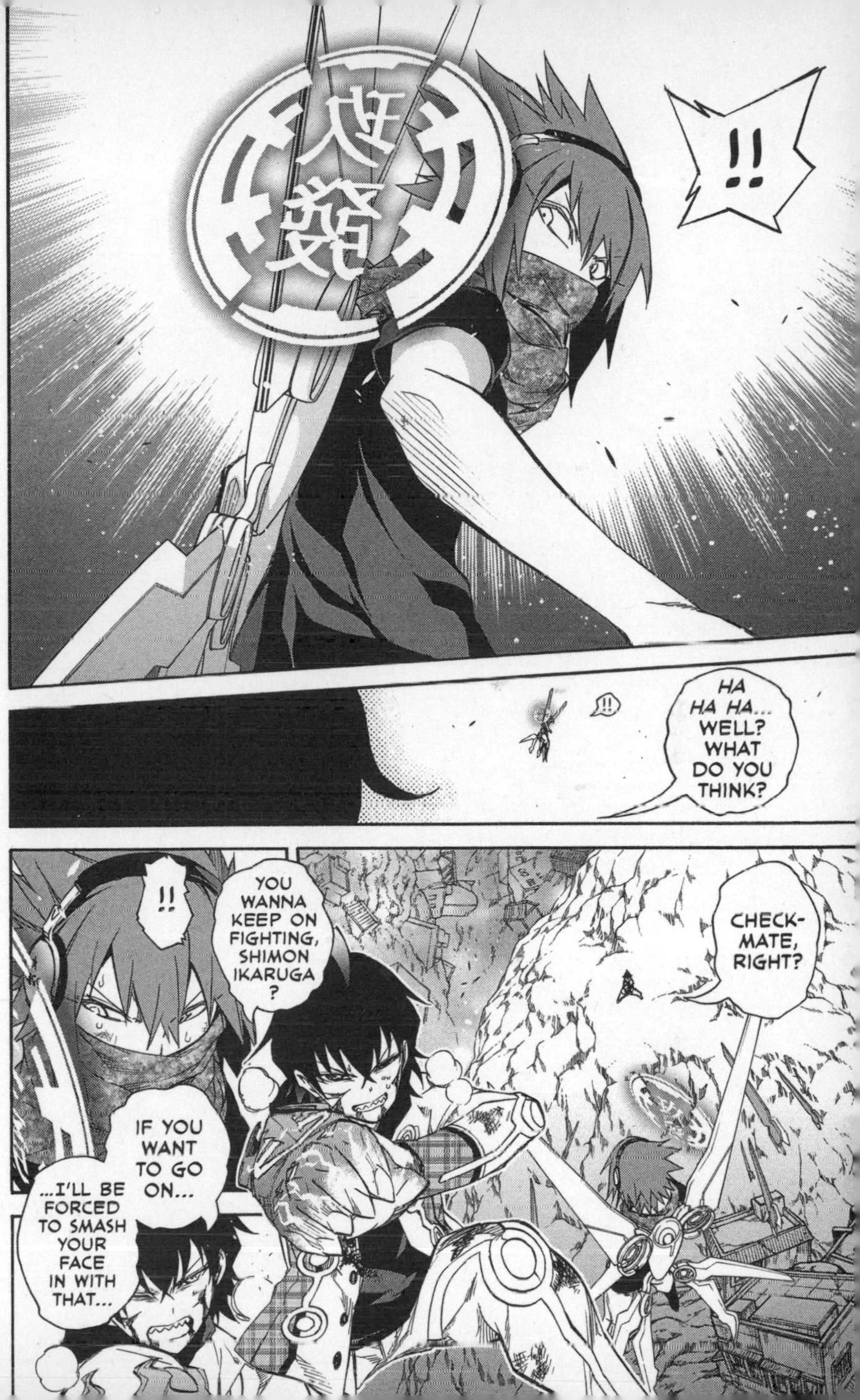
!!
!!
HA HA HA... WELL? WHAT DO YOU THINK?
CHECK-MATE, RIGHT?
YOU WANNA KEEP ON FIGHTING, SHIMON IKARUGA?
!!
IF YOU WANT TO GO ON...
...I'LL BE FORCED TO SMASH YOUR FACE IN WITH THAT...

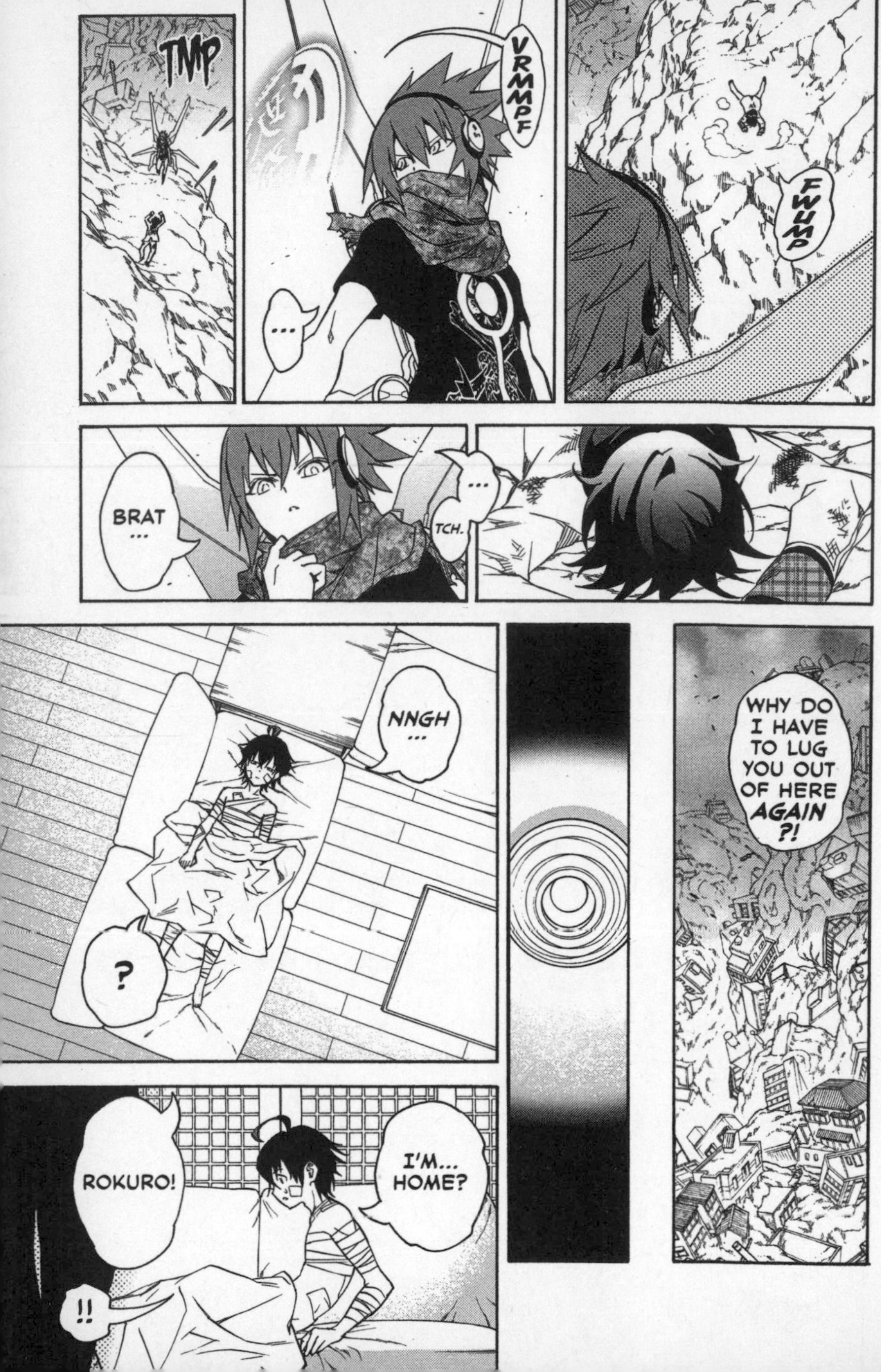
FWUMP
VRMMPF
...
TMP
...
TCH.
BRAT ...
WHY DO I HAVE TO LUG YOU OUT OF HERE AGAIN?!
NNGH ...
?
I'M... HOME?
ROKURO!
!!

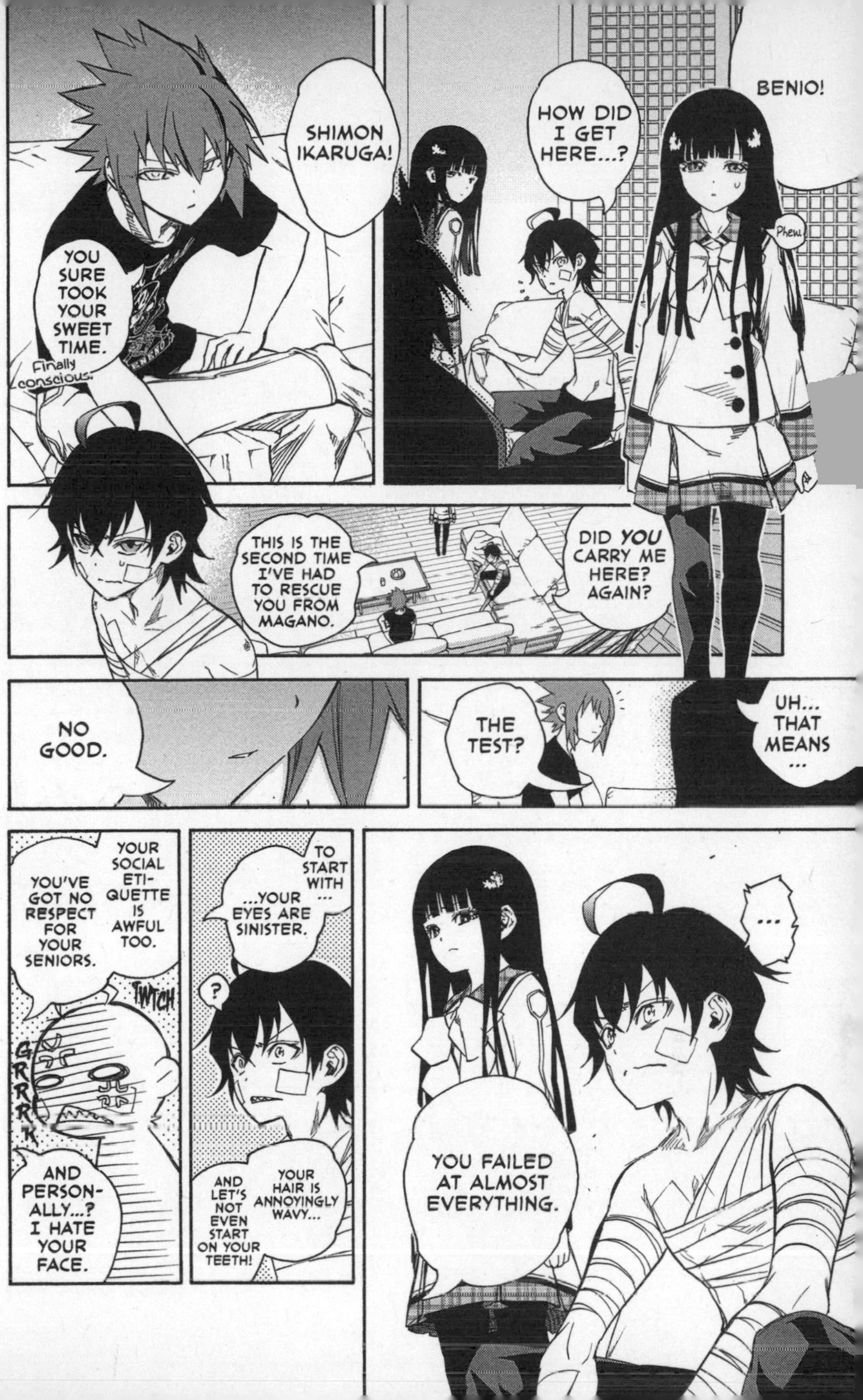
BENIO!
Phew!
HOW DID I GET HERE...?
SHIMON IKARUGA!
YOU SURE TOOK YOUR SWEET TIME.
Finally conscious.
DID *YOU* CARRY ME HERE? AGAIN?
THIS IS THE SECOND TIME I'VE HAD TO RESCUE YOU FROM MAGANO.
UH... THAT MEANS ...
THE TEST?
NO GOOD.
...
YOU FAILED AT ALMOST EVERYTHING.
TO START WITH ...
...YOUR EYES ARE SINISTER.
?
YOUR HAIR IS ANNOYINGLY WAVY...
AND LET'S NOT EVEN START ON YOUR TEETH!
YOUR SOCIAL ETI-QUETTE IS AWFUL TOO.
YOU'VE GOT NO RESPECT FOR YOUR SENIORS.
TWITCH
GRRRK
AND PERSON-ALLY...? I HATE YOUR FACE.

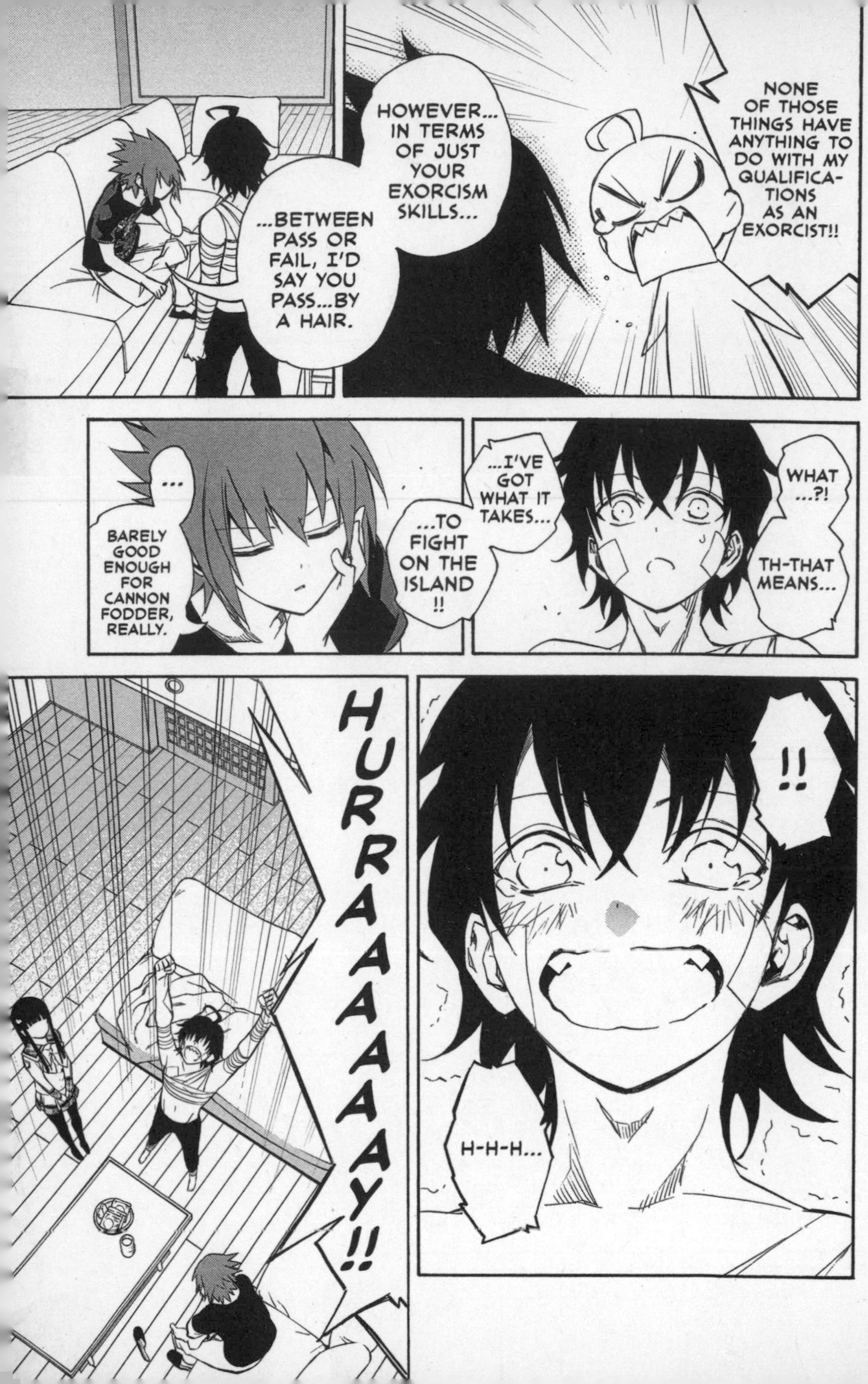

NONE OF THOSE THINGS HAVE ANYTHING TO DO WITH MY QUALIFICATIONS AS AN EXORCIST!!
HOWEVER... IN TERMS OF JUST YOUR EXORCISM SKILLS...
...BETWEEN PASS OR FAIL, I'D SAY YOU PASS...BY A HAIR.
WHAT ...?!
TH-THAT MEANS...
...I'VE GOT WHAT IT TAKES...
...TO FIGHT ON THE ISLAND !!
...
BARELY GOOD ENOUGH FOR CANNON FODDER, REALLY.
!!
H-H-H...
HURRAAAAAAY!!

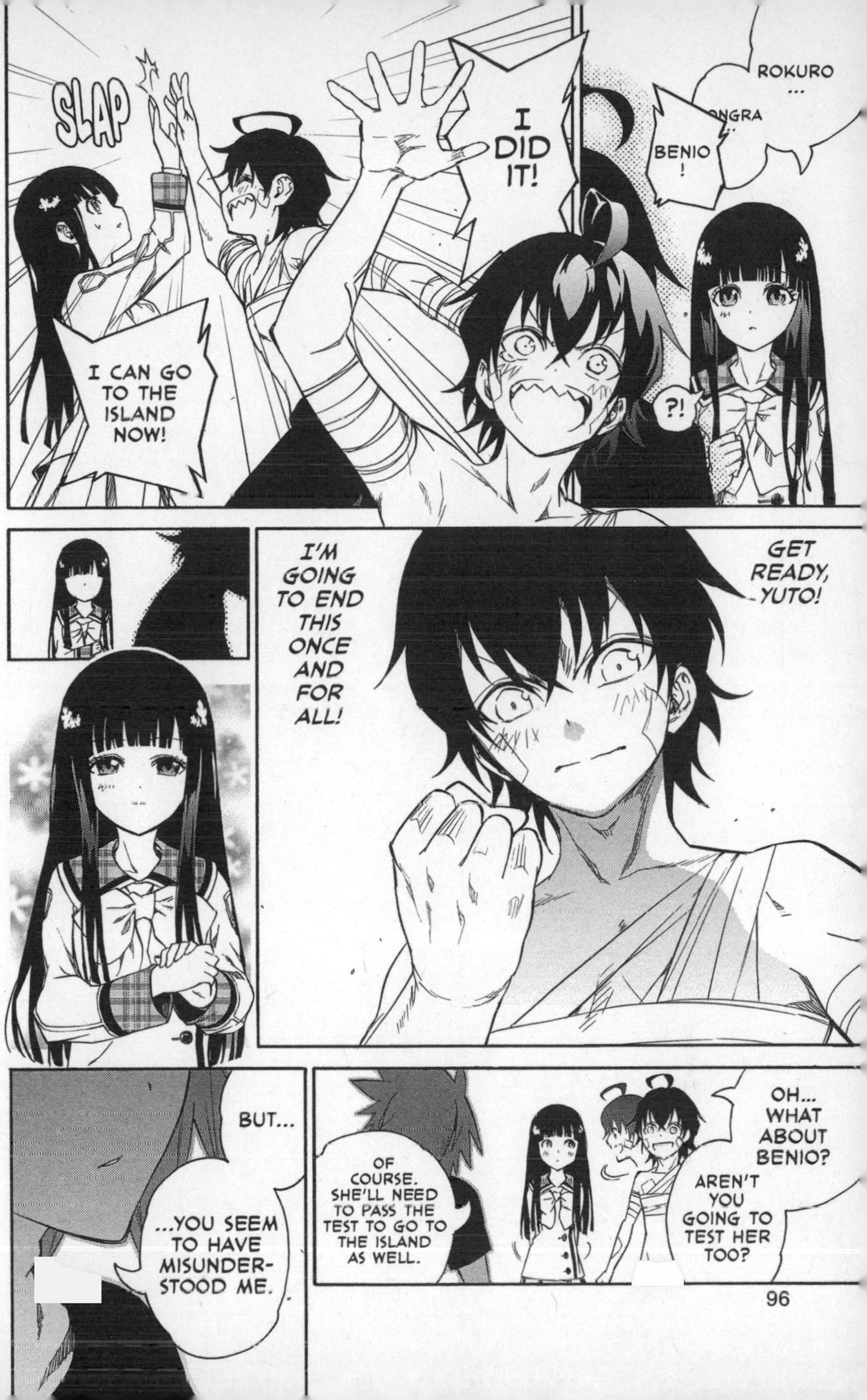
ROKURO...
ONGRA...
BENIO!
?!
I DID IT!
SLAP
I CAN GO TO THE ISLAND NOW!
GET READY, YUTO!
I'M GOING TO END THIS ONCE AND FOR ALL!
OH... WHAT ABOUT BENIO?
AREN'T YOU GOING TO TEST HER TOO?
OF COURSE. SHE'LL NEED TO PASS THE TEST TO GO TO THE ISLAND AS WELL.
BUT...
...YOU SEEM TO HAVE MISUNDER-STOOD ME.

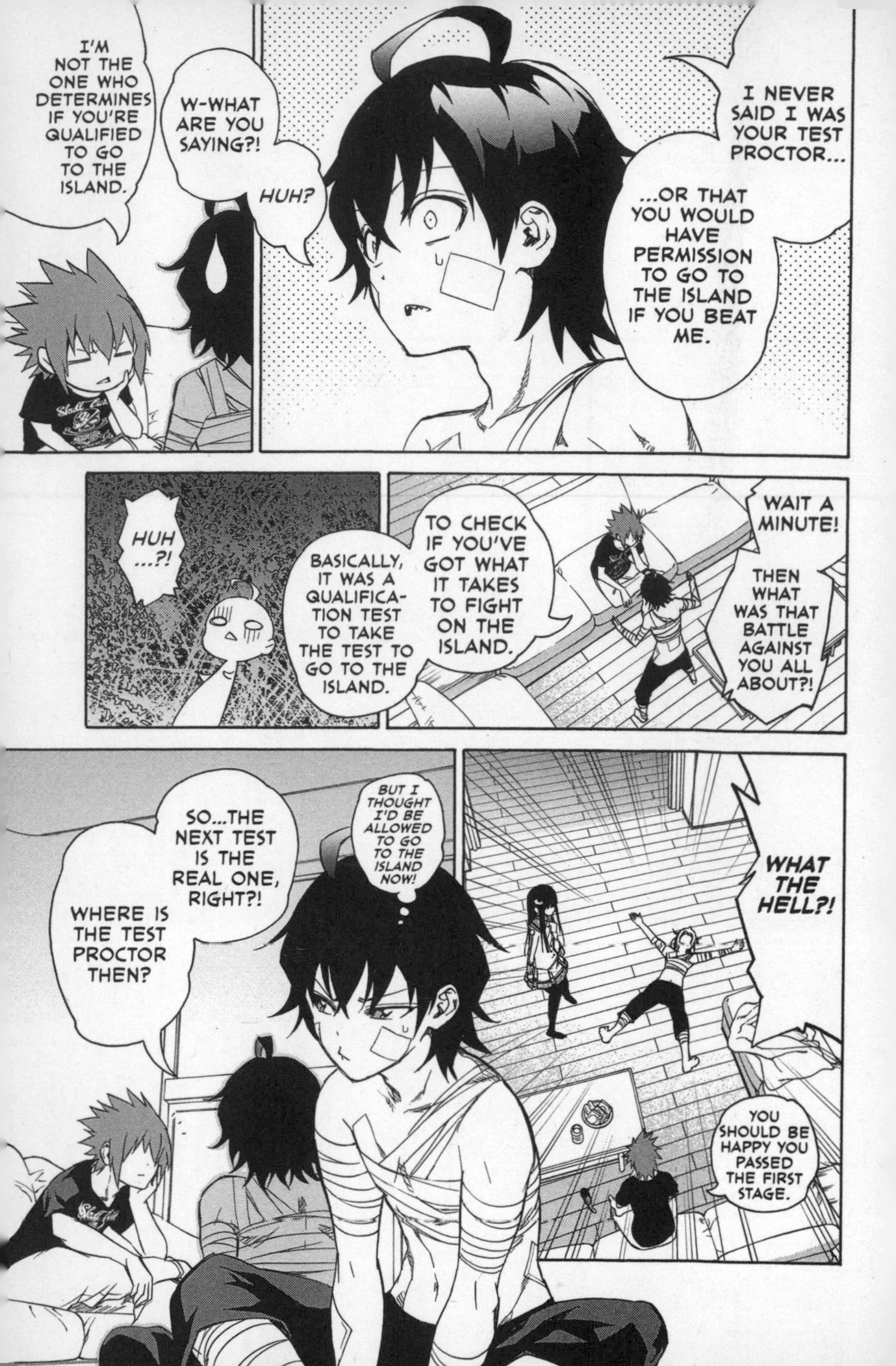
I NEVER SAID I WAS YOUR TEST PROCTOR...
...OR THAT YOU WOULD HAVE PERMISSION TO GO TO THE ISLAND IF YOU BEAT ME.
W-WHAT ARE YOU SAYING?!
HUH?
I'M NOT THE ONE WHO DETERMINES IF YOU'RE QUALIFIED TO GO TO THE ISLAND.
WAIT A MINUTE!
THEN WHAT WAS THAT BATTLE AGAINST YOU ALL ABOUT?!
TO CHECK IF YOU'VE GOT WHAT IT TAKES TO FIGHT ON THE ISLAND.
BASICALLY, IT WAS A QUALIFICATION TEST TO TAKE THE TEST TO GO TO THE ISLAND.
HUH...?!
WHAT THE HELL?!
YOU SHOULD BE HAPPY YOU PASSED THE FIRST STAGE.
BUT I THOUGHT I'D BE ALLOWED TO GO TO THE ISLAND NOW!
SO...THE NEXT TEST IS THE REAL ONE, RIGHT?!
WHERE IS THE TEST PROCTOR THEN?

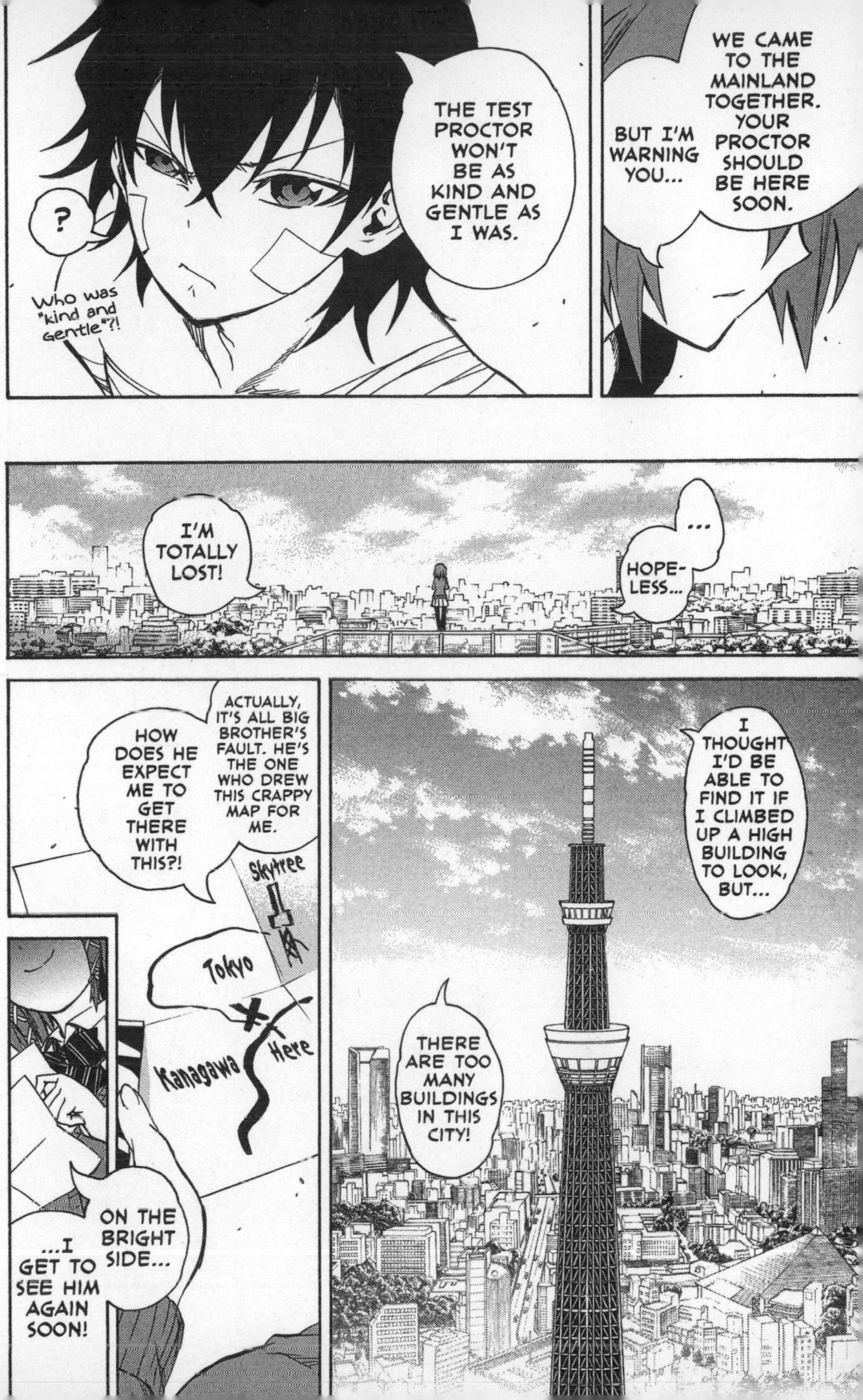
WE CAME TO THE MAINLAND TOGETHER. YOUR PROCTOR SHOULD BE HERE SOON.
BUT I'M WARNING YOU...
THE TEST PROCTOR WON'T BE AS KIND AND GENTLE AS I WAS.
?
Who was "kind and gentle"?!
...
I'M TOTALLY LOST!
HOPE-LESS...
I THOUGHT I'D BE ABLE TO FIND IT IF I CLIMBED UP A HIGH BUILDING TO LOOK, BUT...
THERE ARE TOO MANY BUILDINGS IN THIS CITY!
ACTUALLY, IT'S ALL BIG BROTHER'S FAULT. HE'S THE ONE WHO DREW THIS CRAPPY MAP FOR ME.
HOW DOES HE EXPECT ME TO GET THERE WITH THIS?!
Skytree
Tokyo
Here
Kanagawa
ON THE BRIGHT SIDE...
...I GET TO SEE HIM AGAIN SOON!

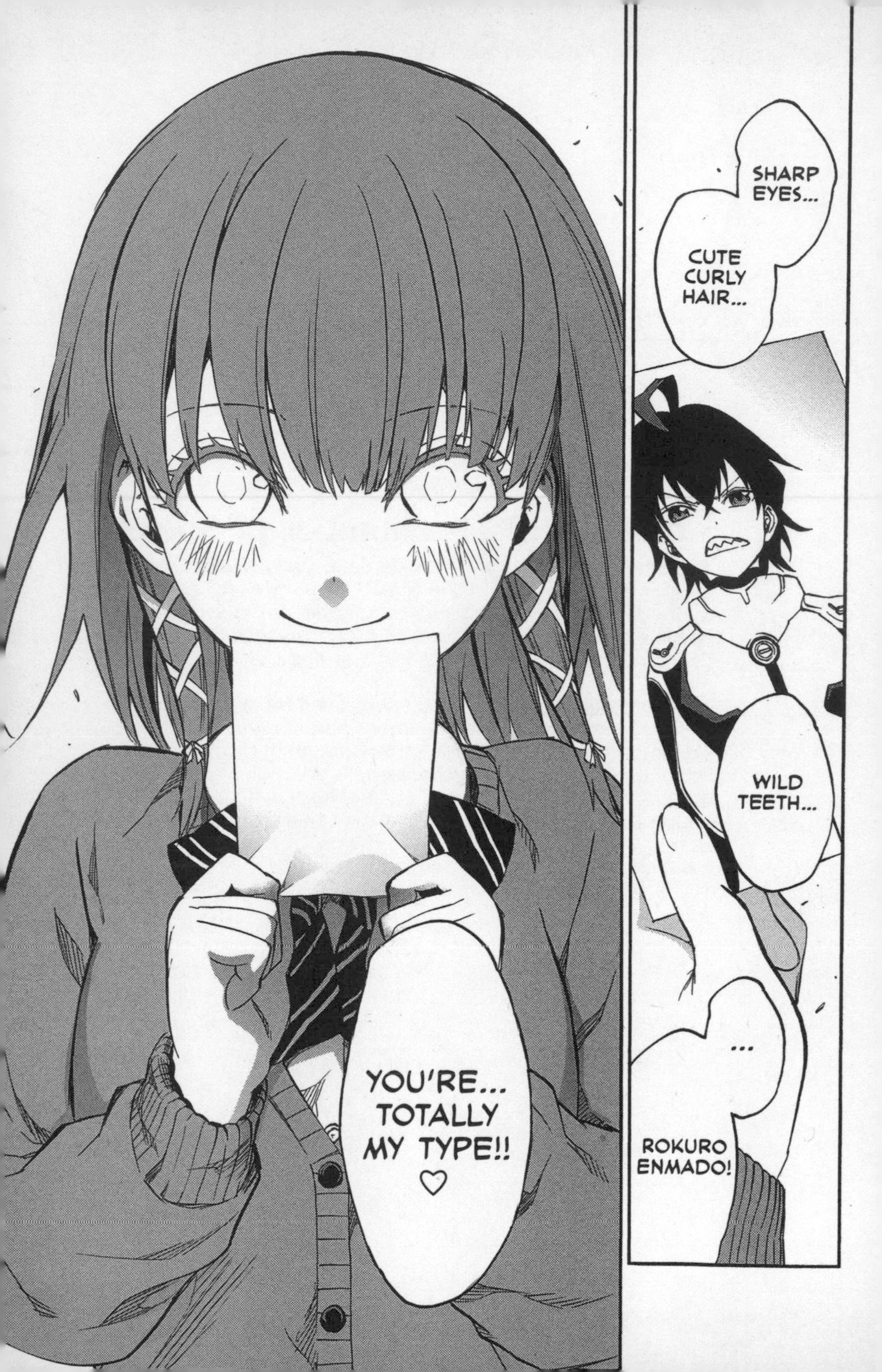
SHARP EYES...
CUTE CURLY HAIR...
WILD TEETH...
...
ROKURO ENMADO!
YOU'RE... TOTALLY MY TYPE!! ♡

Column ⑬ The Number of Spells

The spells in this story are divided into yang style and ying style. I've basically used the term "yang style" for spells used by modern-day exorcists and "ying style" for specialized spells which have been approved by the Association of Unified Exorcists for use in battle against the Kegare.

It is said that there are 1,080 spells used by modern-day exorcists. All I found in a document during my research was the total, though, so I don't know what each of them does (obviously). I'm assuming these spells are mainly used for fortune-telling, exorcism and curses, but I'm a bit concerned... I hope they don't really have a spell in their arsenal that makes them fly. Even though actual flight wouldn't be possible, I have a hunch they could make people float in midair at least...

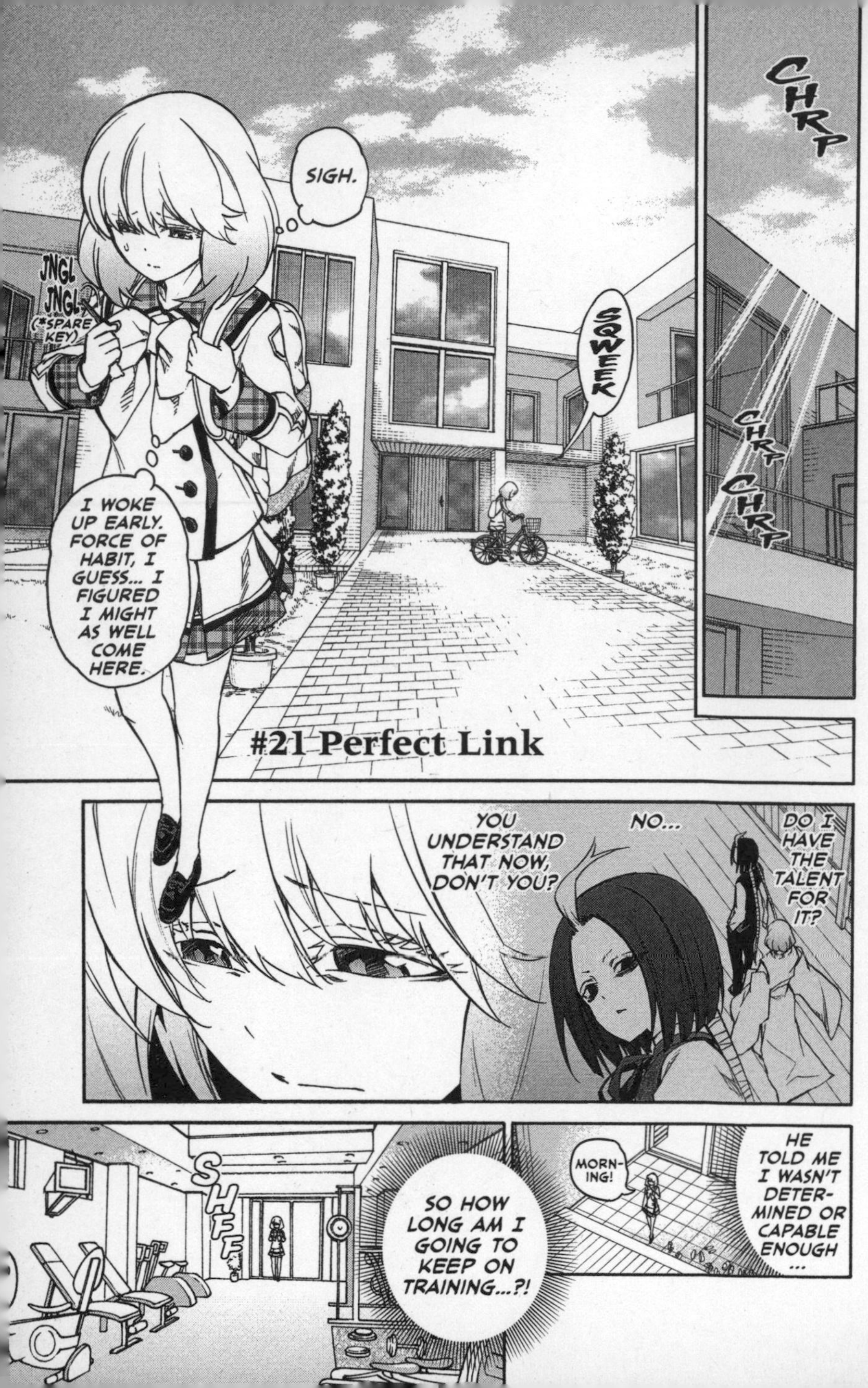
CHRP
CHRP CHRP CHRP
SIGH.
SQWEEK
JNGL JNGL
(*SPARE KEY)
I WOKE UP EARLY. FORCE OF HABIT, I GUESS... I FIGURED I MIGHT AS WELL COME HERE.
#21 Perfect Link
DO I HAVE THE TALENT FOR IT?
NO...
YOU UNDERSTAND THAT NOW, DON'T YOU?
HE TOLD ME I WASN'T DETERMINED OR CAPABLE ENOUGH ...
MORNING!
SHFF
SO HOW LONG AM I GOING TO KEEP ON TRAINING...?!

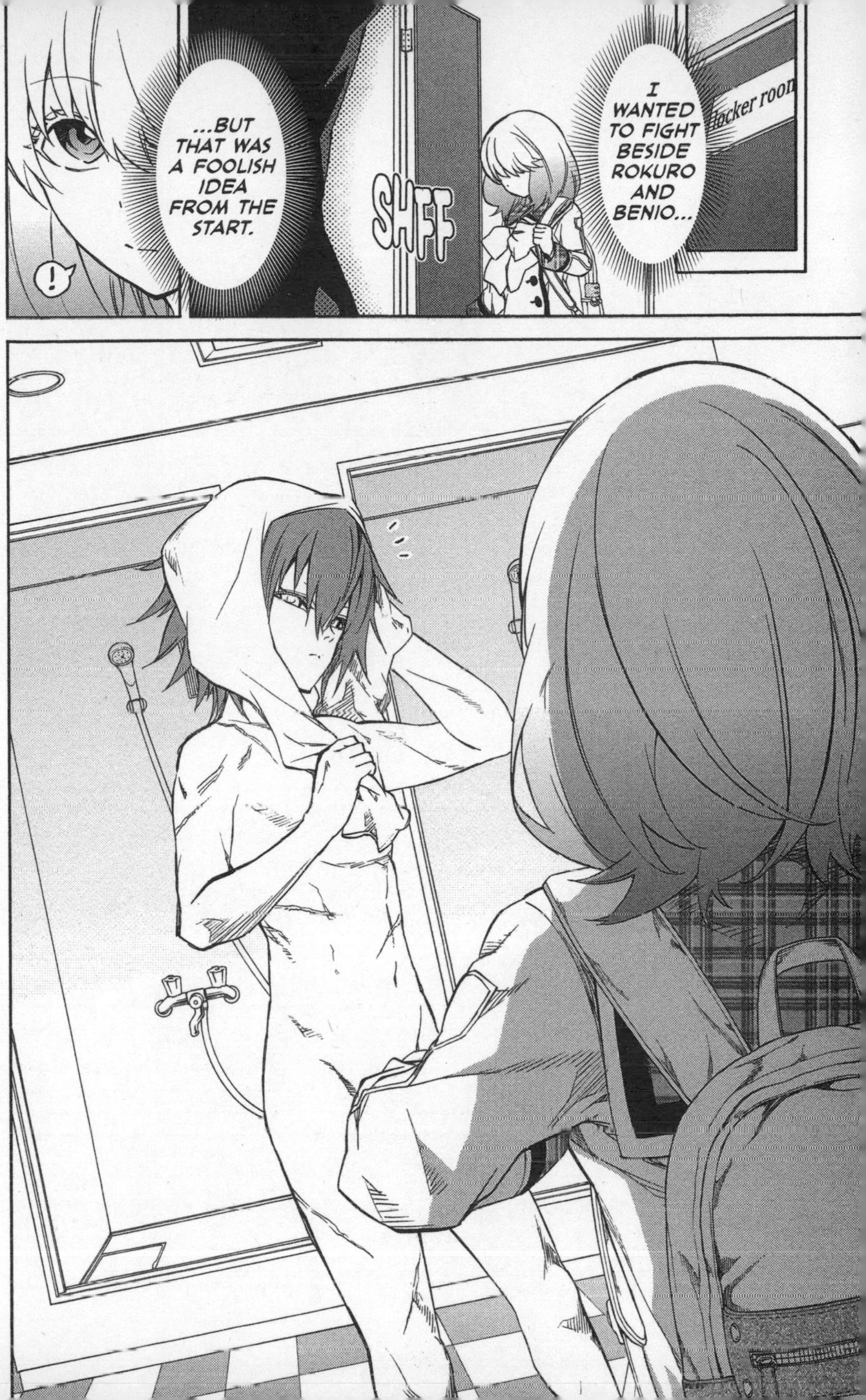
I WANTED TO FIGHT BESIDE ROKURO AND BENIO...
locker room
SHFF
...BUT THAT WAS A FOOLISH IDEA FROM THE START.
!

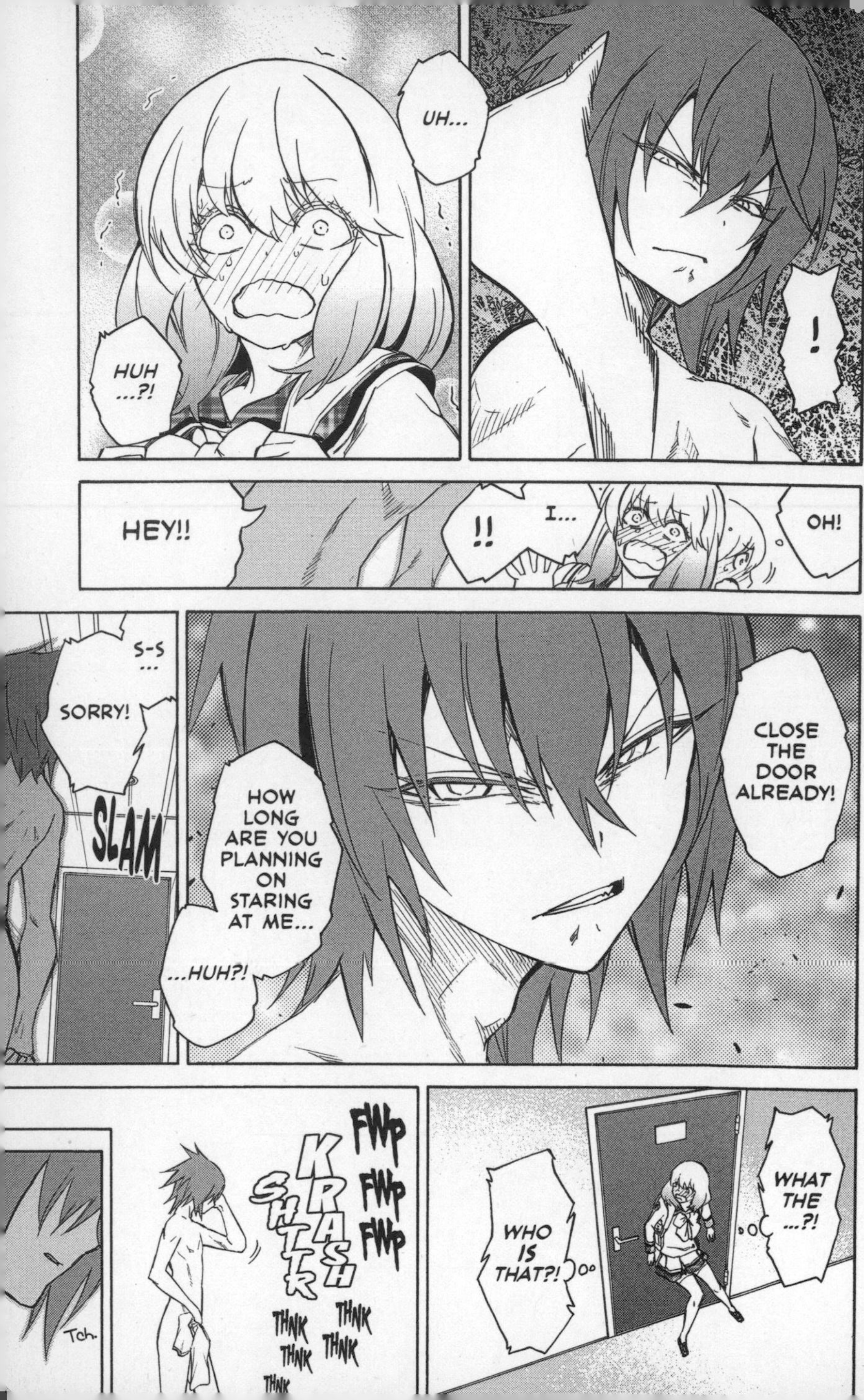
!
UH...
HUH ...?!
OH!
I...
!!
HEY!!
CLOSE THE DOOR ALREADY!
HOW LONG ARE YOU PLANNING ON STARING AT ME...
...HUH?!
S-S ... SORRY!
SLAM
WHAT THE ...?!
WHO IS THAT?!
FWP
FWP
FWP
KRASH
SHLIK
THNK
THNK
THNK
THNK
THNK
Tch.

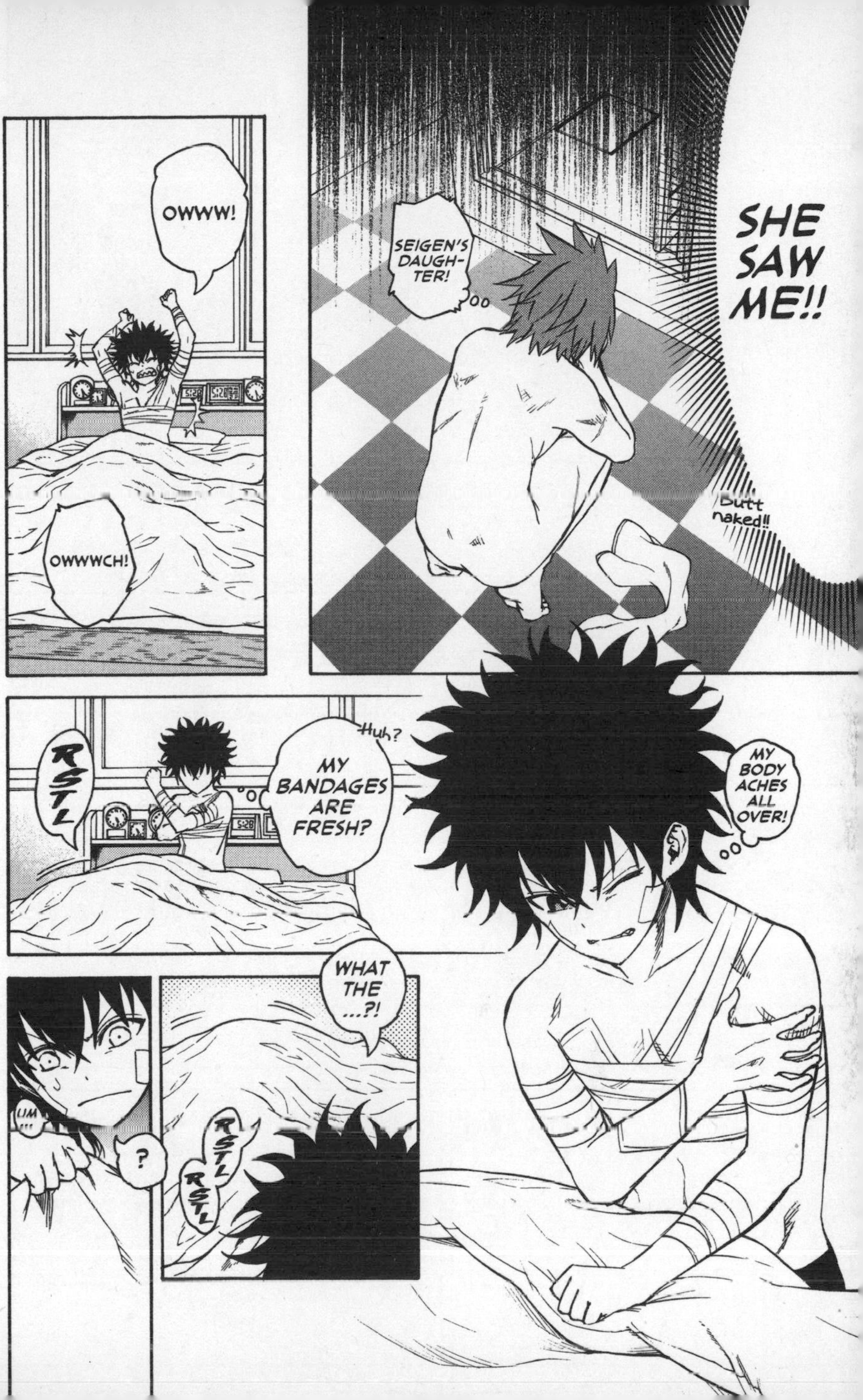
SHE SAW ME!!
SEIGEN'S DAUGH-TER!
Butt naked!!
OWWW!
OWWWCH!
MY BODY ACHES ALL OVER!
RSTL
Huh?
MY BANDAGES ARE FRESH?
WHAT THE ...?!
RSTL
RSTL
UM...
?

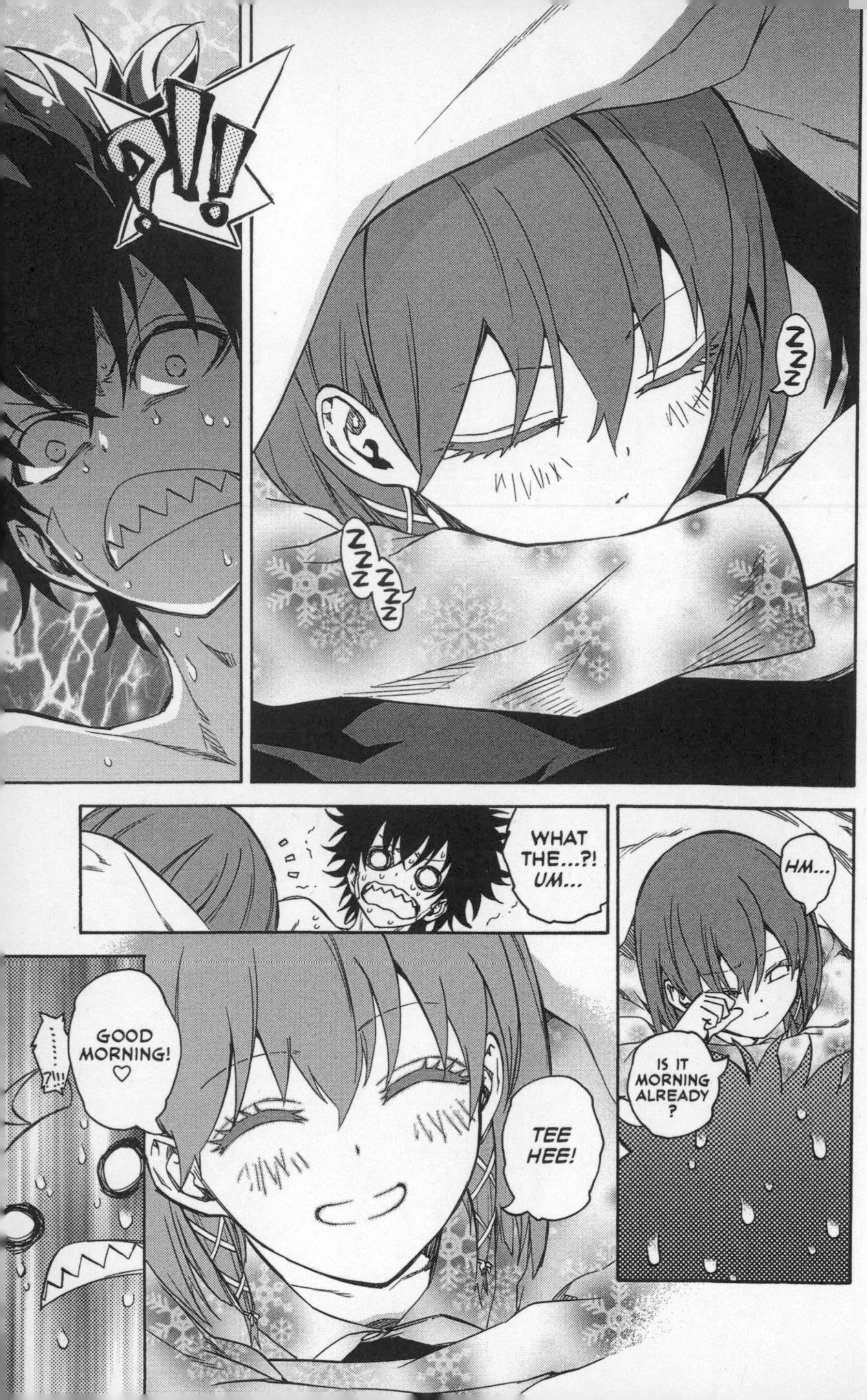
ZZZ
ZZZ ZZZ
?!!
HM...
IS IT MORNING ALREADY?
WHAT THE...?! UM...
TEE HEE!
GOOD MORNING! ♡
...?!!!

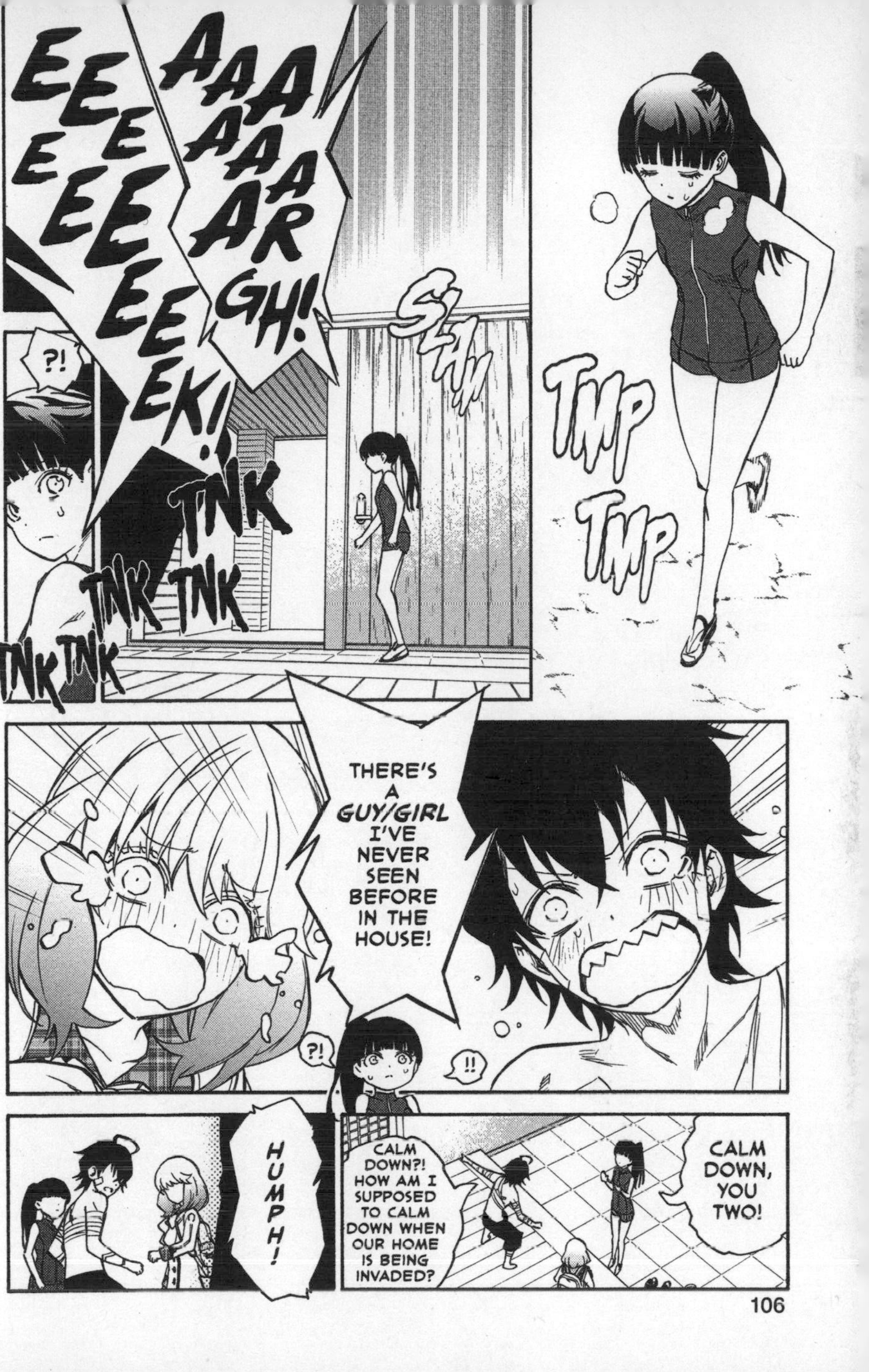
TMP
TMP
AAAAAARGH!
EEEEEEEEEEK!
SLAM
TNK TNK TNK TNK TNK
?!
THERE'S A GUY/GIRL I'VE NEVER SEEN BEFORE IN THE HOUSE!
!!
?!
CALM DOWN, YOU TWO!
CALM DOWN?! HOW AM I SUPPOSED TO CALM DOWN WHEN OUR HOME IS BEING INVADED?
HUMPH!

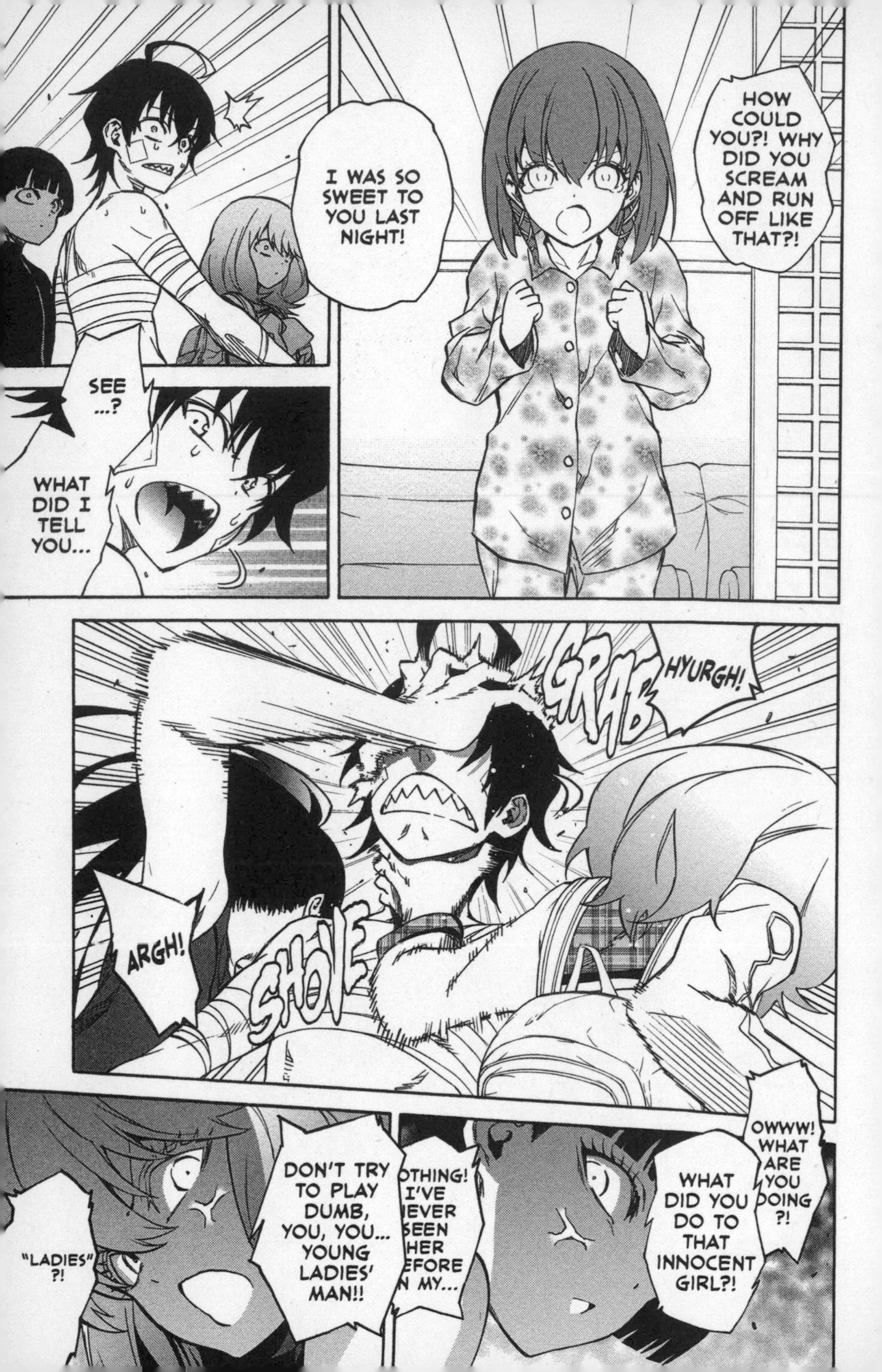
HOW COULD YOU?! WHY DID YOU SCREAM AND RUN OFF LIKE THAT?!
I WAS SO SWEET TO YOU LAST NIGHT!
SEE ...?
WHAT DID I TELL YOU...
HYURGH!
GRAB
SHOVE
ARGH!
OWWW! WHAT ARE YOU DOING ?!
WHAT DID YOU DO TO THAT INNOCENT GIRL?!
OTHING! I'VE IEVER SEEN HER EFORE N MY...
DON'T TRY TO PLAY DUMB, YOU, YOU... YOUNG LADIES' MAN!!
"LADIES" ?!

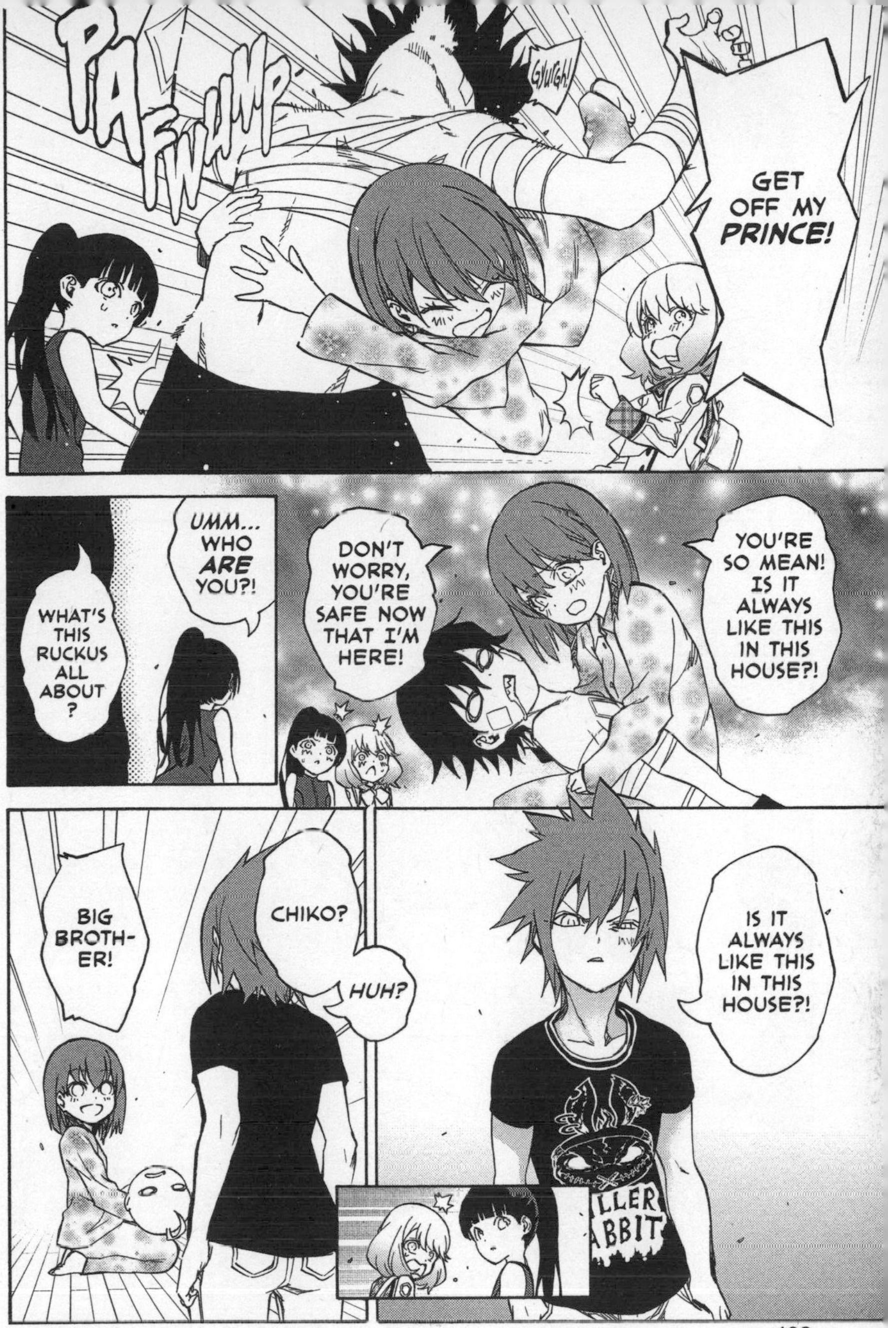
GET OFF MY PRINCE!
GYURGH!
PA FWUMP
YOU'RE SO MEAN! IS IT ALWAYS LIKE THIS IN THIS HOUSE?!
DON'T WORRY, YOU'RE SAFE NOW THAT I'M HERE!
UMM... WHO ARE YOU?!
WHAT'S THIS RUCKUS ALL ABOUT?
IS IT ALWAYS LIKE THIS IN THIS HOUSE?!
CHIKO?
BIG BROTHER!
HUH?

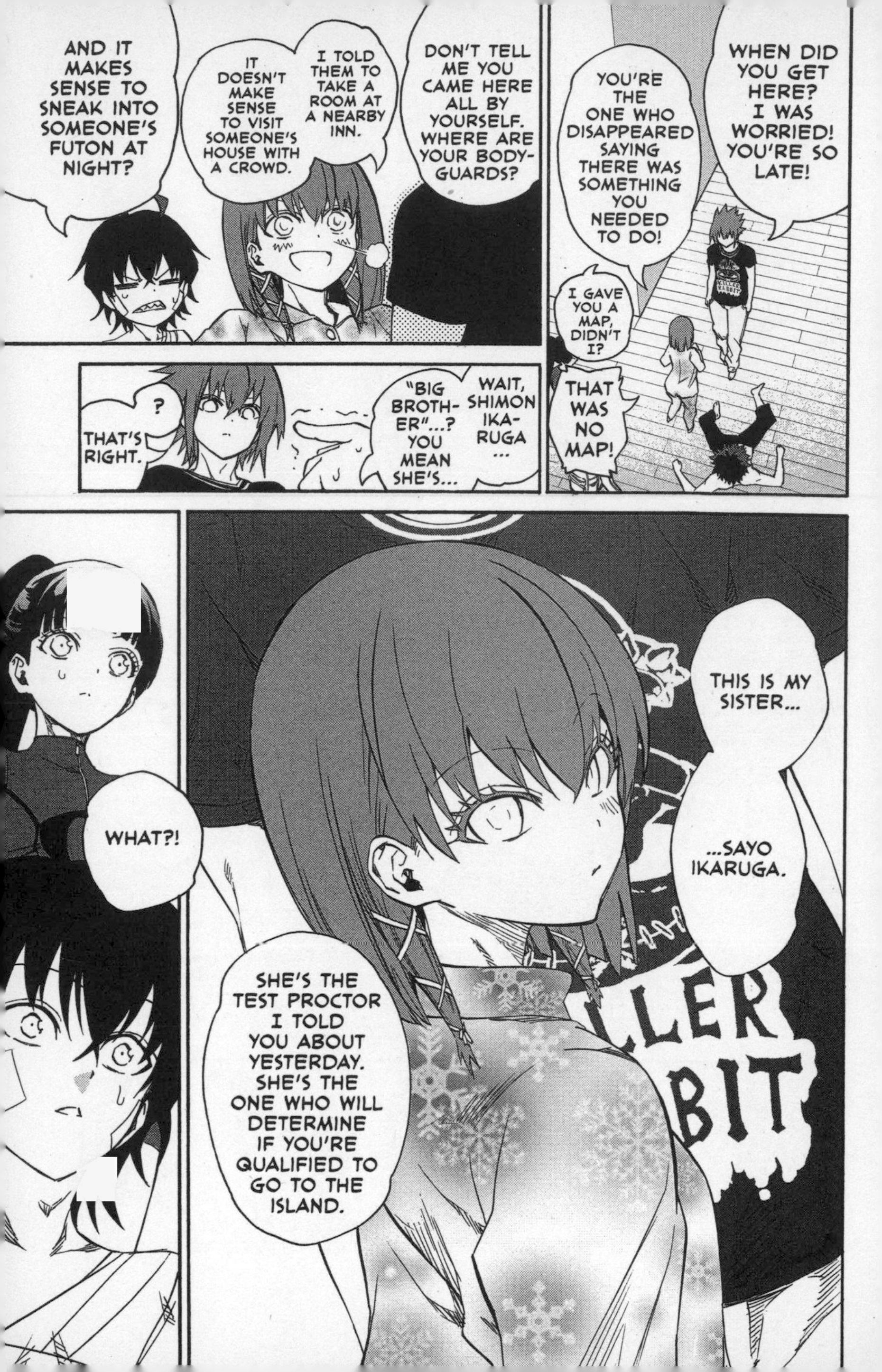
WHEN DID YOU GET HERE? I WAS WORRIED! YOU'RE SO LATE!
YOU'RE THE ONE WHO DISAPPEARED SAYING THERE WAS SOMETHING YOU NEEDED TO DO!
I GAVE YOU A MAP, DIDN'T I?
THAT WAS NO MAP!
DON'T TELL ME YOU CAME HERE ALL BY YOURSELF. WHERE ARE YOUR BODY-GUARDS?
I TOLD THEM TO TAKE A ROOM AT A NEARBY INN.
IT DOESN'T MAKE SENSE TO VISIT SOMEONE'S HOUSE WITH A CROWD.
AND IT MAKES SENSE TO SNEAK INTO SOMEONE'S FUTON AT NIGHT?
WAIT, SHIMON IKARUGA...
"BIG BROTHER"...? YOU MEAN SHE'S...
?
THAT'S RIGHT.
THIS IS MY SISTER...
...SAYO IKARUGA.
SHE'S THE TEST PROCTOR I TOLD YOU ABOUT YESTERDAY. SHE'S THE ONE WHO WILL DETERMINE IF YOU'RE QUALIFIED TO GO TO THE ISLAND.
WHAT?!

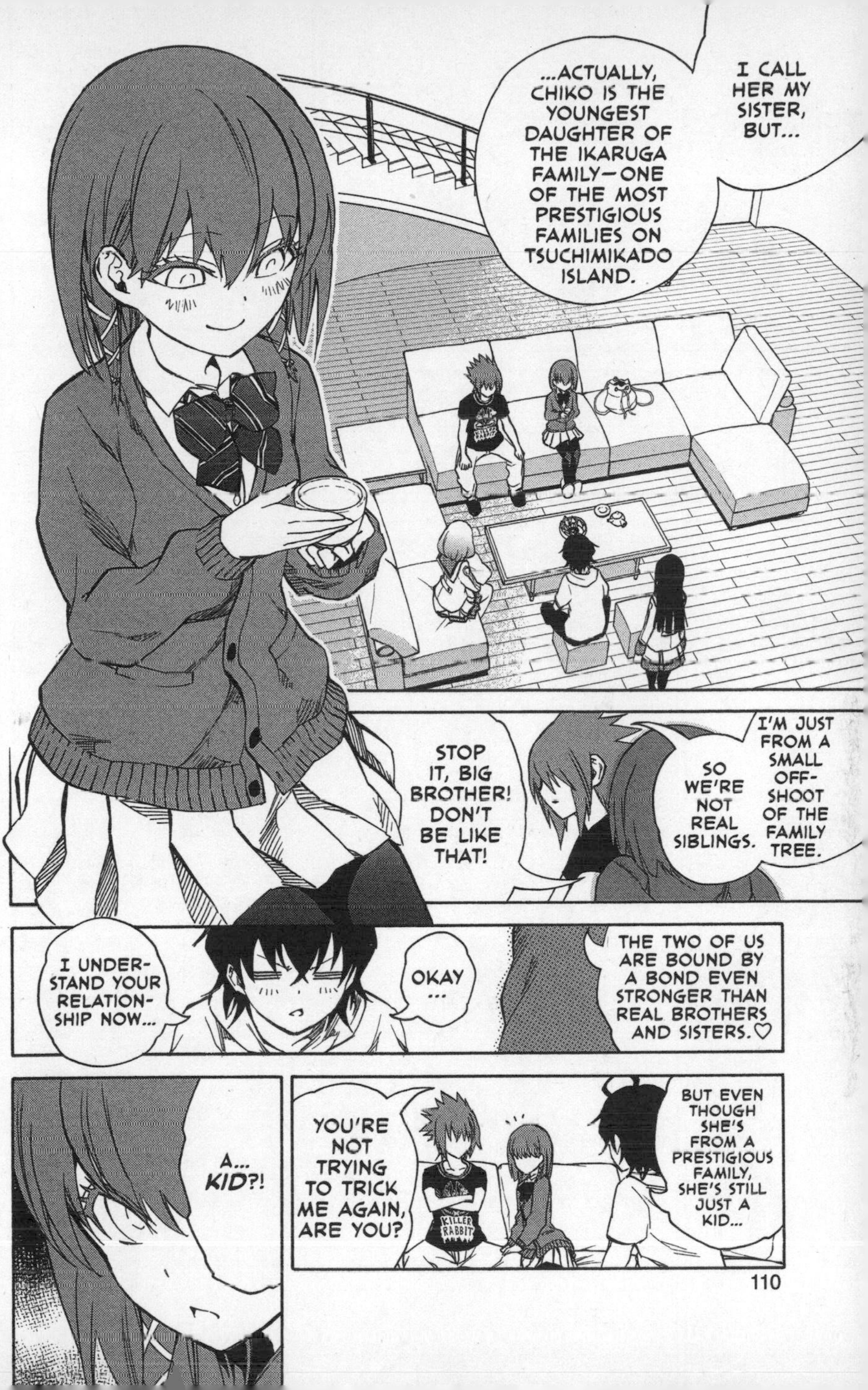
I CALL HER MY SISTER, BUT...
...ACTUALLY, CHIKO IS THE YOUNGEST DAUGHTER OF THE IKARUGA FAMILY—ONE OF THE MOST PRESTIGIOUS FAMILIES ON TSUCHIMIKADO ISLAND.
I'M JUST FROM A SMALL OFF-SHOOT OF THE FAMILY TREE.
SO WE'RE NOT REAL SIBLINGS.
STOP IT, BIG BROTHER! DON'T BE LIKE THAT!
THE TWO OF US ARE BOUND BY A BOND EVEN STRONGER THAN REAL BROTHERS AND SISTERS.♡
OKAY ...
I UNDER-STAND YOUR RELATION-SHIP NOW...
BUT EVEN THOUGH SHE'S FROM A PRESTIGIOUS FAMILY, SHE'S STILL JUST A KID...
KILLER RABBIT
YOU'RE NOT TRYING TO TRICK ME AGAIN, ARE YOU?
A... *KID*?!

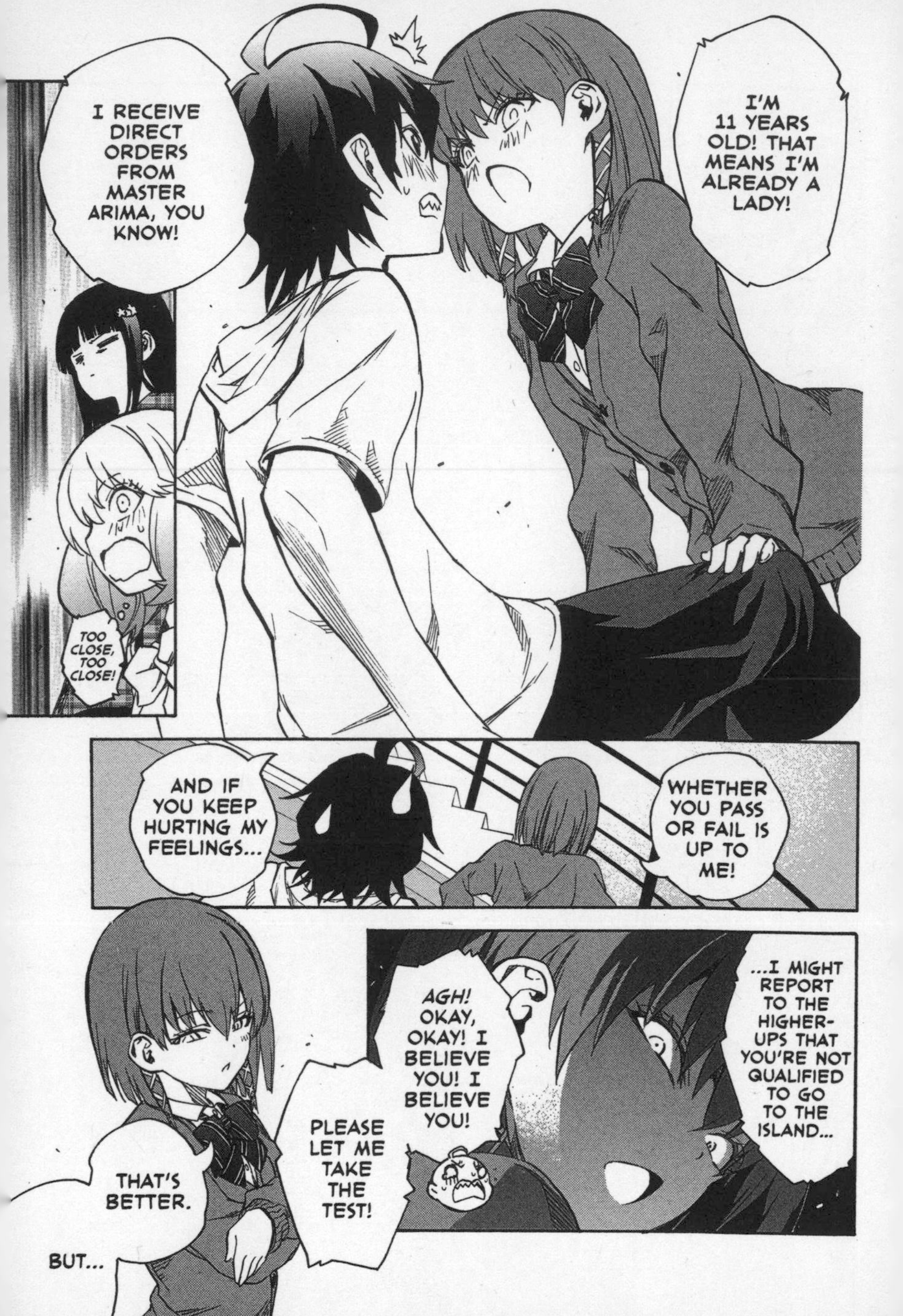
I'M 11 YEARS OLD! THAT MEANS I'M ALREADY A LADY!
I RECEIVE DIRECT ORDERS FROM MASTER ARIMA, YOU KNOW!
TOO CLOSE, TOO CLOSE!
WHETHER YOU PASS OR FAIL IS UP TO ME!
AND IF YOU KEEP HURTING MY FEELINGS...
...I MIGHT REPORT TO THE HIGHER-UPS THAT YOU'RE NOT QUALIFIED TO GO TO THE ISLAND...
AGH! OKAY, OKAY! I BELIEVE YOU! I BELIEVE YOU!
PLEASE LET ME TAKE THE TEST!
THAT'S BETTER.
BUT...

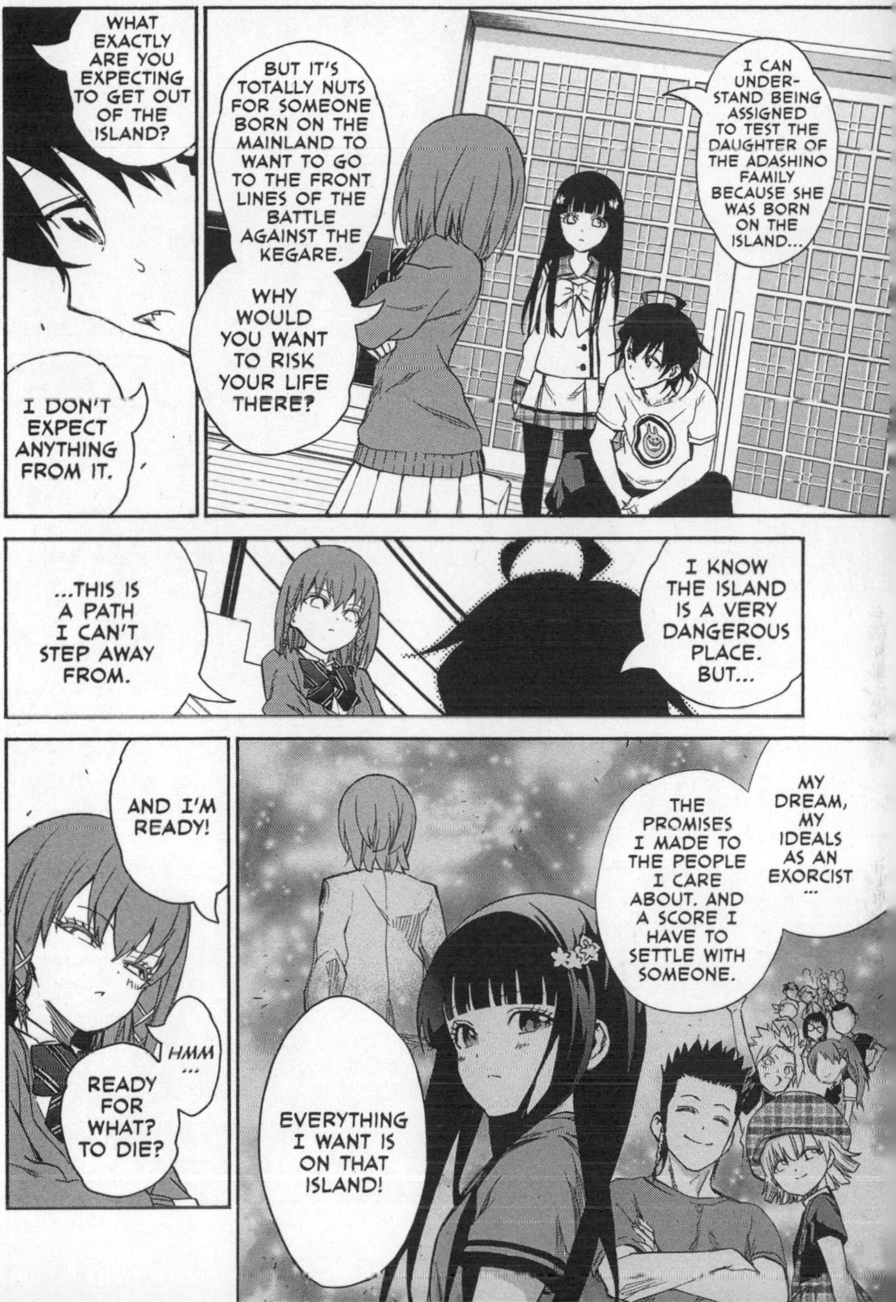
I CAN UNDER-STAND BEING ASSIGNED TO TEST THE DAUGHTER OF THE ADASHINO FAMILY BECAUSE SHE WAS BORN ON THE ISLAND...
BUT IT'S TOTALLY NUTS FOR SOMEONE BORN ON THE MAINLAND TO WANT TO GO TO THE FRONT LINES OF THE BATTLE AGAINST THE KEGARE.
WHY WOULD YOU WANT TO RISK YOUR LIFE THERE?
WHAT EXACTLY ARE YOU EXPECTING TO GET OUT OF THE ISLAND?
I DON'T EXPECT ANYTHING FROM IT.
I KNOW THE ISLAND IS A VERY DANGEROUS PLACE. BUT...
...THIS IS A PATH I CAN'T STEP AWAY FROM.
MY DREAM, MY IDEALS AS AN EXORCIST ...
THE PROMISES I MADE TO THE PEOPLE I CARE ABOUT. AND A SCORE I HAVE TO SETTLE WITH SOMEONE.
EVERYTHING I WANT IS ON THAT ISLAND!
AND I'M READY!
HMM ...
READY FOR WHAT? TO DIE?

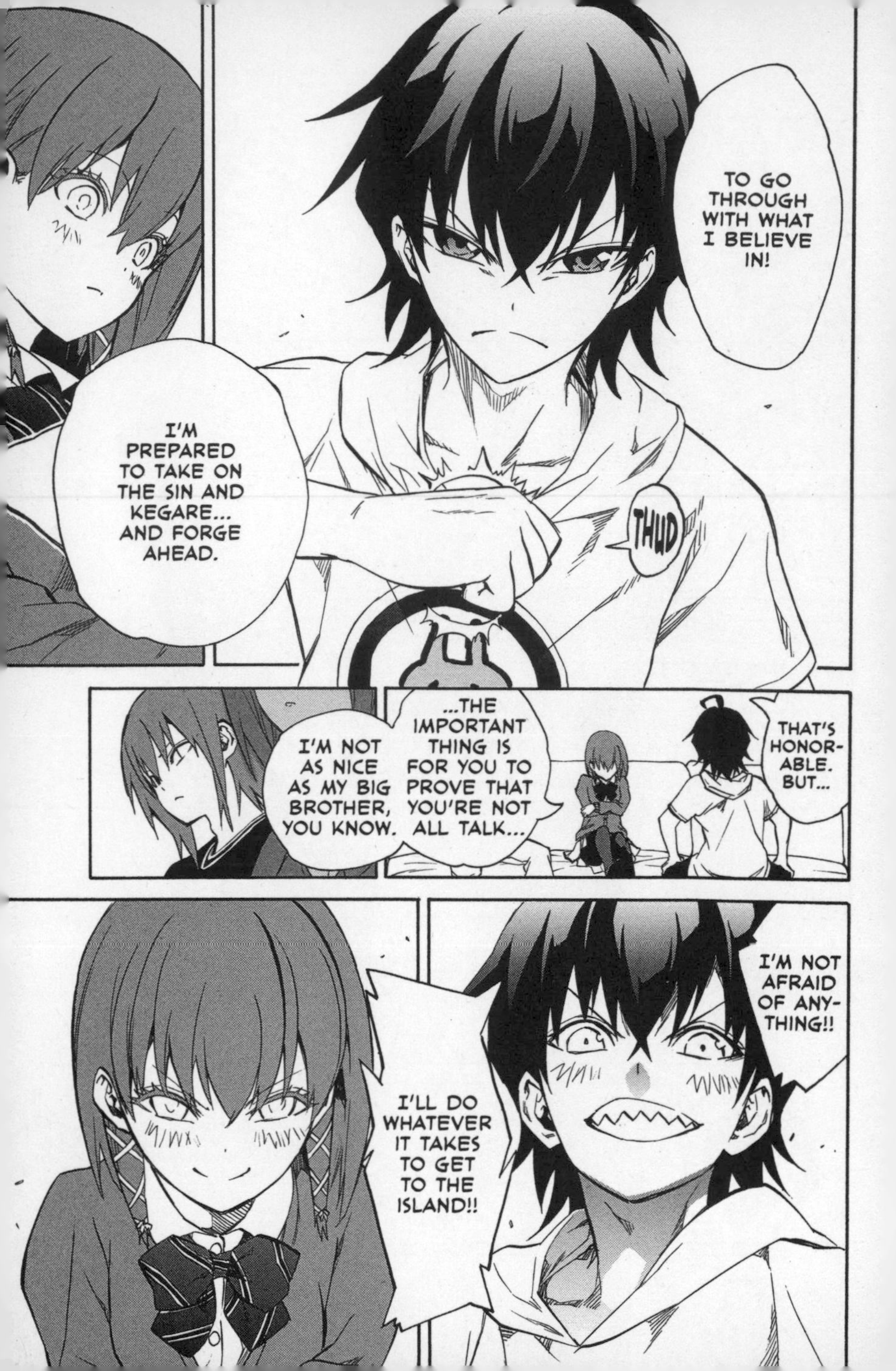
TO GO THROUGH WITH WHAT I BELIEVE IN!
I'M PREPARED TO TAKE ON THE SIN AND KEGARE... AND FORGE AHEAD.
THUD
THAT'S HONOR-ABLE. BUT...
...THE IMPORTANT THING IS FOR YOU TO PROVE THAT YOU'RE NOT ALL TALK...
I'M NOT AS NICE AS MY BIG BROTHER, YOU KNOW.
I'M NOT AFRAID OF ANY-THING!!
I'LL DO WHATEVER IT TAKES TO GET TO THE ISLAND!!

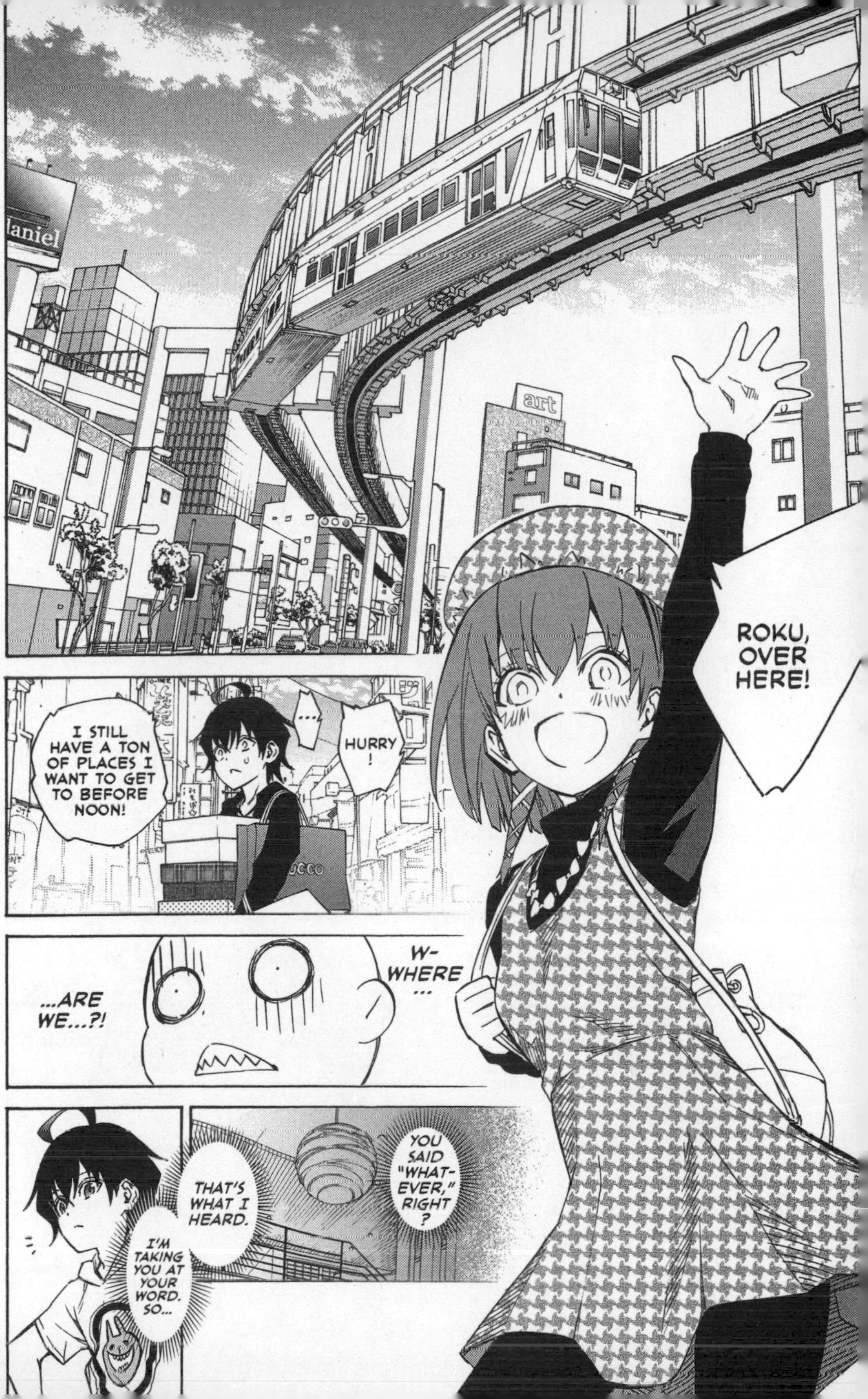

daniel
art
ROKU, OVER HERE!
HURRY!
...
I STILL HAVE A TON OF PLACES I WANT TO GET TO BEFORE NOON!
W-WHERE...
...ARE WE...?!
YOU SAID "WHATEVER," RIGHT?
THAT'S WHAT I HEARD.
I'M TAKING YOU AT YOUR WORD. SO...

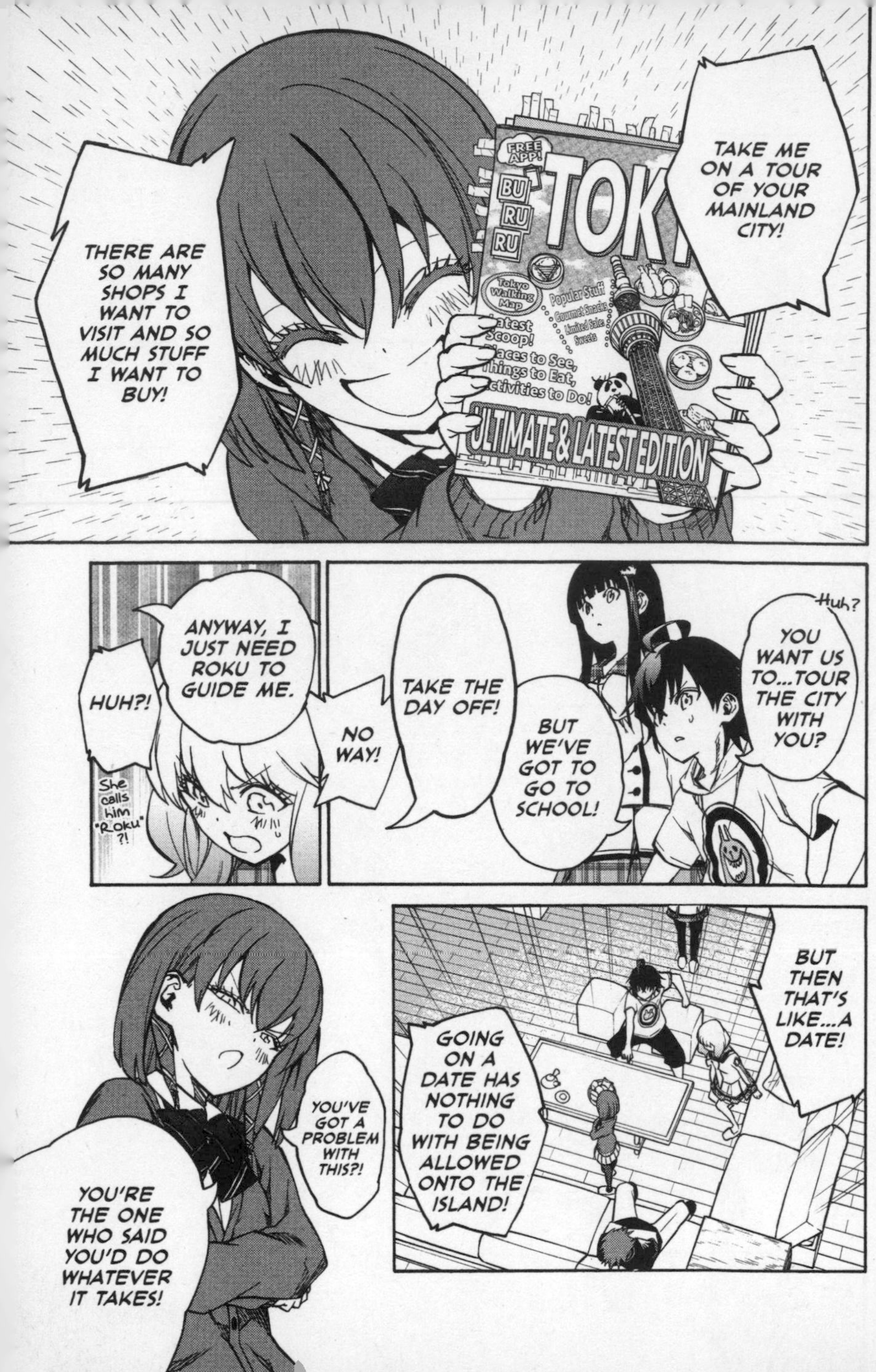
TAKE ME ON A TOUR OF YOUR MAINLAND CITY!
FREE APP!
BU RU RU
TOK
Tokyo Walking Map
Popular Stuff
Gourmet Snacks
Limited Sale
Sweets
ULTIMATE & LATEST EDITION
THERE ARE SO MANY SHOPS I WANT TO VISIT AND SO MUCH STUFF I WANT TO BUY!
Huh?
YOU WANT US TO...TOUR THE CITY WITH YOU?
BUT WE'VE GOT TO GO TO SCHOOL!
TAKE THE DAY OFF!
NO WAY!
ANYWAY, I JUST NEED ROKU TO GUIDE ME.
HUH?!
She calls him "Roku"?!
BUT THEN THAT'S LIKE...A DATE!
GOING ON A DATE HAS NOTHING TO DO WITH BEING ALLOWED ONTO THE ISLAND!
YOU'VE GOT A PROBLEM WITH THIS?!
YOU'RE THE ONE WHO SAID YOU'D DO WHATEVER IT TAKES!

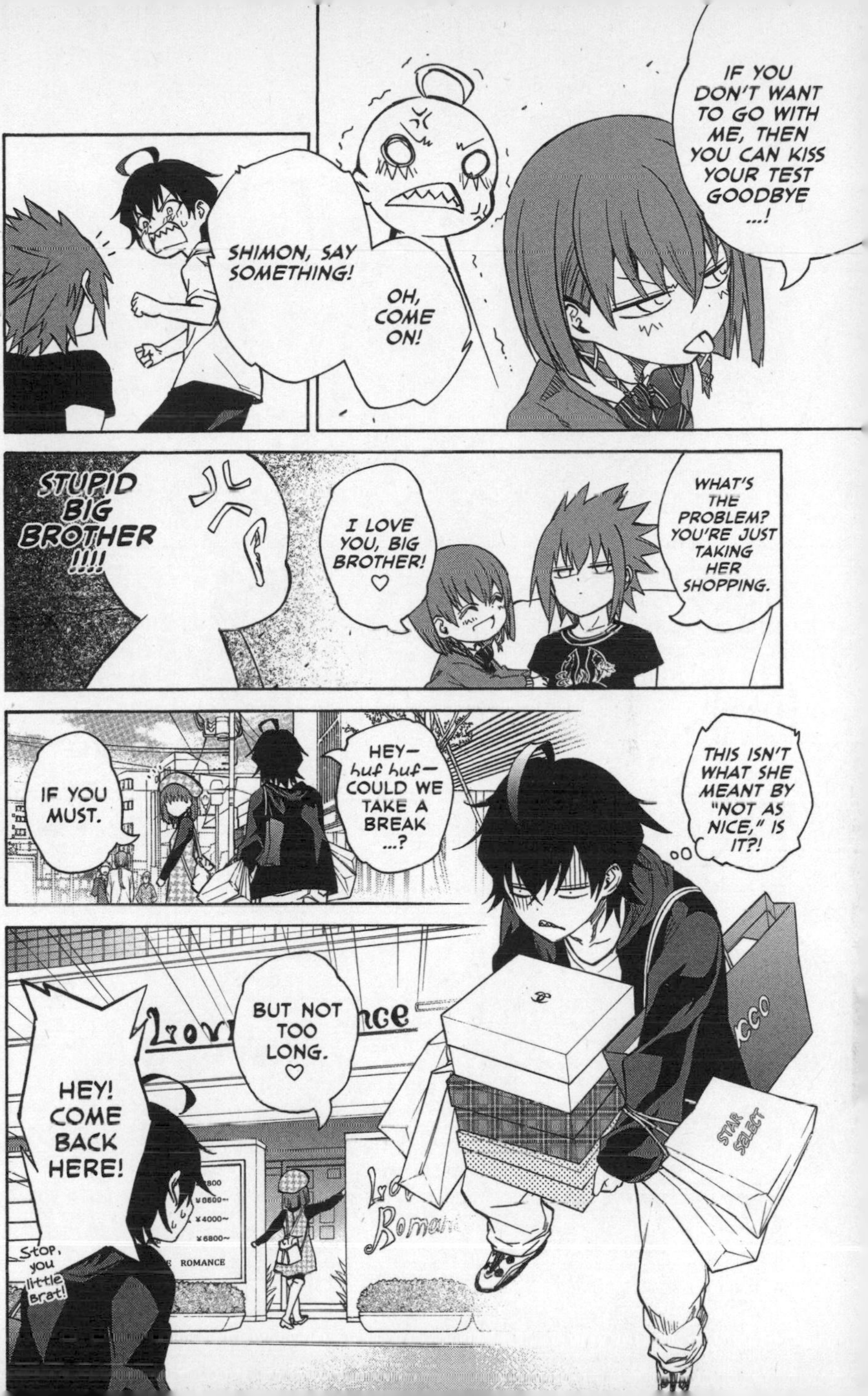
IF YOU DON'T WANT TO GO WITH ME, THEN YOU CAN KISS YOUR TEST GOODBYE ...!
SHIMON, SAY SOMETHING!
OH, COME ON!
WHAT'S THE PROBLEM? YOU'RE JUST TAKING HER SHOPPING.
I LOVE YOU, BIG BROTHER! ♡
STUPID BIG BROTHER!!!!
THIS ISN'T WHAT SHE MEANT BY "NOT AS NICE," IS IT?!
STAR SELECT
HEY— huf huf— COULD WE TAKE A BREAK ...?
IF YOU MUST.
BUT NOT TOO LONG. ♡
HEY! COME BACK HERE!
Stop, you little Brat!

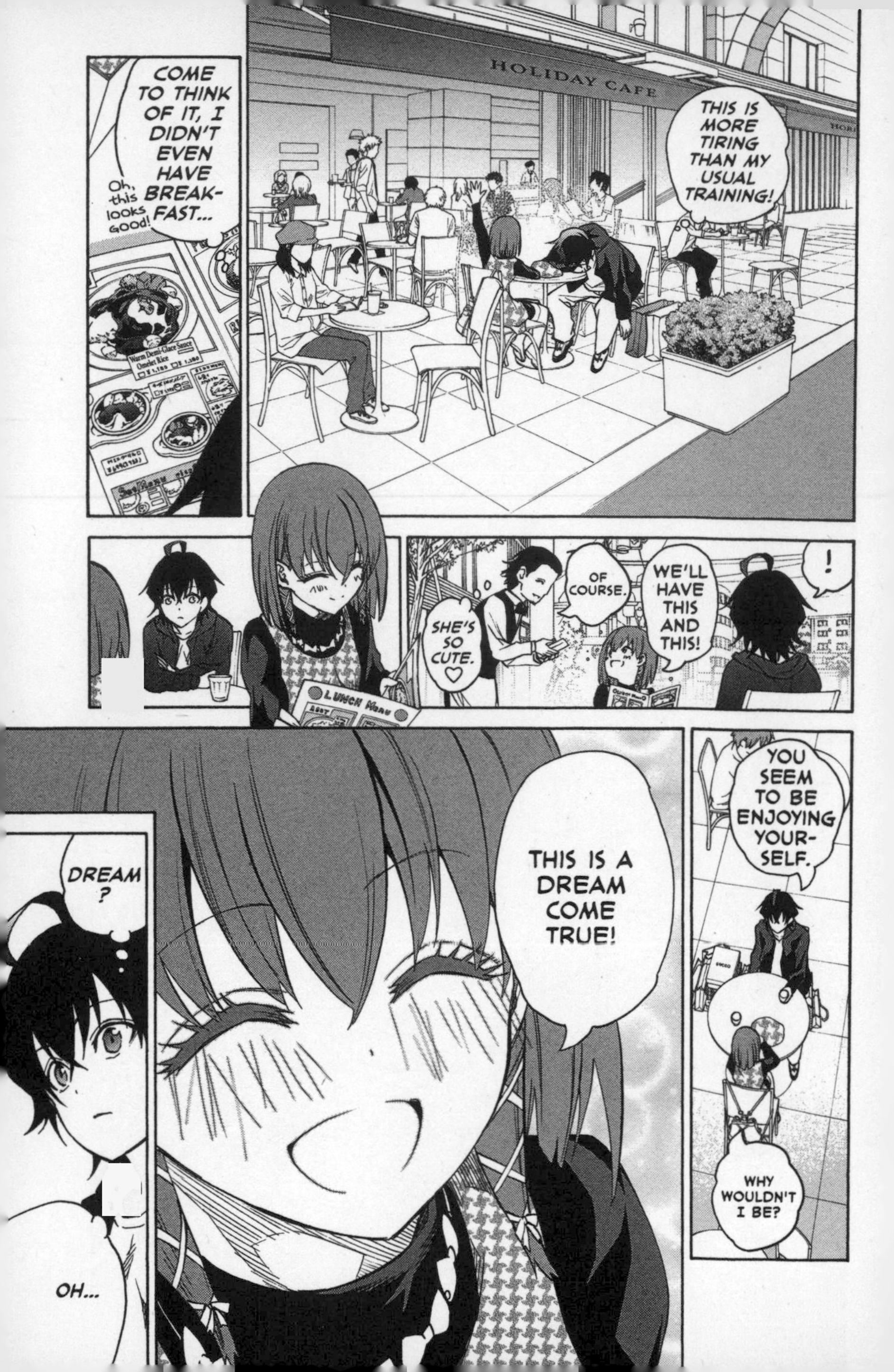
HOLIDAY CAFE
THIS IS MORE TIRING THAN MY USUAL TRAINING!
COME TO THINK OF IT, I DIDN'T EVEN HAVE BREAKFAST...
Oh, this looks good!
Warm Demi-Glace Sauce Omelet Rice
!
WE'LL HAVE THIS AND THIS!
OF COURSE.
SHE'S SO CUTE. ♡
LUNCH MENU
YOU SEEM TO BE ENJOYING YOURSELF.
WHY WOULDN'T I BE?
THIS IS A DREAM COME TRUE!
DREAM?
OH...

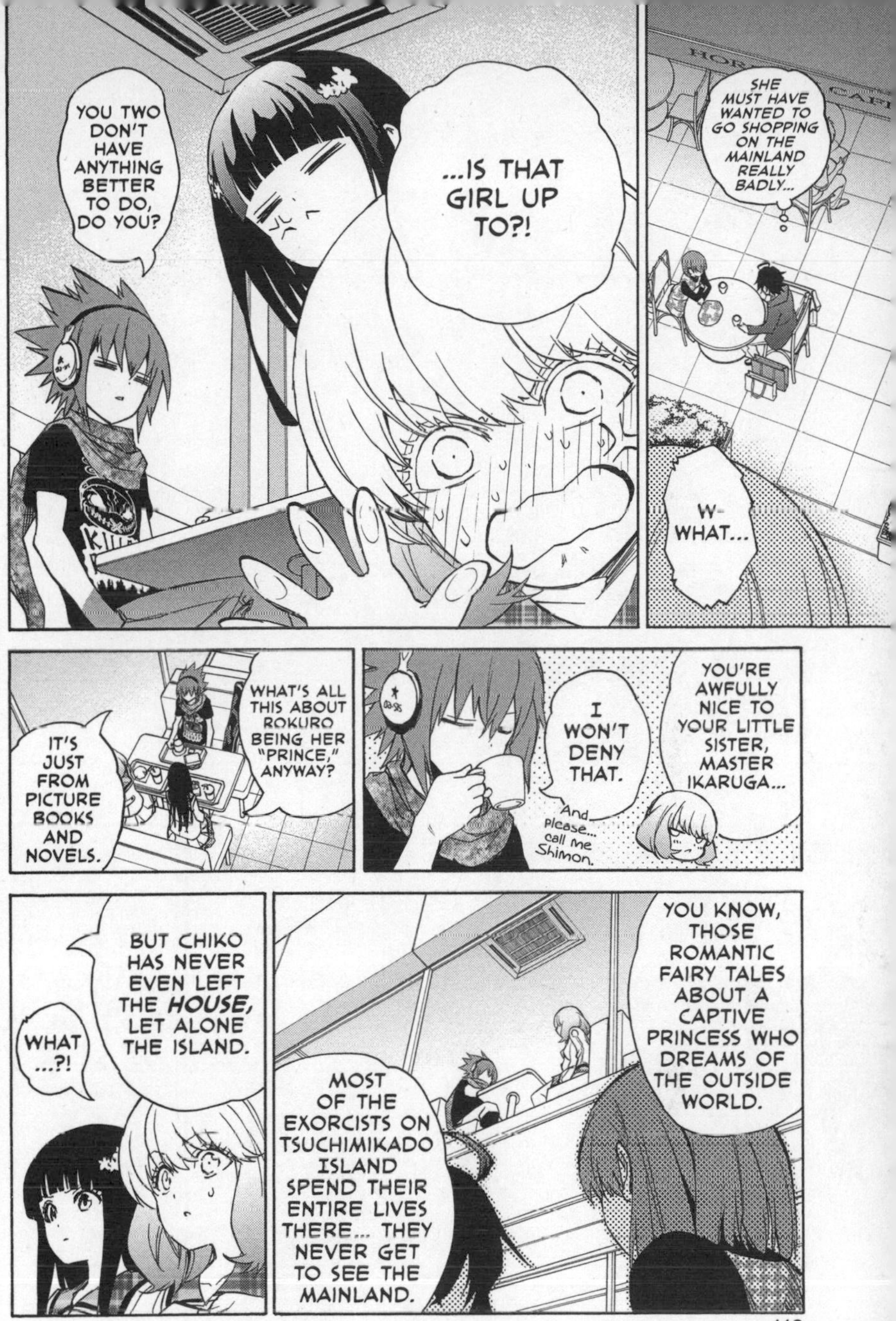
SHE MUST HAVE WANTED TO GO SHOPPING ON THE MAINLAND REALLY BADLY...
W-WHAT...
...IS THAT GIRL UP TO?!
YOU TWO DON'T HAVE ANYTHING BETTER TO DO, DO YOU?
YOU'RE AWFULLY NICE TO YOUR LITTLE SISTER, MASTER IKARUGA...
I WON'T DENY THAT.
And please... call me Shimon.
WHAT'S ALL THIS ABOUT ROKURO BEING HER "PRINCE," ANYWAY?
IT'S JUST FROM PICTURE BOOKS AND NOVELS.
YOU KNOW, THOSE ROMANTIC FAIRY TALES ABOUT A CAPTIVE PRINCESS WHO DREAMS OF THE OUTSIDE WORLD.
MOST OF THE EXORCISTS ON TSUCHIMIKADO ISLAND SPEND THEIR ENTIRE LIVES THERE... THEY NEVER GET TO SEE THE MAINLAND.
BUT CHIKO HAS NEVER EVEN LEFT THE *HOUSE*, LET ALONE THE ISLAND.
WHAT ...?!

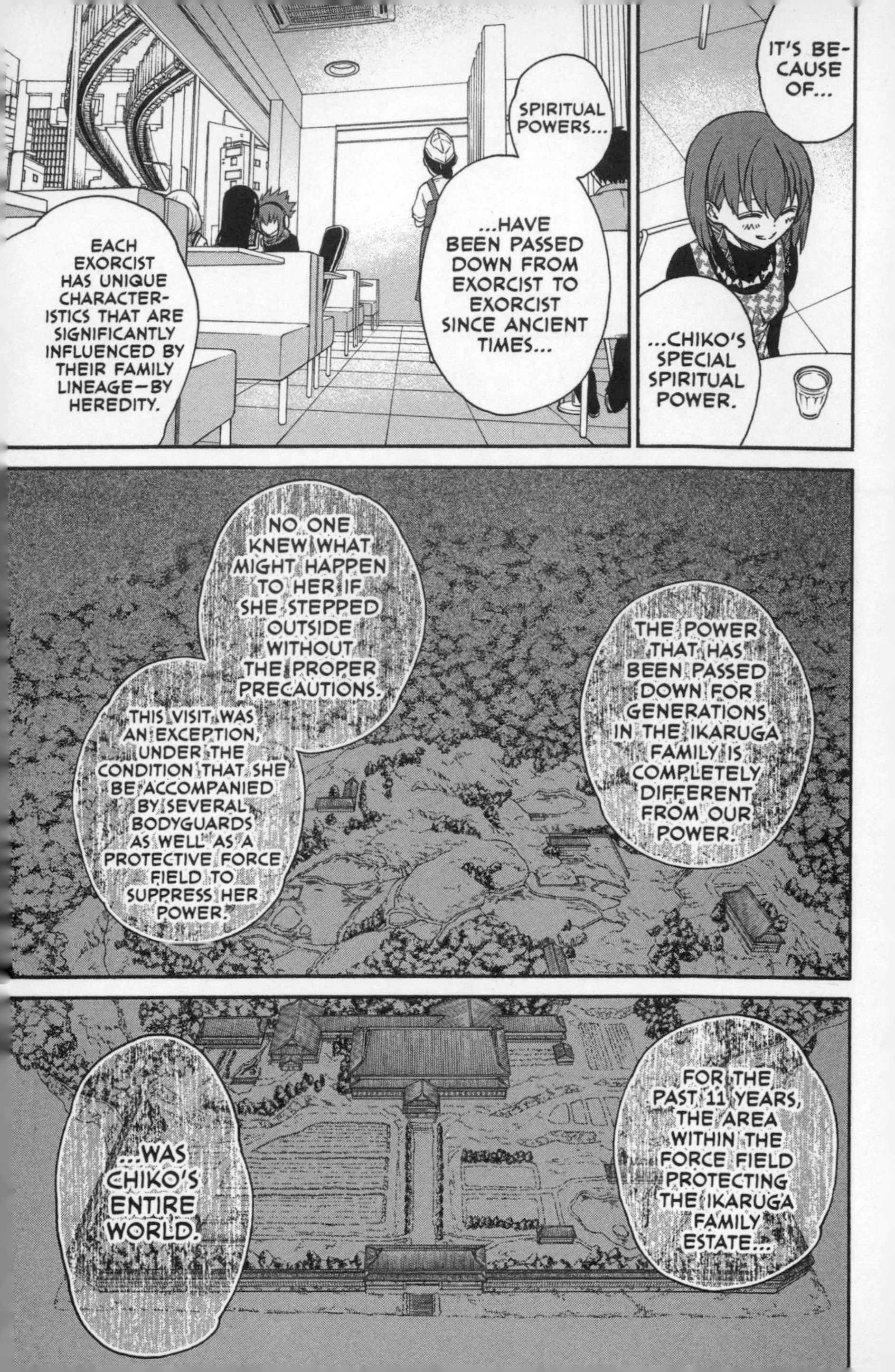
IT'S BE-CAUSE OF...
...CHIKO'S SPECIAL SPIRITUAL POWER.
SPIRITUAL POWERS...
...HAVE BEEN PASSED DOWN FROM EXORCIST TO EXORCIST SINCE ANCIENT TIMES...
EACH EXORCIST HAS UNIQUE CHARACTER-ISTICS THAT ARE SIGNIFICANTLY INFLUENCED BY THEIR FAMILY LINEAGE—BY HEREDITY.
THE POWER THAT HAS BEEN PASSED DOWN FOR GENERATIONS IN THE IKARUGA FAMILY IS COMPLETELY DIFFERENT FROM OUR POWER.
NO ONE KNEW WHAT MIGHT HAPPEN TO HER IF SHE STEPPED OUTSIDE WITHOUT THE PROPER PRECAUTIONS.
THIS VISIT WAS AN EXCEPTION, UNDER THE CONDITION THAT SHE BE ACCOMPANIED BY SEVERAL BODYGUARDS AS WELL AS A PROTECTIVE FORCE FIELD TO SUPPRESS HER POWER.
FOR THE PAST 11 YEARS, THE AREA WITHIN THE FORCE FIELD PROTECTING THE IKARUGA FAMILY ESTATE...
...WAS CHIKO'S ENTIRE WORLD.

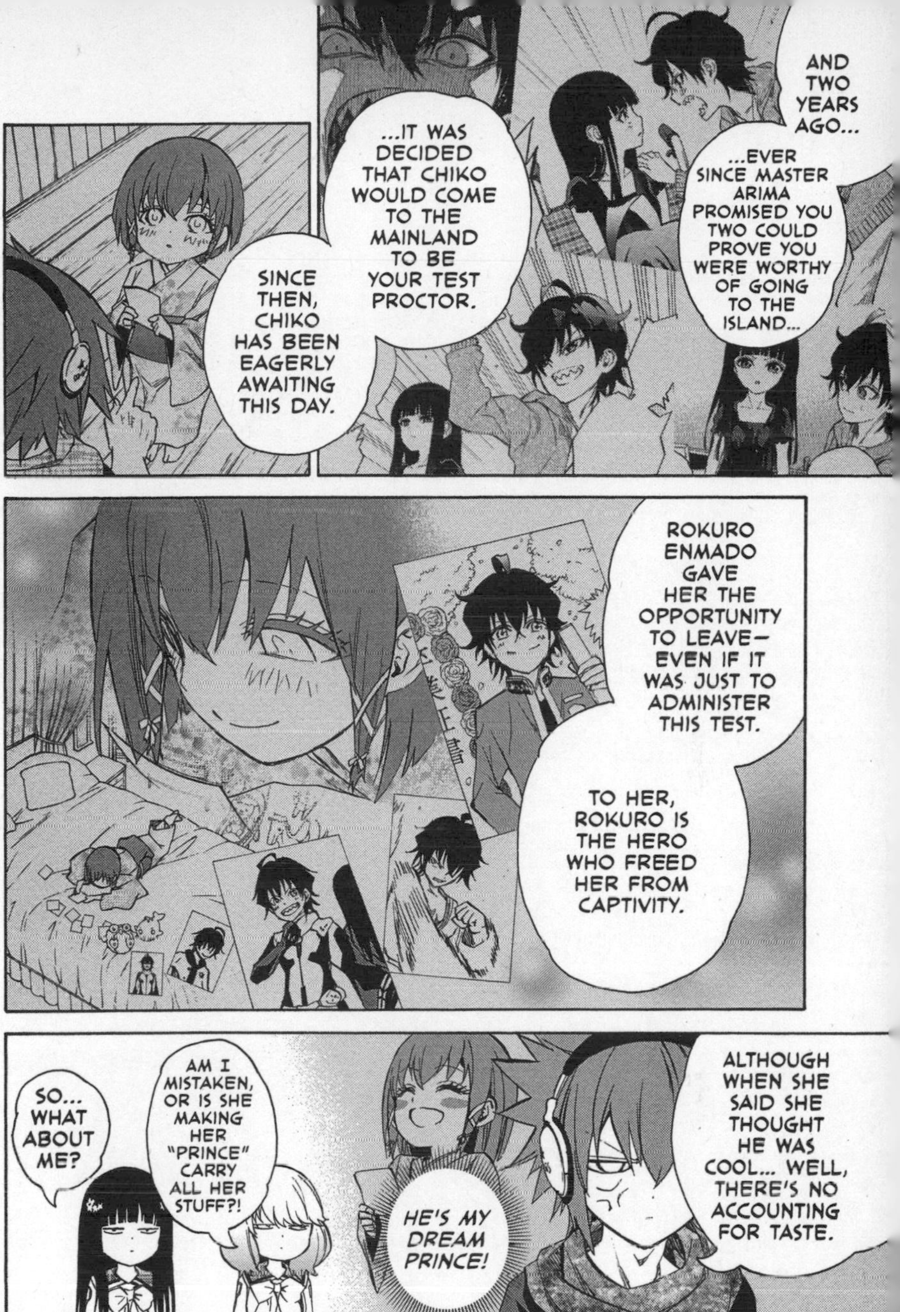
AND TWO YEARS AGO...
...EVER SINCE MASTER ARIMA PROMISED YOU TWO COULD PROVE YOU WERE WORTHY OF GOING TO THE ISLAND...
...IT WAS DECIDED THAT CHIKO WOULD COME TO THE MAINLAND TO BE YOUR TEST PROCTOR.
SINCE THEN, CHIKO HAS BEEN EAGERLY AWAITING THIS DAY.
ROKURO ENMADO GAVE HER THE OPPORTUNITY TO LEAVE—EVEN IF IT WAS JUST TO ADMINISTER THIS TEST.
TO HER, ROKURO IS THE HERO WHO FREED HER FROM CAPTIVITY.
ALTHOUGH WHEN SHE SAID SHE THOUGHT HE WAS COOL... WELL, THERE'S NO ACCOUNTING FOR TASTE.
HE'S MY DREAM PRINCE!
AM I MISTAKEN, OR IS SHE MAKING HER "PRINCE" CARRY ALL HER STUFF?!
SO... WHAT ABOUT ME?

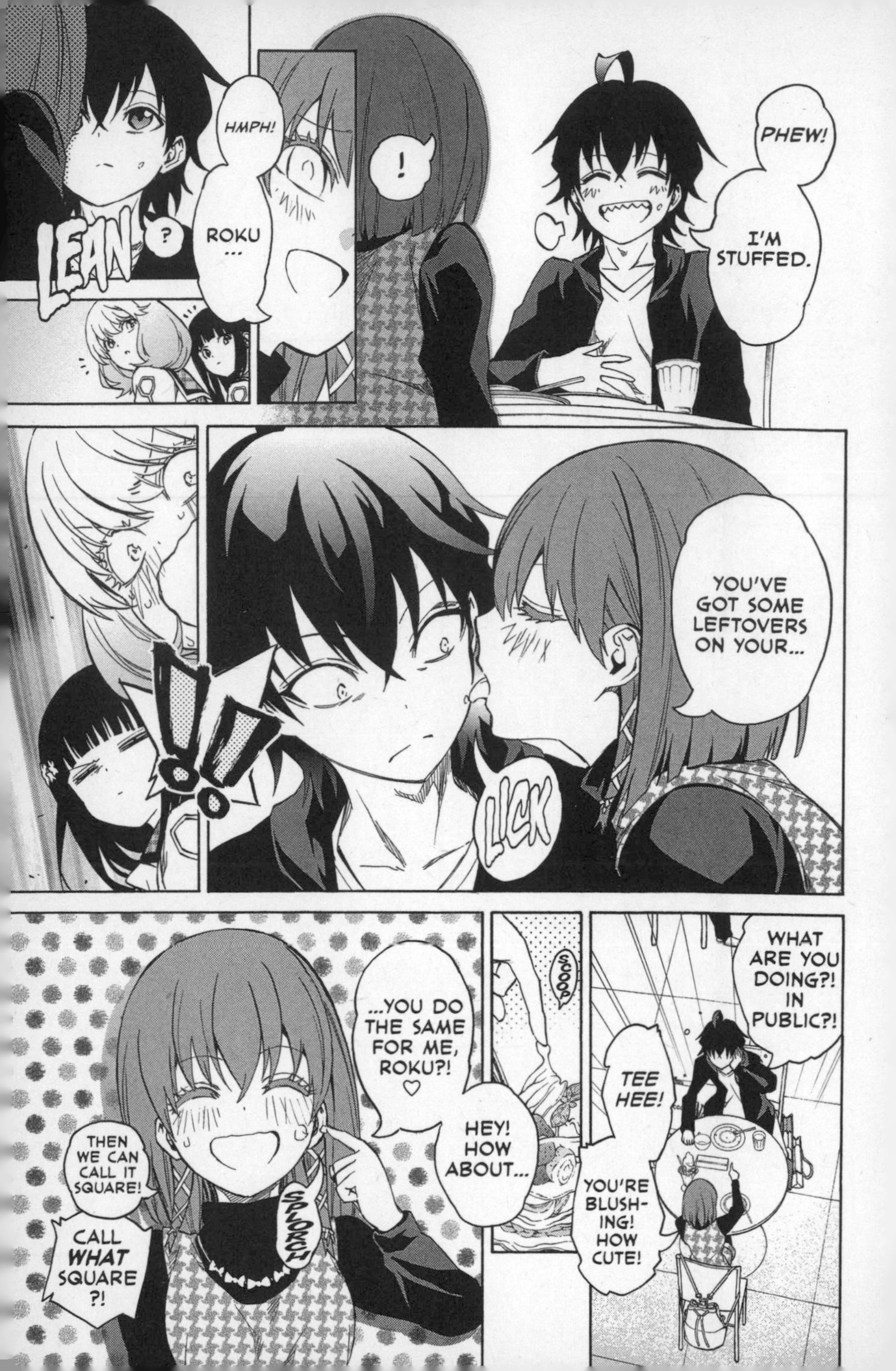
PHEW!
I'M STUFFED.
!
ROKU...
HMPH!
LEAN
?
YOU'VE GOT SOME LEFTOVERS ON YOUR...
LICK
WHAT ARE YOU DOING?! IN PUBLIC?!
TEE HEE!
YOU'RE BLUSHING! HOW CUTE!
SCOOP
HEY! HOW ABOUT...
...YOU DO THE SAME FOR ME, ROKU?! ♡
SPLORCH
THEN WE CAN CALL IT SQUARE!
CALL WHAT SQUARE?!

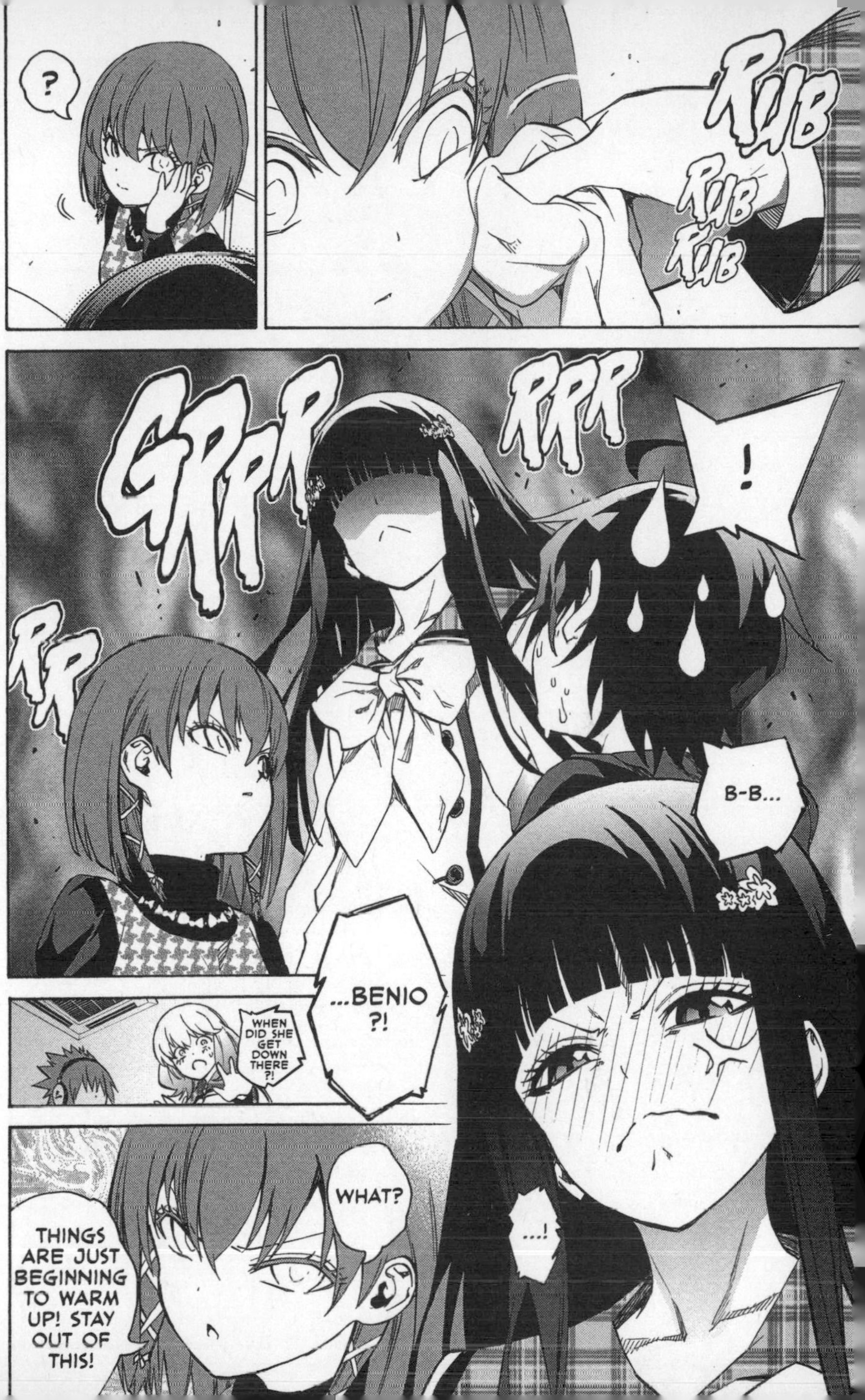
RUB
RUB
RUB
?
!
RRR
GRRR
B-B...
RR
...BENIO ?!
WHEN DID SHE GET DOWN THERE ?!
...!
WHAT?
THINGS ARE JUST BEGINNING TO WARM UP! STAY OUT OF THIS!

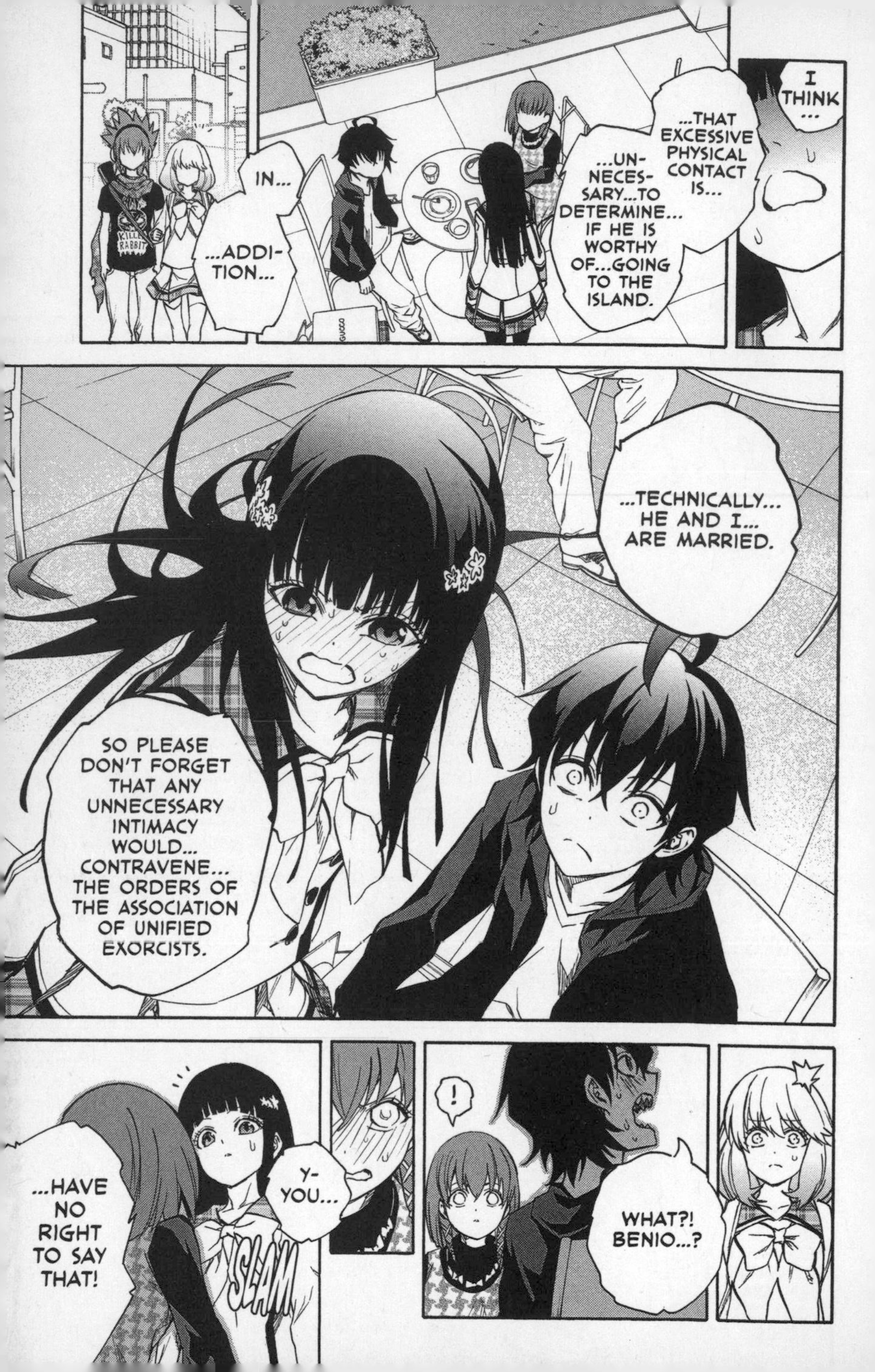
I THINK...
...THAT EXCESSIVE PHYSICAL CONTACT IS...
...UN-NECES-SARY...TO DETERMINE... IF HE IS WORTHY OF...GOING TO THE ISLAND.
IN...
...ADDI-TION...
...TECHNICALLY... HE AND I... ARE MARRIED.
SO PLEASE DON'T FORGET THAT ANY UNNECESSARY INTIMACY WOULD... CONTRAVENE... THE ORDERS OF THE ASSOCIATION OF UNIFIED EXORCISTS.
!
WHAT?! BENIO...?
Y-YOU...
...HAVE NO RIGHT TO SAY THAT!
SLAM

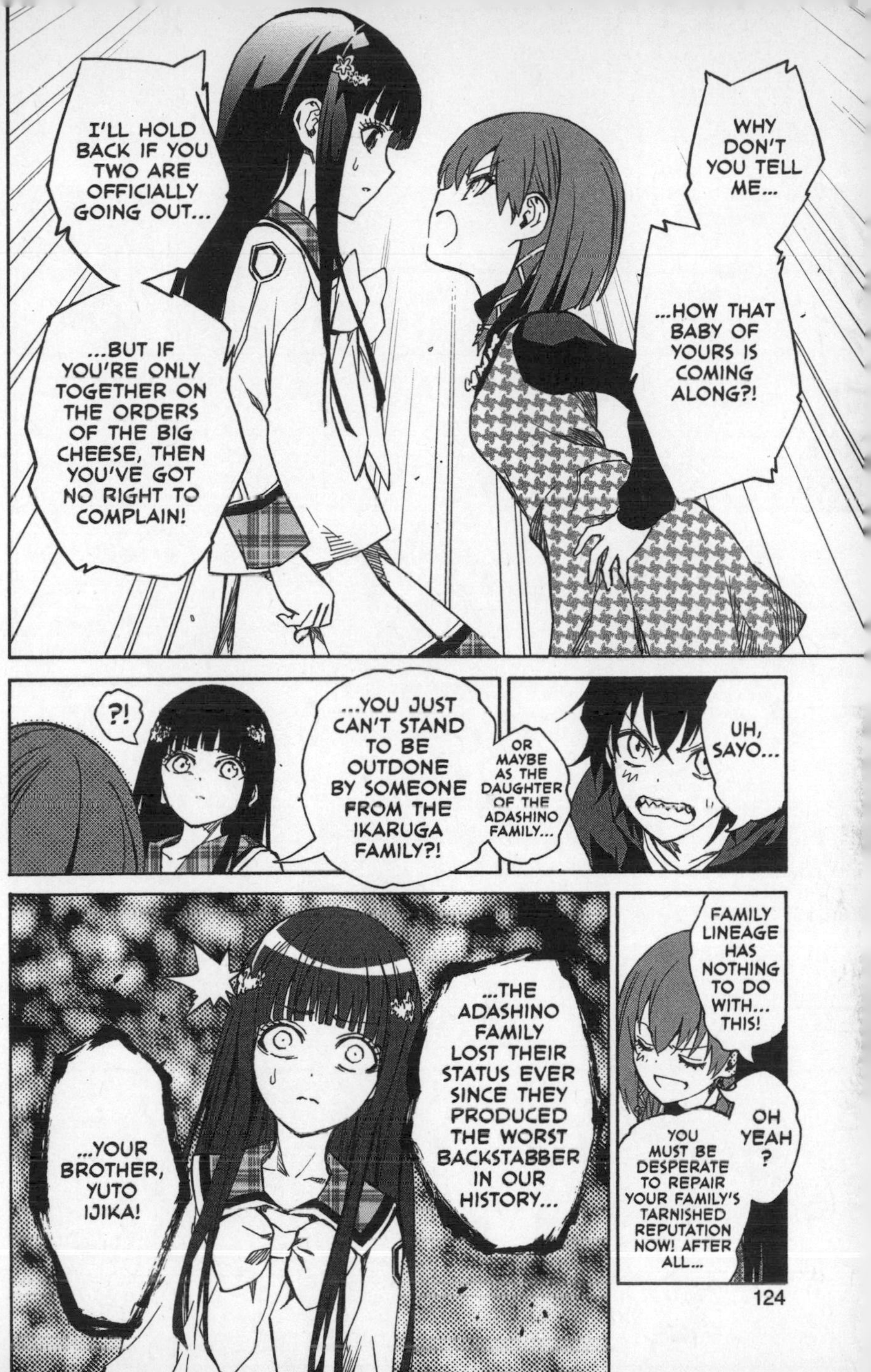
WHY DON'T YOU TELL ME...
...HOW THAT BABY OF YOURS IS COMING ALONG?!
I'LL HOLD BACK IF YOU TWO ARE OFFICIALLY GOING OUT...
...BUT IF YOU'RE ONLY TOGETHER ON THE ORDERS OF THE BIG CHEESE, THEN YOU'VE GOT NO RIGHT TO COMPLAIN!
UH, SAYO...
OR MAYBE AS THE DAUGHTER OF THE ADASHINO FAMILY...
...YOU JUST CAN'T STAND TO BE OUTDONE BY SOMEONE FROM THE IKARUGA FAMILY?!
?!
FAMILY LINEAGE HAS NOTHING TO DO WITH... THIS!
OH YEAH?
YOU MUST BE DESPERATE TO REPAIR YOUR FAMILY'S TARNISHED REPUTATION NOW! AFTER ALL...
...THE ADASHINO FAMILY LOST THEIR STATUS EVER SINCE THEY PRODUCED THE WORST BACKSTABBER IN OUR HISTORY...
...YOUR BROTHER, YUTO IJIKA!

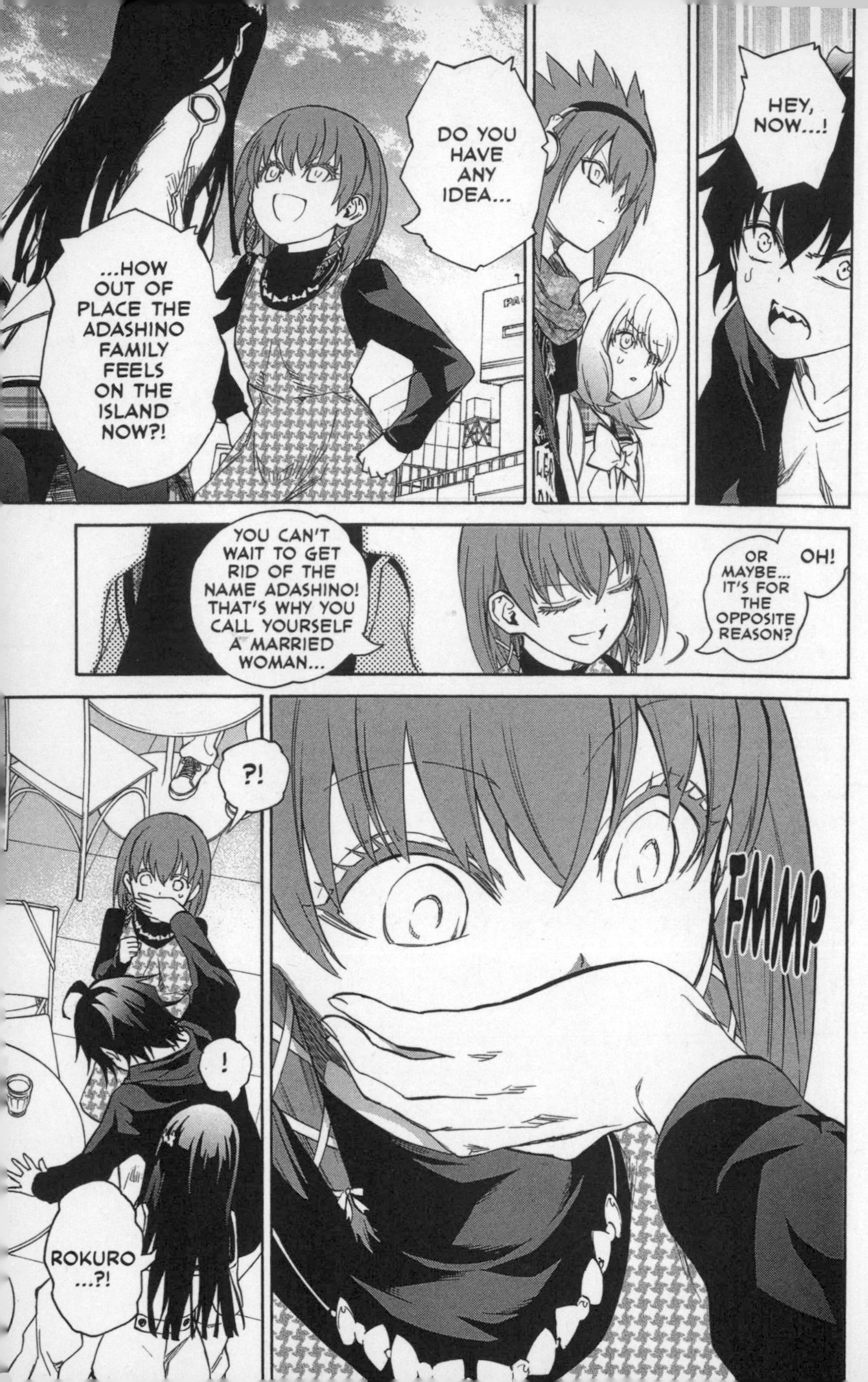
HEY, NOW...!
DO YOU HAVE ANY IDEA...
...HOW OUT OF PLACE THE ADASHINO FAMILY FEELS ON THE ISLAND NOW?!
OH!
OR MAYBE... IT'S FOR THE OPPOSITE REASON?
YOU CAN'T WAIT TO GET RID OF THE NAME ADASHINO! THAT'S WHY YOU CALL YOURSELF A MARRIED WOMAN...
FMMP
?!
!
ROKURO ...?!

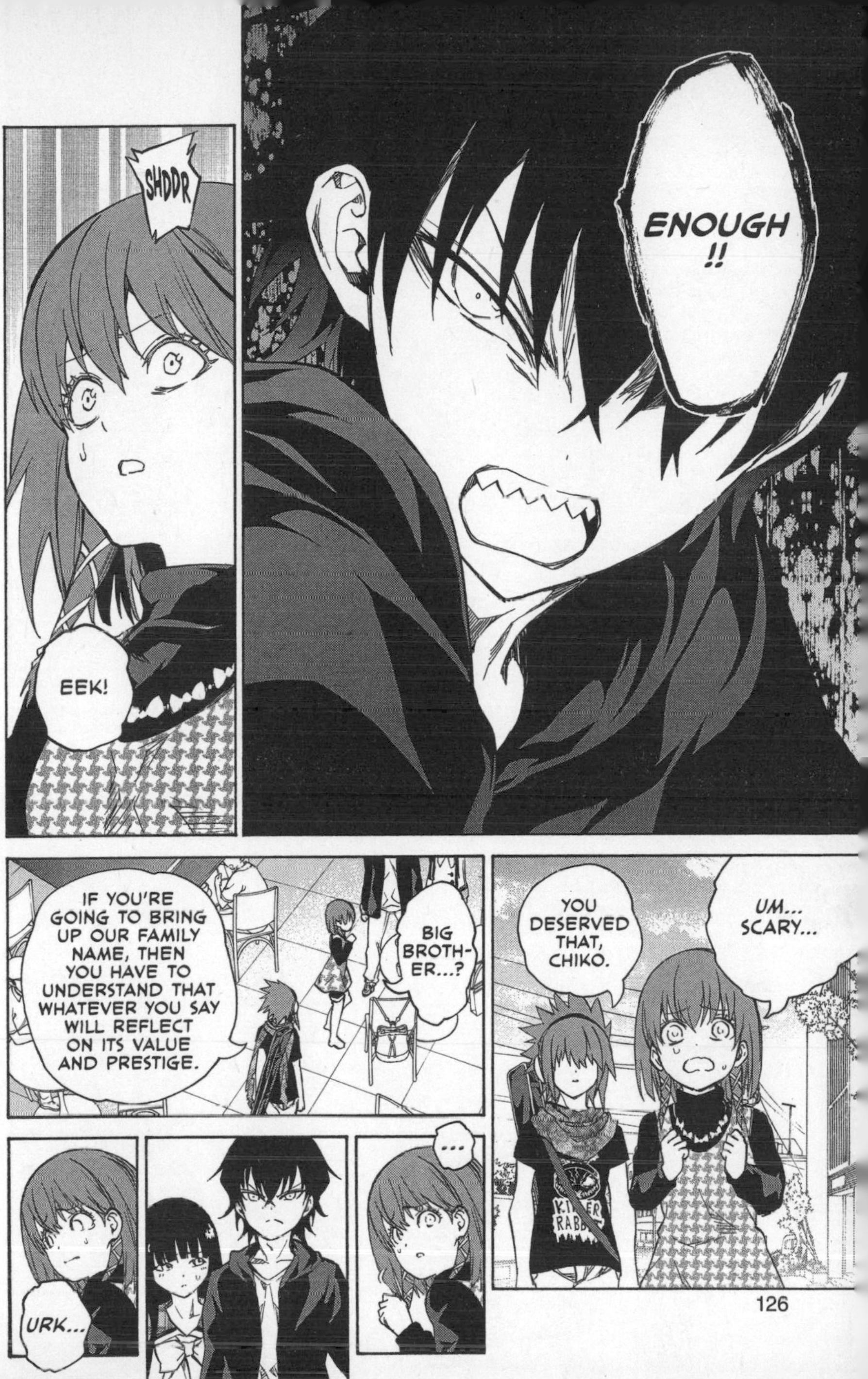
ENOUGH !!
SHDDR
EEK!
UM... SCARY...
YOU DESERVED THAT, CHIKO.
BIG BROTHER...?
IF YOU'RE GOING TO BRING UP OUR FAMILY NAME, THEN YOU HAVE TO UNDERSTAND THAT WHATEVER YOU SAY WILL REFLECT ON ITS VALUE AND PRESTIGE.
...
URK...

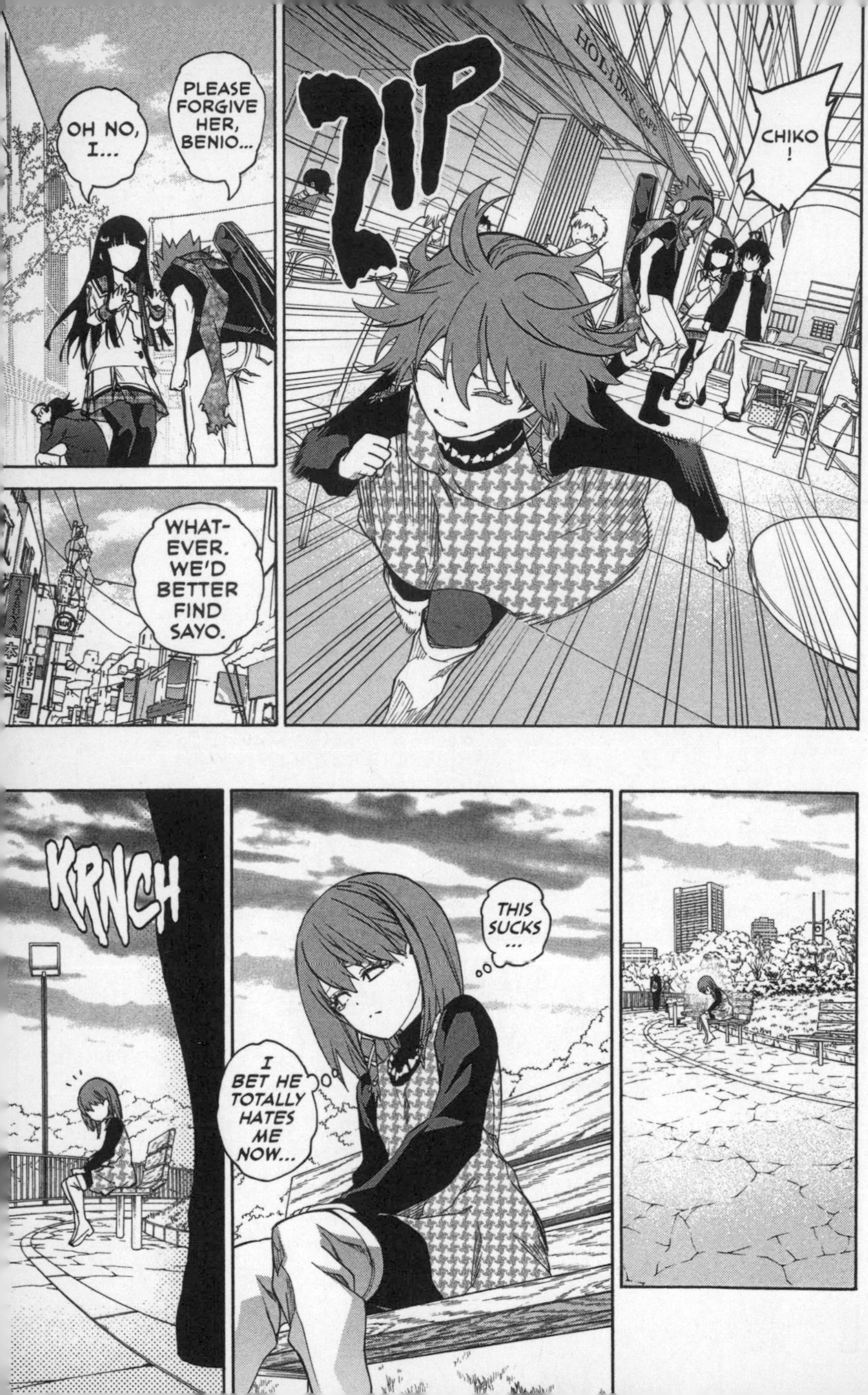
CHIKO!
ZIP
PLEASE FORGIVE HER, BENIO...
OH NO, I...
WHATEVER. WE'D BETTER FIND SAYO.
THIS SUCKS...
I BET HE TOTALLY HATES ME NOW...
KRNCH

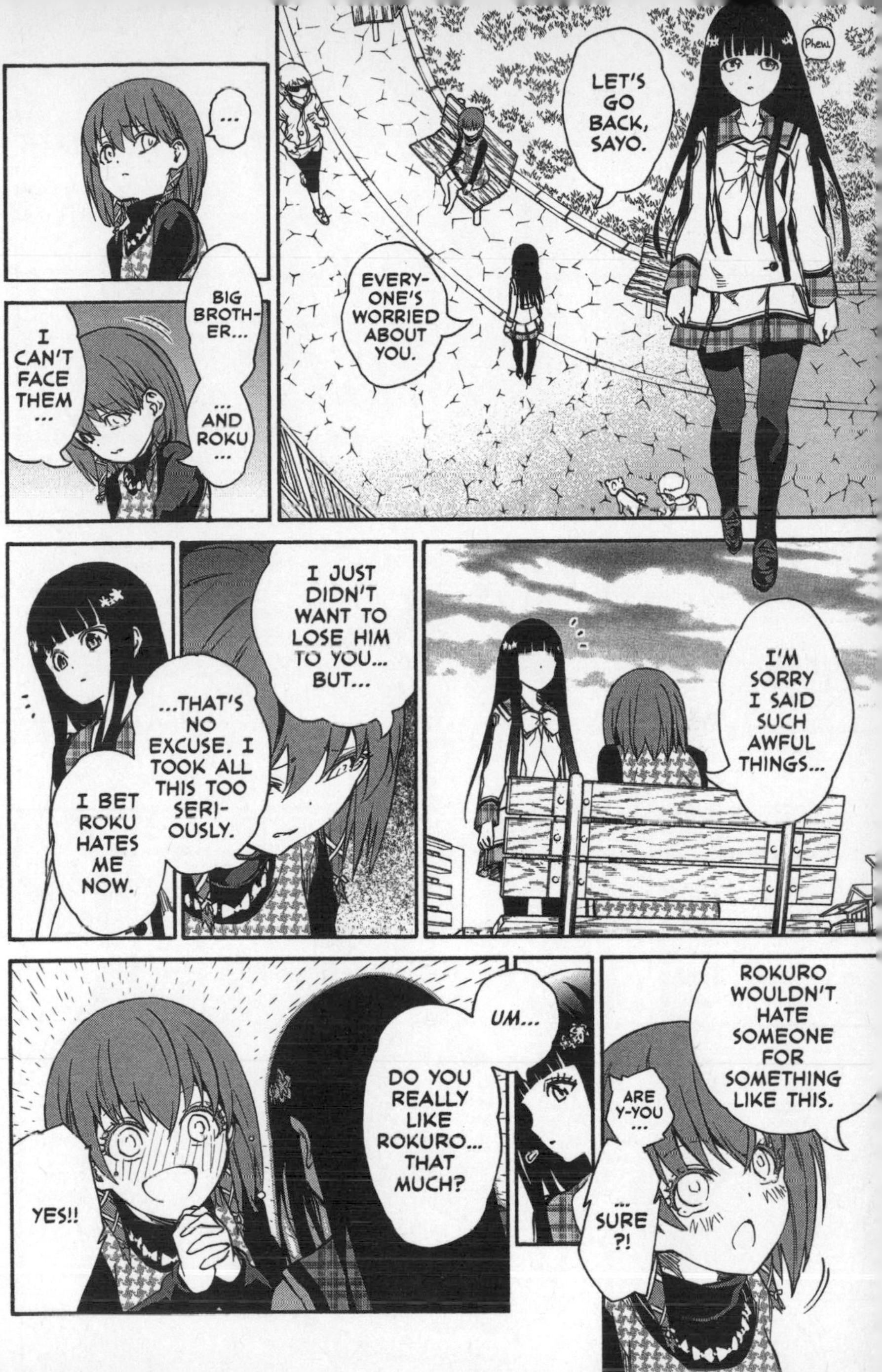
Phew
LET'S GO BACK, SAYO.
EVERYONE'S WORRIED ABOUT YOU.
...
BIG BROTHER...
...AND ROKU...
I CAN'T FACE THEM...
I'M SORRY I SAID SUCH AWFUL THINGS...
I JUST DIDN'T WANT TO LOSE HIM TO YOU... BUT...
...THAT'S NO EXCUSE. I TOOK ALL THIS TOO SERIOUSLY.
I BET ROKU HATES ME NOW.
ROKURO WOULDN'T HATE SOMEONE FOR SOMETHING LIKE THIS.
ARE Y-YOU...
...SURE?!
UM...
DO YOU REALLY LIKE ROKURO... THAT MUCH?
YES!!

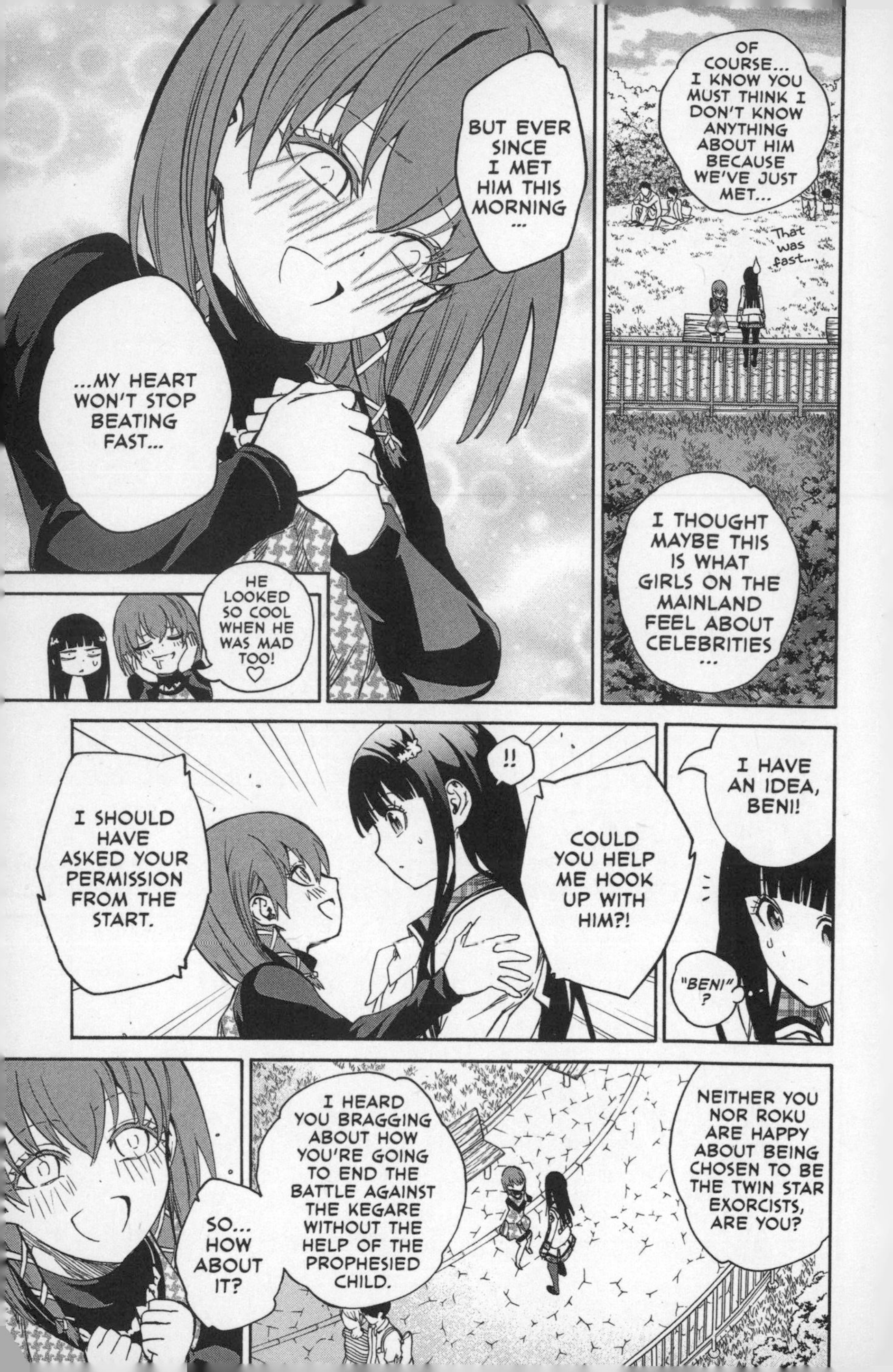
OF COURSE... I KNOW YOU MUST THINK I DON'T KNOW ANYTHING ABOUT HIM BECAUSE WE'VE JUST MET...
That was fast...
I THOUGHT MAYBE THIS IS WHAT GIRLS ON THE MAINLAND FEEL ABOUT CELEBRITIES...
BUT EVER SINCE I MET HIM THIS MORNING...
...MY HEART WON'T STOP BEATING FAST...
HE LOOKED SO COOL WHEN HE WAS MAD TOO! ♡
I HAVE AN IDEA, BENI!
"BENI"?
COULD YOU HELP ME HOOK UP WITH HIM?!
!!
I SHOULD HAVE ASKED YOUR PERMISSION FROM THE START.
NEITHER YOU NOR ROKU ARE HAPPY ABOUT BEING CHOSEN TO BE THE TWIN STAR EXORCISTS, ARE YOU?
I HEARD YOU BRAGGING ABOUT HOW YOU'RE GOING TO END THE BATTLE AGAINST THE KEGARE WITHOUT THE HELP OF THE PROPHESIED CHILD.
SO... HOW ABOUT IT?

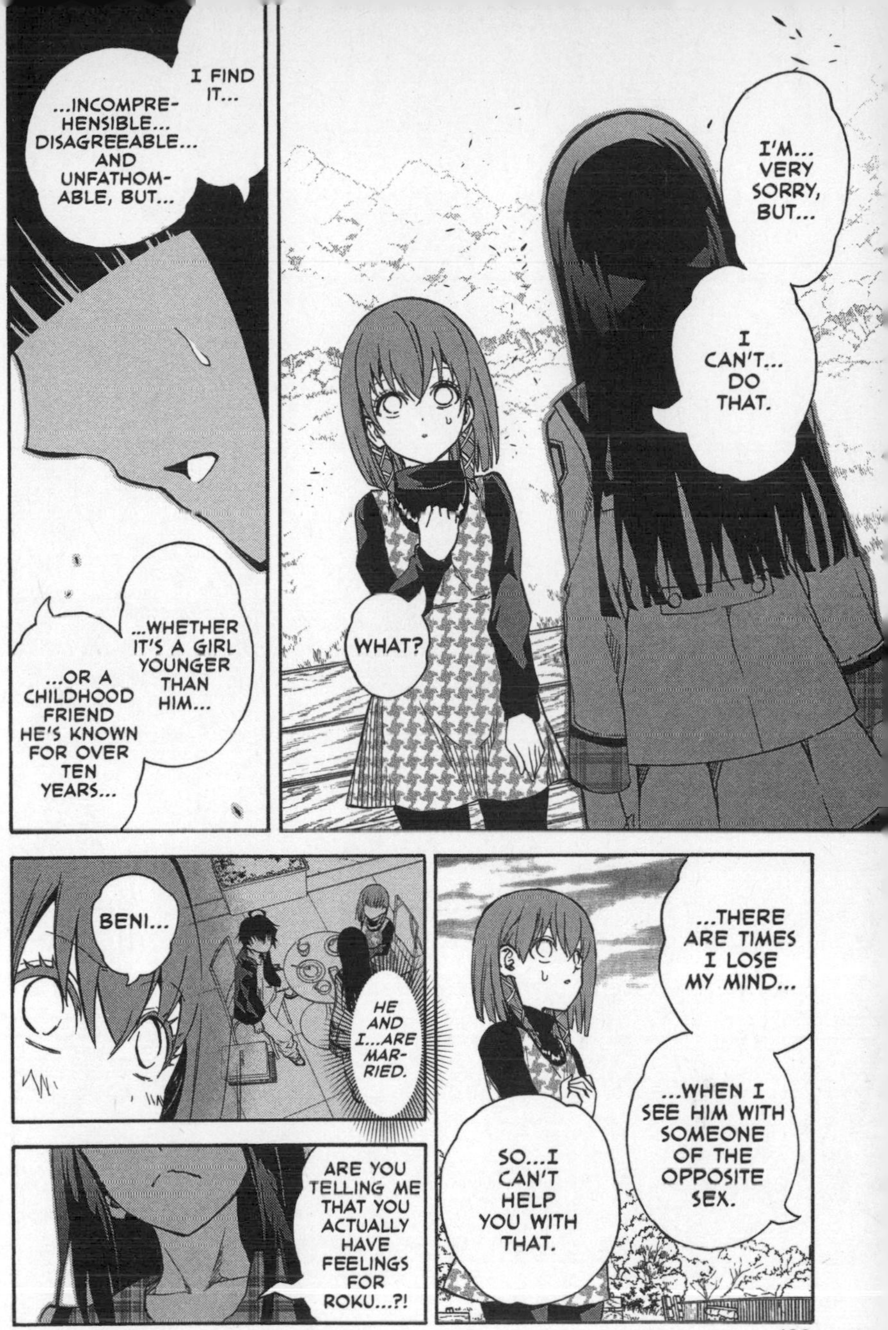
I'M... VERY SORRY, BUT...
I CAN'T... DO THAT.
WHAT?
I FIND IT...
...INCOMPREHENSIBLE... DISAGREEABLE... AND UNFATHOMABLE, BUT...
...WHETHER IT'S A GIRL YOUNGER THAN HIM...
...OR A CHILDHOOD FRIEND HE'S KNOWN FOR OVER TEN YEARS...
...THERE ARE TIMES I LOSE MY MIND...
...WHEN I SEE HIM WITH SOMEONE OF THE OPPOSITE SEX.
SO...I CAN'T HELP YOU WITH THAT.
HE AND I...ARE MARRIED.
BENI...
ARE YOU TELLING ME THAT YOU ACTUALLY HAVE FEELINGS FOR ROKU...?!

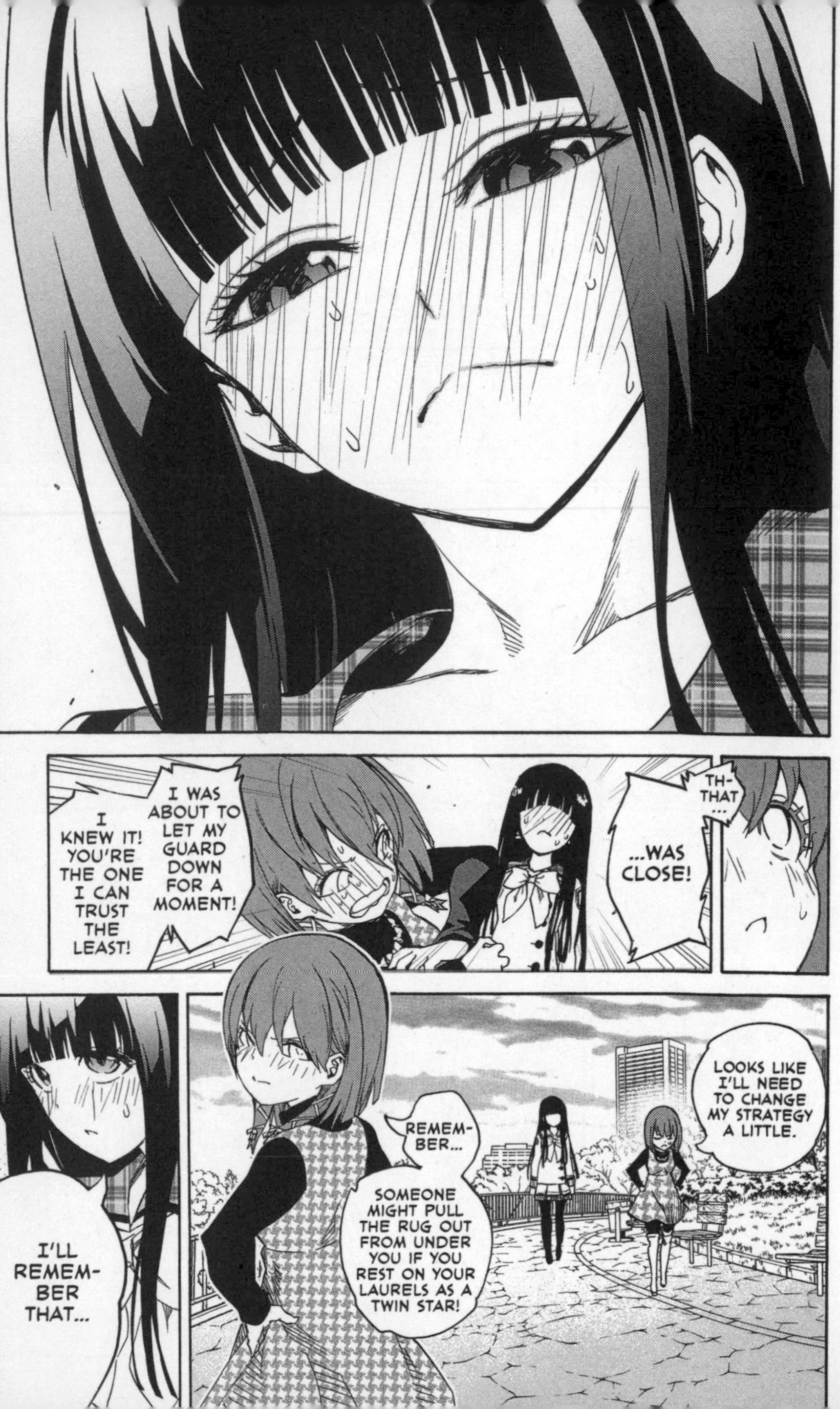
TH-THAT...
...WAS CLOSE!
I WAS ABOUT TO LET MY GUARD DOWN FOR A MOMENT!
I KNEW IT! YOU'RE THE ONE I CAN TRUST THE LEAST!
LOOKS LIKE I'LL NEED TO CHANGE MY STRATEGY A LITTLE.
REMEMBER...
SOMEONE MIGHT PULL THE RUG OUT FROM UNDER YOU IF YOU REST ON YOUR LAURELS AS A TWIN STAR!
I'LL REMEMBER THAT...

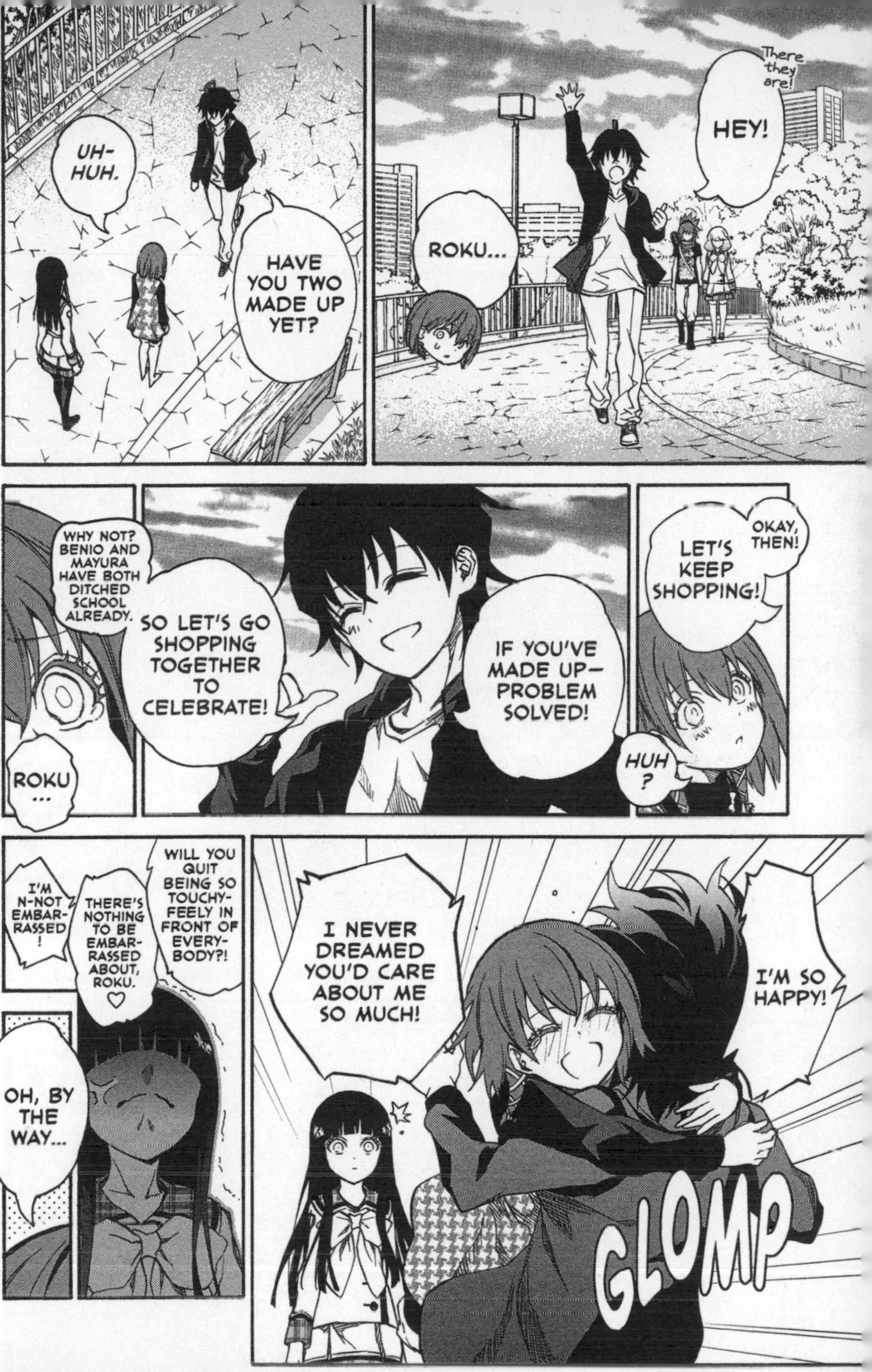
There they are!
HEY!
ROKU...
HAVE YOU TWO MADE UP YET?
UH-HUH.
OKAY, THEN!
LET'S KEEP SHOPPING!
HUH?
IF YOU'VE MADE UP—PROBLEM SOLVED!
SO LET'S GO SHOPPING TOGETHER TO CELEBRATE!
WHY NOT? BENIO AND MAYURA HAVE BOTH DITCHED SCHOOL ALREADY.
ROKU...
I'M SO HAPPY!
I NEVER DREAMED YOU'D CARE ABOUT ME SO MUCH!
GLOMP
WILL YOU QUIT BEING SO TOUCHY-FEELY IN FRONT OF EVERY-BODY?!
THERE'S NOTHING TO BE EMBAR-RASSED ABOUT, ROKU. ♡
I'M N-NOT EMBAR-RASSED!
OH, BY THE WAY...

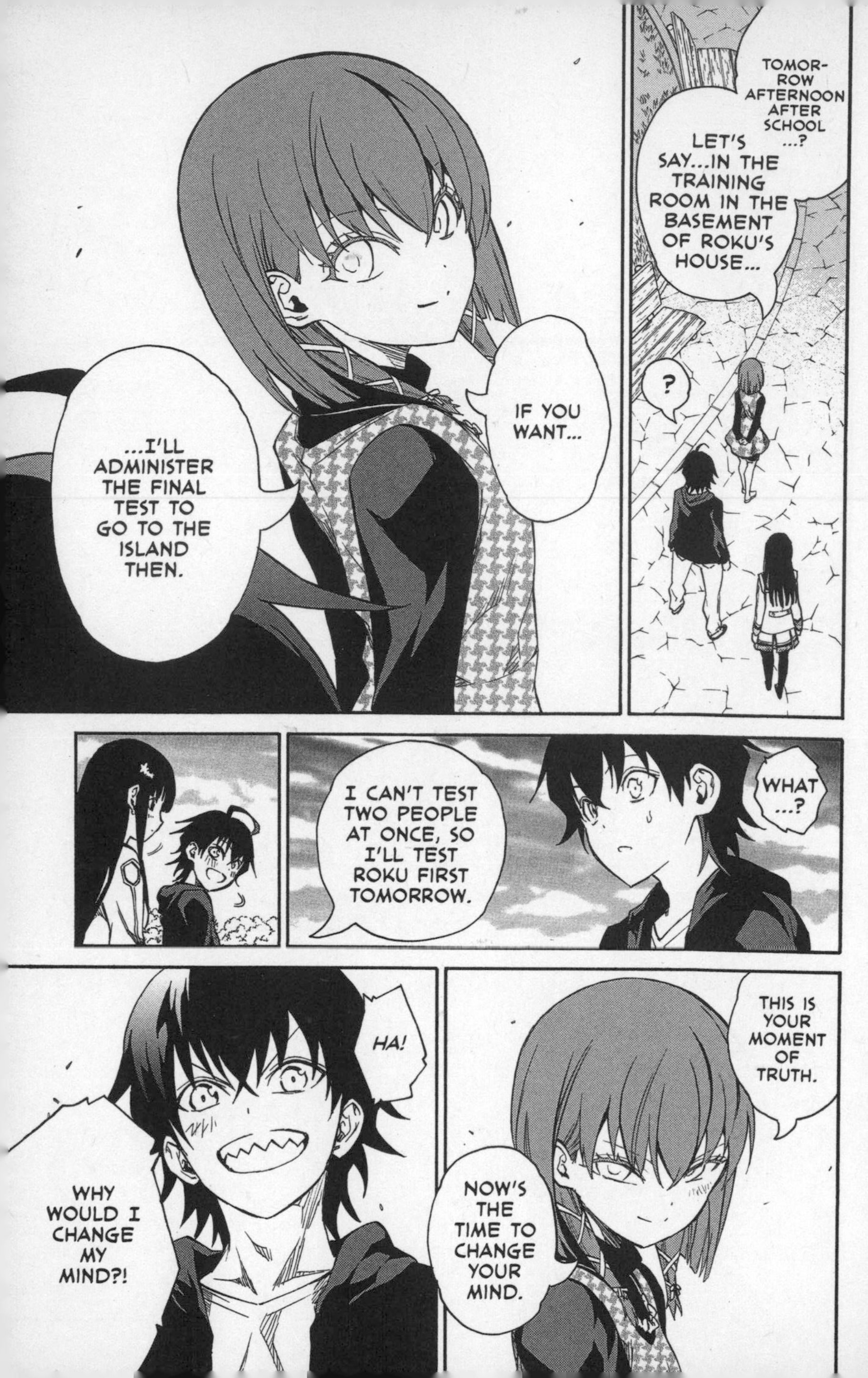
TOMORROW AFTERNOON AFTER SCHOOL ...?
LET'S SAY...IN THE TRAINING ROOM IN THE BASEMENT OF ROKU'S HOUSE...
?
IF YOU WANT...
...I'LL ADMINISTER THE FINAL TEST TO GO TO THE ISLAND THEN.
WHAT ...?
I CAN'T TEST TWO PEOPLE AT ONCE, SO I'LL TEST ROKU FIRST TOMORROW.
THIS IS YOUR MOMENT OF TRUTH.
NOW'S THE TIME TO CHANGE YOUR MIND.
HA!
WHY WOULD I CHANGE MY MIND?!

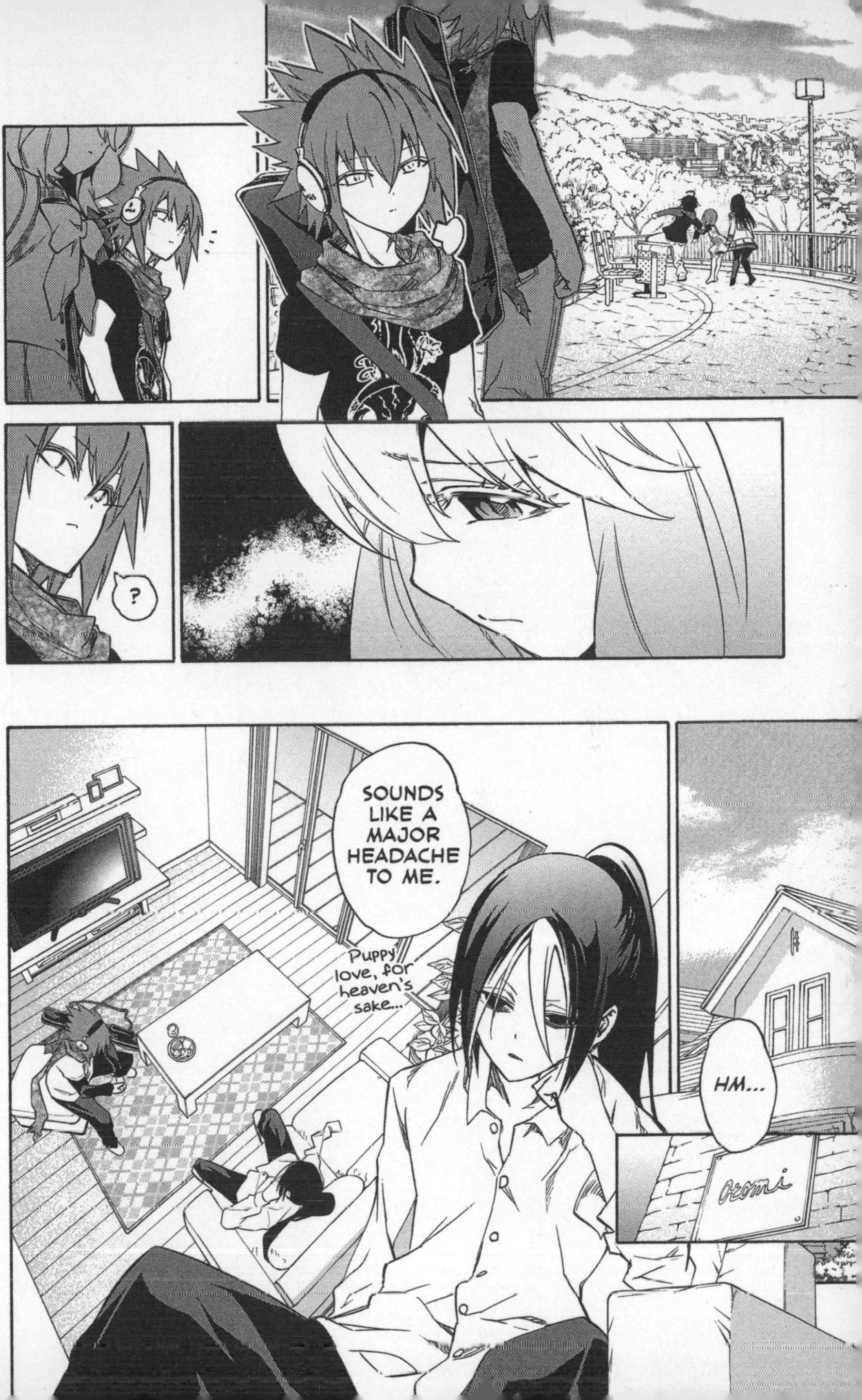
?
HM...
Otomi
SOUNDS LIKE A MAJOR HEADACHE TO ME.
Puppy love, for heaven's sake...

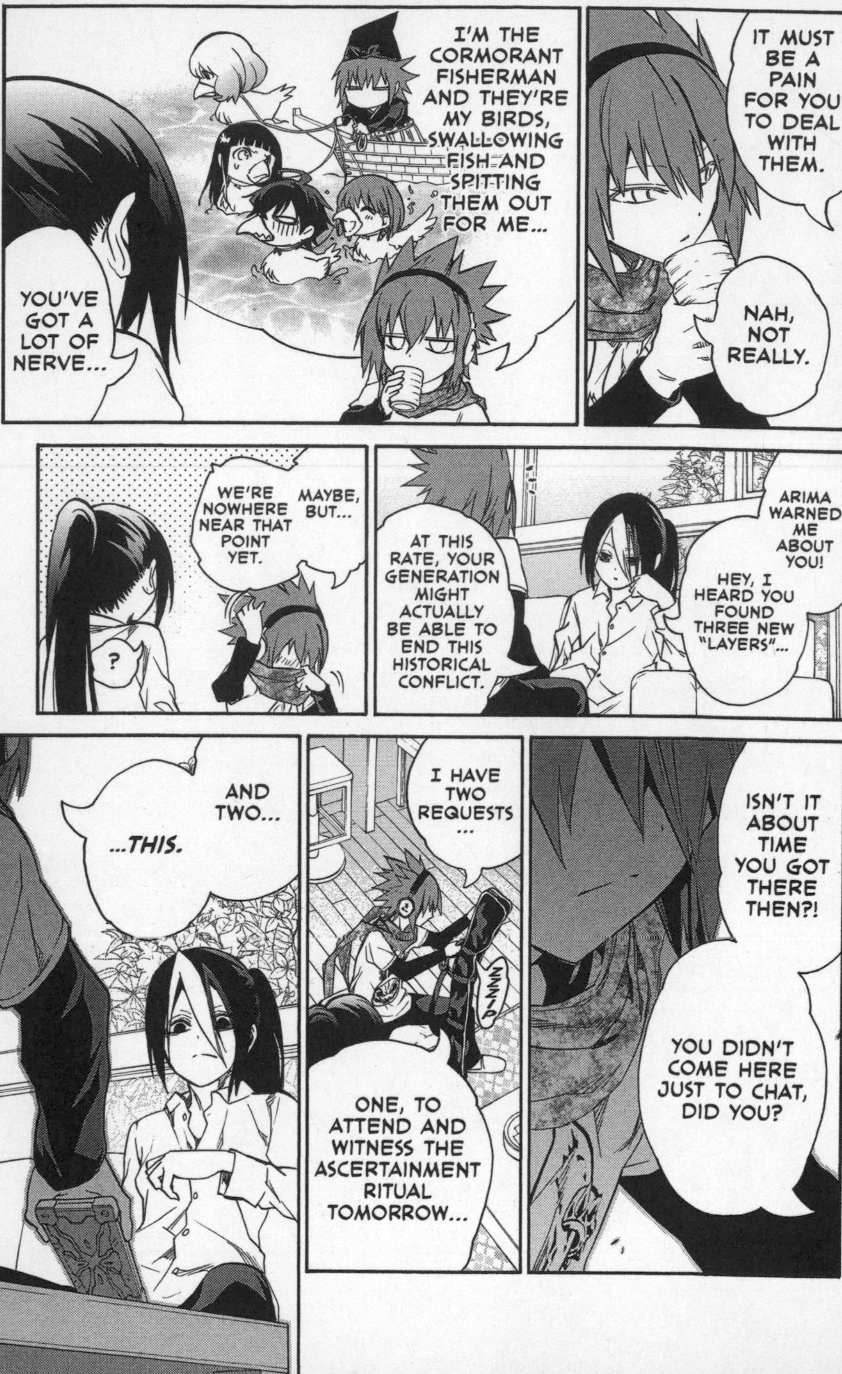
IT MUST BE A PAIN FOR YOU TO DEAL WITH THEM.
NAH, NOT REALLY.
I'M THE CORMORANT FISHERMAN AND THEY'RE MY BIRDS, SWALLOWING FISH AND SPITTING THEM OUT FOR ME...
YOU'VE GOT A LOT OF NERVE...
ARIMA WARNED ME ABOUT YOU!
HEY, I HEARD YOU FOUND THREE NEW "LAYERS"...
AT THIS RATE, YOUR GENERATION MIGHT ACTUALLY BE ABLE TO END THIS HISTORICAL CONFLICT.
MAYBE, BUT...
WE'RE NOWHERE NEAR THAT POINT YET.
?
ISN'T IT ABOUT TIME YOU GOT THERE THEN?!
YOU DIDN'T COME HERE JUST TO CHAT, DID YOU?
I HAVE TWO REQUESTS...
ZZZIP
ONE, TO ATTEND AND WITNESS THE ASCERTAINMENT RITUAL TOMORROW...
AND TWO...
...THIS.

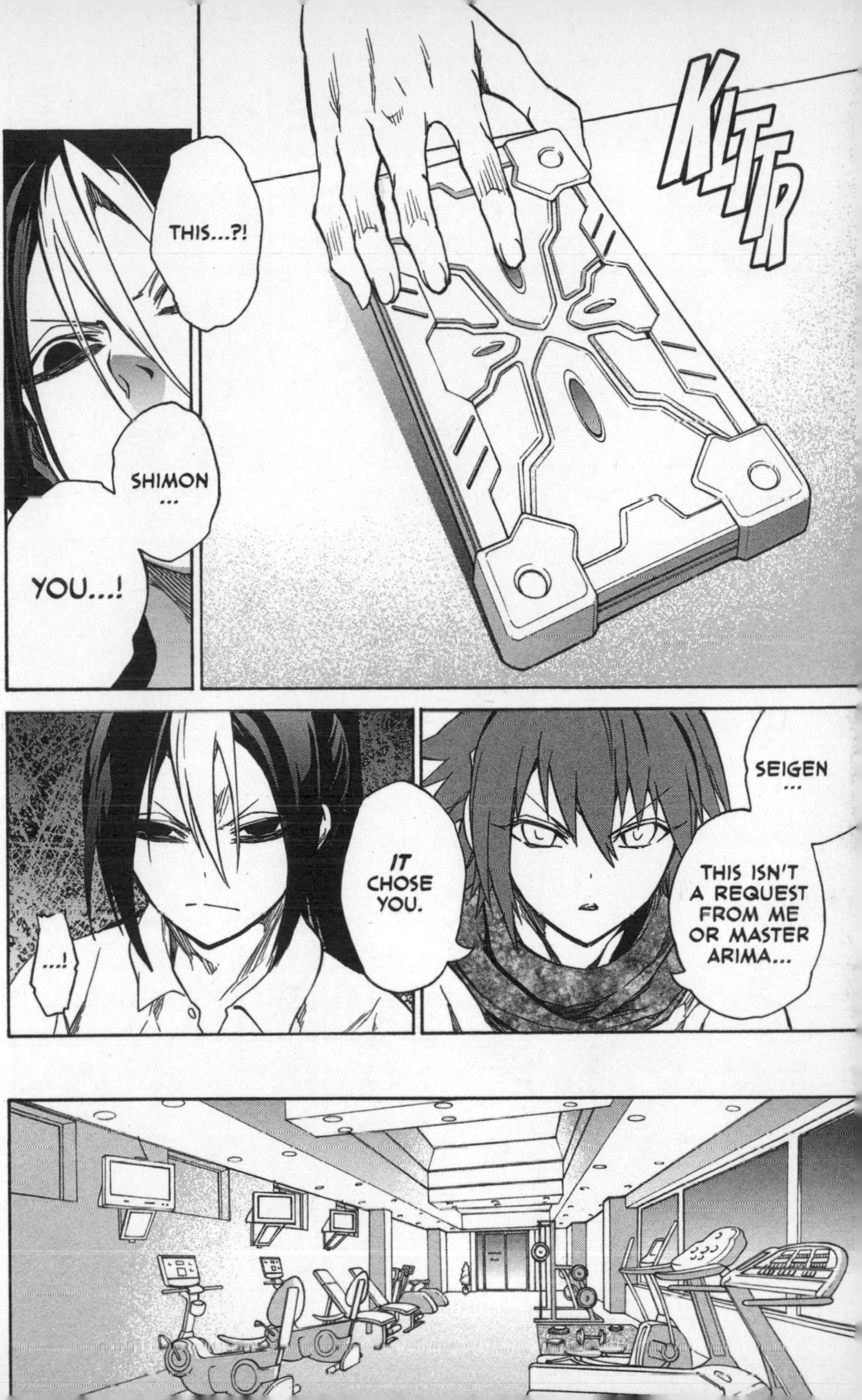
KLTTR
THIS...?!
SHIMON ...
YOU...!
SEIGEN ...
THIS ISN'T A REQUEST FROM ME OR MASTER ARIMA...
IT CHOSE YOU.
...!

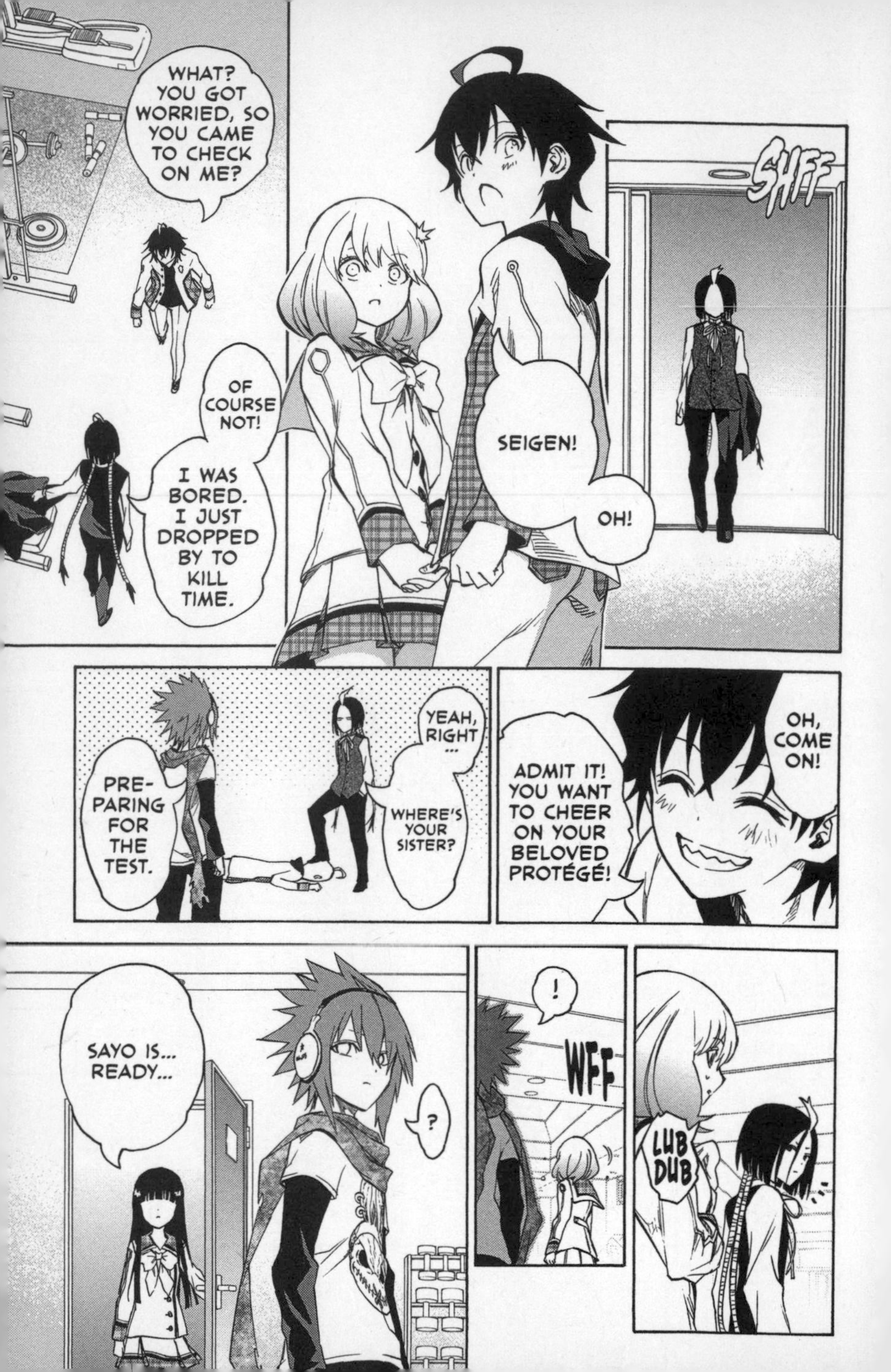
SHFF
OH!
SEIGEN!
WHAT? YOU GOT WORRIED, SO YOU CAME TO CHECK ON ME?
OF COURSE NOT!
I WAS BORED. I JUST DROPPED BY TO KILL TIME.
OH, COME ON!
ADMIT IT! YOU WANT TO CHEER ON YOUR BELOVED PROTÉGÉ!
YEAH, RIGHT...
WHERE'S YOUR SISTER?
PRE-PARING FOR THE TEST.
LUB DUB
!
WFF
?
SAYO IS... READY...

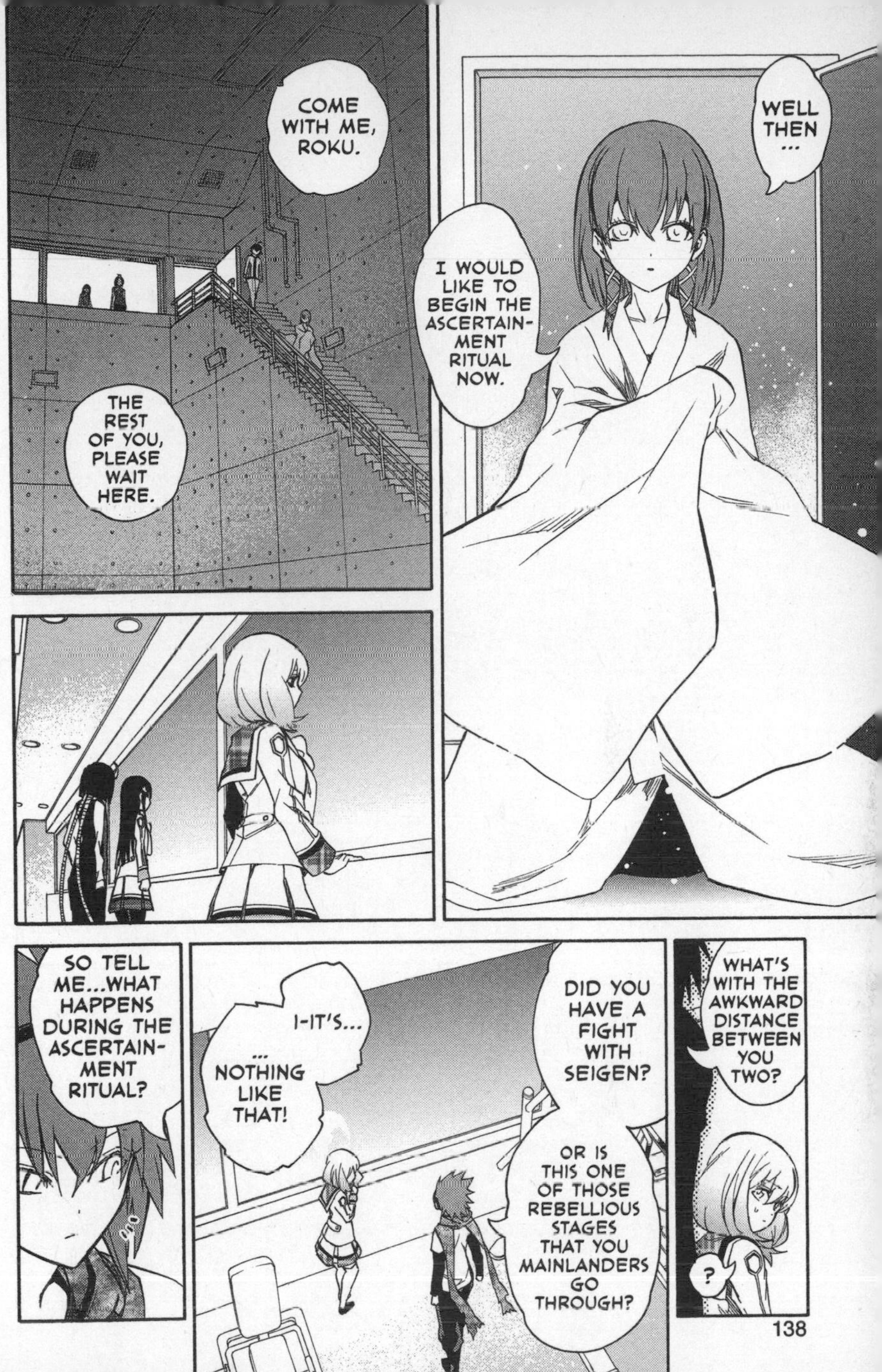
WELL THEN ...
I WOULD LIKE TO BEGIN THE ASCERTAINMENT RITUAL NOW.
COME WITH ME, ROKU.
THE REST OF YOU, PLEASE WAIT HERE.
WHAT'S WITH THE AWKWARD DISTANCE BETWEEN YOU TWO?
?
DID YOU HAVE A FIGHT WITH SEIGEN?
OR IS THIS ONE OF THOSE REBELLIOUS STAGES THAT YOU MAINLANDERS GO THROUGH?
I-IT'S...
... NOTHING LIKE THAT!
SO TELL ME...WHAT HAPPENS DURING THE ASCERTAINMENT RITUAL?

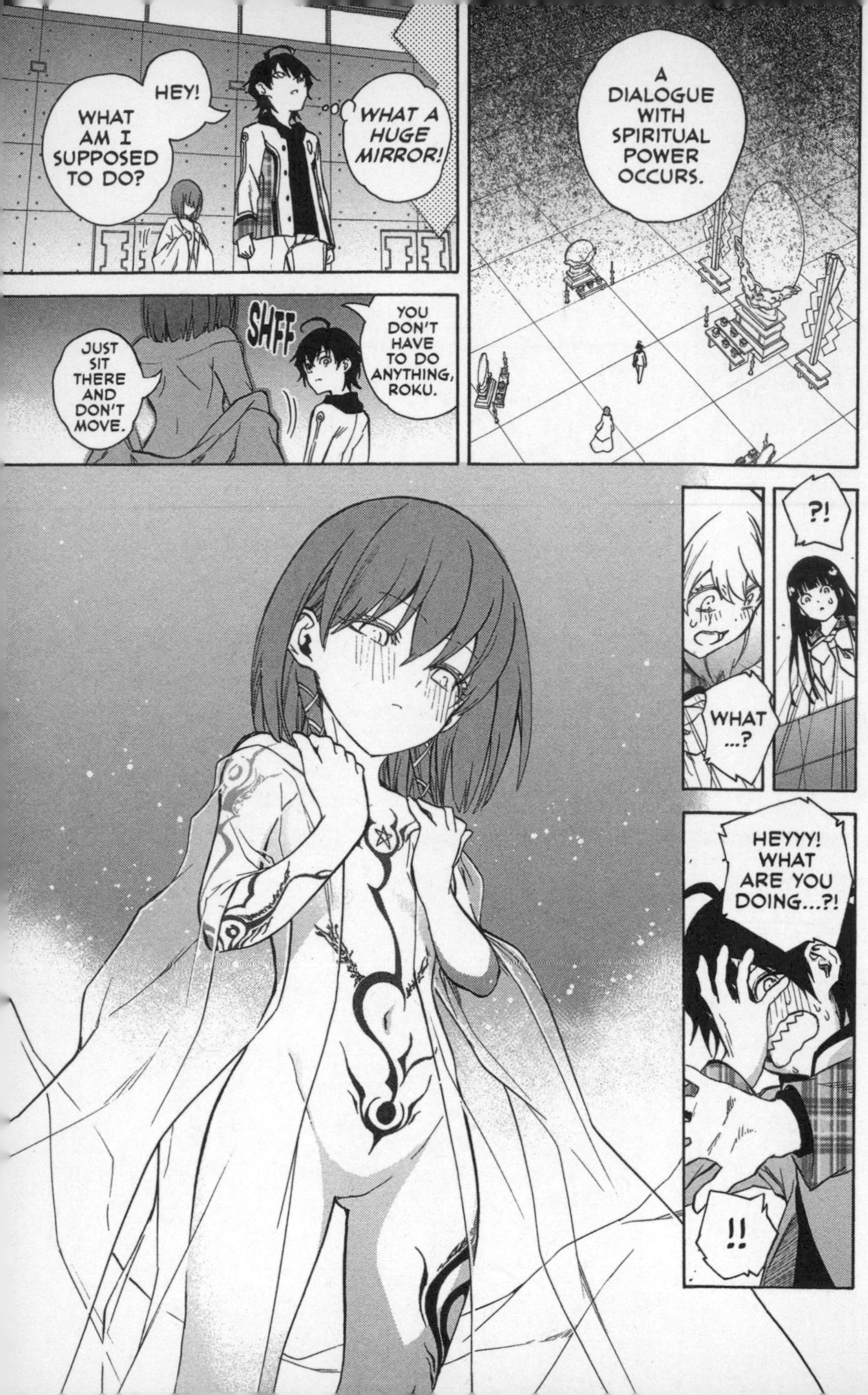
A DIALOGUE WITH SPIRITUAL POWER OCCURS.
WHAT A HUGE MIRROR!
HEY! WHAT AM I SUPPOSED TO DO?
YOU DON'T HAVE TO DO ANYTHING, ROKU.
SHFF
JUST SIT THERE AND DON'T MOVE.
?!
WHAT ...?
HEYYY! WHAT ARE YOU DOING...?!
!!

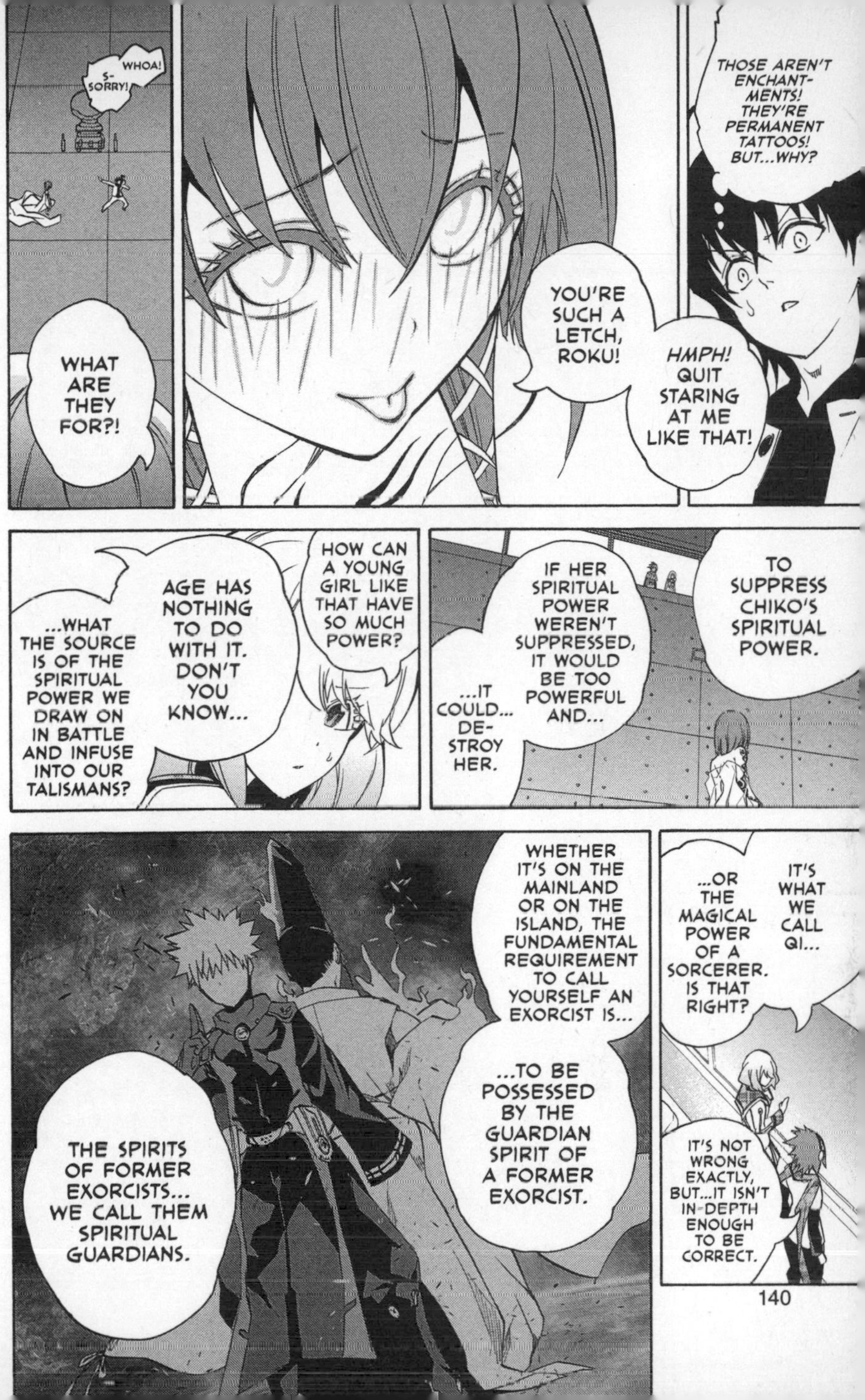
THOSE AREN'T ENCHANT-MENTS! THEY'RE PERMANENT TATTOOS! BUT...WHY?
HMPH! QUIT STARING AT ME LIKE THAT!
YOU'RE SUCH A LETCH, ROKU!
WHOA!
S-SORRY!
WHAT ARE THEY FOR?!
TO SUPPRESS CHIKO'S SPIRITUAL POWER.
IF HER SPIRITUAL POWER WEREN'T SUPPRESSED, IT WOULD BE TOO POWERFUL AND...
...IT COULD... DE-STROY HER.
HOW CAN A YOUNG GIRL LIKE THAT HAVE SO MUCH POWER?
AGE HAS NOTHING TO DO WITH IT. DON'T YOU KNOW...
...WHAT THE SOURCE IS OF THE SPIRITUAL POWER WE DRAW ON IN BATTLE AND INFUSE INTO OUR TALISMANS?
IT'S WHAT WE CALL QI...
...OR THE MAGICAL POWER OF A SORCERER. IS THAT RIGHT?
IT'S NOT WRONG EXACTLY, BUT...IT ISN'T IN-DEPTH ENOUGH TO BE CORRECT.
WHETHER IT'S ON THE MAINLAND OR ON THE ISLAND, THE FUNDAMENTAL REQUIREMENT TO CALL YOURSELF AN EXORCIST IS...
...TO BE POSSESSED BY THE GUARDIAN SPIRIT OF A FORMER EXORCIST.
THE SPIRITS OF FORMER EXORCISTS... WE CALL THEM SPIRITUAL GUARDIANS.

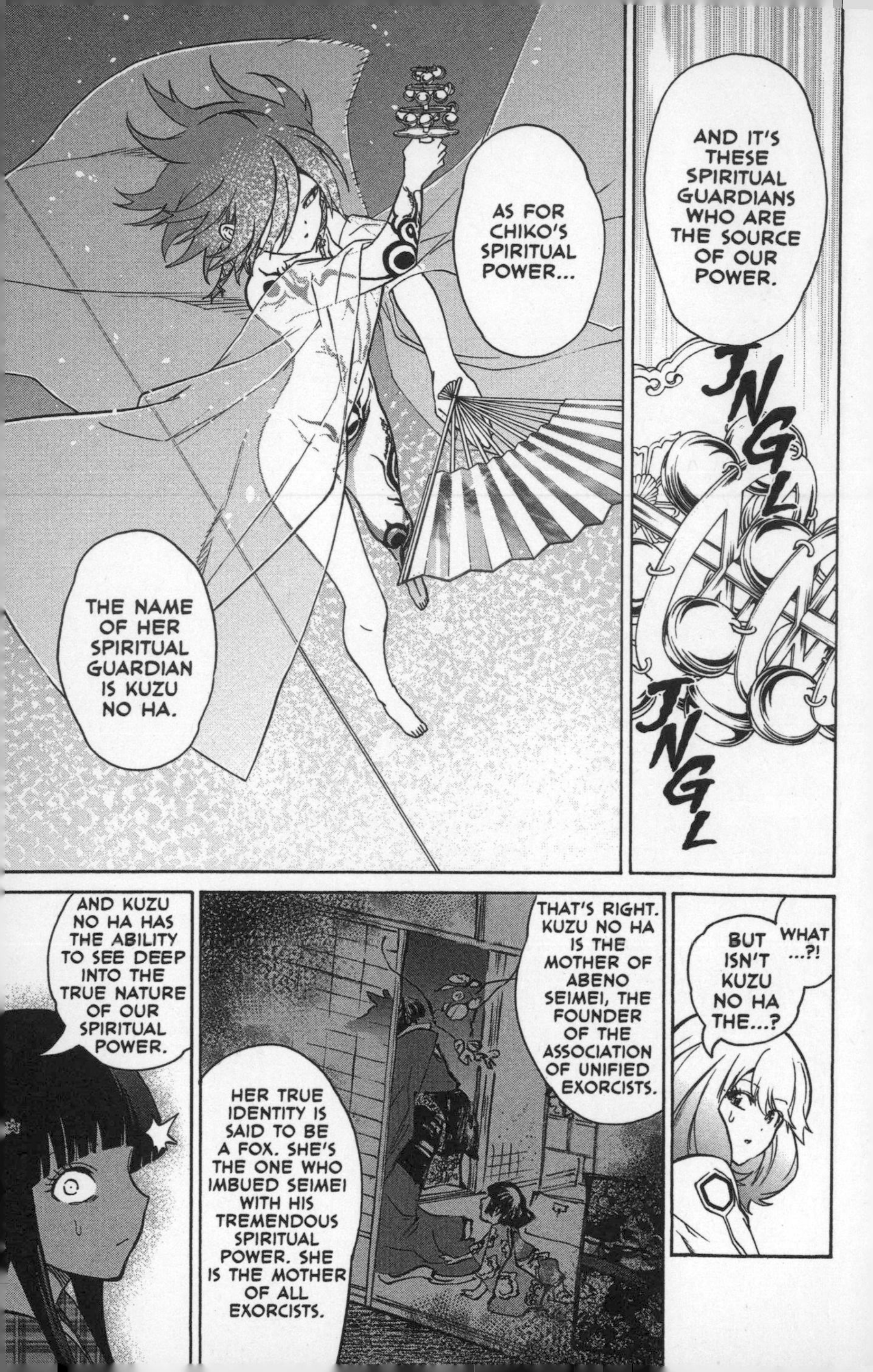
AND IT'S THESE SPIRITUAL GUARDIANS WHO ARE THE SOURCE OF OUR POWER.
JNGL
JNGL
AS FOR CHIKO'S SPIRITUAL POWER...
THE NAME OF HER SPIRITUAL GUARDIAN IS KUZU NO HA.
WHAT ...?!
BUT ISN'T KUZU NO HA THE...?
THAT'S RIGHT. KUZU NO HA IS THE MOTHER OF ABENO SEIMEI, THE FOUNDER OF THE ASSOCIATION OF UNIFIED EXORCISTS.
HER TRUE IDENTITY IS SAID TO BE A FOX. SHE'S THE ONE WHO IMBUED SEIMEI WITH HIS TREMENDOUS SPIRITUAL POWER. SHE IS THE MOTHER OF ALL EXORCISTS.
AND KUZU NO HA HAS THE ABILITY TO SEE DEEP INTO THE TRUE NATURE OF OUR SPIRITUAL POWER.

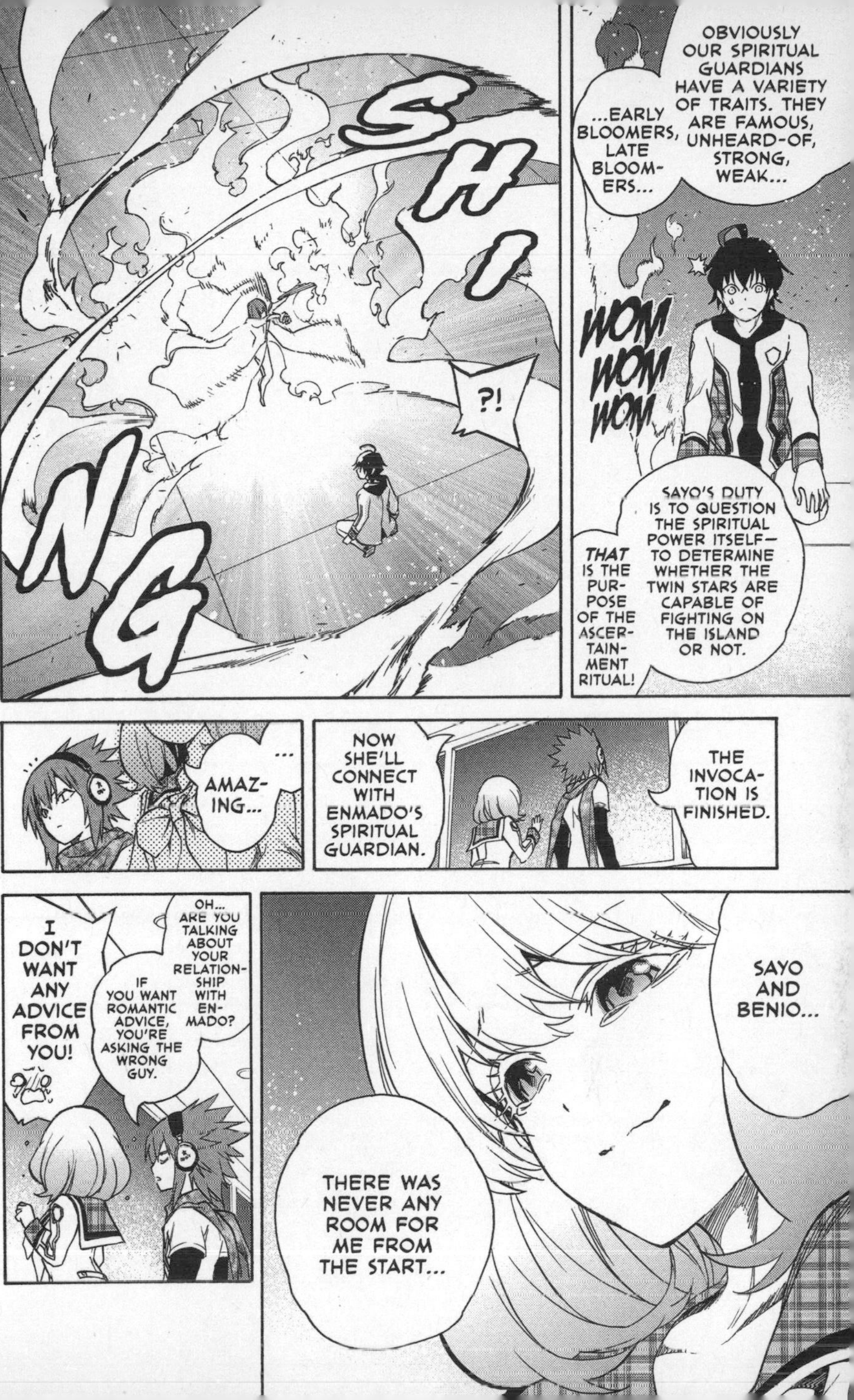
OBVIOUSLY OUR SPIRITUAL GUARDIANS HAVE A VARIETY OF TRAITS. THEY ARE FAMOUS, UNHEARD-OF, STRONG, WEAK...
...EARLY BLOOMERS, LATE BLOOM-ERS...
WOM WOM WOM
SAYO'S DUTY IS TO QUESTION THE SPIRITUAL POWER ITSELF— TO DETERMINE WHETHER THE TWIN STARS ARE CAPABLE OF FIGHTING ON THE ISLAND OR NOT.
THAT IS THE PUR-POSE OF THE ASCER-TAIN-MENT RITUAL!
SHING
?!
THE INVOCA-TION IS FINISHED.
NOW SHE'LL CONNECT WITH ENMADO'S SPIRITUAL GUARDIAN.
...
AMAZ-ING...
SAYO AND BENIO...
THERE WAS NEVER ANY ROOM FOR ME FROM THE START...
OH... ARE YOU TALKING ABOUT YOUR RELATION-SHIP WITH EN-MADO?
IF YOU WANT ROMANTIC ADVICE, YOU'RE ASKING THE WRONG GUY.
I DON'T WANT ANY ADVICE FROM YOU!

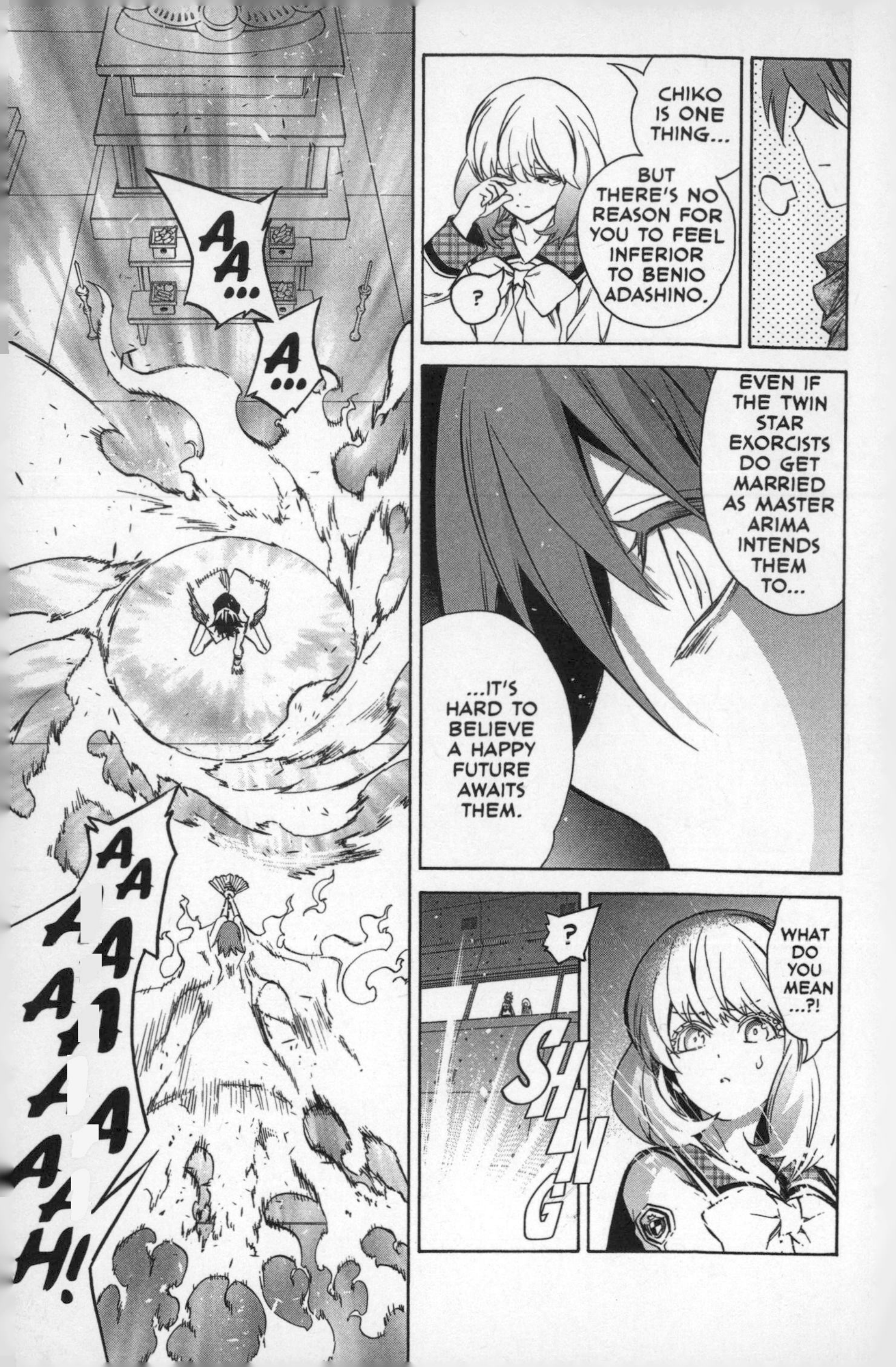
CHIKO IS ONE THING...
BUT THERE'S NO REASON FOR YOU TO FEEL INFERIOR TO BENIO ADASHINO.
?
EVEN IF THE TWIN STAR EXORCISTS DO GET MARRIED AS MASTER ARIMA INTENDS THEM TO...
...IT'S HARD TO BELIEVE A HAPPY FUTURE AWAITS THEM.
WHAT DO YOU MEAN...?!
?
SHING
AA...
A...
AAAAAAAAAAH!

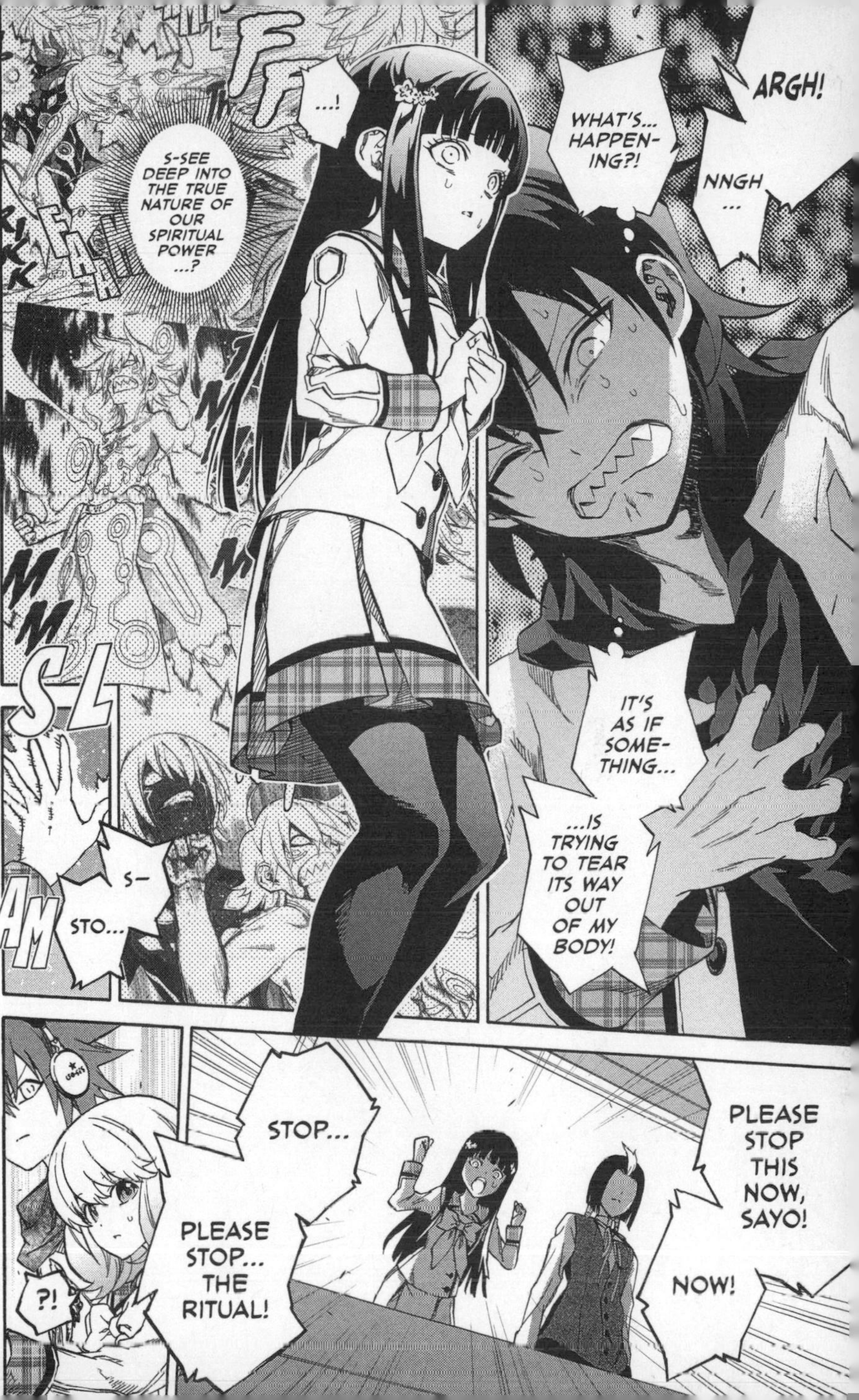
ARGH!
WHAT'S... HAPPENING?!
NNGH...
IT'S AS IF SOMETHING...
...IS TRYING TO TEAR ITS WAY OUT OF MY BODY!
...!
S-SEE DEEP INTO THE TRUE NATURE OF OUR SPIRITUAL POWER...?
SL
AM
S—
STO...
PLEASE STOP THIS NOW, SAYO!
NOW!
STOP...
PLEASE STOP... THE RITUAL!
?!

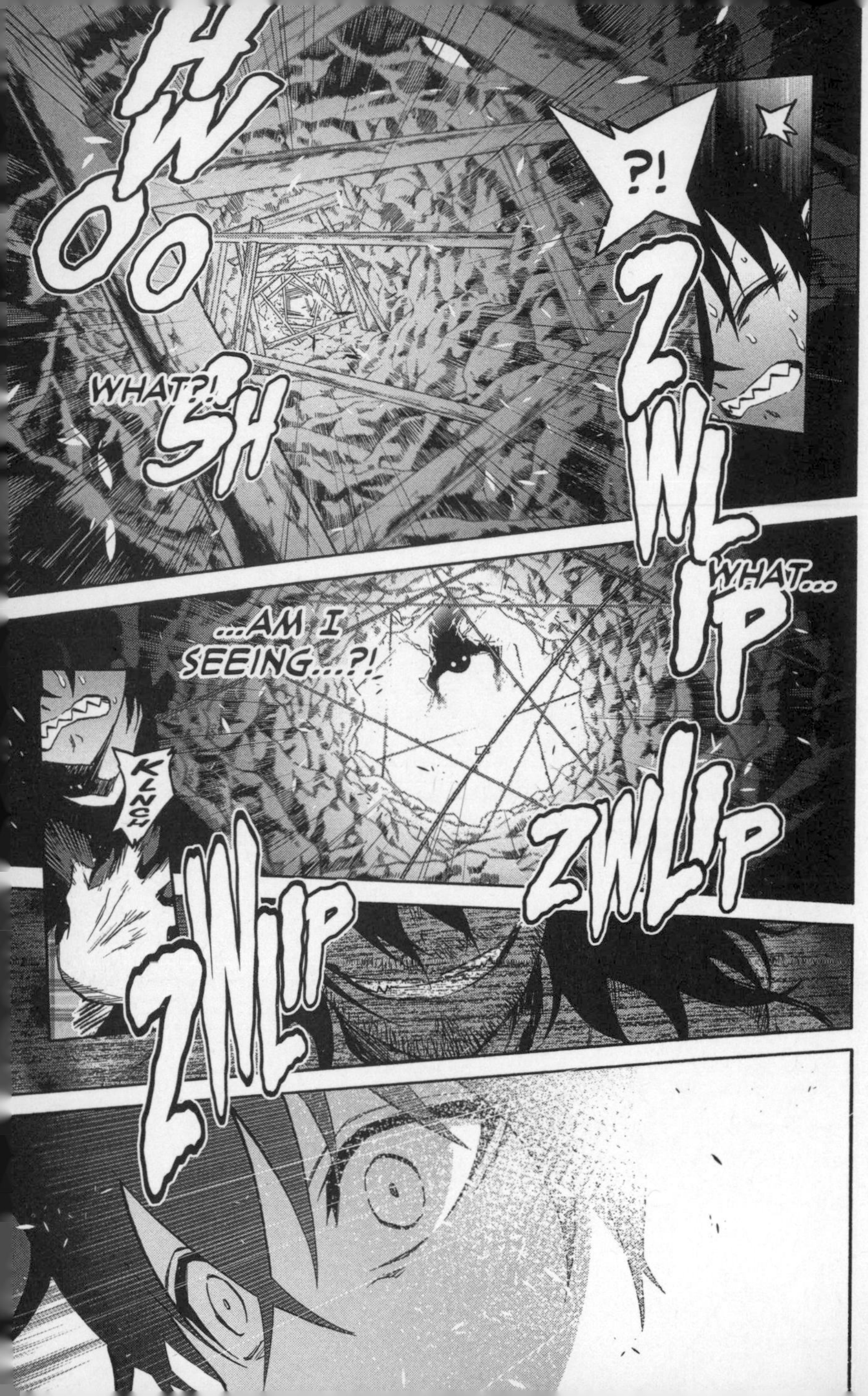
?!
ZWLIP
WHOOSH
WHAT?!
WHAT...
...AM I SEEING...?!
ZWLIP
KLNCH
ZWLIP

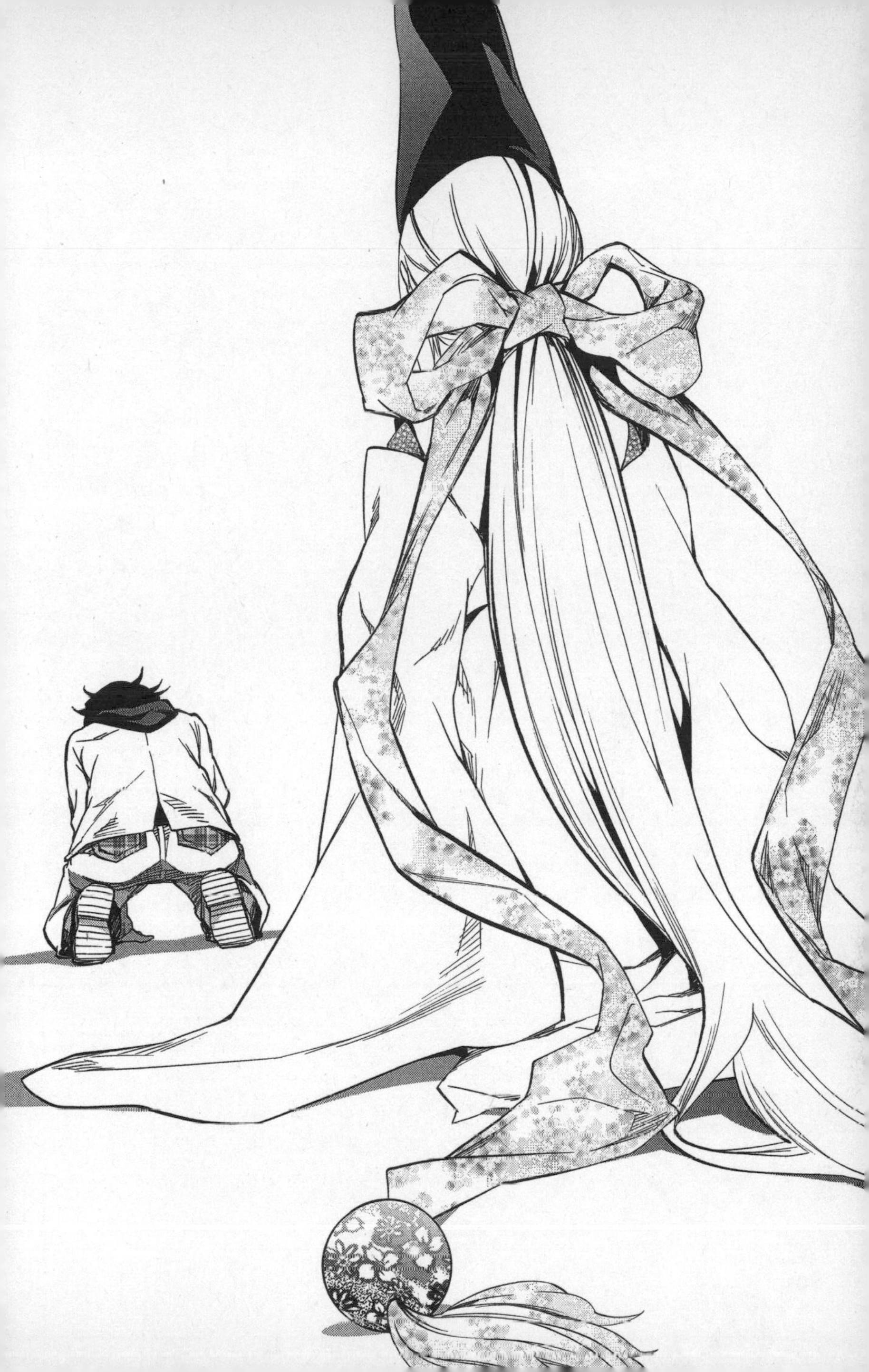

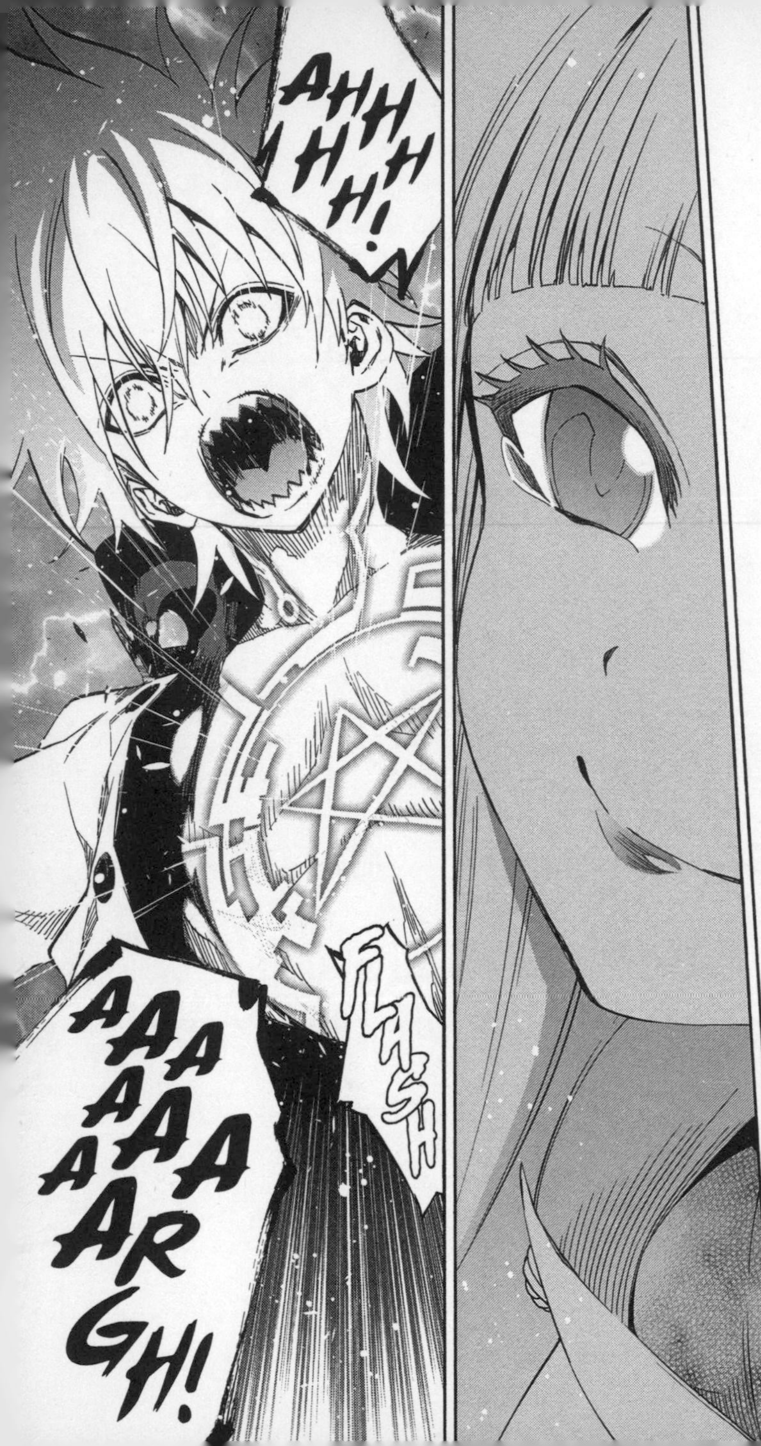
AHHHHHHH!
FLASH
AAAAAAAAARGH!

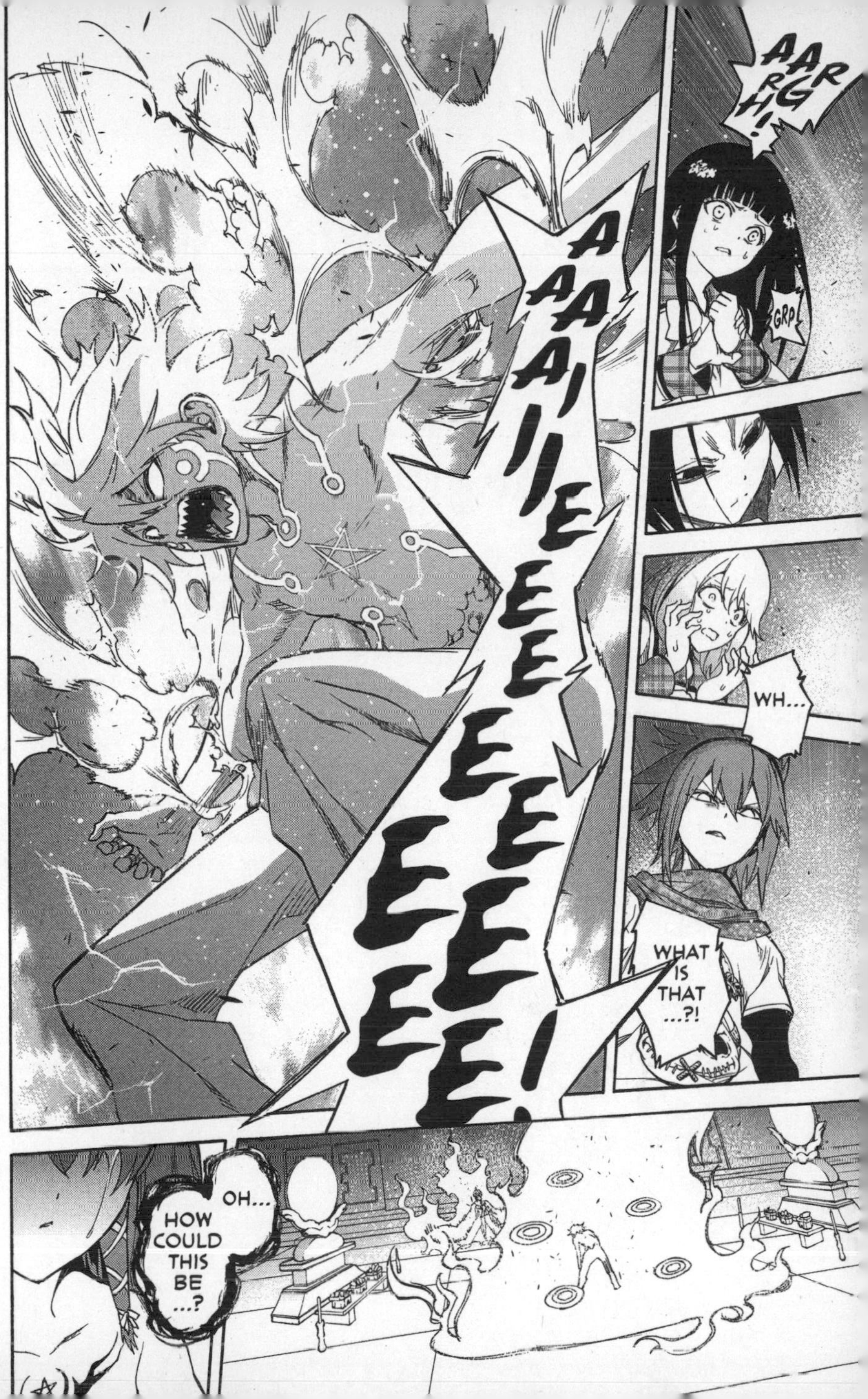
AARGH!
GRP
WH...
WHAT IS THAT ...?!
AAAIIEEEEEEEEEE!
OH... HOW COULD THIS BE ...?

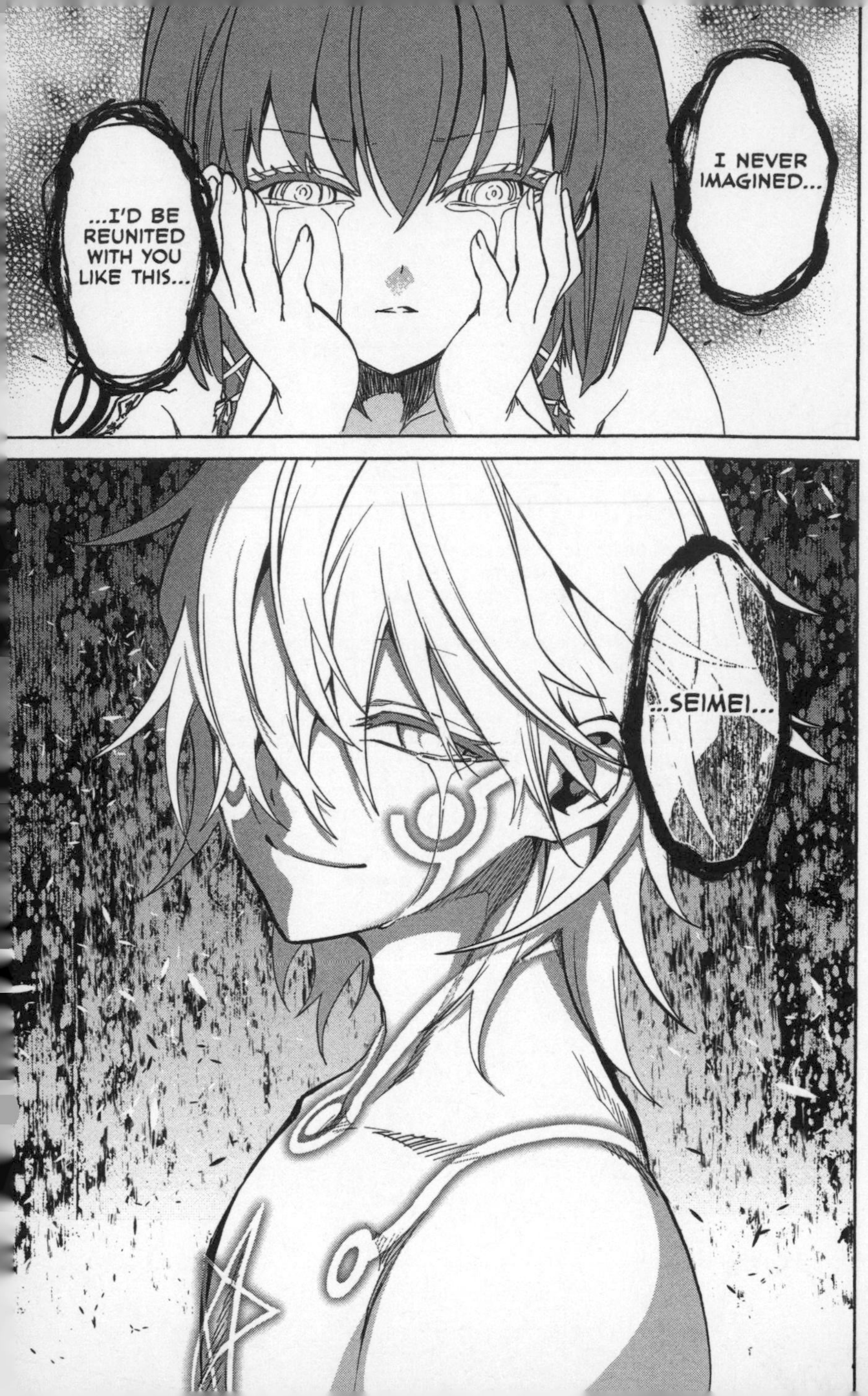
I NEVER IMAGINED...
...I'D BE REUNITED WITH YOU LIKE THIS...
...SEIMEI...

Column ⑭ Ascertainment Ritual

For modern-day exorcists—especially within the six families (Wood family, Fire family, Earth family, Metal family, Water family and the Head family)—who have passed down the exorcism arts of Abeno Seimei from the family head to the rightful heir, the Ascertainment Ritual is used to decide the heir of the family.

The real ritual is the same as in the manga. A person is examined to see if they are possessed by an exorcist from the past, and if so, they become the rightful heir of the family.

In real life, this ritual is performed on the candidates when they are around the age of three. From that day on, they are trained to become the family heir. Exorcists truly live in a very different world from us...!

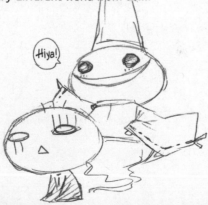

Hiya!

Twin Star Exorcists

O N M Y O J I

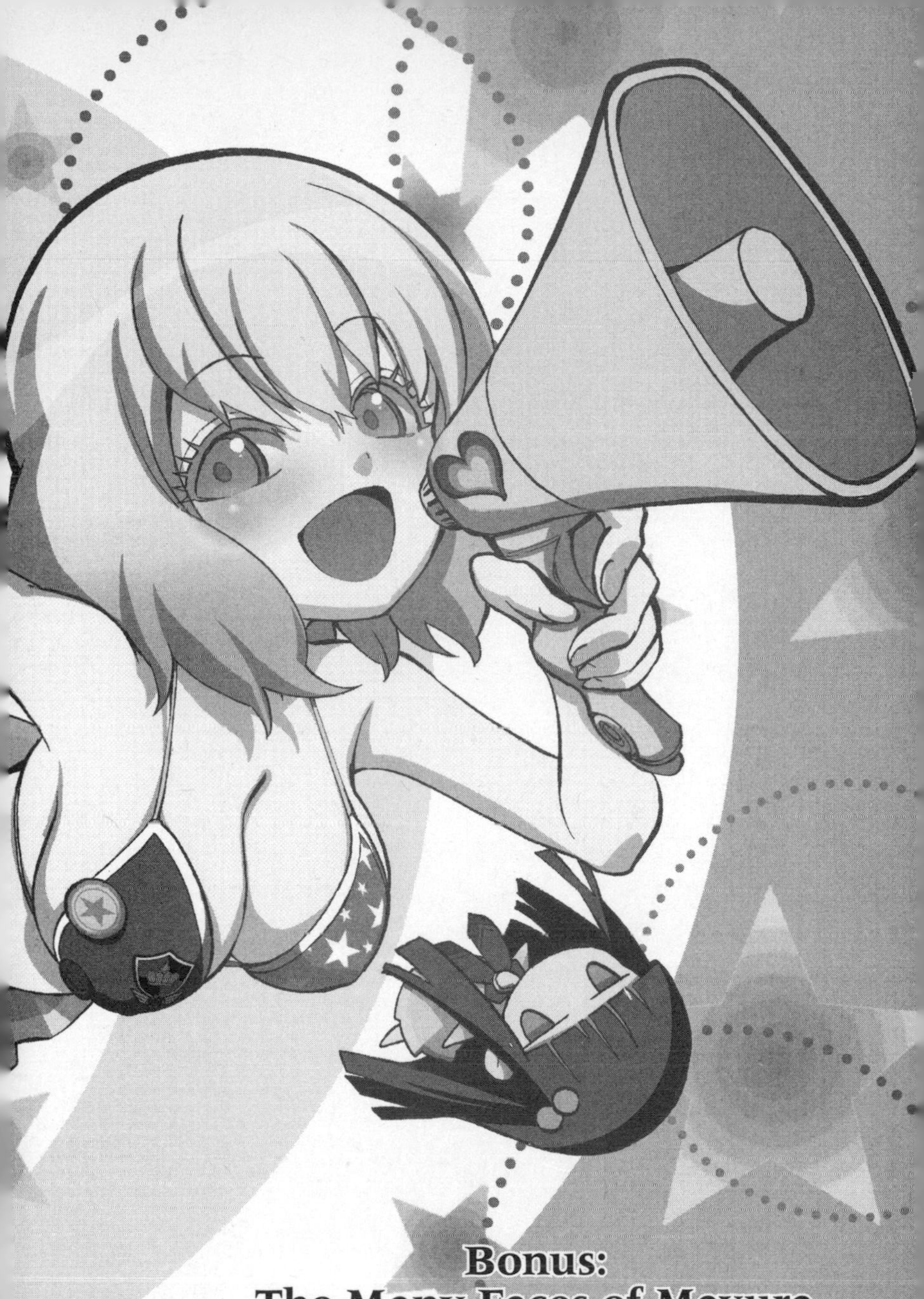

Bonus: The Many Faces of Mayura

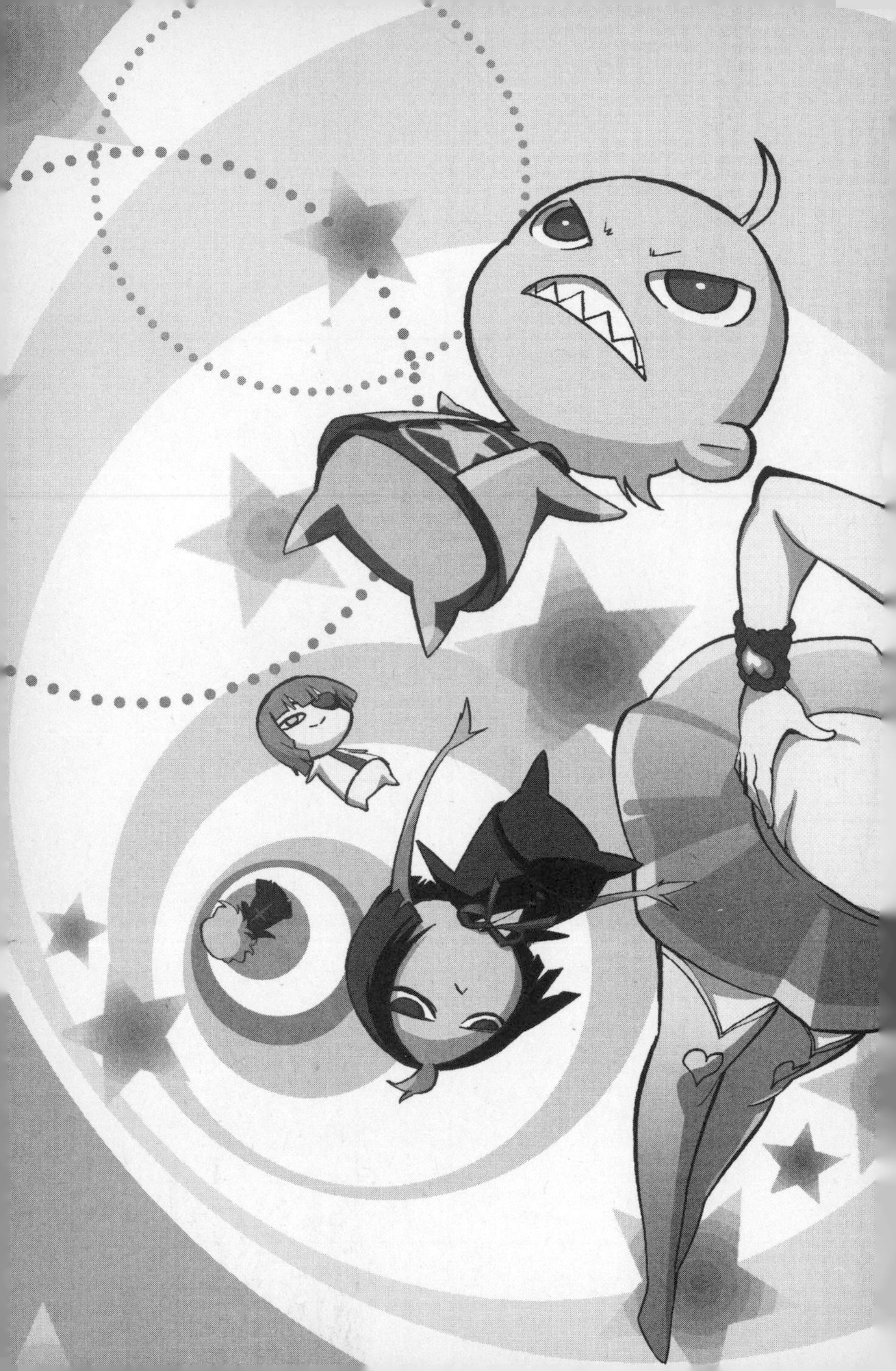

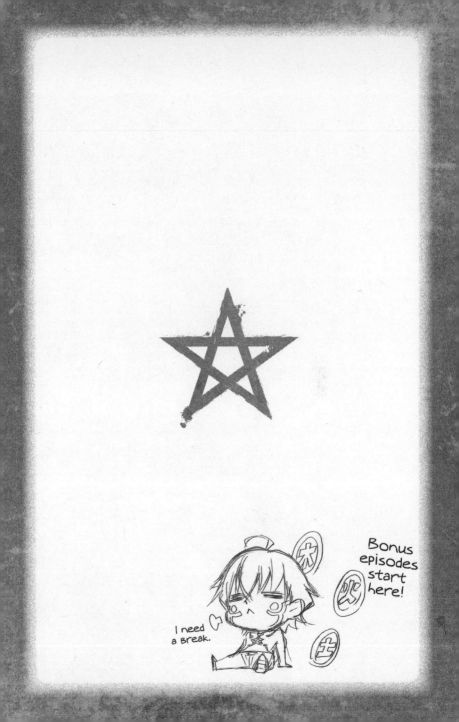

Bonus episodes start here!

I need a break.

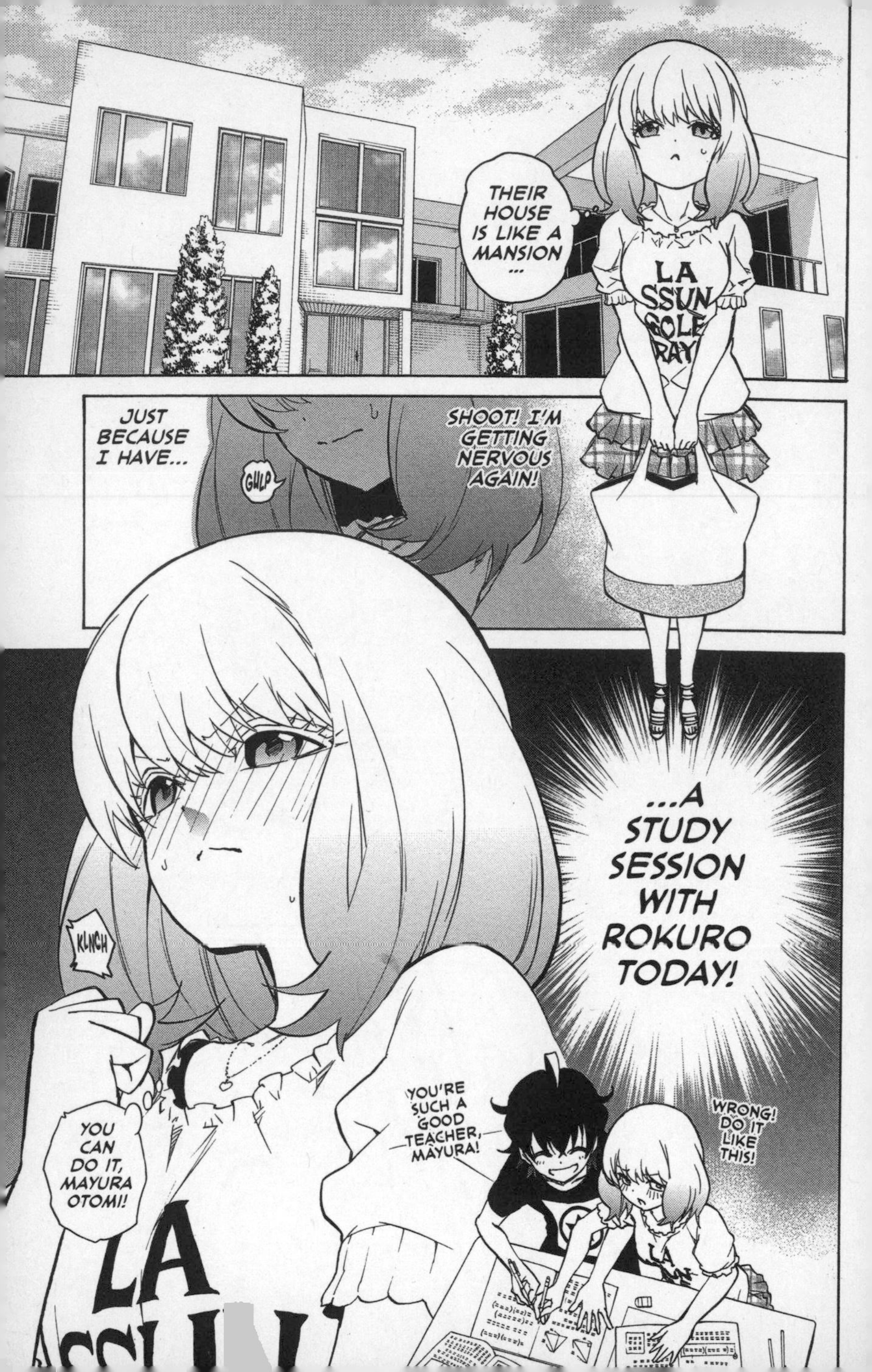
THEIR HOUSE IS LIKE A MANSION ...
LA SSUN GOLE RAY!
SHOOT! I'M GETTING NERVOUS AGAIN!
GULP
JUST BECAUSE I HAVE...
...A STUDY SESSION WITH ROKURO TODAY!
KLNCH
WRONG! DO IT LIKE THIS!
YOU'RE SUCH A GOOD TEACHER, MAYURA!
YOU CAN DO IT, MAYURA OTOMI!

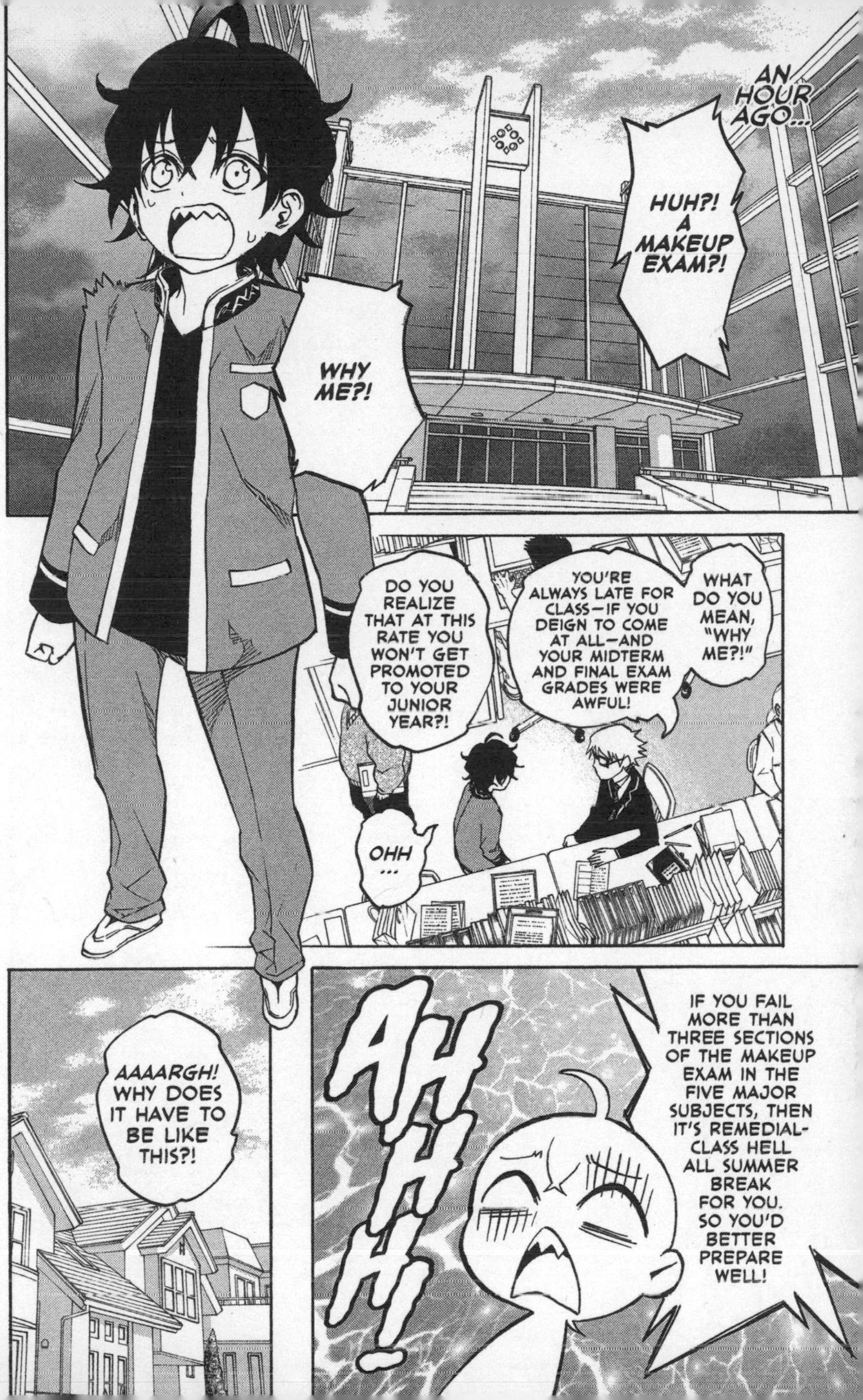
AN HOUR AGO...
HUH?! A MAKEUP EXAM?!
WHY ME?!
WHAT DO YOU MEAN, "WHY ME?!"
YOU'RE ALWAYS LATE FOR CLASS—IF YOU DEIGN TO COME AT ALL—AND YOUR MIDTERM AND FINAL EXAM GRADES WERE AWFUL!
DO YOU REALIZE THAT AT THIS RATE YOU WON'T GET PROMOTED TO YOUR JUNIOR YEAR?!
OHH ...
IF YOU FAIL MORE THAN THREE SECTIONS OF THE MAKEUP EXAM IN THE FIVE MAJOR SUBJECTS, THEN IT'S REMEDIAL-CLASS HELL ALL SUMMER BREAK FOR YOU. SO YOU'D BETTER PREPARE WELL!
AHHH!
AAAARGH! WHY DOES IT HAVE TO BE LIKE THIS?!

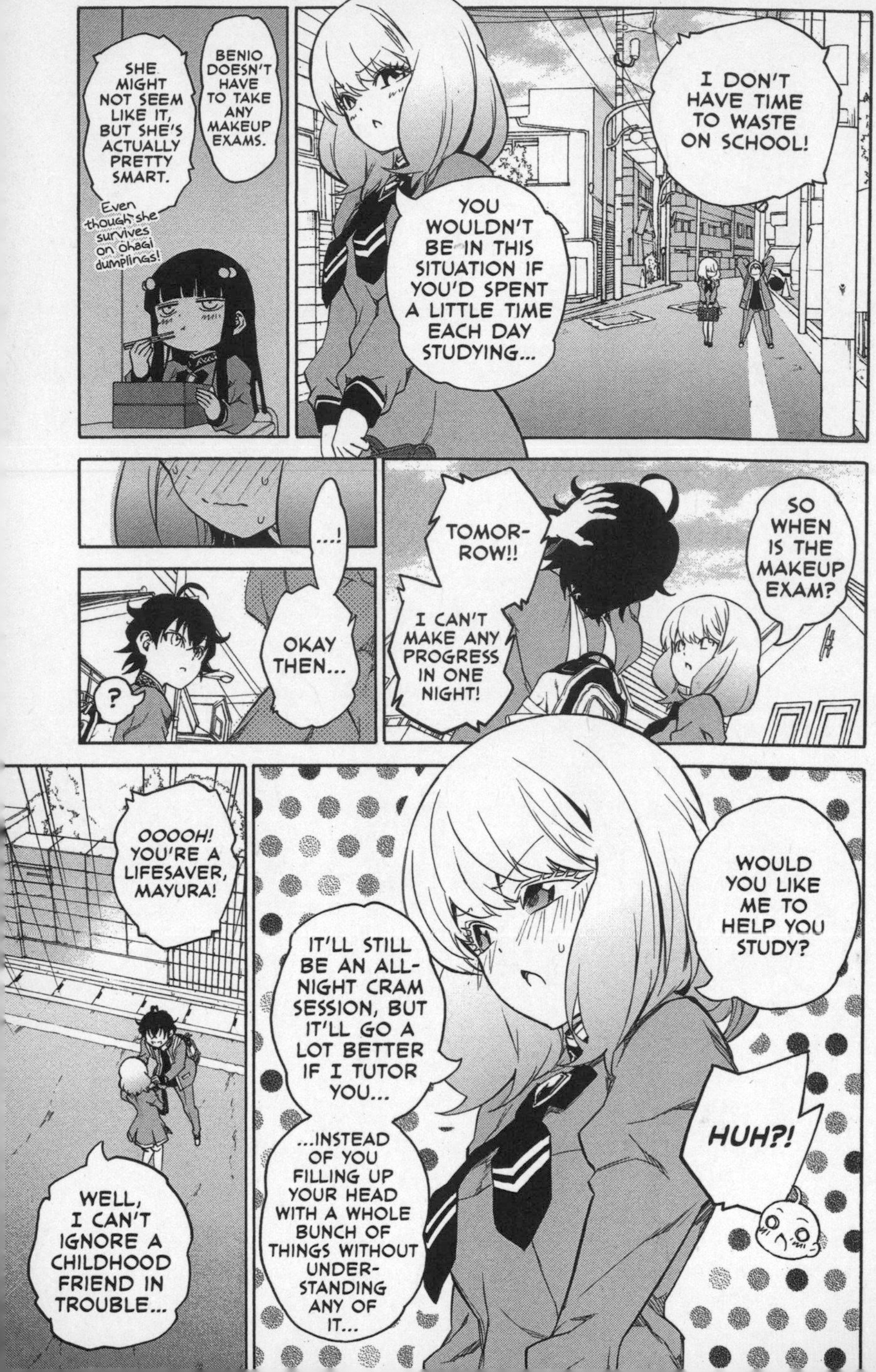
I DON'T HAVE TIME TO WASTE ON SCHOOL!
YOU WOULDN'T BE IN THIS SITUATION IF YOU'D SPENT A LITTLE TIME EACH DAY STUDYING...
BENIO DOESN'T HAVE TO TAKE ANY MAKEUP EXAMS.
SHE MIGHT NOT SEEM LIKE IT, BUT SHE'S ACTUALLY PRETTY SMART.
Even though she survives on ohagi dumplings!
SO WHEN IS THE MAKEUP EXAM?
TOMORROW!!
I CAN'T MAKE ANY PROGRESS IN ONE NIGHT!
...!
OKAY THEN...
?
WOULD YOU LIKE ME TO HELP YOU STUDY?
IT'LL STILL BE AN ALL-NIGHT CRAM SESSION, BUT IT'LL GO A LOT BETTER IF I TUTOR YOU...
...INSTEAD OF YOU FILLING UP YOUR HEAD WITH A WHOLE BUNCH OF THINGS WITHOUT UNDER-STANDING ANY OF IT...
HUH?!
OOOOH! YOU'RE A LIFESAVER, MAYURA!
WELL, I CAN'T IGNORE A CHILDHOOD FRIEND IN TROUBLE...

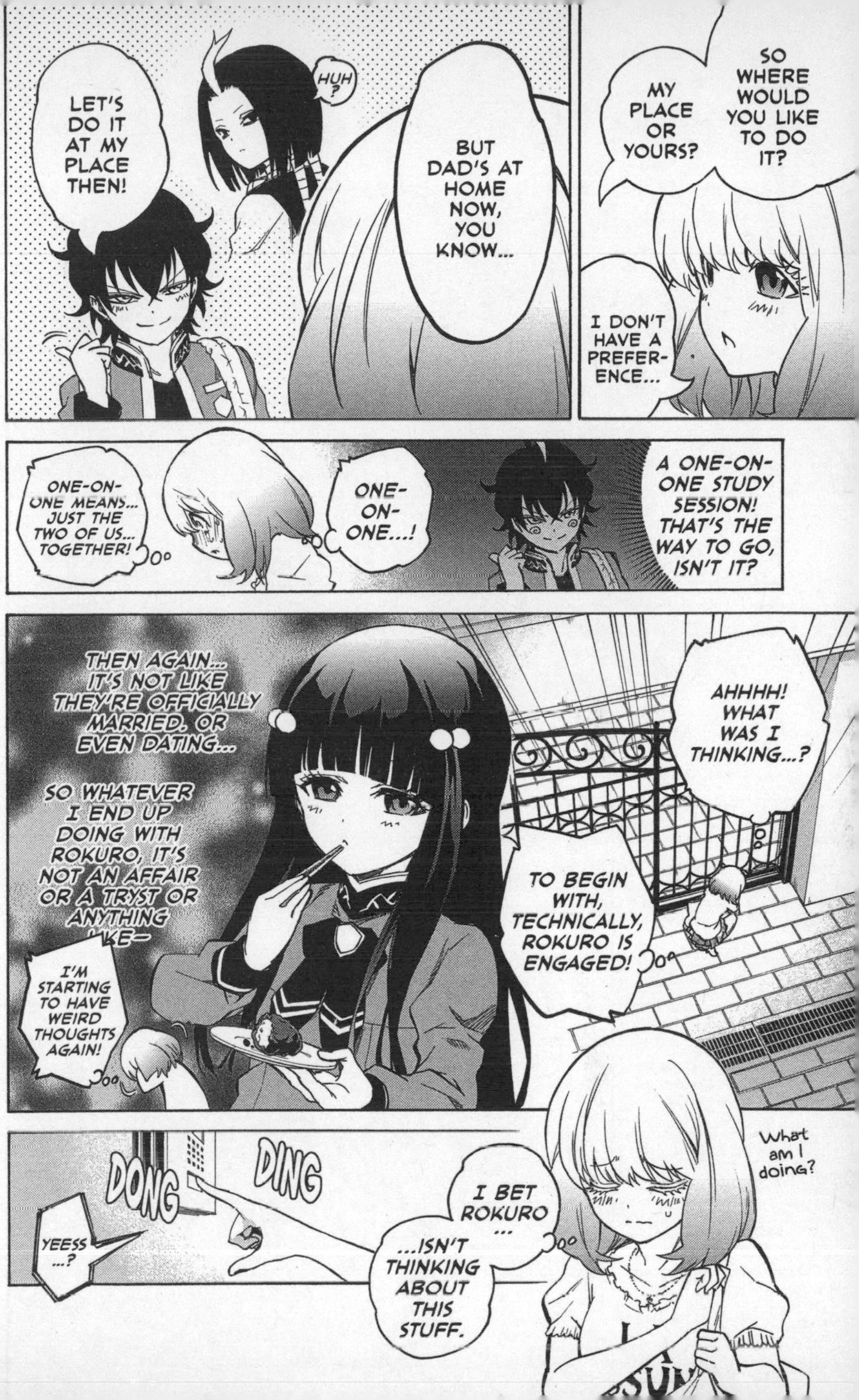
SO WHERE WOULD YOU LIKE TO DO IT?
MY PLACE OR YOURS?
I DON'T HAVE A PREFERENCE...
BUT DAD'S AT HOME NOW, YOU KNOW...
HUH?
LET'S DO IT AT MY PLACE THEN!
A ONE-ON-ONE STUDY SESSION! THAT'S THE WAY TO GO, ISN'T IT?
ONE-ON-ONE...!
ONE-ON-ONE MEANS... JUST THE TWO OF US... TOGETHER!
AHHHH! WHAT WAS I THINKING...?
TO BEGIN WITH, TECHNICALLY, ROKURO IS ENGAGED!
THEN AGAIN... IT'S NOT LIKE THEY'RE OFFICIALLY MARRIED. OR EVEN DATING...
SO WHATEVER I END UP DOING WITH ROKURO, IT'S NOT AN AFFAIR OR A TRYST OR ANYTHING LIKE—
I'M STARTING TO HAVE WEIRD THOUGHTS AGAIN!
What am I doing?
I BET ROKURO ...
...ISN'T THINKING ABOUT THIS STUFF.
DING
DONG
YEESS ...?

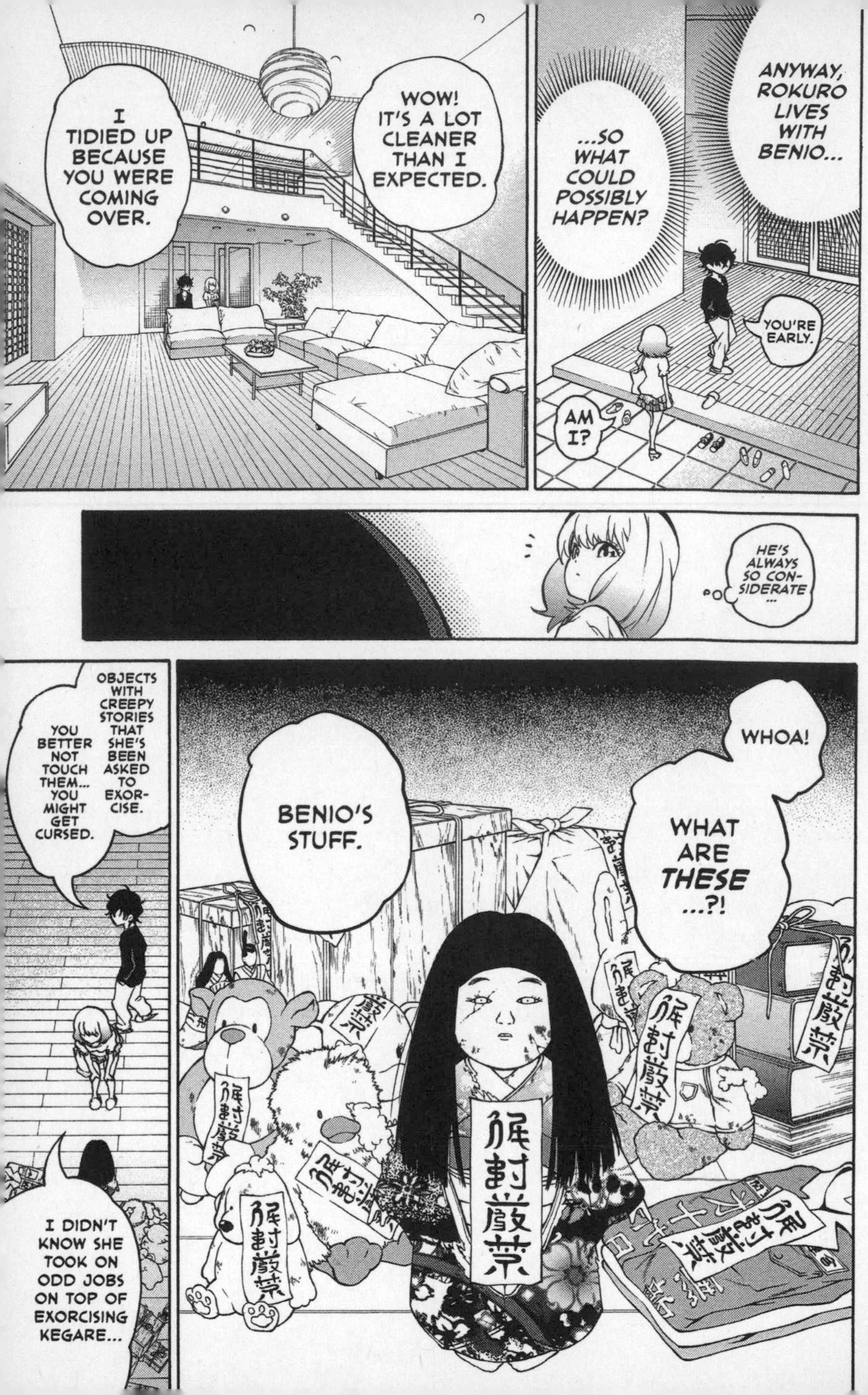
ANYWAY, ROKURO LIVES WITH BENIO...
...SO WHAT COULD POSSIBLY HAPPEN?
YOU'RE EARLY.
AM I?
WOW! IT'S A LOT CLEANER THAN I EXPECTED.
I TIDIED UP BECAUSE YOU WERE COMING OVER.
HE'S ALWAYS SO CONSIDERATE...
WHOA!
WHAT ARE *THESE*...?!
BENIO'S STUFF.
OBJECTS WITH CREEPY STORIES THAT SHE'S BEEN ASKED TO EXORCISE.
YOU BETTER NOT TOUCH THEM... YOU MIGHT GET CURSED.
I DIDN'T KNOW SHE TOOK ON ODD JOBS ON TOP OF EXORCISING KEGARE...

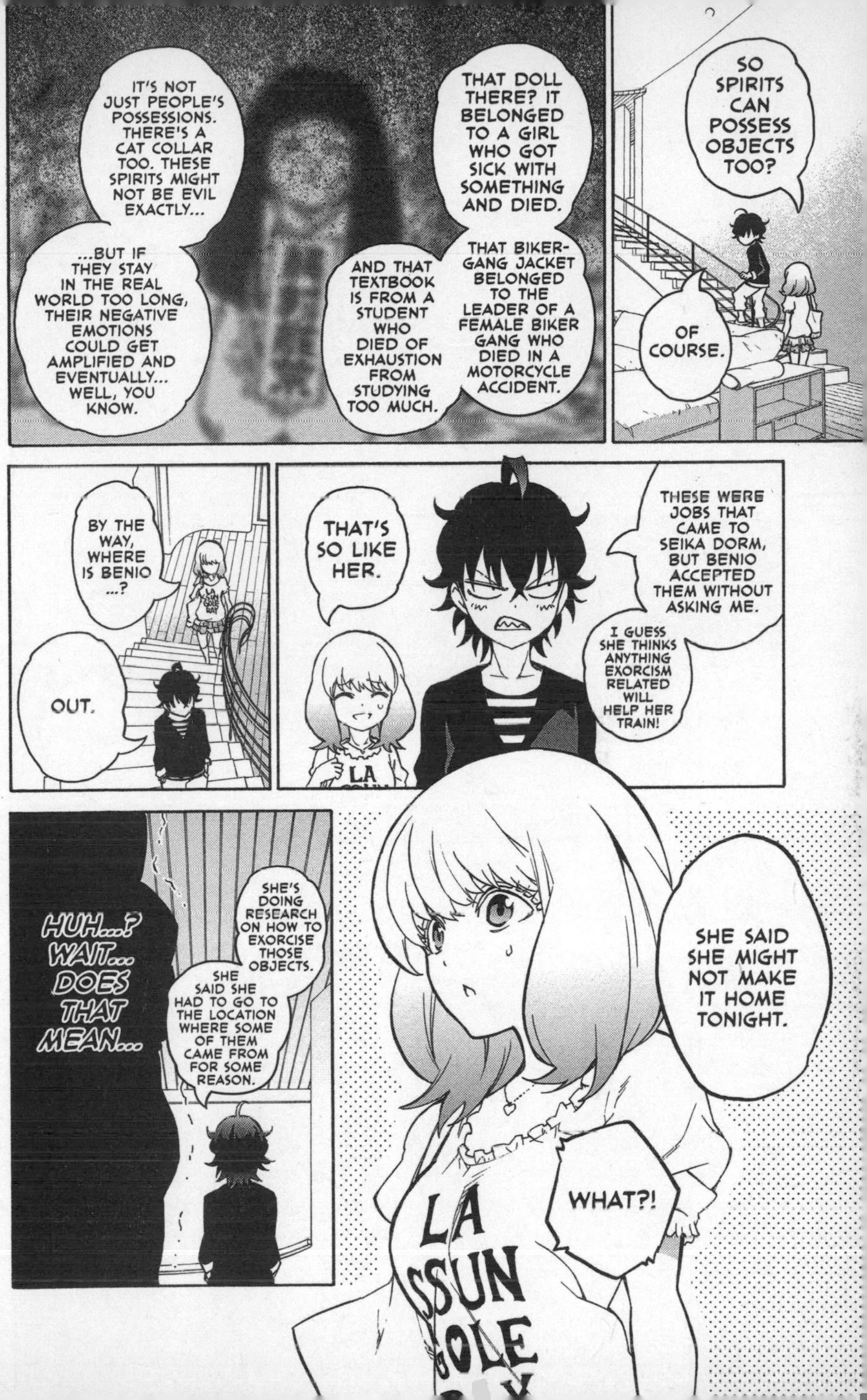
SO SPIRITS CAN POSSESS OBJECTS TOO?
OF COURSE.
THAT DOLL THERE? IT BELONGED TO A GIRL WHO GOT SICK WITH SOMETHING AND DIED.
THAT BIKER-GANG JACKET BELONGED TO THE LEADER OF A FEMALE BIKER GANG WHO DIED IN A MOTORCYCLE ACCIDENT.
AND THAT TEXTBOOK IS FROM A STUDENT WHO DIED OF EXHAUSTION FROM STUDYING TOO MUCH.
IT'S NOT JUST PEOPLE'S POSSESSIONS. THERE'S A CAT COLLAR TOO. THESE SPIRITS MIGHT NOT BE EVIL EXACTLY...
...BUT IF THEY STAY IN THE REAL WORLD TOO LONG, THEIR NEGATIVE EMOTIONS COULD GET AMPLIFIED AND EVENTUALLY... WELL, YOU KNOW.
THESE WERE JOBS THAT CAME TO SEIKA DORM, BUT BENIO ACCEPTED THEM WITHOUT ASKING ME.
I GUESS SHE THINKS ANYTHING EXORCISM RELATED WILL HELP HER TRAIN!
THAT'S SO LIKE HER.
BY THE WAY, WHERE IS BENIO ...?
OUT.
SHE SAID SHE MIGHT NOT MAKE IT HOME TONIGHT.
WHAT?!
SHE'S DOING RESEARCH ON HOW TO EXORCISE THOSE OBJECTS.
SHE SAID SHE HAD TO GO TO THE LOCATION WHERE SOME OF THEM CAME FROM FOR SOME REASON.
HUH...? WAIT... DOES THAT MEAN...

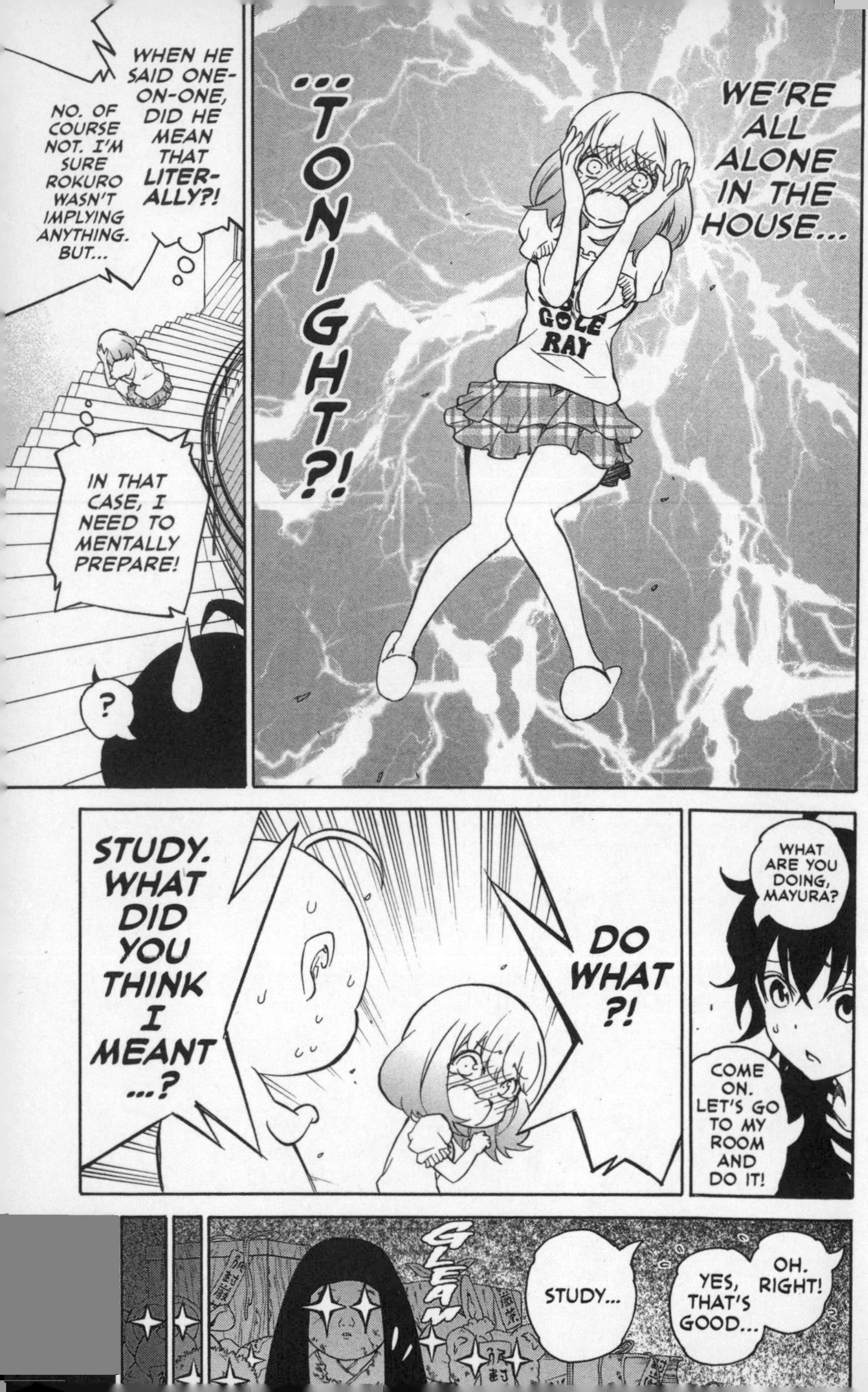
WE'RE ALL ALONE IN THE HOUSE...
...TONIGHT?!
WHEN HE SAID ONE-ON-ONE, DID HE MEAN THAT LITERALLY?!
NO. OF COURSE NOT. I'M SURE ROKURO WASN'T IMPLYING ANYTHING. BUT...
IN THAT CASE, I NEED TO MENTALLY PREPARE!
?
WHAT ARE YOU DOING, MAYURA?
COME ON. LET'S GO TO MY ROOM AND DO IT!
DO WHAT?!
STUDY. WHAT DID YOU THINK I MEANT...?
OH. RIGHT!
YES, THAT'S GOOD...
STUDY...
GLEAM

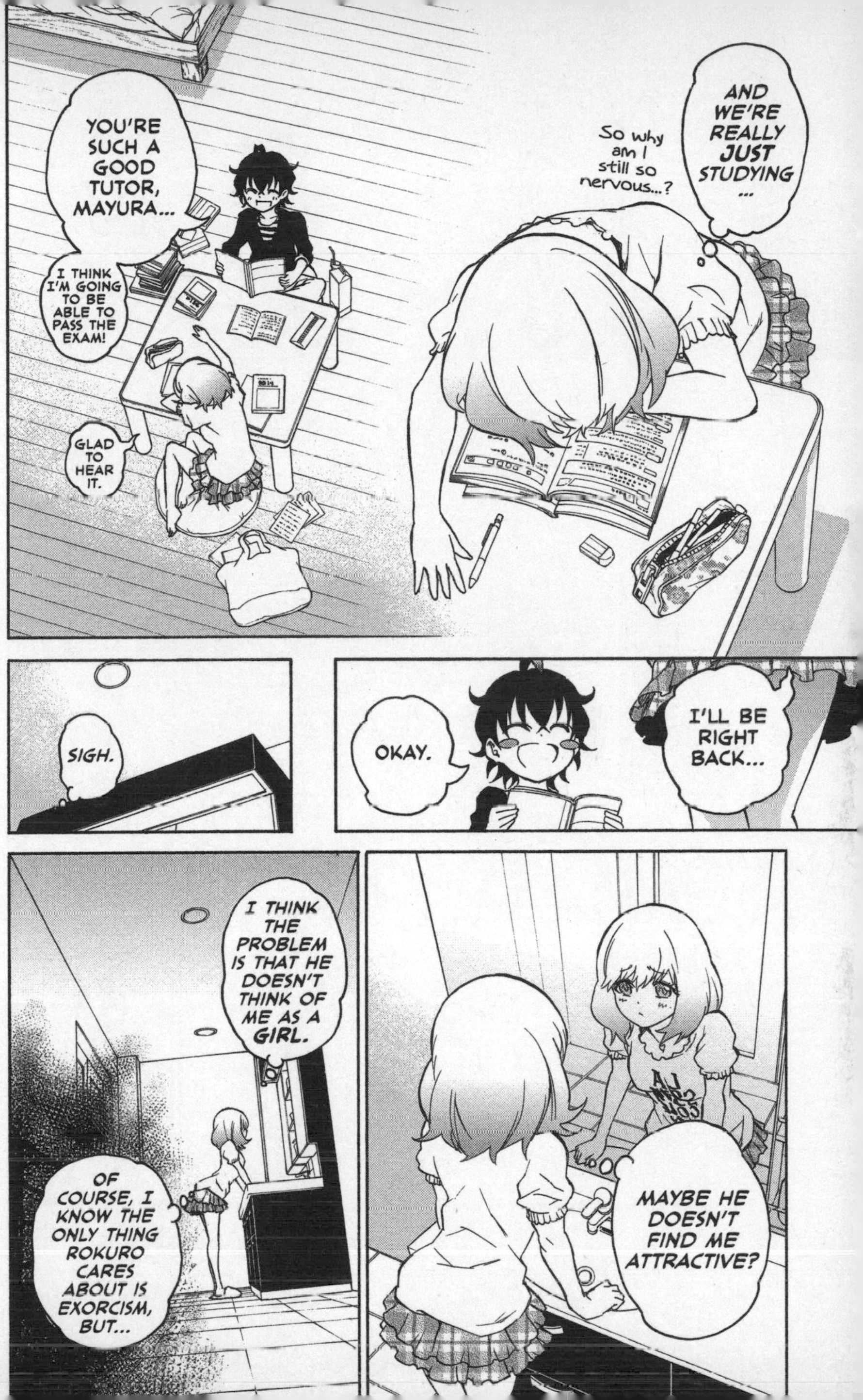
AND WE'RE REALLY JUST STUDYING...
So why am I still so nervous...?
YOU'RE SUCH A GOOD TUTOR, MAYURA...
I THINK I'M GOING TO BE ABLE TO PASS THE EXAM!
GLAD TO HEAR IT.
I'LL BE RIGHT BACK...
OKAY.
SIGH.
MAYBE HE DOESN'T FIND ME ATTRACTIVE?
I THINK THE PROBLEM IS THAT HE DOESN'T THINK OF ME AS A GIRL.
OF COURSE, I KNOW THE ONLY THING ROKURO CARES ABOUT IS EXORCISM, BUT...

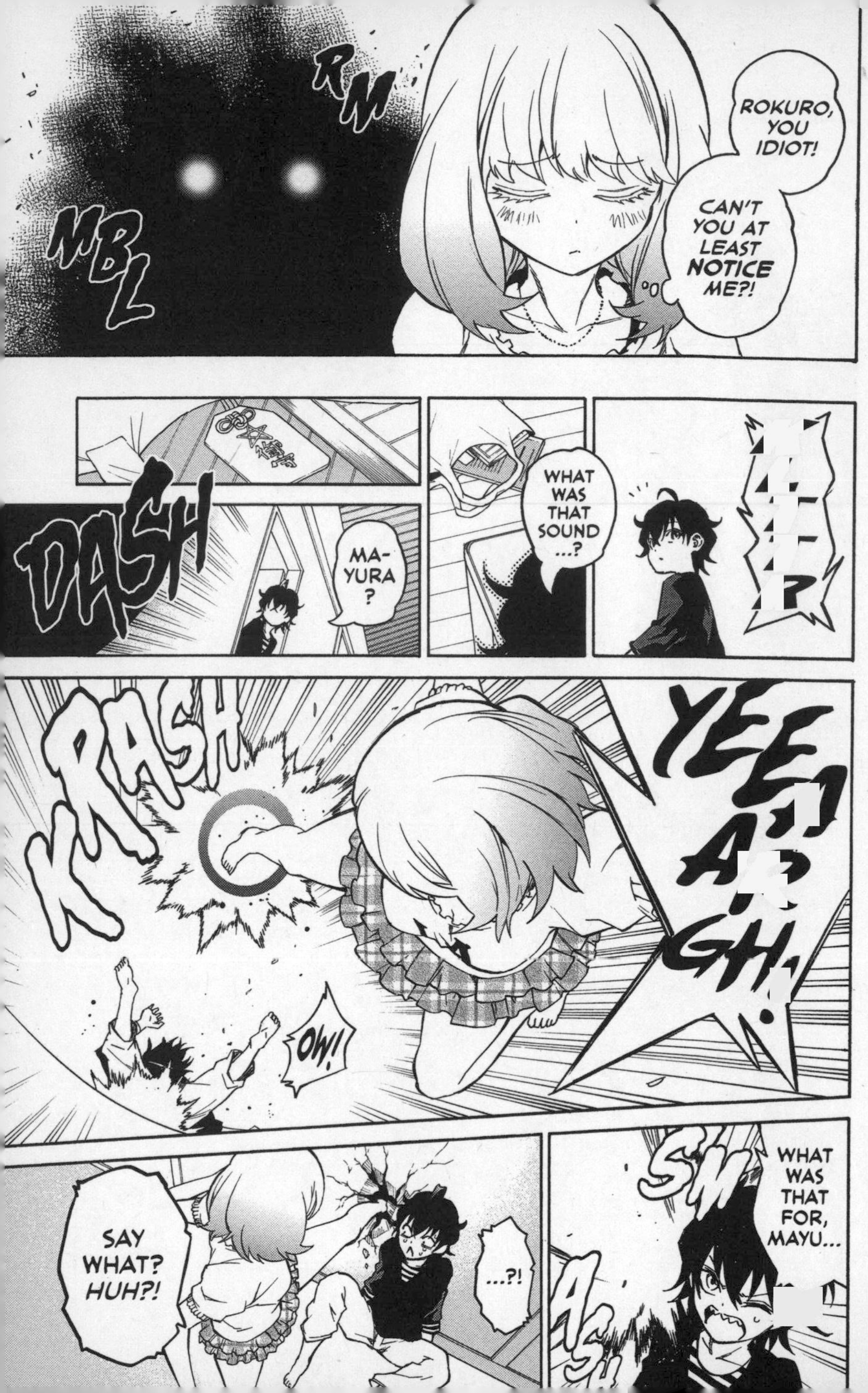
ROKURO, YOU IDIOT!
CAN'T YOU AT LEAST NOTICE ME?!
RM
MBL
WHAT WAS THAT SOUND ...?
MA-YURA ?
DASH
KRASH
OW!
WHAT WAS THAT FOR, MAYU...
...?!
SAY WHAT? HUH?!

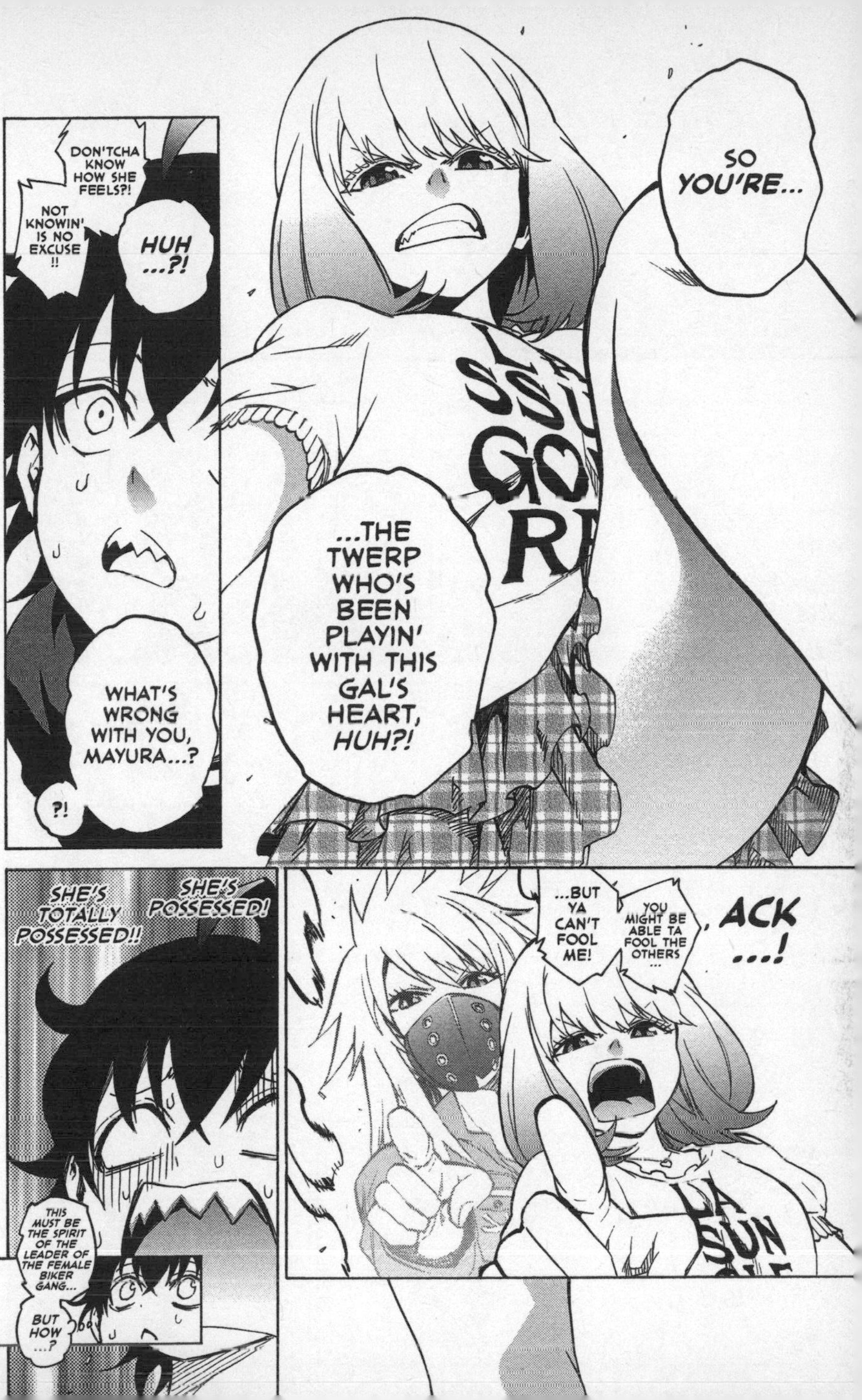
SO YOU'RE...
...THE TWERP WHO'S BEEN PLAYIN' WITH THIS GAL'S HEART, HUH?!
HUH ...?!
DON'TCHA KNOW HOW SHE FEELS?!
NOT KNOWIN' IS NO EXCUSE !!
WHAT'S WRONG WITH YOU, MAYURA...?
?!
ACK ...!
YOU MIGHT BE ABLE TA FOOL THE OTHERS ...
...BUT YA CAN'T FOOL ME!
SHE'S POSSESSED!
SHE'S TOTALLY POSSESSED!!
THIS MUST BE THE SPIRIT OF THE LEADER OF THE FEMALE BIKER GANG...
BUT HOW ...?

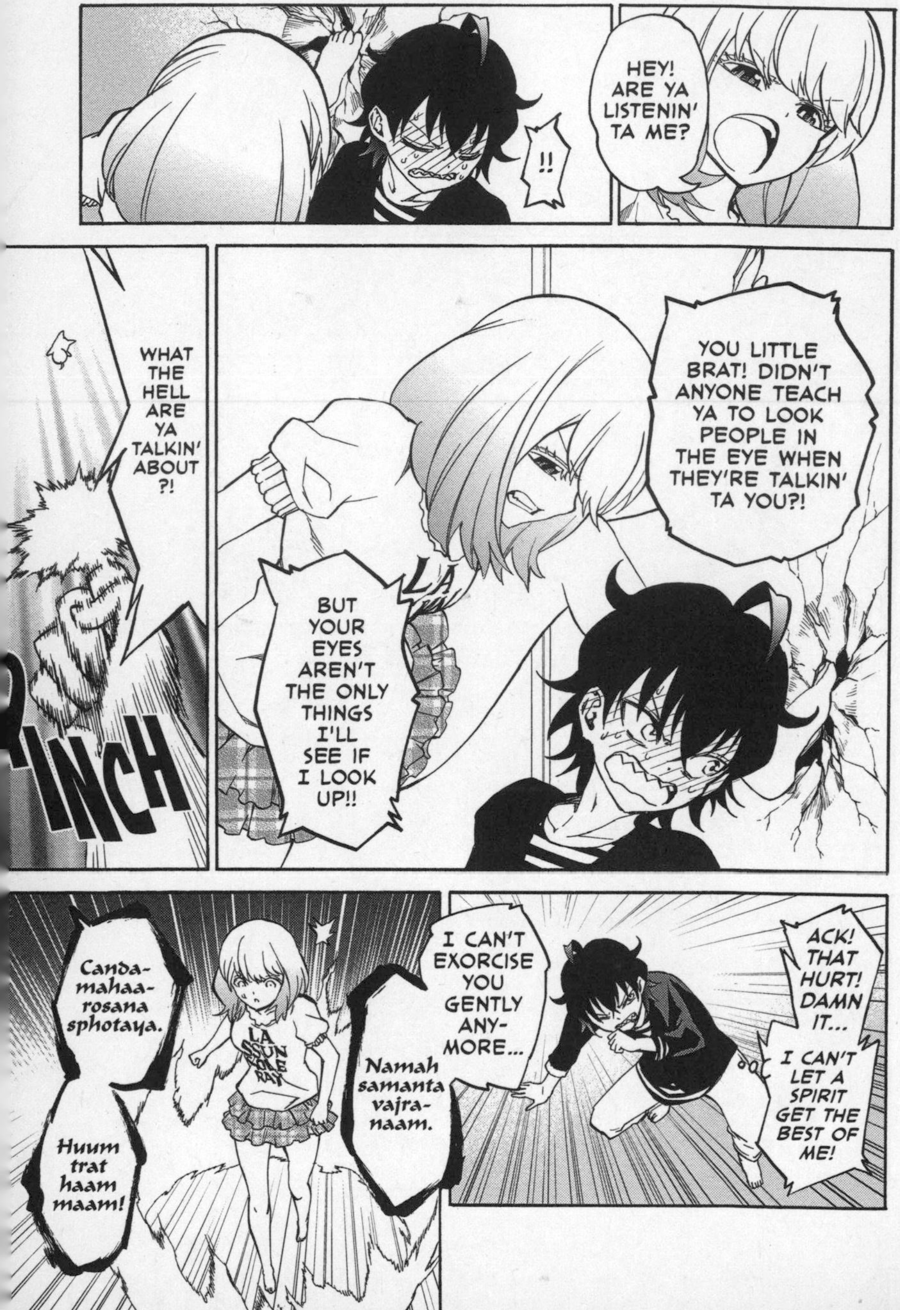
HEY! ARE YA LISTENIN' TA ME?
!!
YOU LITTLE BRAT! DIDN'T ANYONE TEACH YA TO LOOK PEOPLE IN THE EYE WHEN THEY'RE TALKIN' TA YOU?!
BUT YOUR EYES AREN'T THE ONLY THINGS I'LL SEE IF I LOOK UP!!
WHAT THE HELL ARE YA TALKIN' ABOUT?!
INCH
ACK! THAT HURT! DAMN IT...
I CAN'T LET A SPIRIT GET THE BEST OF ME!
I CAN'T EXORCISE YOU GENTLY ANYMORE...
Namah samanta vajra-naam.
Canda-mahaa-rosana sphotaya.
Huum trat haam maam!

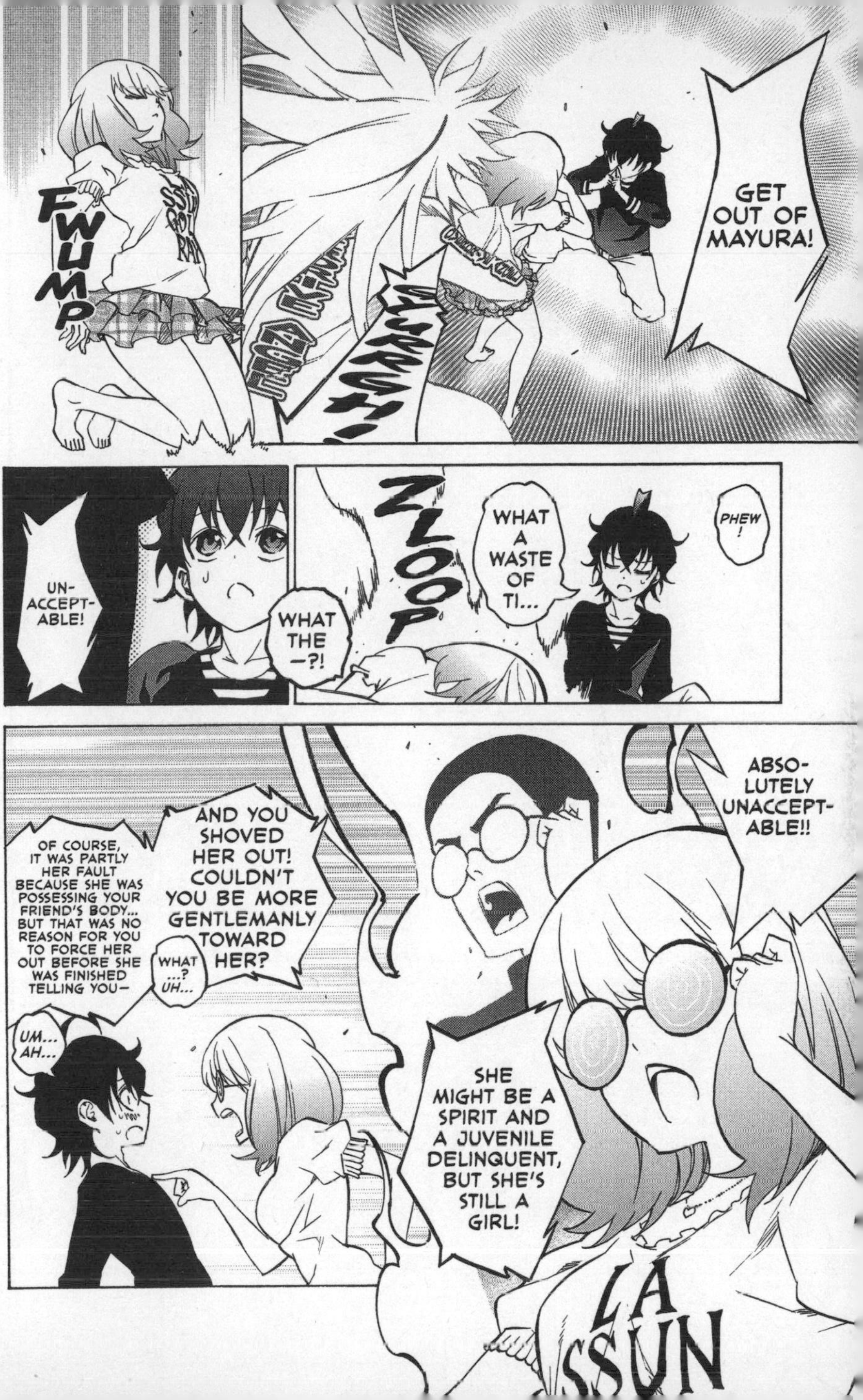
GET OUT OF MAYURA!
SWURRSH!!
FWUMP
PHEW!
WHAT A WASTE OF TI...
ZLOOP
WHAT THE—?!
UN-ACCEPT-ABLE!
ABSO-LUTELY UNACCEPT-ABLE!!
AND YOU SHOVED HER OUT! COULDN'T YOU BE MORE GENTLEMANLY TOWARD HER?
OF COURSE, IT WAS PARTLY HER FAULT BECAUSE SHE WAS POSSESSING YOUR FRIEND'S BODY... BUT THAT WAS NO REASON FOR YOU TO FORCE HER OUT BEFORE SHE WAS FINISHED TELLING YOU—
WHAT ...? UH...
SHE MIGHT BE A SPIRIT AND A JUVENILE DELINQUENT, BUT SHE'S STILL A GIRL!
UM... AH...
LA SSUN

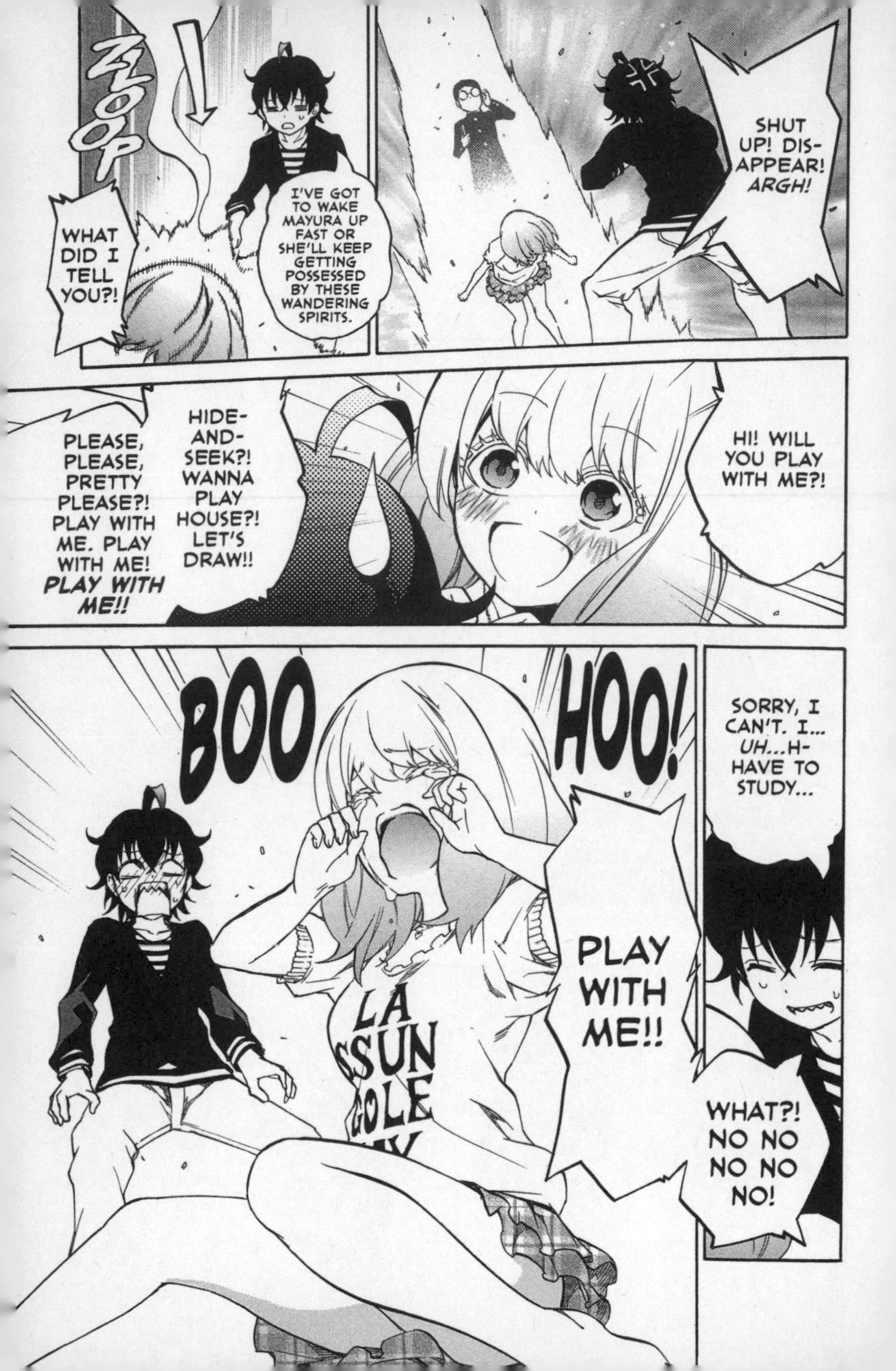
SHUT UP! DIS-APPEAR! *ARGH!*
I'VE GOT TO WAKE MAYURA UP FAST OR SHE'LL KEEP GETTING POSSESSED BY THESE WANDERING SPIRITS.
ZLOOP
WHAT DID I TELL YOU?!
HI! WILL YOU PLAY WITH ME?!
HIDE-AND-SEEK?! WANNA PLAY HOUSE?! LET'S DRAW!!
PLEASE, PLEASE, PRETTY PLEASE?! PLAY WITH ME. PLAY WITH ME! ***PLAY WITH ME!!***
SORRY, I CAN'T. I... *UH*...H-HAVE TO STUDY...
WHAT?! NO NO NO NO NO!
BOO HOO!
PLAY WITH ME!!

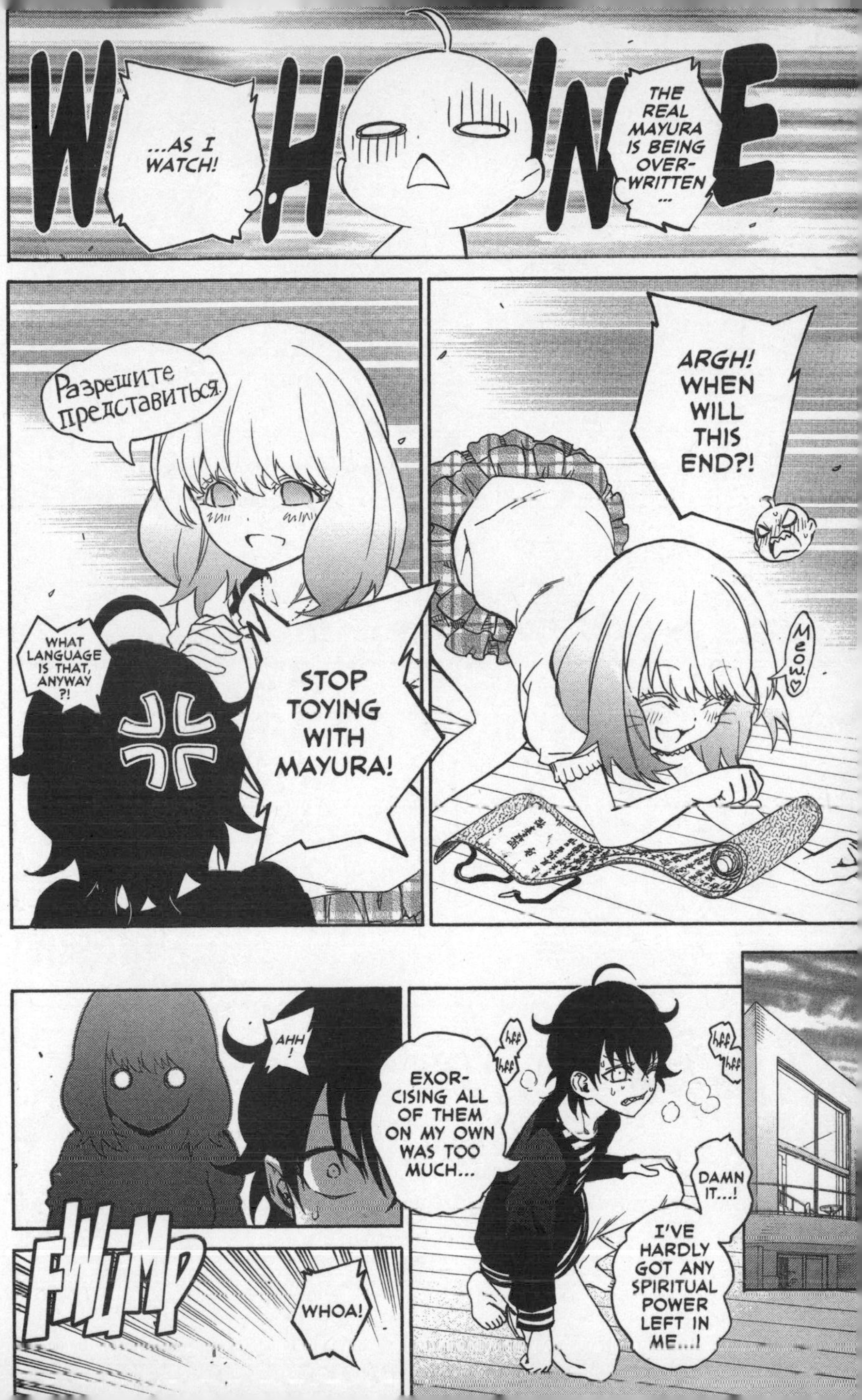
THE REAL MAYURA IS BEING OVER-WRITTEN...
...AS I WATCH!
ARGH! WHEN WILL THIS END?!
MEOW.♡
Разрешите представиться.
STOP TOYING WITH MAYURA!
WHAT LANGUAGE IS THAT, ANYWAY?!
hff hff
hff hff
EXOR-CISING ALL OF THEM ON MY OWN WAS TOO MUCH...
DAMN IT...!
I'VE HARDLY GOT ANY SPIRITUAL POWER LEFT IN ME...!
AHH!
FWUMP
WHOA!

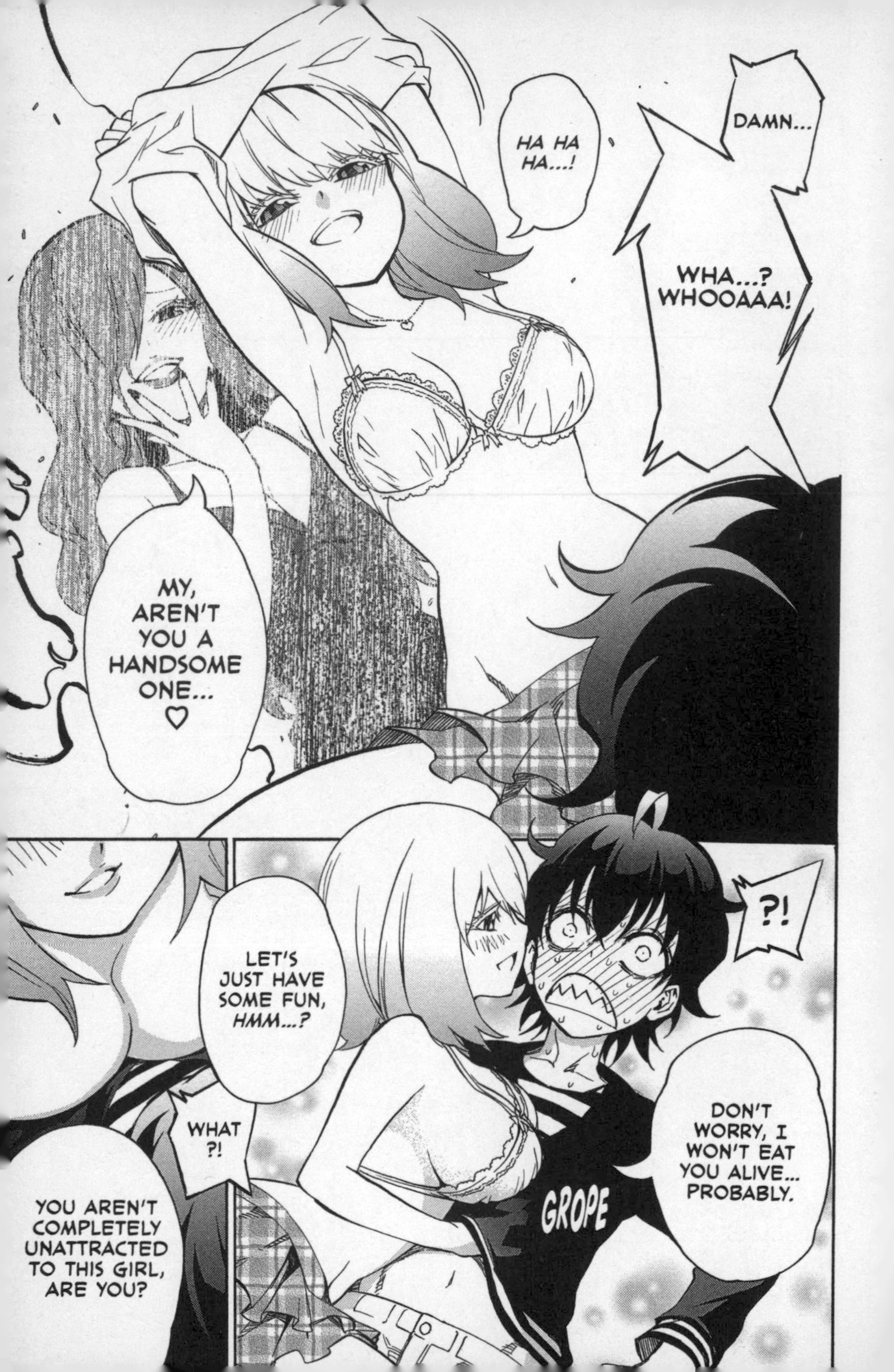

DAMN...
HA HA HA...!
WHA...? WHOOAAA!
MY, AREN'T YOU A HANDSOME ONE... ♡
?!
LET'S JUST HAVE SOME FUN, *HMM...?*
DON'T WORRY, I WON'T EAT YOU ALIVE... PROBABLY.
GROPE
WHAT ?!
YOU AREN'T COMPLETELY UNATTRACTED TO THIS GIRL, ARE YOU?

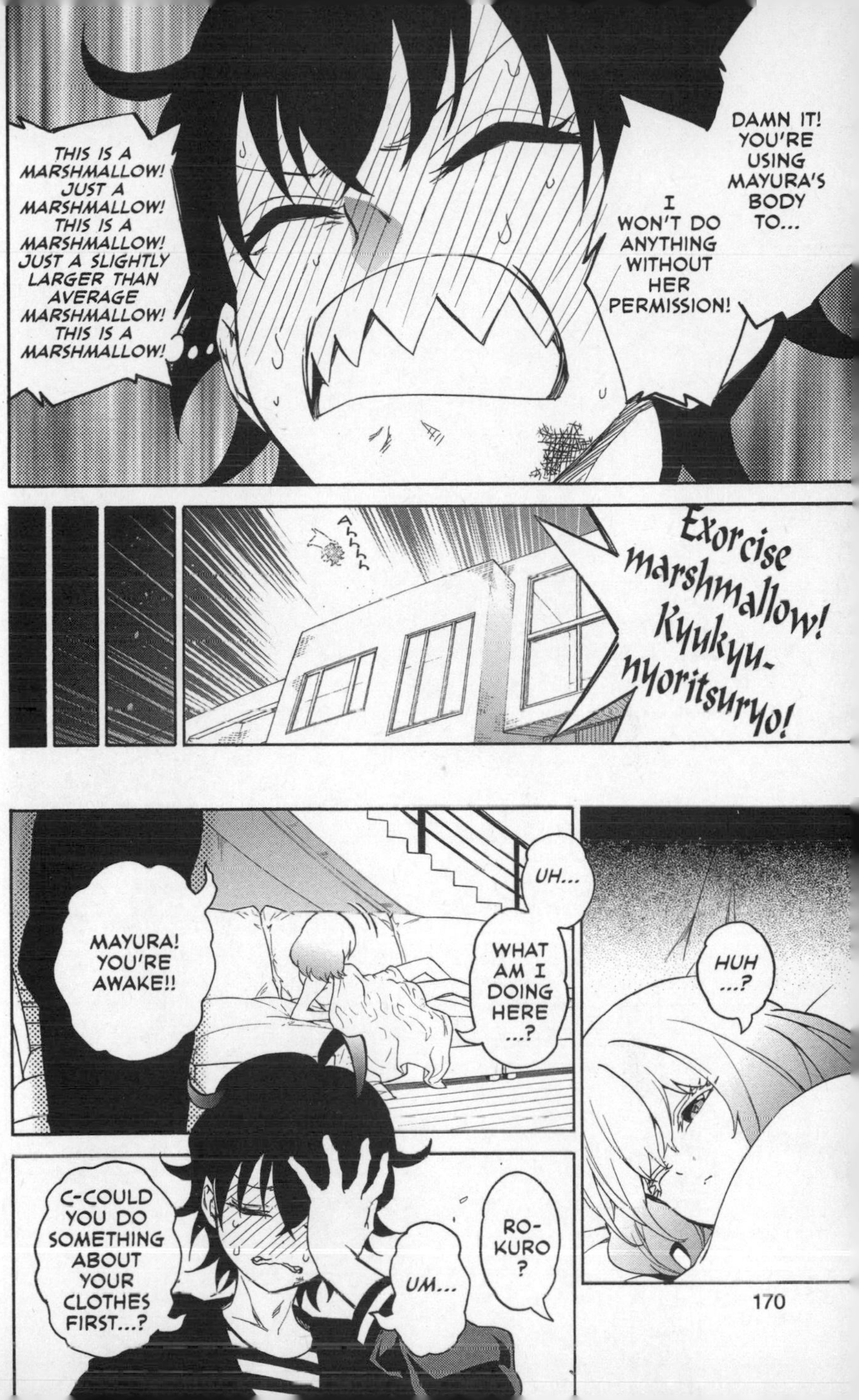
DAMN IT! YOU'RE USING MAYURA'S BODY TO...
I WON'T DO ANYTHING WITHOUT HER PERMISSION!
THIS IS A MARSHMALLOW! JUST A MARSHMALLOW! THIS IS A MARSHMALLOW! JUST A SLIGHTLY LARGER THAN AVERAGE MARSHMALLOW! THIS IS A MARSHMALLOW!
Exorcise marshmallow! Kyukyu-nyoritsuryo!
Ahhhh
HUH ...?
UH...
WHAT AM I DOING HERE ...?
MAYURA! YOU'RE AWAKE!!
RO-KURO ?
UM...
C-COULD YOU DO SOMETHING ABOUT YOUR CLOTHES FIRST...?

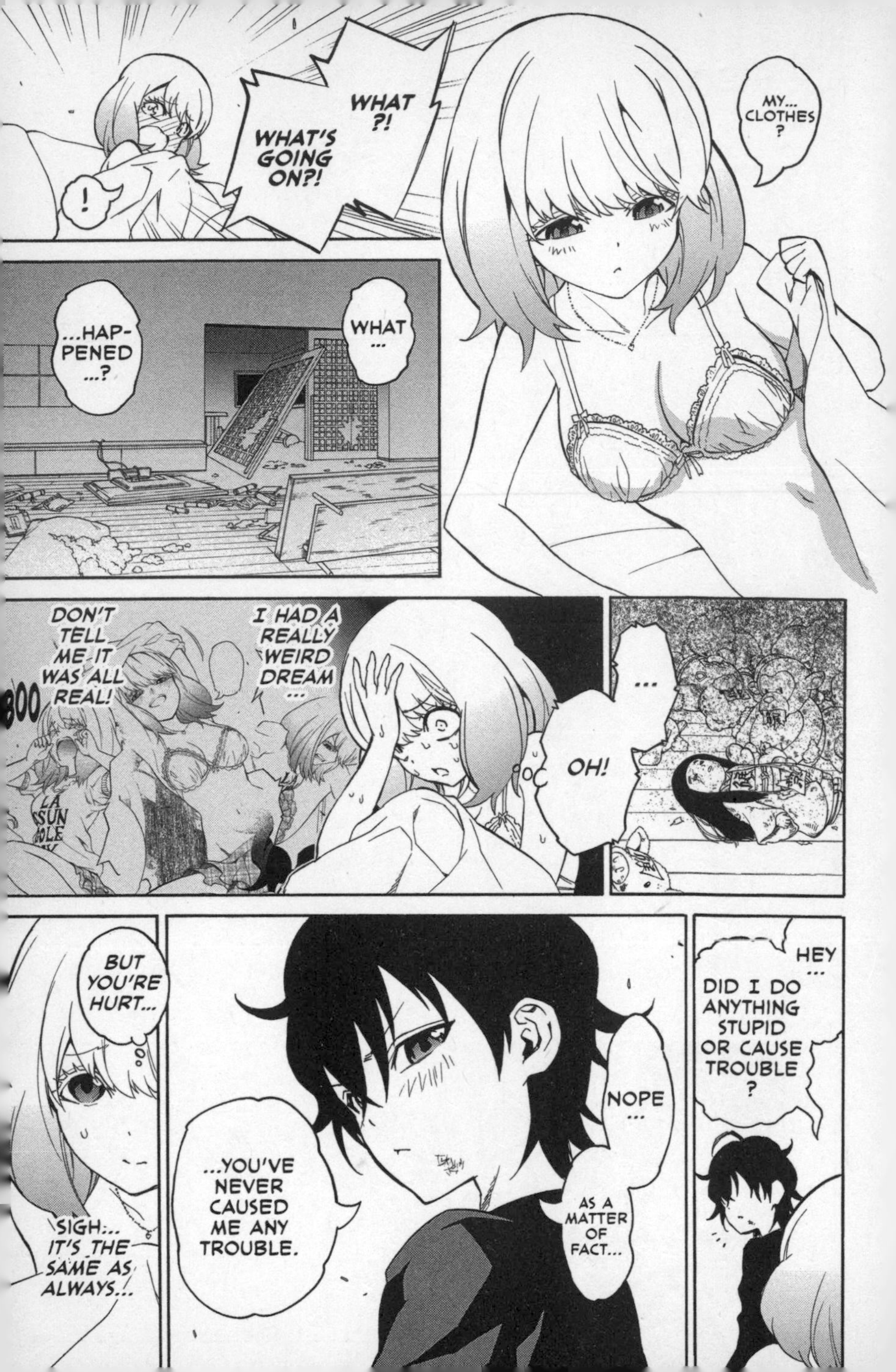
MY... CLOTHES ?
WHAT ?!
WHAT'S GOING ON?!
!
WHAT ...
...HAP-PENED ...?
...
OH!
I HAD A REALLY WEIRD DREAM ...
DON'T TELL ME IT WAS ALL REAL!
HEY ...
DID I DO ANYTHING STUPID OR CAUSE TROUBLE ?
NOPE ...
AS A MATTER OF FACT...
...YOU'VE NEVER CAUSED ME ANY TROUBLE.
BUT YOU'RE HURT...
SIGH... IT'S THE SAME AS ALWAYS...

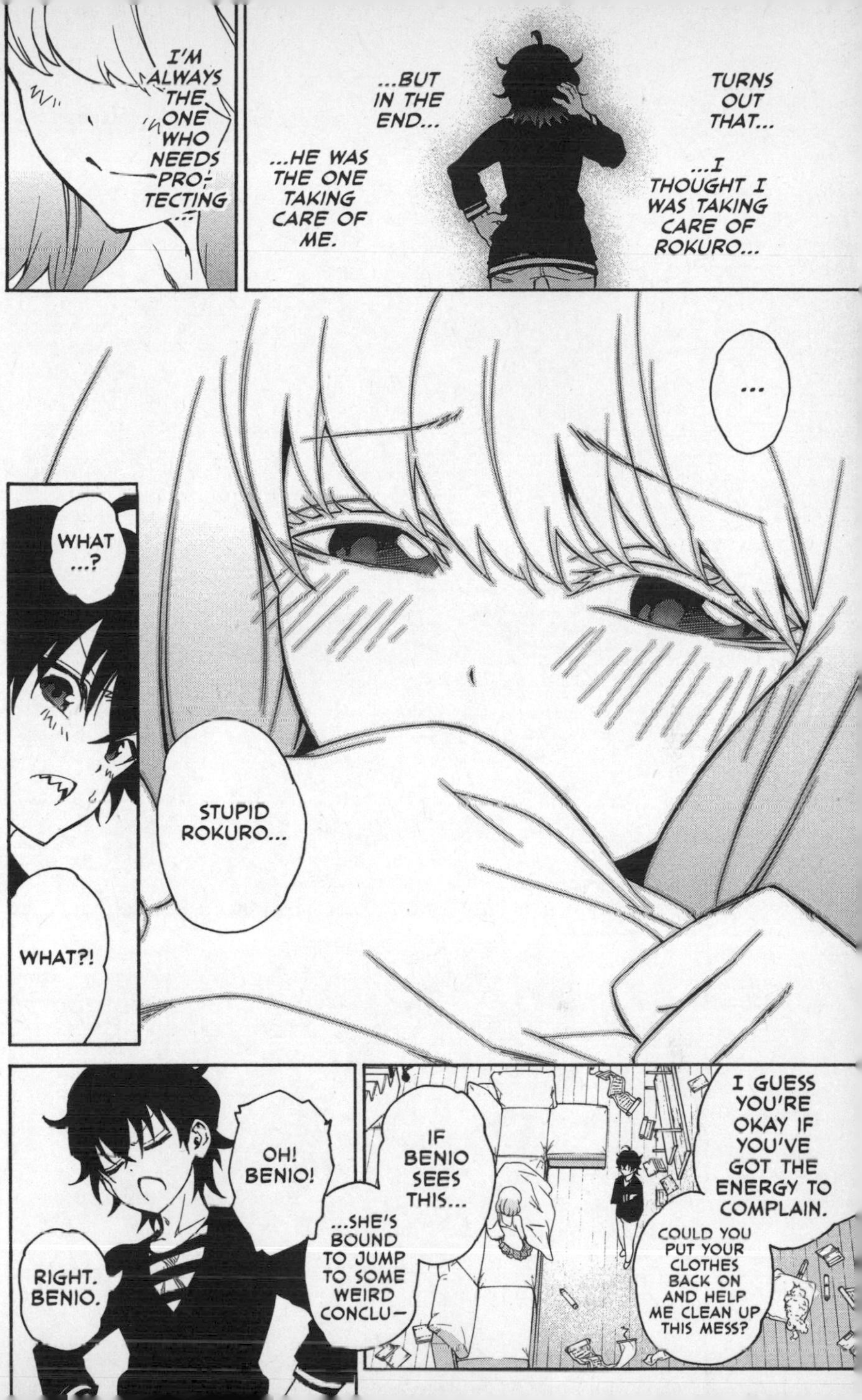
TURNS OUT THAT...
...I THOUGHT I WAS TAKING CARE OF ROKURO...
...BUT IN THE END...
...HE WAS THE ONE TAKING CARE OF ME.
I'M ALWAYS THE ONE WHO NEEDS PRO-TECTING...
...
STUPID ROKURO...
WHAT...?
WHAT?!
I GUESS YOU'RE OKAY IF YOU'VE GOT THE ENERGY TO COMPLAIN.
COULD YOU PUT YOUR CLOTHES BACK ON AND HELP ME CLEAN UP THIS MESS?
IF BENIO SEES THIS...
...SHE'S BOUND TO JUMP TO SOME WEIRD CONCLU—
OH! BENIO!
RIGHT. BENIO.

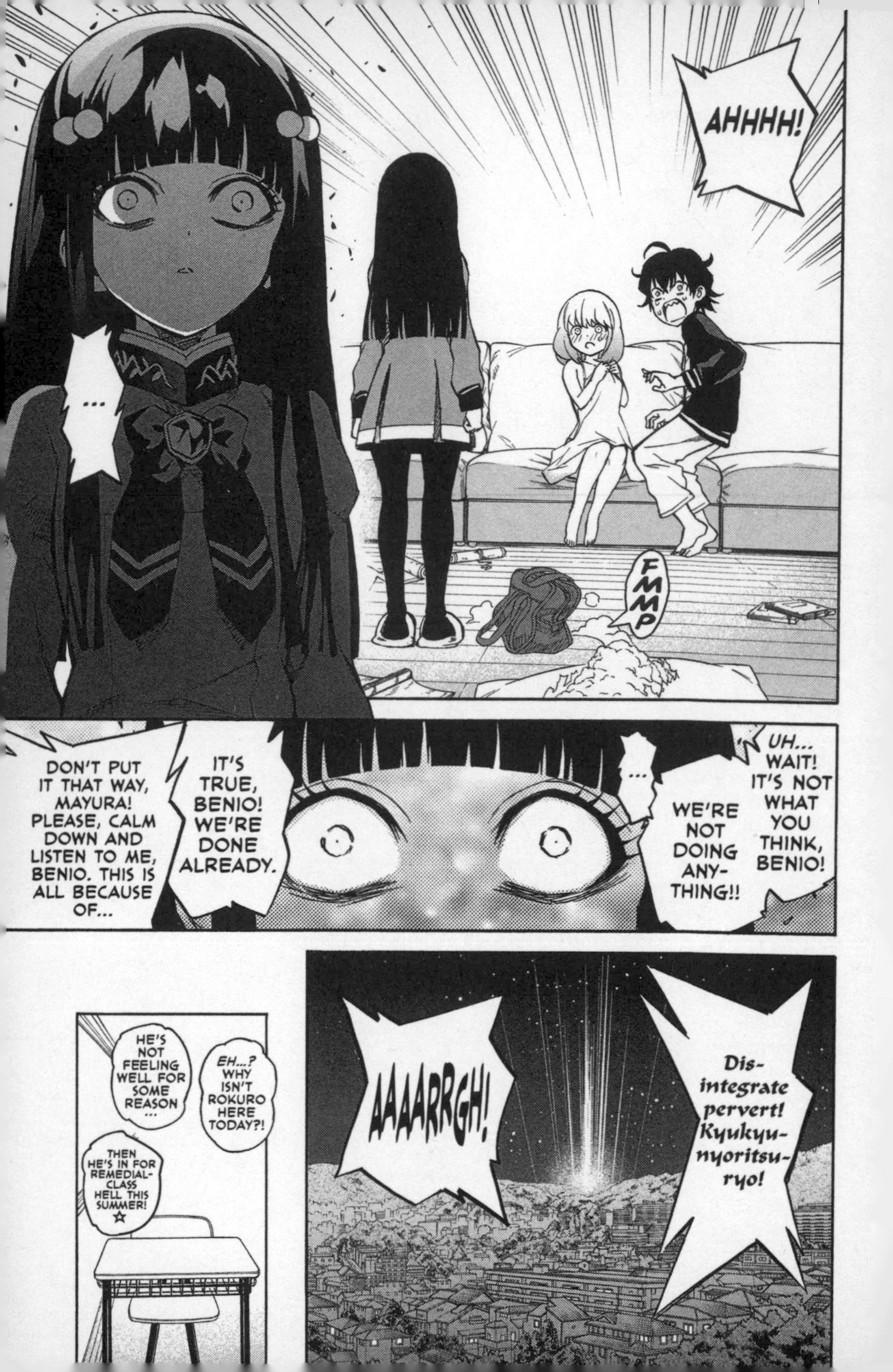
AHHHH!
FMMP
...
UH... WAIT! IT'S NOT WHAT YOU THINK, BENIO!
WE'RE NOT DOING ANY-THING!!
...
IT'S TRUE, BENIO! WE'RE DONE ALREADY.
DON'T PUT IT THAT WAY, MAYURA! PLEASE, CALM DOWN AND LISTEN TO ME, BENIO. THIS IS ALL BECAUSE OF...
Dis-integrate pervert! Kyukyu-nyoritsu-ryo!
AAAARRGH!
EH...? WHY ISN'T ROKURO HERE TODAY?!
HE'S NOT FEELING WELL FOR SOME REASON...
THEN HE'S IN FOR REMEDIAL-CLASS HELL THIS SUMMER! ☆

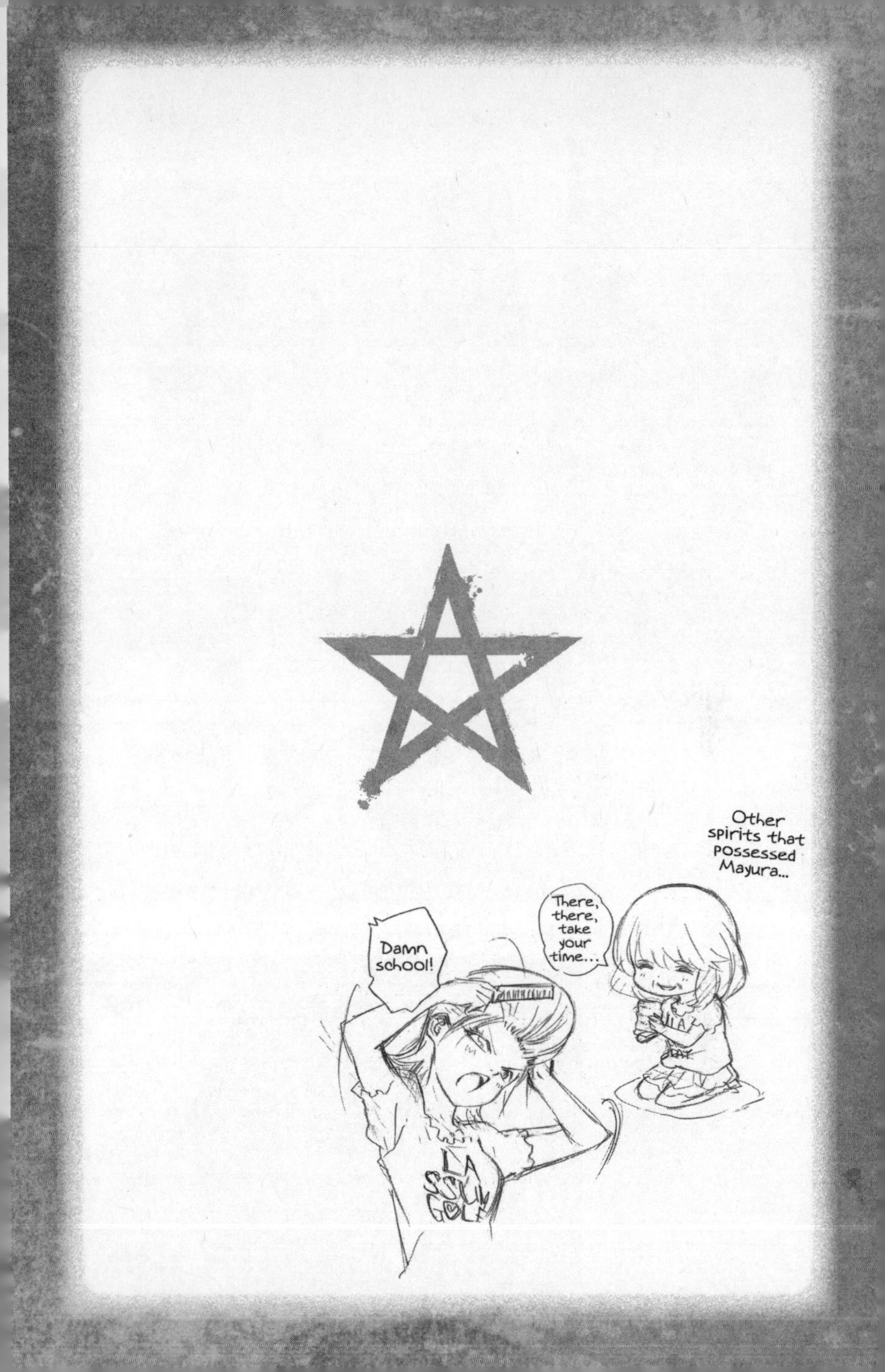
Other spirits that possessed Mayura...
There, there, take your time...
Damn school!

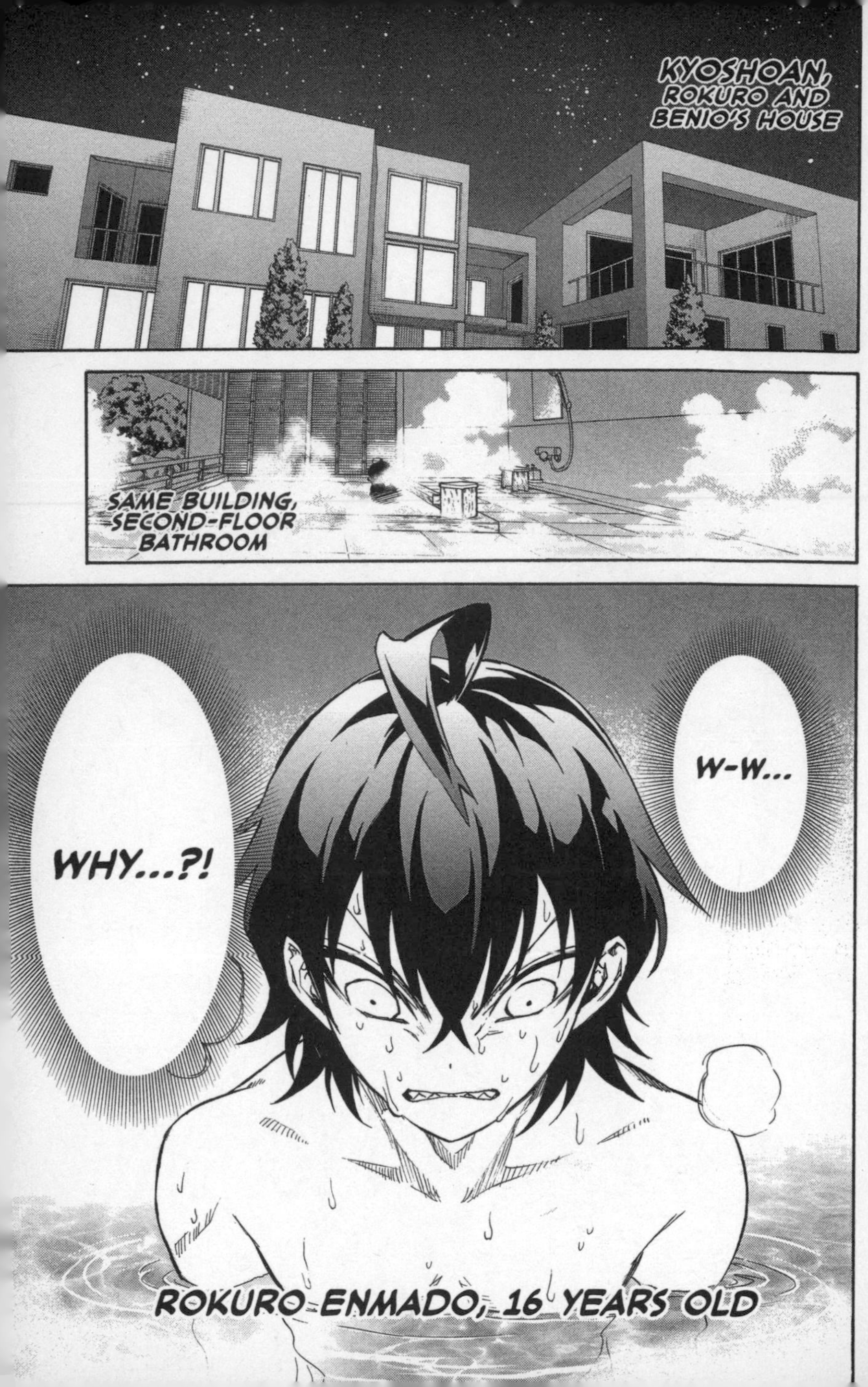
KYOSHOAN, ROKURO AND BENIO'S HOUSE
SAME BUILDING, SECOND-FLOOR BATHROOM
W-W...
WHY...?!
ROKURO ENMADO, 16 YEARS OLD

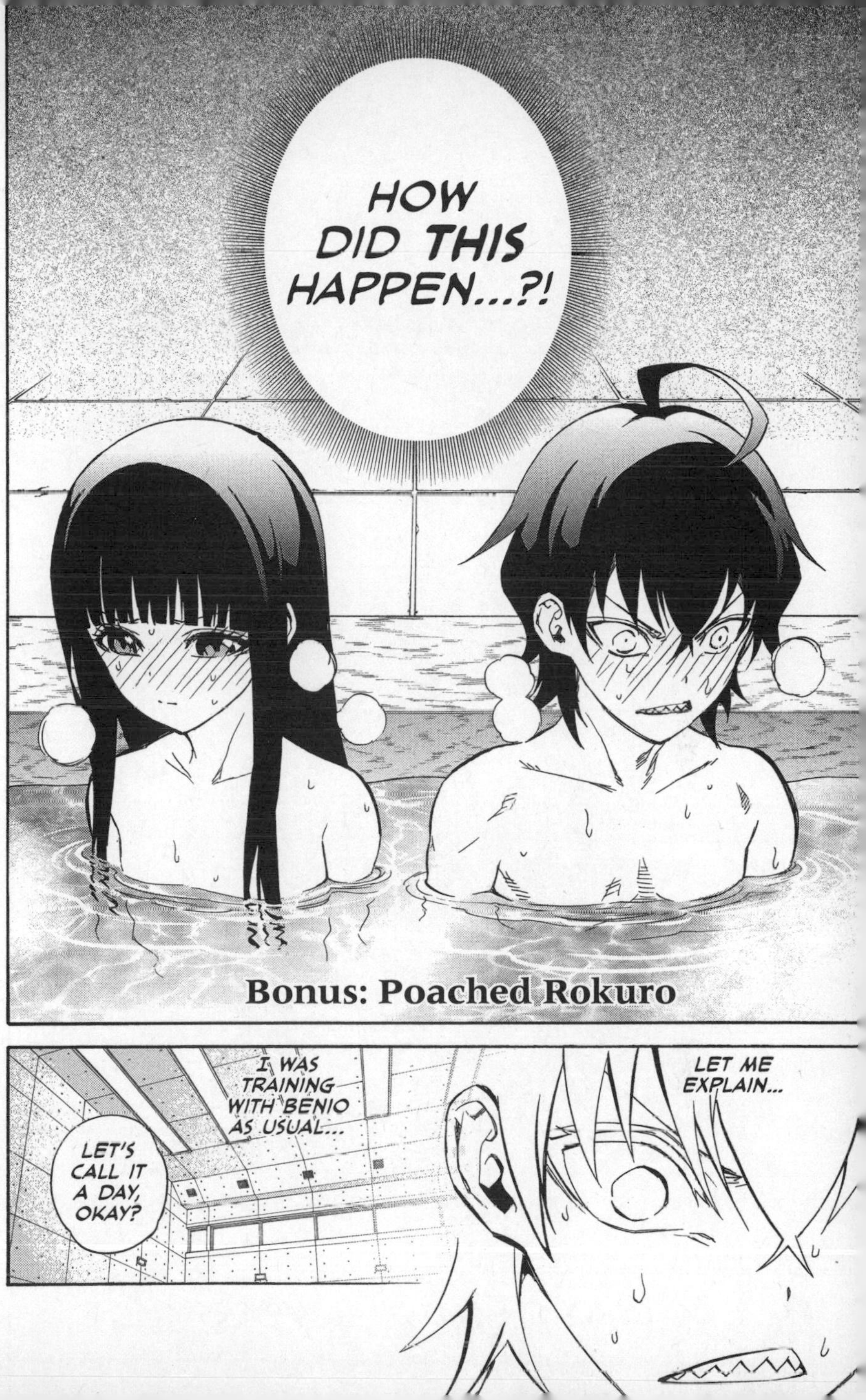
HOW DID THIS HAPPEN...?!
Bonus: Poached Rokuro
LET ME EXPLAIN...
I WAS TRAINING WITH BENIO AS USUAL...
LET'S CALL IT A DAY, OKAY?

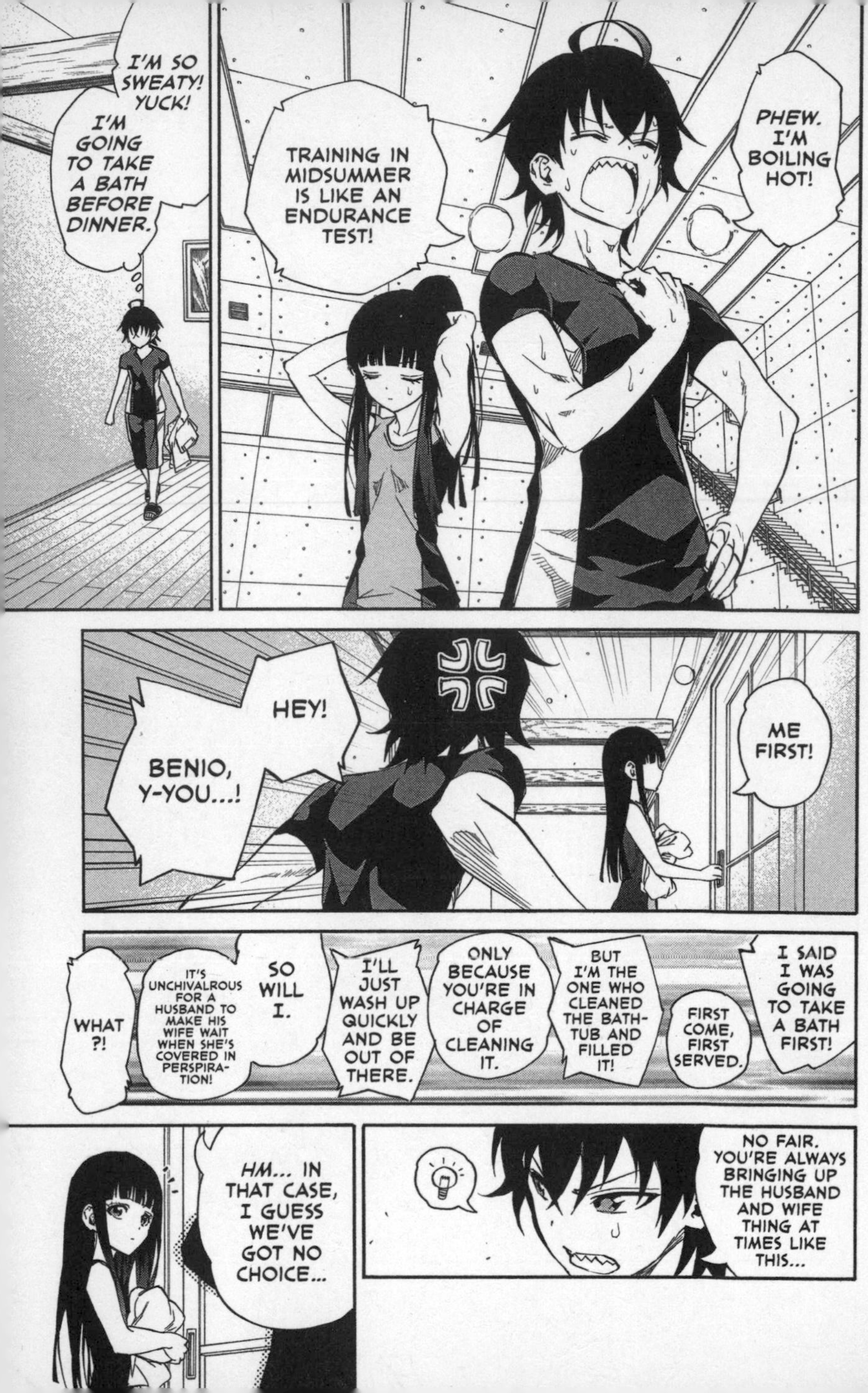
PHEW. I'M BOILING HOT!
TRAINING IN MIDSUMMER IS LIKE AN ENDURANCE TEST!
I'M SO SWEATY! YUCK!
I'M GOING TO TAKE A BATH BEFORE DINNER.
ME FIRST!
HEY!
BENIO, Y-YOU...!
I SAID I WAS GOING TO TAKE A BATH FIRST!
FIRST COME, FIRST SERVED.
BUT I'M THE ONE WHO CLEANED THE BATH-TUB AND FILLED IT!
ONLY BECAUSE YOU'RE IN CHARGE OF CLEANING IT.
I'LL JUST WASH UP QUICKLY AND BE OUT OF THERE.
SO WILL I.
IT'S UNCHIVALROUS FOR A HUSBAND TO MAKE HIS WIFE WAIT WHEN SHE'S COVERED IN PERSPIRA-TION!
WHAT?!
NO FAIR. YOU'RE ALWAYS BRINGING UP THE HUSBAND AND WIFE THING AT TIMES LIKE THIS...
HM... IN THAT CASE, I GUESS WE'VE GOT NO CHOICE...

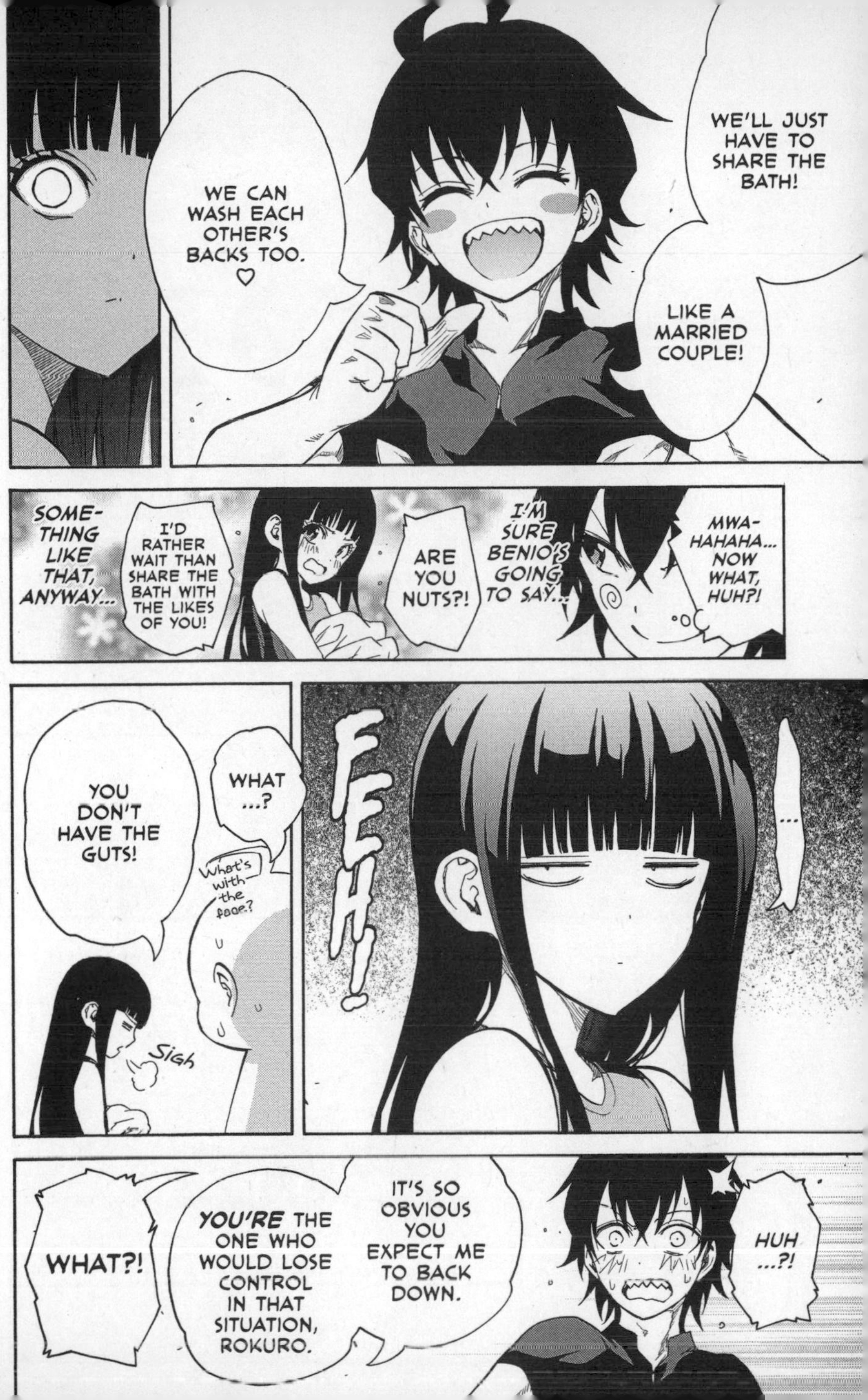
WE'LL JUST HAVE TO SHARE THE BATH!
LIKE A MARRIED COUPLE!
WE CAN WASH EACH OTHER'S BACKS TOO. ♡
MWA-HAHAHA... NOW WHAT, HUH?!
I'M SURE BENIO'S GOING TO SAY...
ARE YOU NUTS?!
I'D RATHER WAIT THAN SHARE THE BATH WITH THE LIKES OF YOU!
SOME-THING LIKE THAT, ANYWAY...
...
FEH!
WHAT ...?
What's with the face?
YOU DON'T HAVE THE GUTS!
Sigh
HUH ...?!
IT'S SO OBVIOUS YOU EXPECT ME TO BACK DOWN.
YOU'RE THE ONE WHO WOULD LOSE CONTROL IN THAT SITUATION, ROKURO.
WHAT?!

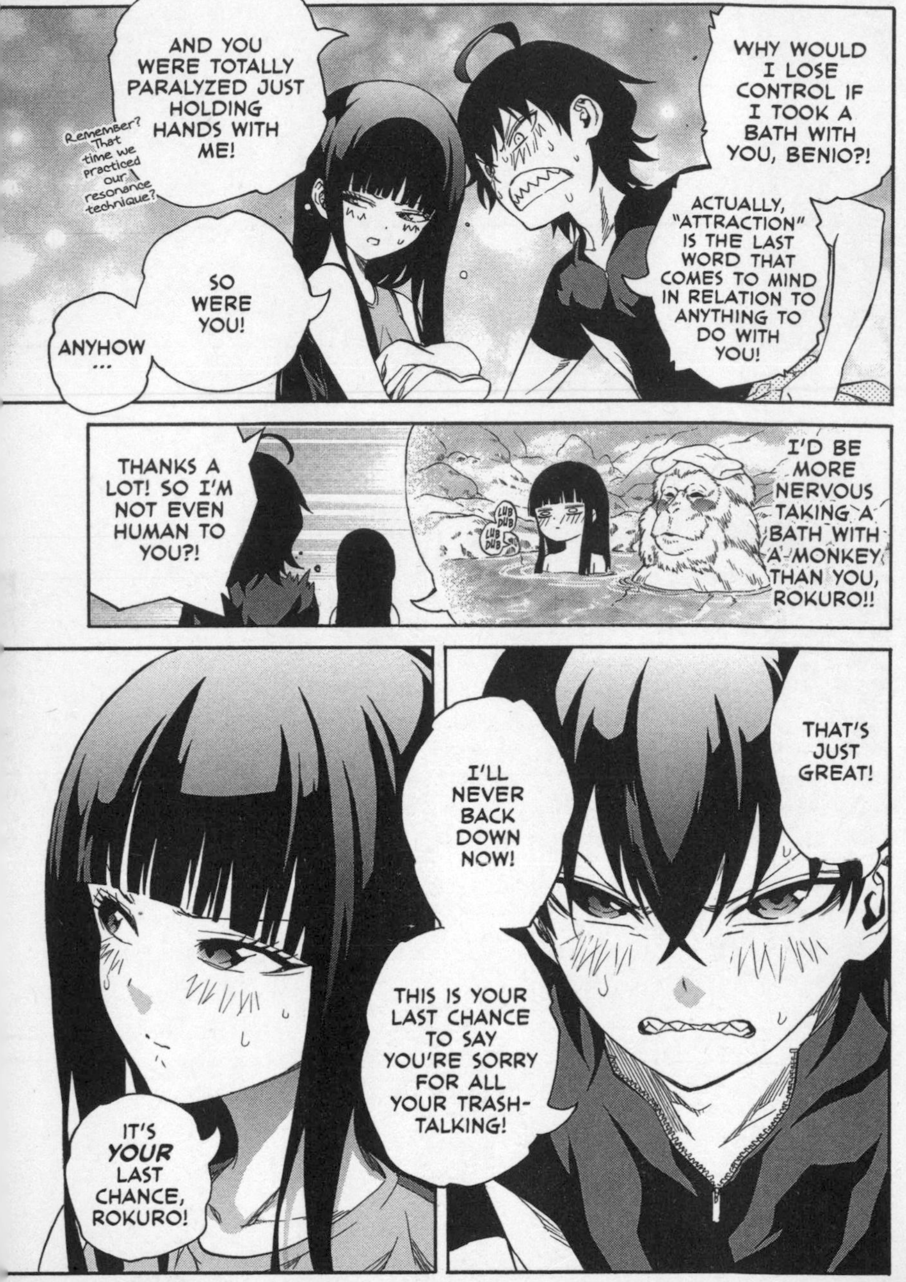
WHY WOULD I LOSE CONTROL IF I TOOK A BATH WITH YOU, BENIO?!
AND YOU WERE TOTALLY PARALYZED JUST HOLDING HANDS WITH ME!
Remember? That time we practiced our resonance technique?
ACTUALLY, "ATTRACTION" IS THE LAST WORD THAT COMES TO MIND IN RELATION TO ANYTHING TO DO WITH YOU!
SO WERE YOU!
ANYHOW...
I'D BE MORE NERVOUS TAKING A BATH WITH A MONKEY THAN YOU, ROKURO!!
LUB DUB
LUB DUB
THANKS A LOT! SO I'M NOT EVEN HUMAN TO YOU?!
THAT'S JUST GREAT!
I'LL NEVER BACK DOWN NOW!
THIS IS YOUR LAST CHANCE TO SAY YOU'RE SORRY FOR ALL YOUR TRASH-TALKING!
IT'S *YOUR* LAST CHANCE, ROKURO!

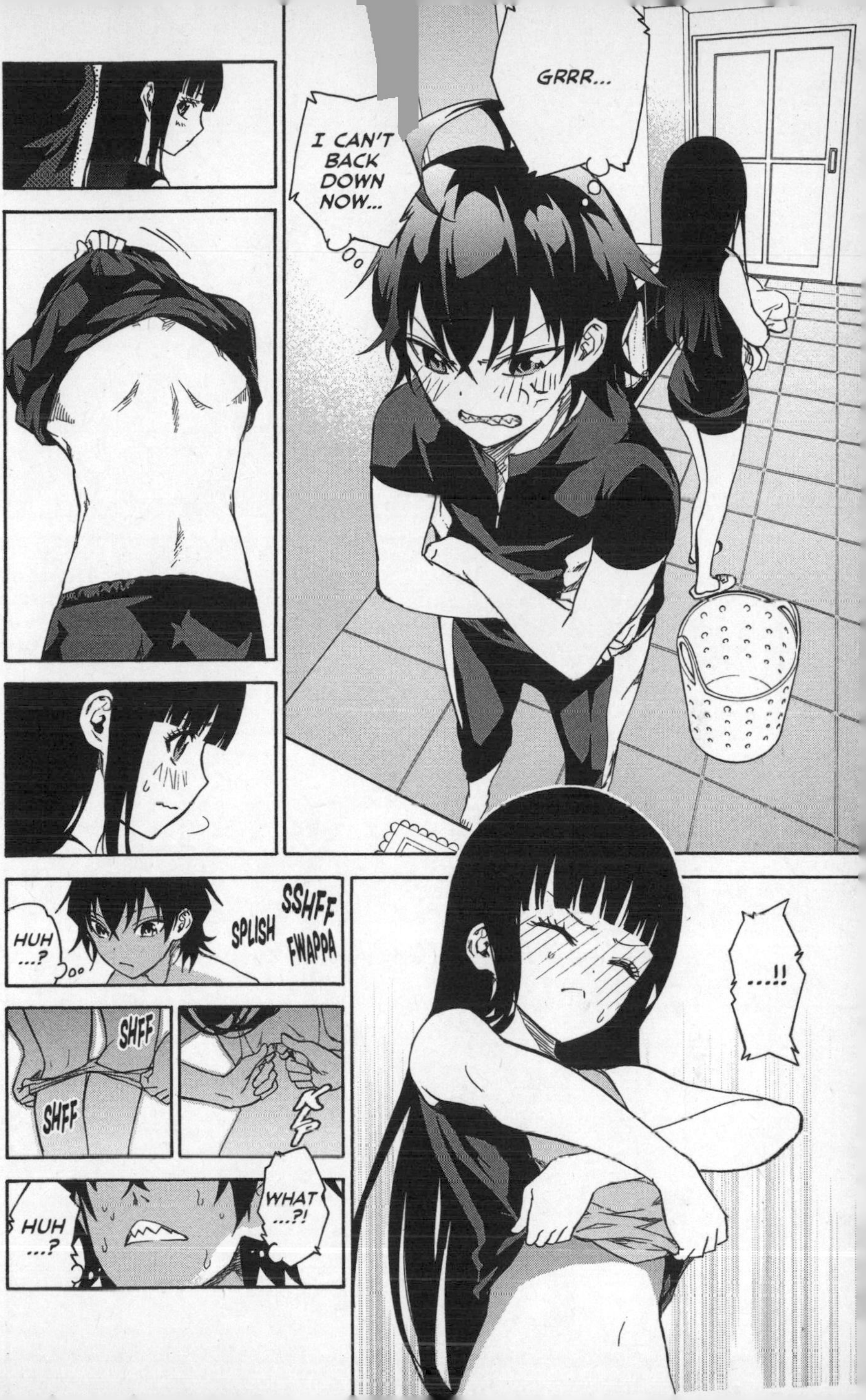
GRRR...
I CAN'T BACK DOWN NOW...
...!!
SSHFF
FWAPPA
SPLISH
HUH ...?
SHFF
SHFF
WHAT ...?!
HUH ...?

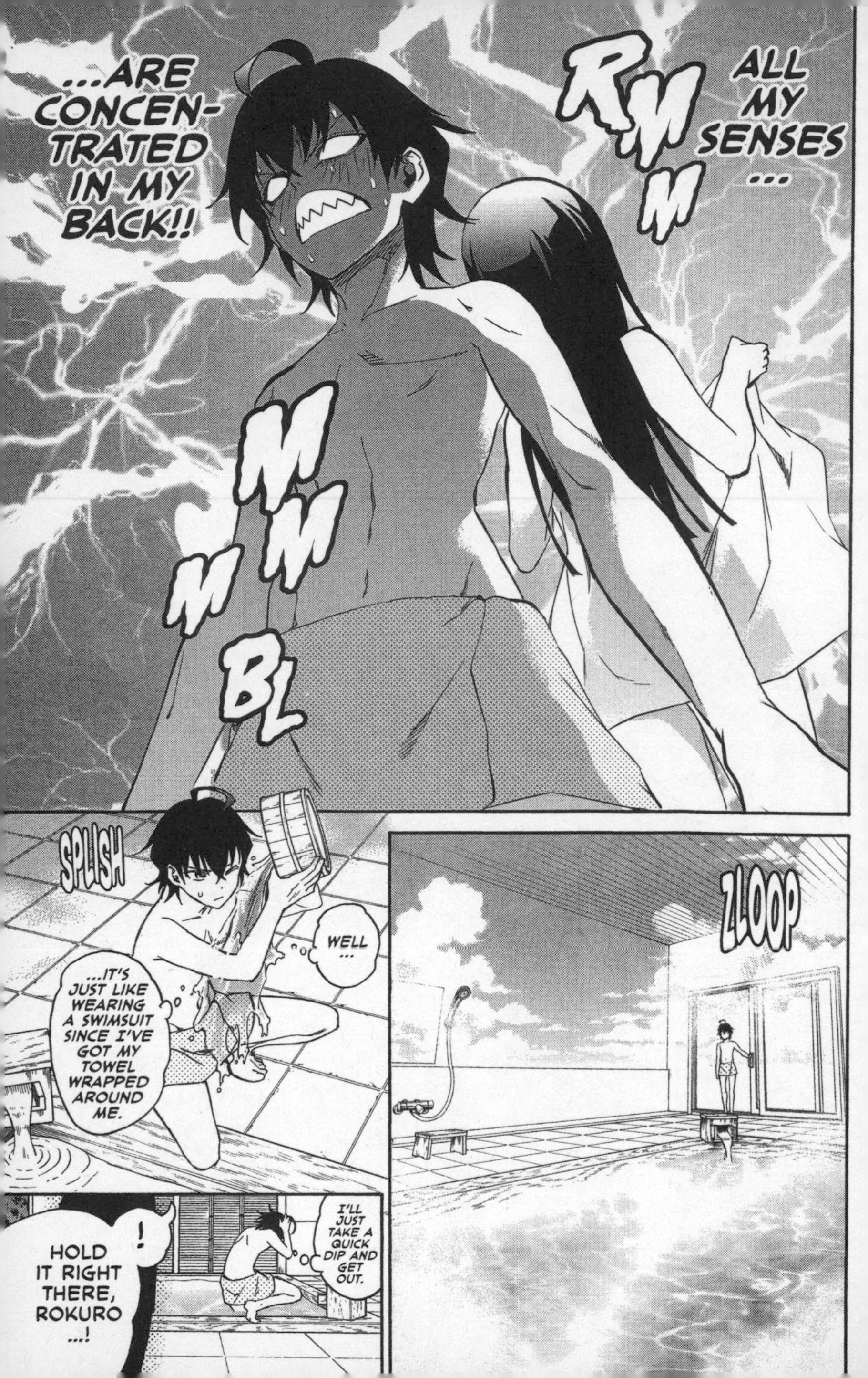
ALL MY SENSES ...
RMM
...ARE CONCEN-TRATED IN MY BACK!!
MMM
BL
ZLOOP
SPLISH
WELL ...
...IT'S JUST LIKE WEARING A SWIMSUIT SINCE I'VE GOT MY TOWEL WRAPPED AROUND ME.
I'LL JUST TAKE A QUICK DIP AND GET OUT.
!
HOLD IT RIGHT THERE, ROKURO ...!

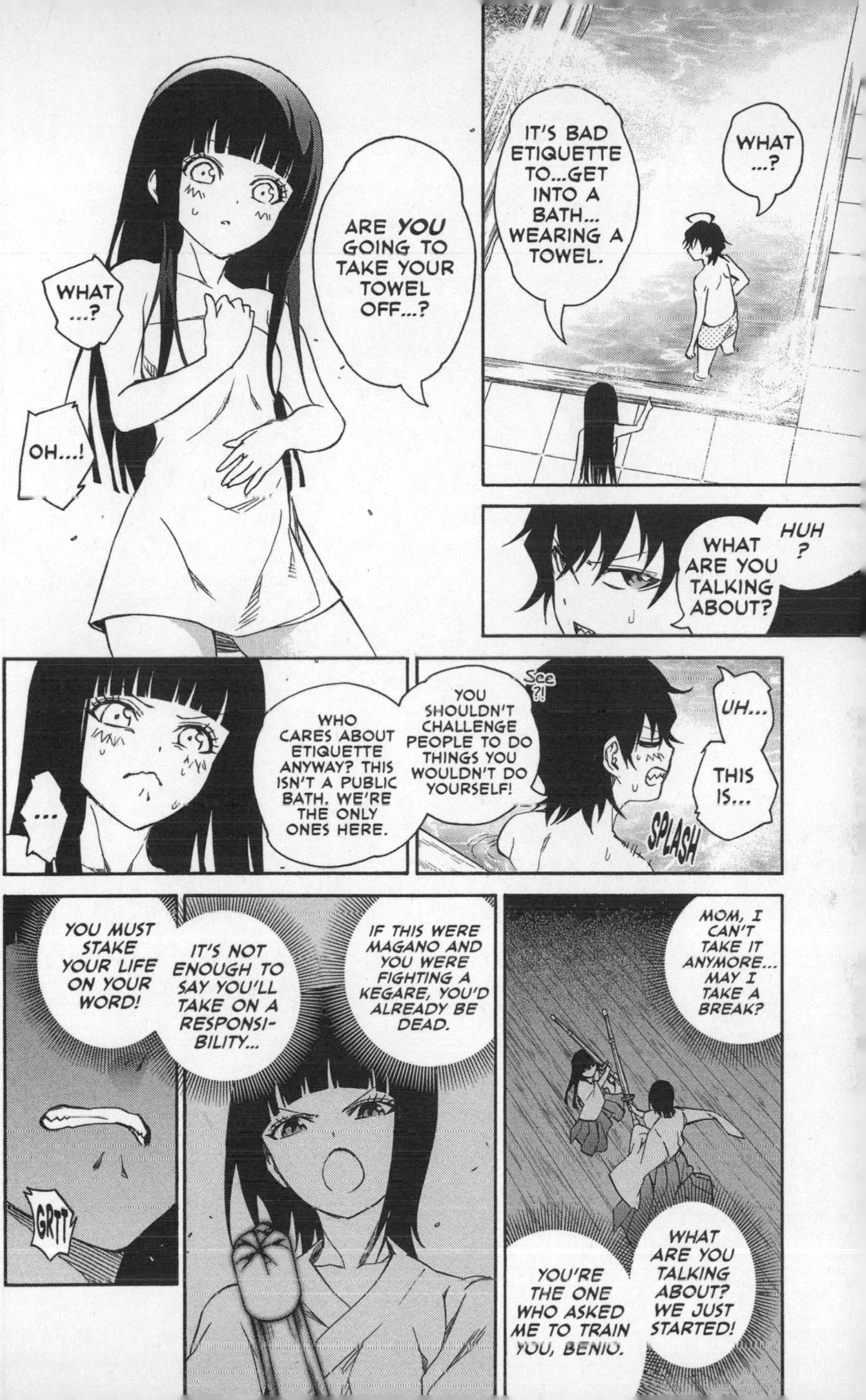
WHAT ...?
IT'S BAD ETIQUETTE TO...GET INTO A BATH... WEARING A TOWEL.
HUH ?
WHAT ARE YOU TALKING ABOUT?
ARE YOU GOING TO TAKE YOUR TOWEL OFF...?
WHAT ...?
OH...!
UH...
THIS IS...
SPLASH
See ?!
YOU SHOULDN'T CHALLENGE PEOPLE TO DO THINGS YOU WOULDN'T DO YOURSELF!
WHO CARES ABOUT ETIQUETTE ANYWAY? THIS ISN'T A PUBLIC BATH. WE'RE THE ONLY ONES HERE.
...
MOM, I CAN'T TAKE IT ANYMORE... MAY I TAKE A BREAK?
WHAT ARE YOU TALKING ABOUT? WE JUST STARTED!
YOU'RE THE ONE WHO ASKED ME TO TRAIN YOU, BENIO.
IF THIS WERE MAGANO AND YOU WERE FIGHTING A KEGARE, YOU'D ALREADY BE DEAD.
IT'S NOT ENOUGH TO SAY YOU'LL TAKE ON A RESPONSI-BILITY...
YOU MUST STAKE YOUR LIFE ON YOUR WORD!
GRTT

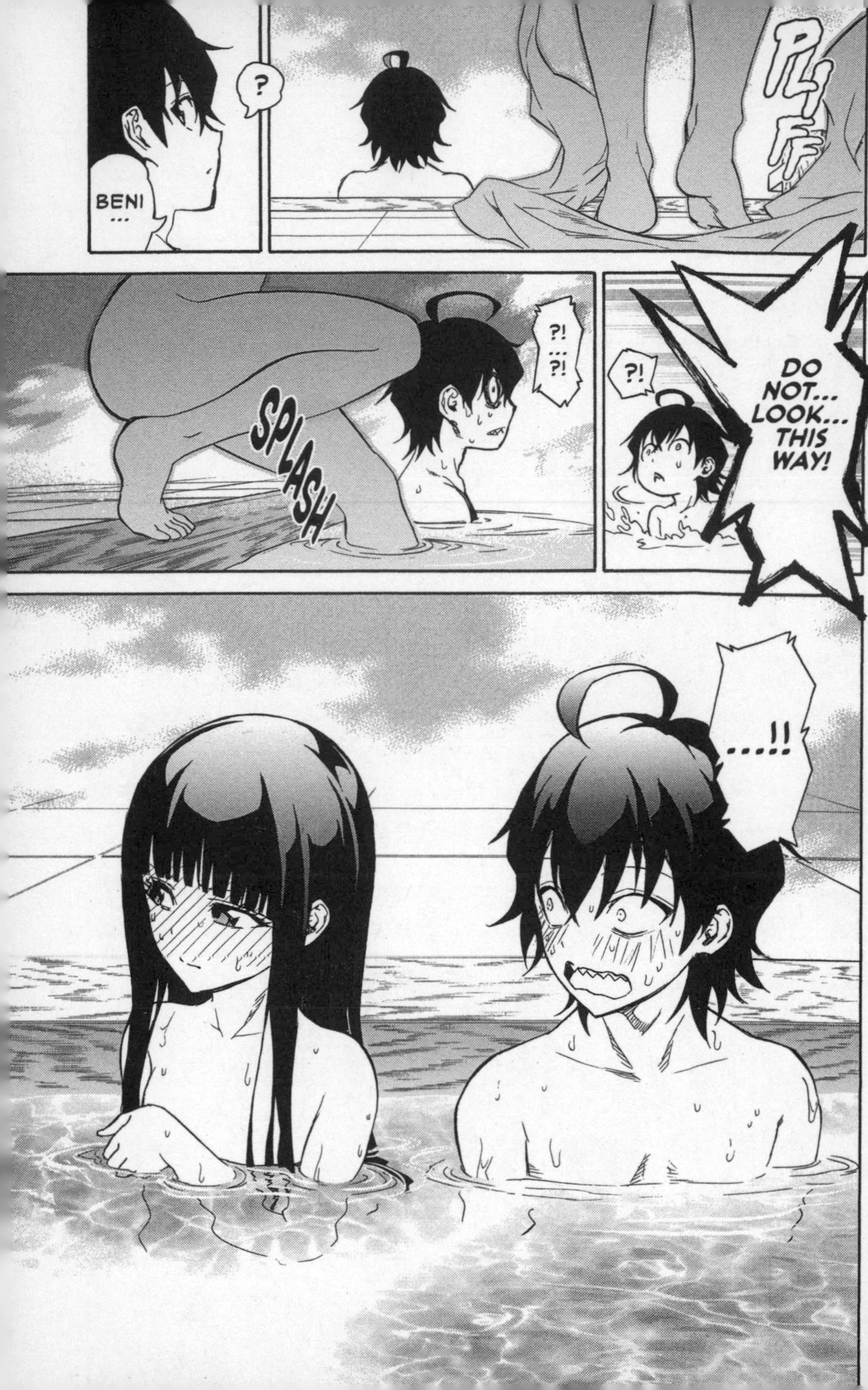
PLIFF
?
BENI...
DO NOT... LOOK... THIS WAY!
?!
?! ... ?!
SPLASH
...!!

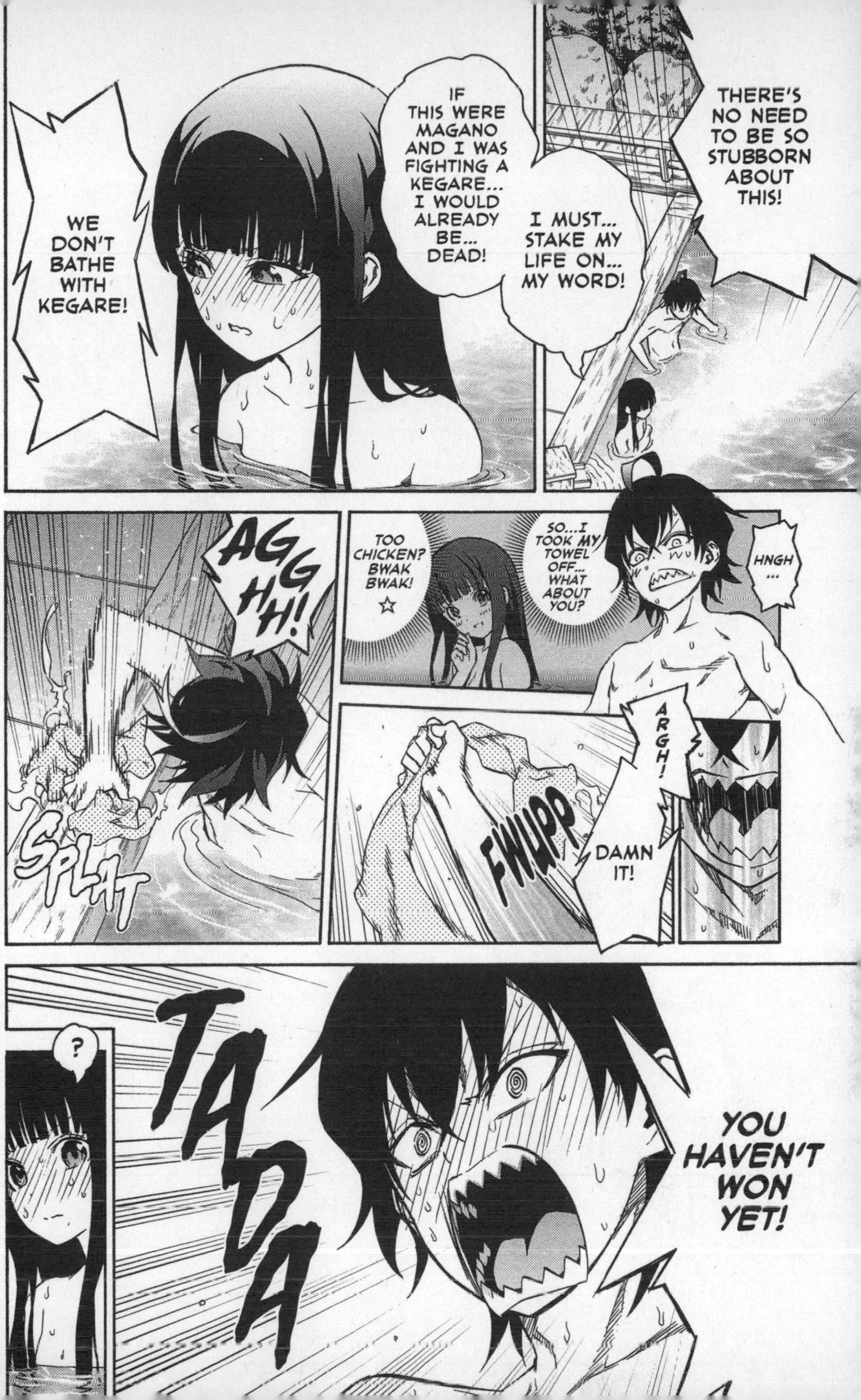
THERE'S NO NEED TO BE SO STUBBORN ABOUT THIS!
I MUST... STAKE MY LIFE ON... MY WORD!
IF THIS WERE MAGANO AND I WAS FIGHTING A KEGARE... I WOULD ALREADY BE... DEAD!
WE DON'T BATHE WITH KEGARE!
HNGH...
SO...I TOOK MY TOWEL OFF... WHAT ABOUT YOU?
TOO CHICKEN? BWAK BWAK! ☆
ARGH!
DAMN IT!
FWUPP
AGGHH!
SPLAT
YOU HAVEN'T WON YET!
TADA
?

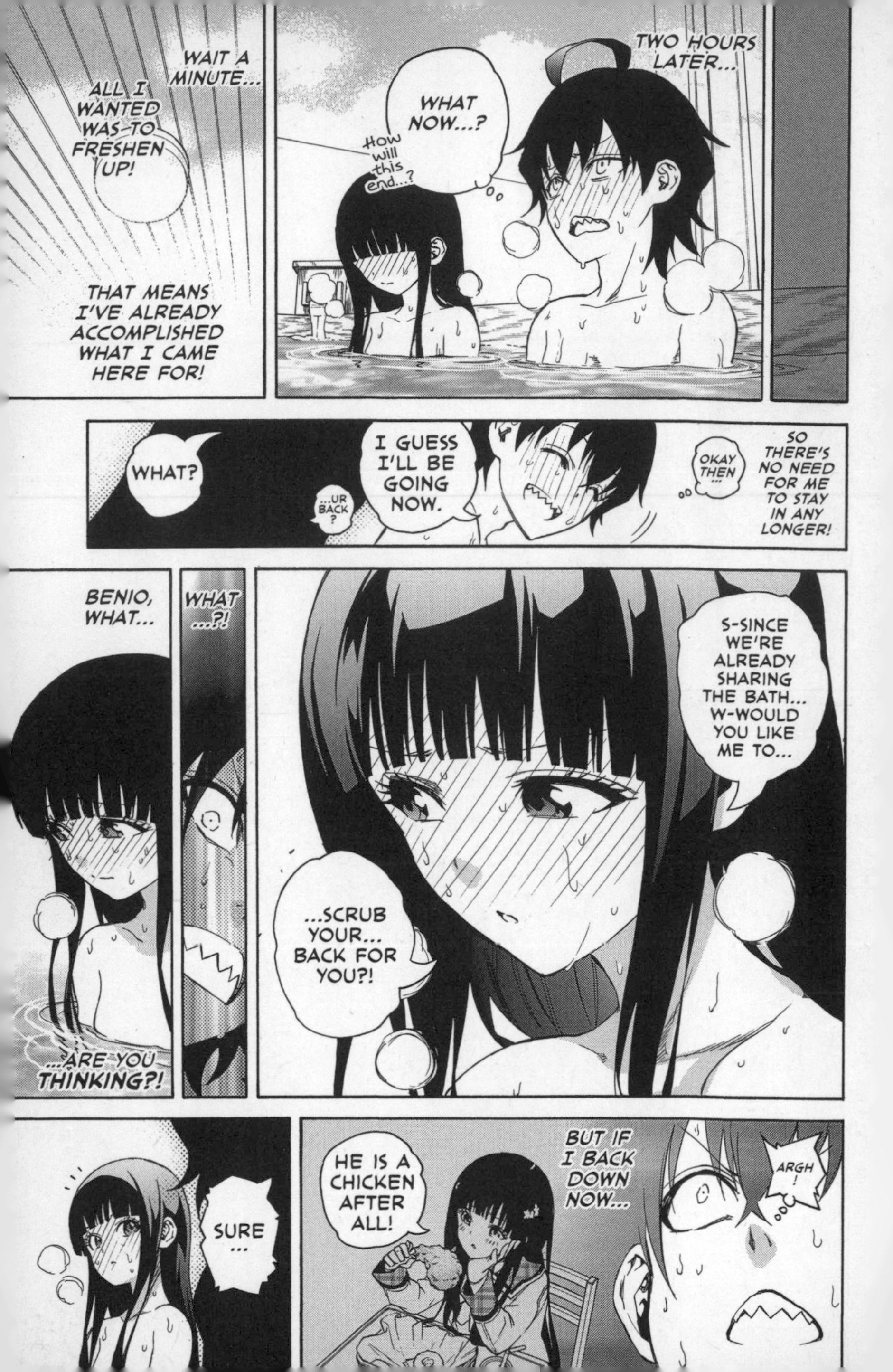
TWO HOURS LATER...
WHAT NOW...?
How will this end...?
WAIT A MINUTE...
ALL I WANTED WAS TO FRESHEN UP!
THAT MEANS I'VE ALREADY ACCOMPLISHED WHAT I CAME HERE FOR!
SO THERE'S NO NEED FOR ME TO STAY IN ANY LONGER!
OKAY THEN ...
I GUESS I'LL BE GOING NOW.
...UR BACK ?
WHAT?
S-SINCE WE'RE ALREADY SHARING THE BATH... W-WOULD YOU LIKE ME TO...
...SCRUB YOUR... BACK FOR YOU?!
WHAT ...?!
BENIO, WHAT...
...ARE YOU THINKING?!
BUT IF I BACK DOWN NOW...
ARGH !
HE IS A CHICKEN AFTER ALL!
SURE ...

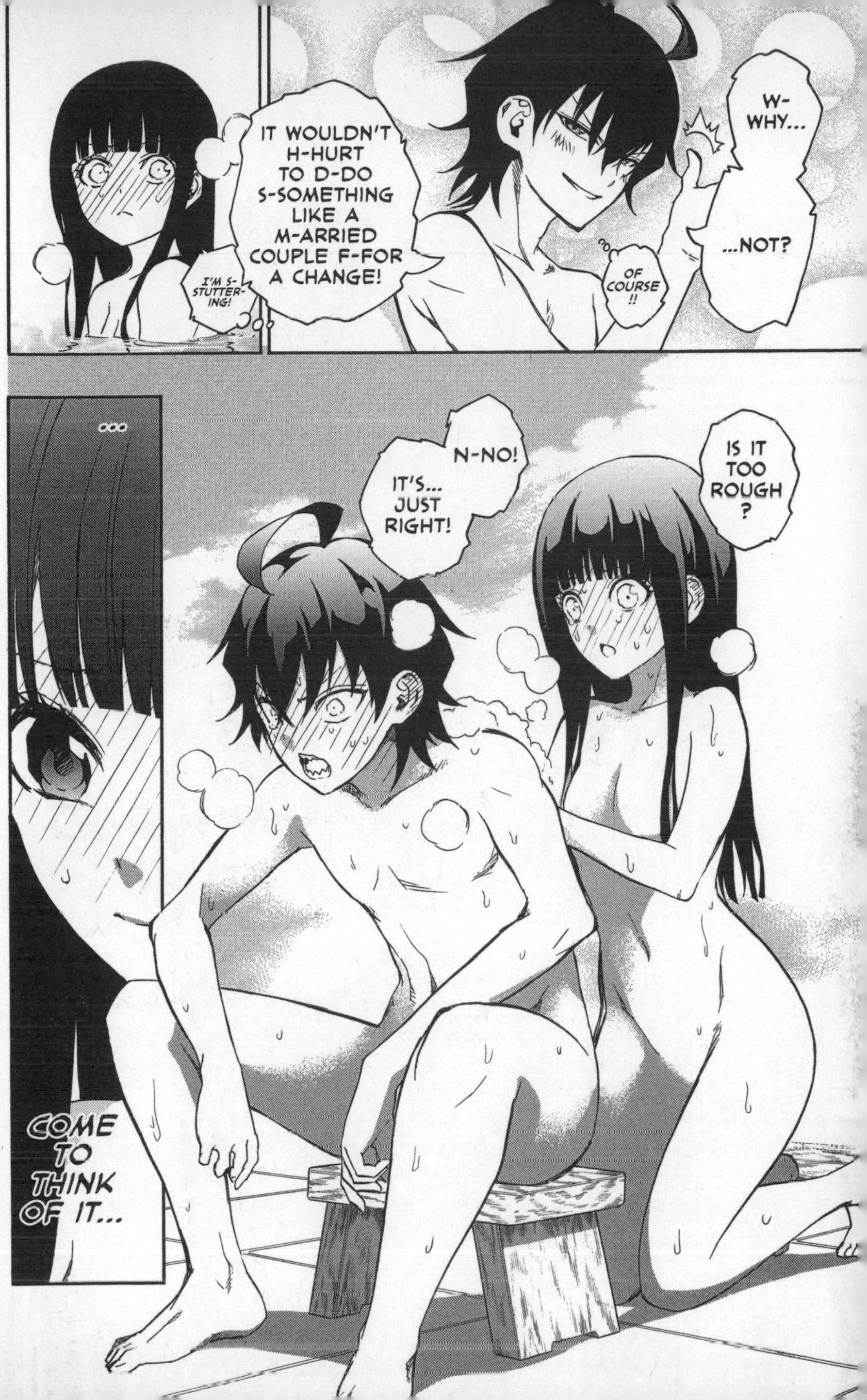
W-WHY... ...NOT?
OF COURSE!!
IT WOULDN'T H-HURT TO D-DO S-SOMETHING LIKE A M-ARRIED COUPLE F-FOR A CHANGE!
I'M S-STUTTERING!
IS IT TOO ROUGH?
N-NO! IT'S... JUST RIGHT!
...
COME TO THINK OF IT...

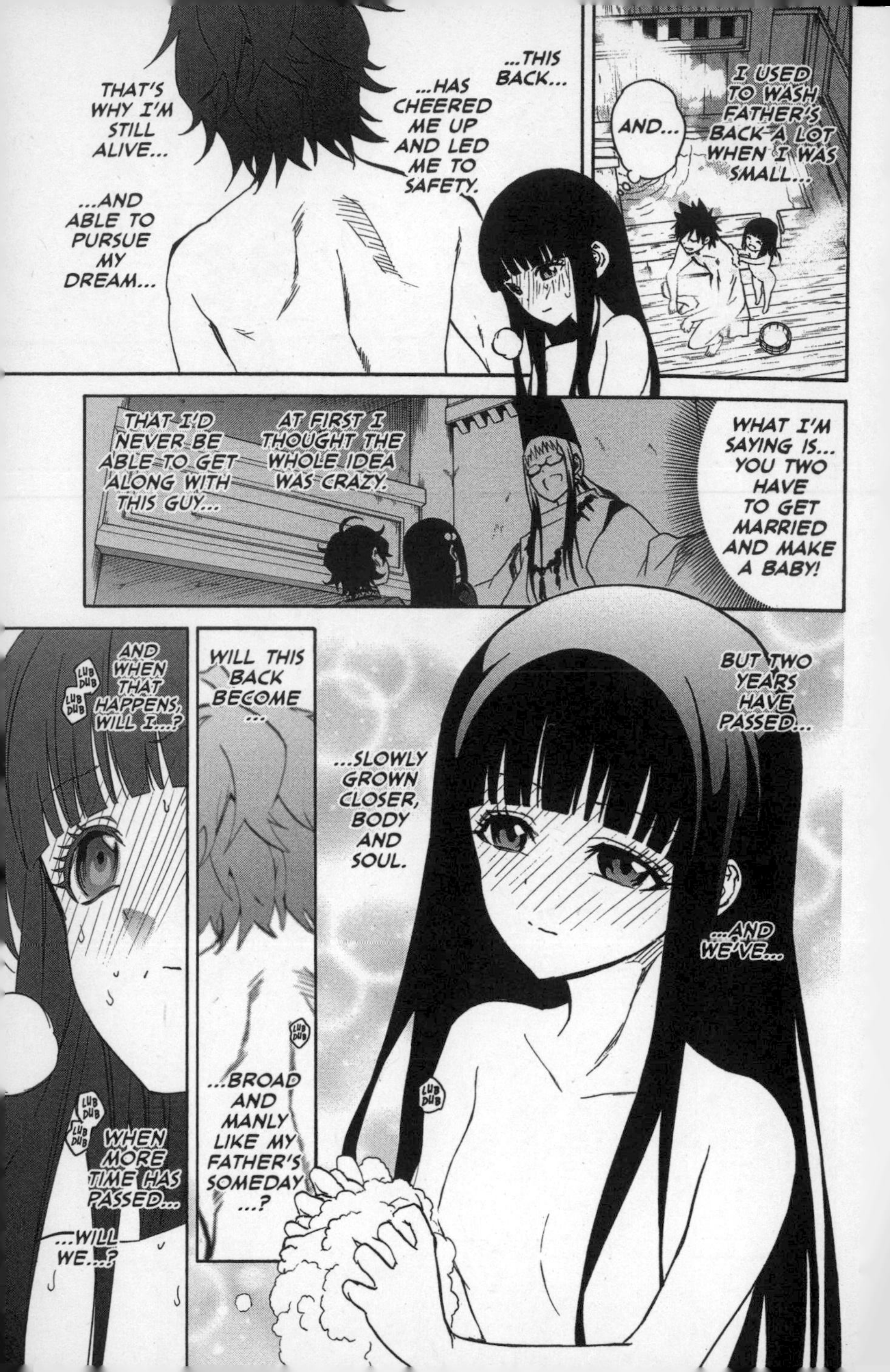

I USED TO WASH FATHER'S BACK A LOT WHEN I WAS SMALL...
AND...
...THIS BACK...
...HAS CHEERED ME UP AND LED ME TO SAFETY.
THAT'S WHY I'M STILL ALIVE...
...AND ABLE TO PURSUE MY DREAM...
WHAT I'M SAYING IS... YOU TWO HAVE TO GET MARRIED AND MAKE A BABY!
AT FIRST I THOUGHT THE WHOLE IDEA WAS CRAZY.
THAT I'D NEVER BE ABLE TO GET ALONG WITH THIS GUY...
BUT TWO YEARS HAVE PASSED...
...AND WE'VE...
...SLOWLY GROWN CLOSER, BODY AND SOUL.
LUB DUB
WILL THIS BACK BECOME ...
...BROAD AND MANLY LIKE MY FATHER'S SOMEDAY ...?
LUB DUB
AND WHEN THAT HAPPENS, WILL I...?
LUB DUB
LUB DUB
LUB DUB
LUB DUB
WHEN MORE TIME HAS PASSED...
...WILL WE...?

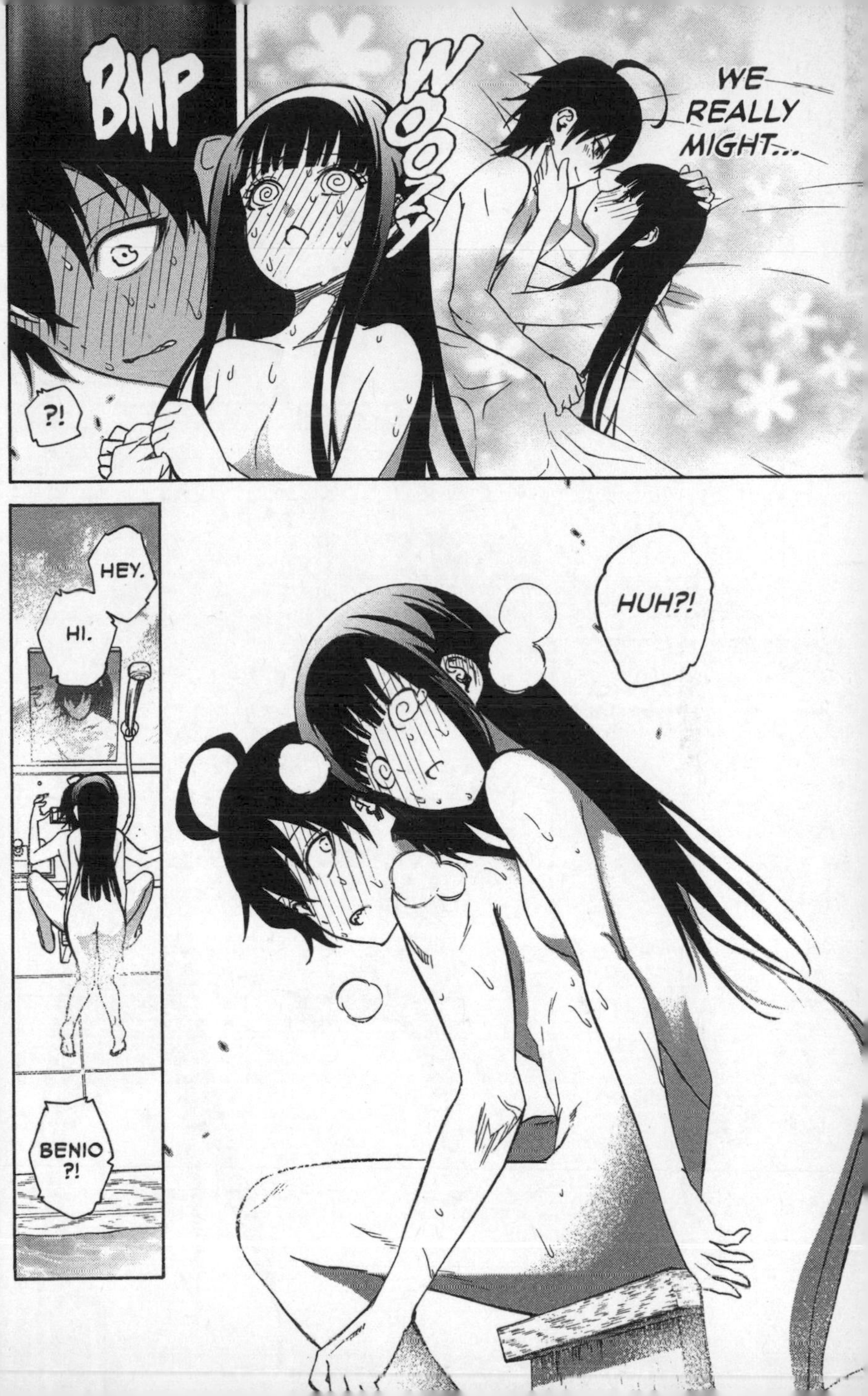
WE REALLY MIGHT...
WOOZY
BMP
?!
HUH?!
HEY.
HI.
BENIO ?!

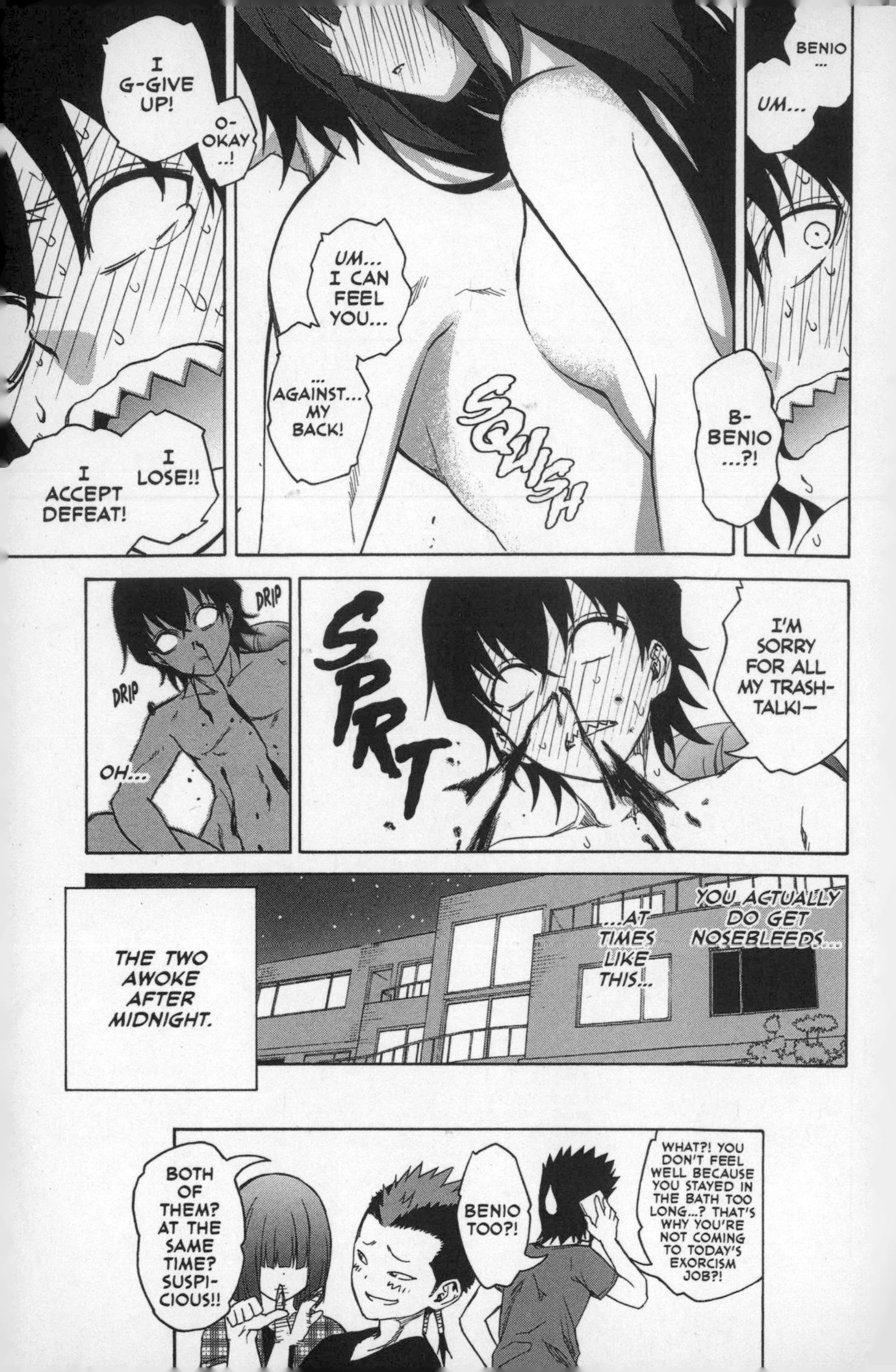
BENIO ...
UM...
B-BENIO ...?!
UM... I CAN FEEL YOU...
... AGAINST... MY BACK!
SQUISH
I G-GIVE UP!
O-OKAY ...!
I LOSE!!
I ACCEPT DEFEAT!
I'M SORRY FOR ALL MY TRASH-TALKI—
SPRT
DRIP
DRIP
OH...
YOU ACTUALLY DO GET NOSEBLEEDS...
...AT TIMES LIKE THIS...
THE TWO AWOKE AFTER MIDNIGHT.
WHAT?! YOU DON'T FEEL WELL BECAUSE YOU STAYED IN THE BATH TOO LONG...? THAT'S WHY YOU'RE NOT COMING TO TODAY'S EXORCISM JOB?!
BENIO TOO?!
BOTH OF THEM? AT THE SAME TIME? SUSPI-CIOUS!!

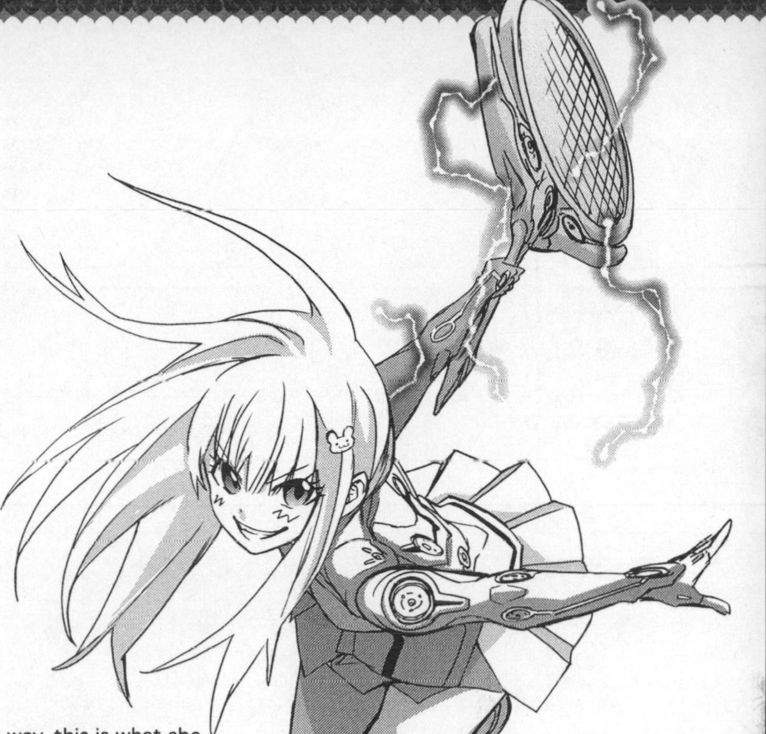

By the way, this is what she looked like in the magazine.

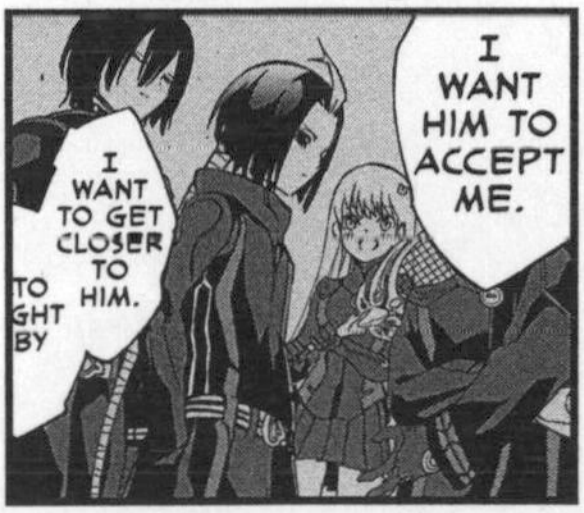
I WANT HIM TO ACCEPT ME.
I WANT TO GET CLOSER TO HIM.

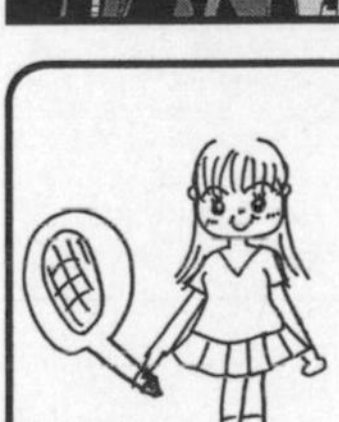

The tennis racket!

The racket changes size, and she defeats Kegare by beating them with it.

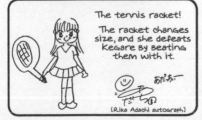

[Rika Adachi autograph]

This character was created for a TV program called *Jump Undercover Mission Police* (a show that introduces *Jump* magazine manga) by Rika Adashi, a regular contributor to the show. The idea was to create an original exorcist on the show and have that character make an appearance in the manga. But because of the story line, I was only able to have her appear in a small panel in the magazine version. I decided to draw her character larger in the graphic novel. This brought back memories for me because we often had our readers create an original character for *Good Luck Girl!* (*Bimbo Gami Ga*), and I would draw the final image of it...

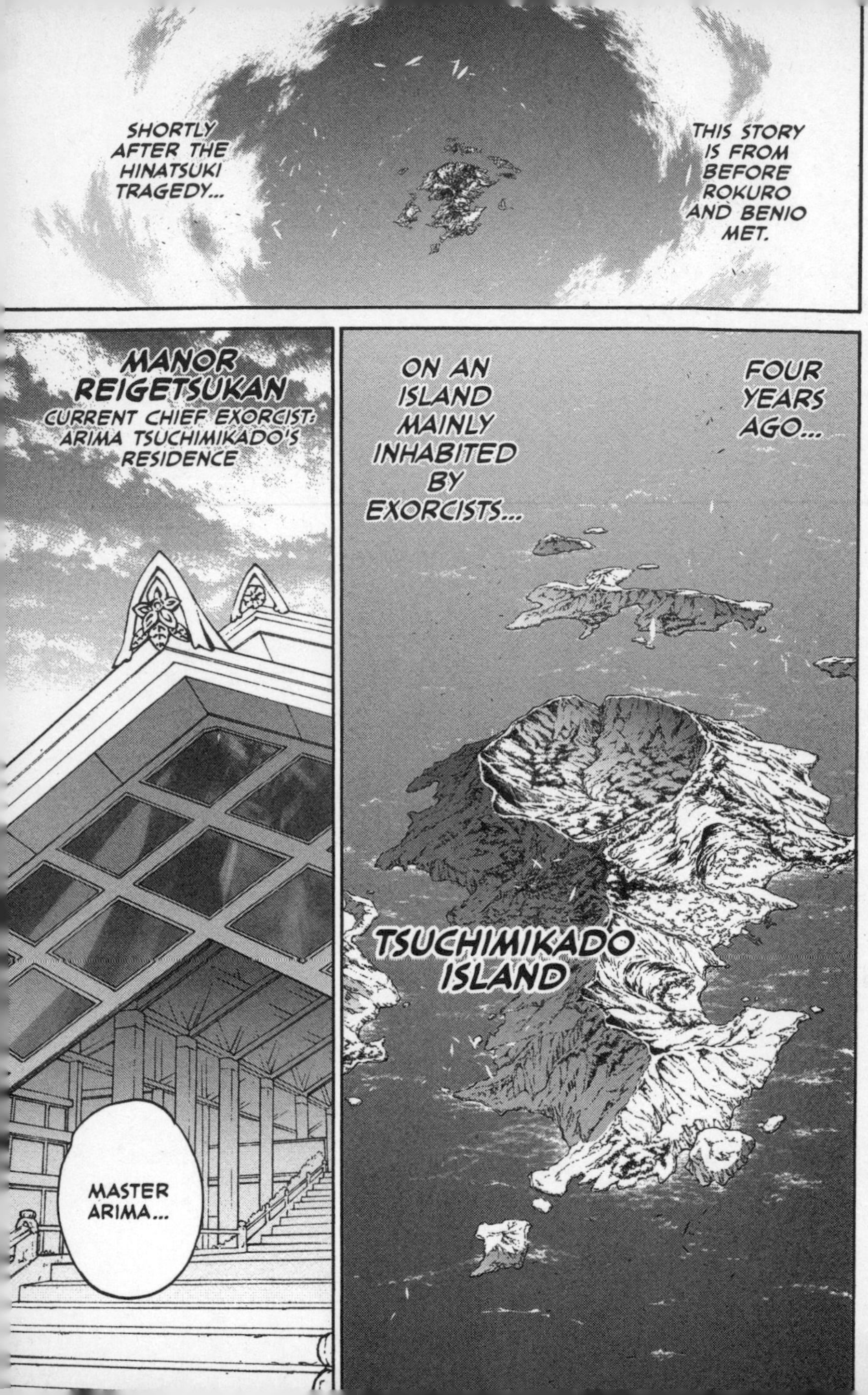
THIS STORY IS FROM BEFORE ROKURO AND BENIO MET.
SHORTLY AFTER THE HINATSUKI TRAGEDY...
FOUR YEARS AGO...
ON AN ISLAND MAINLY INHABITED BY EXORCISTS...
TSUCHIMIKADO ISLAND
MANOR REIGETSUKAN
CURRENT CHIEF EXORCIST: ARIMA TSUCHIMIKADO'S RESIDENCE
MASTER ARIMA...

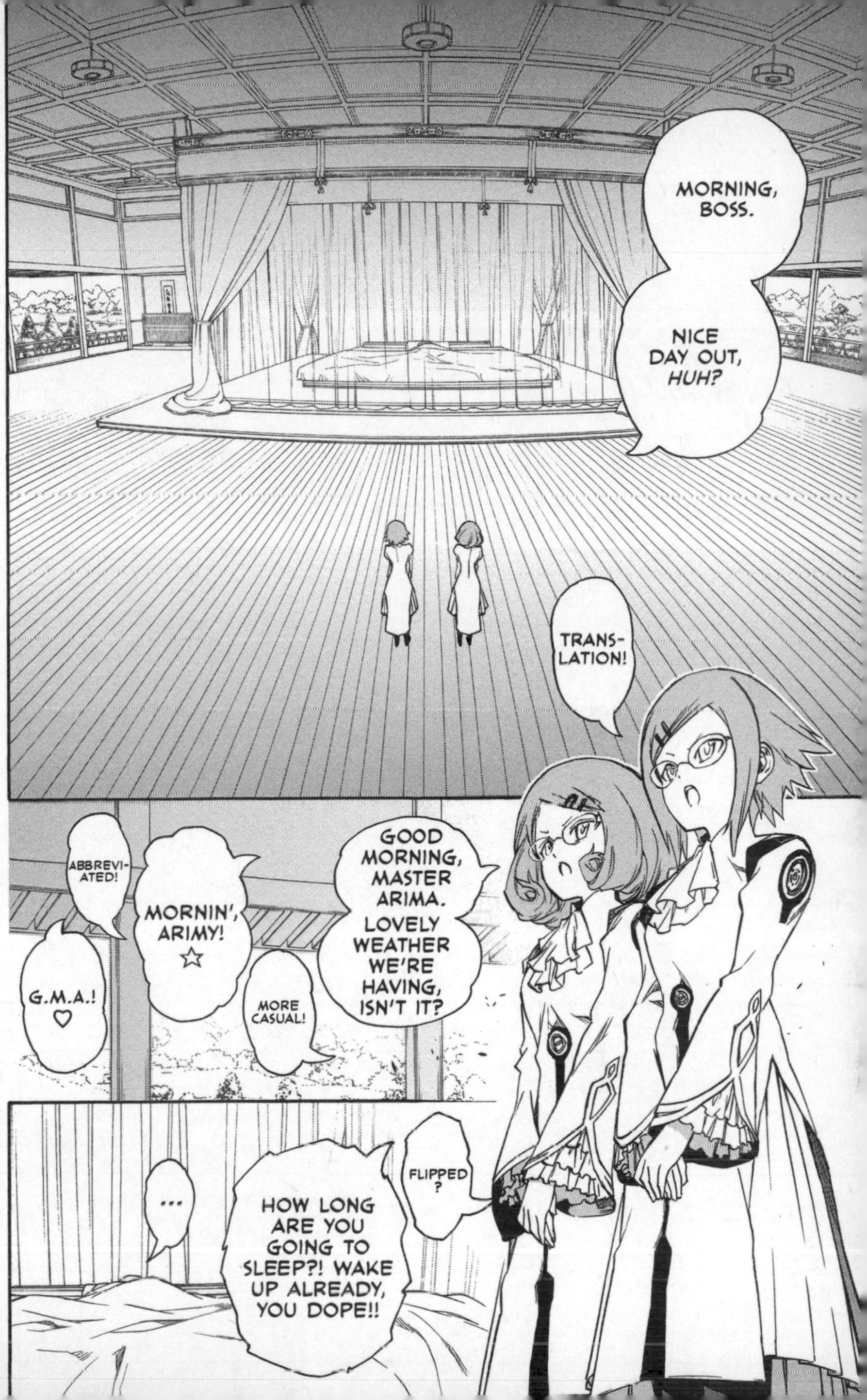
MORNING, BOSS.
NICE DAY OUT, HUH?
TRANS-LATION!
GOOD MORNING, MASTER ARIMA. LOVELY WEATHER WE'RE HAVING, ISN'T IT?
MORE CASUAL!
MORNIN', ARIMY! ☆
ABBREVI-ATED!
G.M.A.! ♡
FLIPPED?
HOW LONG ARE YOU GOING TO SLEEP?! WAKE UP ALREADY, YOU DOPE!!
...

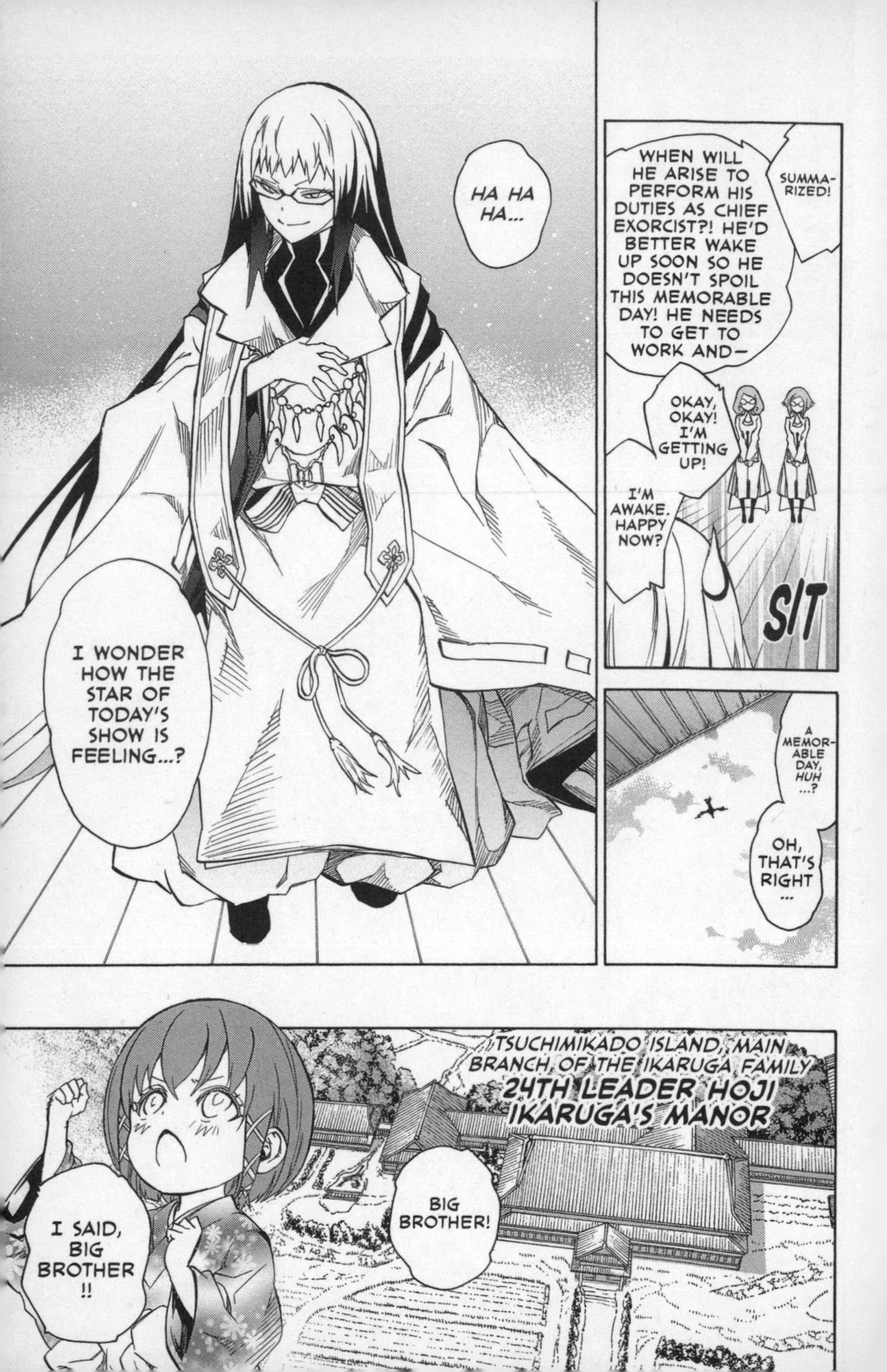
SUMMA-RIZED!
WHEN WILL HE ARISE TO PERFORM HIS DUTIES AS CHIEF EXORCIST?! HE'D BETTER WAKE UP SOON SO HE DOESN'T SPOIL THIS MEMORABLE DAY! HE NEEDS TO GET TO WORK AND—
OKAY, OKAY! I'M GETTING UP!
I'M AWAKE. HAPPY NOW?
SIT
A MEMOR-ABLE DAY, HUH ...?
OH, THAT'S RIGHT ...
HA HA HA...
I WONDER HOW THE STAR OF TODAY'S SHOW IS FEELING...?
TSUCHIMIKADO ISLAND, MAIN BRANCH OF THE IKARUGA FAMILY
24TH LEADER HOJI IKARUGA'S MANOR
BIG BROTHER!
I SAID, BIG BROTHER !!

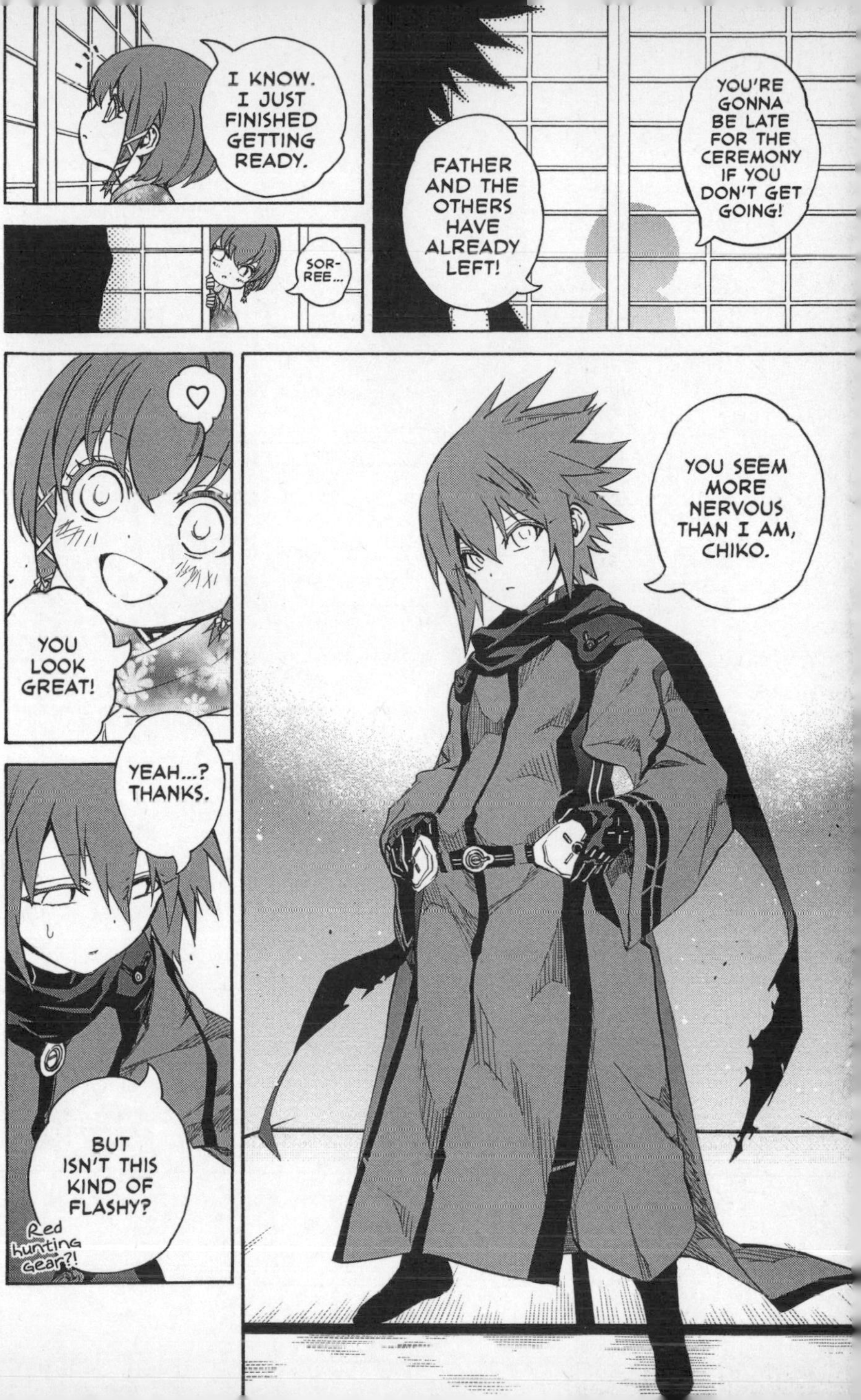
YOU'RE GONNA BE LATE FOR THE CEREMONY IF YOU DON'T GET GOING!
FATHER AND THE OTHERS HAVE ALREADY LEFT!
I KNOW. I JUST FINISHED GETTING READY.
SOR-REE...
YOU SEEM MORE NERVOUS THAN I AM, CHIKO.
YOU LOOK GREAT!
YEAH...? THANKS.
BUT ISN'T THIS KIND OF FLASHY?
Red hunting gear?!

Bonus: Suzaku's Ceremony of Accession to the Twelve Guardians

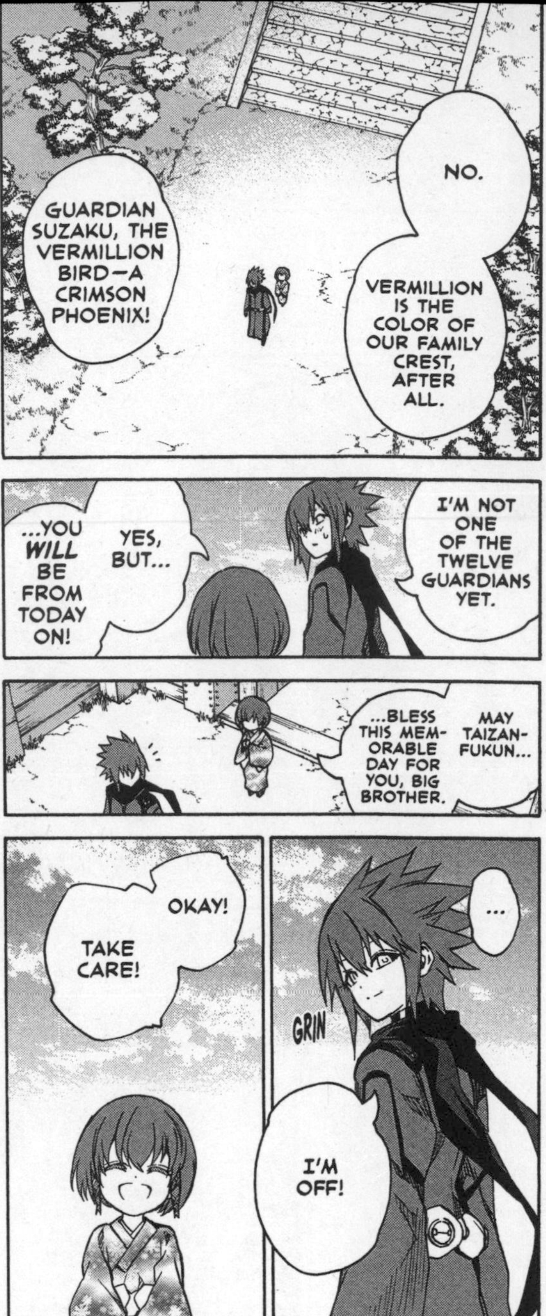
NO.
VERMILLION IS THE COLOR OF OUR FAMILY CREST, AFTER ALL.
GUARDIAN SUZAKU, THE VERMILLION BIRD—A CRIMSON PHOENIX!
I'M NOT ONE OF THE TWELVE GUARDIANS YET.
YES, BUT...
...YOU *WILL* BE FROM TODAY ON!
MAY TAIZAN-FUKUN...
...BLESS THIS MEM-ORABLE DAY FOR YOU, BIG BROTHER.
...
GRIN
I'M OFF!
OKAY!
TAKE CARE!

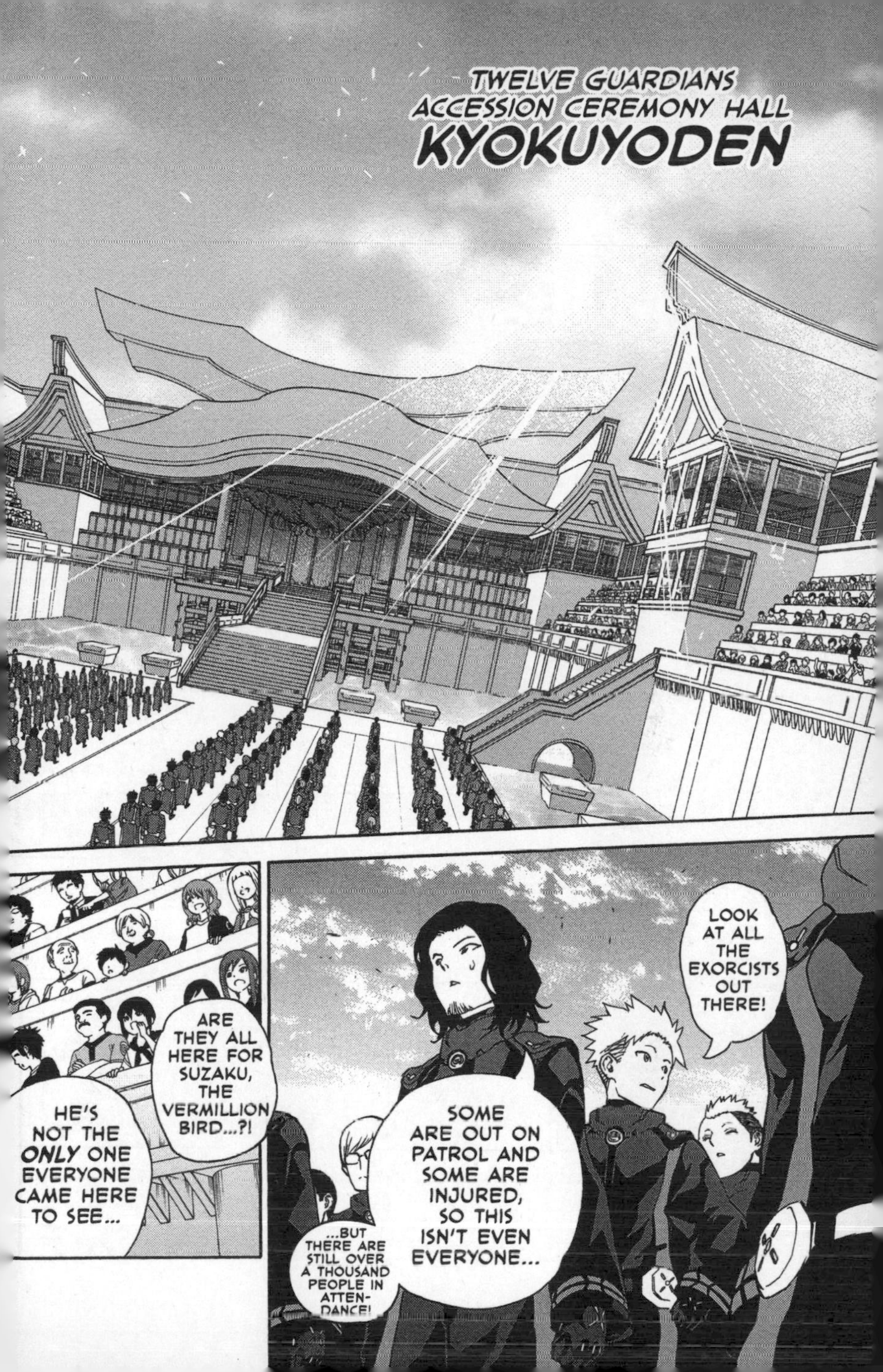
TWELVE GUARDIANS ACCESSION CEREMONY HALL
KYOKUYODEN
LOOK AT ALL THE EXORCISTS OUT THERE!
SOME ARE OUT ON PATROL AND SOME ARE INJURED, SO THIS ISN'T EVEN EVERYONE...
...BUT THERE ARE STILL OVER A THOUSAND PEOPLE IN ATTEN-DANCE!
ARE THEY ALL HERE FOR SUZAKU, THE VERMILLION BIRD...?!
HE'S NOT THE *ONLY* ONE EVERYONE CAME HERE TO SEE...

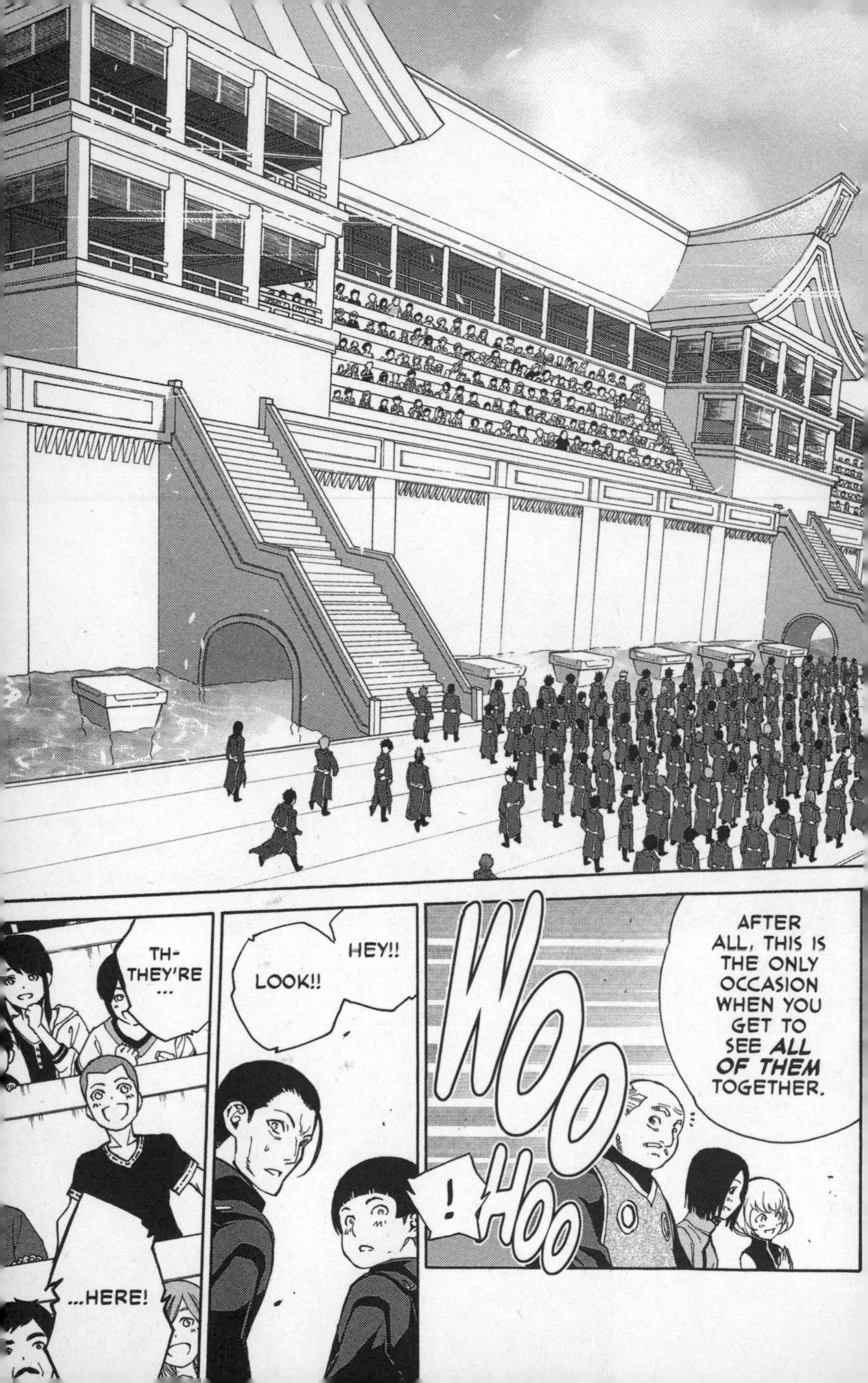
AFTER ALL, THIS IS THE ONLY OCCASION WHEN YOU GET TO SEE *ALL OF THEM* TOGETHER.
WOO HOO
!
HEY!! LOOK!!
TH- THEY'RE ...
...HERE!

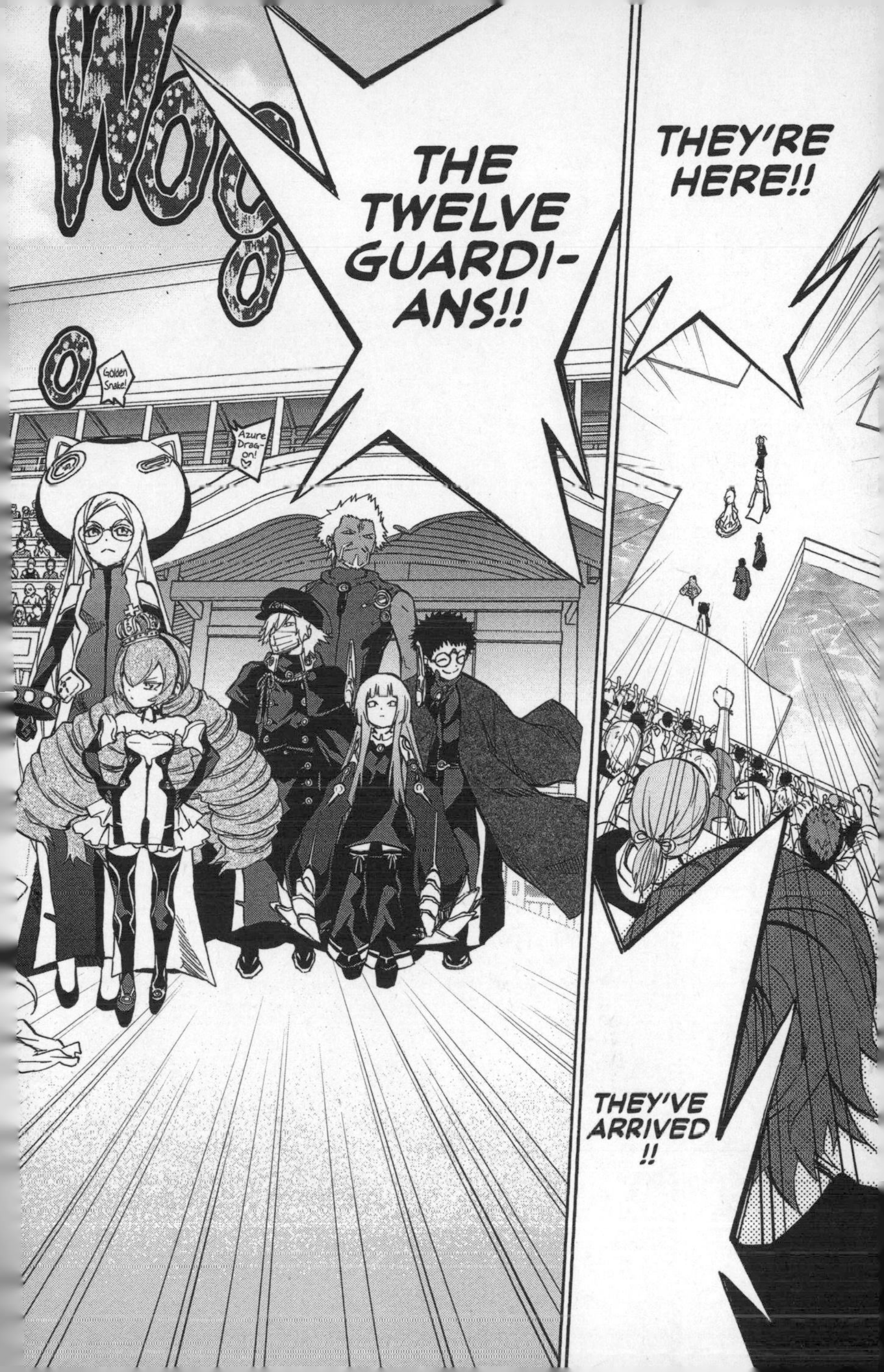
THEY'RE HERE!!
THEY'VE ARRIVED !!
WOOOOO
THE TWELVE GUARDI-ANS!!
Golden Snake!
Azure Drag-on! ♡

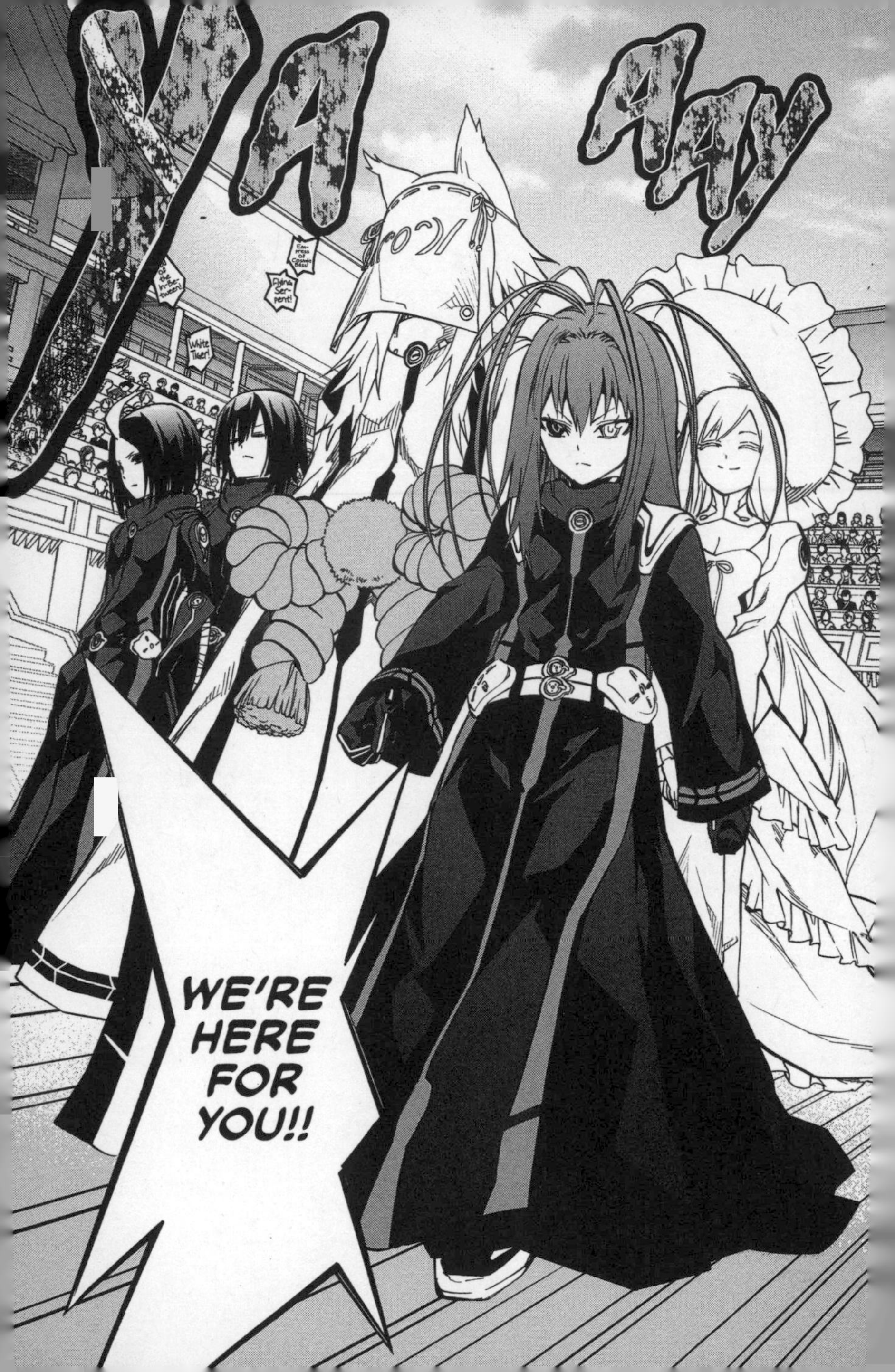
YAAAY
Empress of Cosmic Bliss!
Flying Serpent!
of the In-Between!
White Tiger!
WE'RE HERE FOR YOU!!

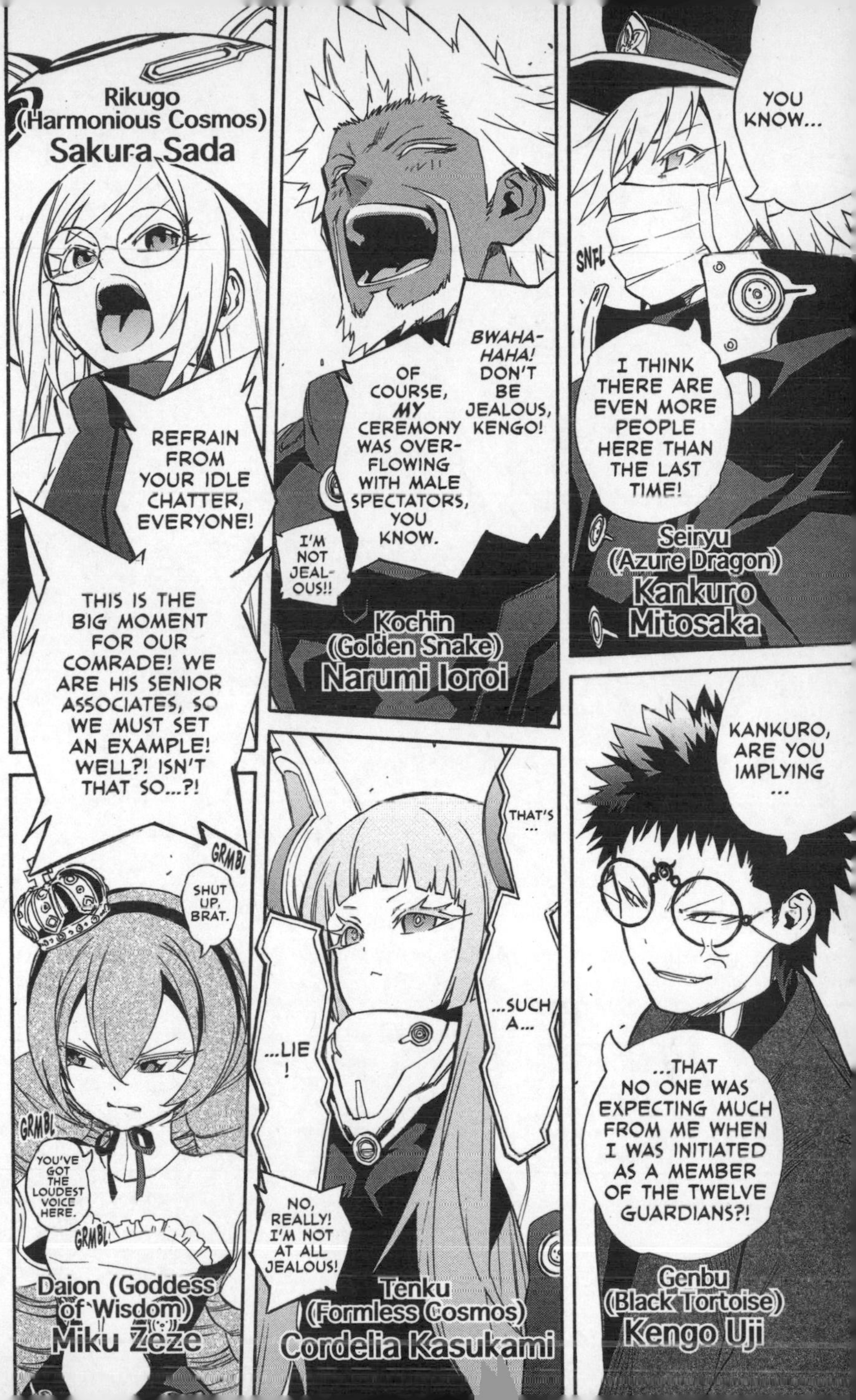
YOU KNOW...
SNFL
I THINK THERE ARE EVEN MORE PEOPLE HERE THAN THE LAST TIME!
Seiryu (Azure Dragon) Kankuro Mitosaka
BWAHAHAHA! DON'T BE JEALOUS, KENGO!
OF COURSE, MY CEREMONY WAS OVERFLOWING WITH MALE SPECTATORS, YOU KNOW.
I'M NOT JEALOUS!!
Kochin (Golden Snake) Narumi Ioroi
Rikugo (Harmonious Cosmos) Sakura Sada
REFRAIN FROM YOUR IDLE CHATTER, EVERYONE!
THIS IS THE BIG MOMENT FOR OUR COMRADE! WE ARE HIS SENIOR ASSOCIATES, SO WE MUST SET AN EXAMPLE! WELL?! ISN'T THAT SO...?!
KANKURO, ARE YOU IMPLYING ...
...THAT NO ONE WAS EXPECTING MUCH FROM ME WHEN I WAS INITIATED AS A MEMBER OF THE TWELVE GUARDIANS?!
Genbu (Black Tortoise) Kengo Uji
THAT'S ...
...SUCH A...
...LIE !
NO, REALLY! I'M NOT AT ALL JEALOUS!
Tenku (Formless Cosmos) Cordelia Kasukami
GRMBL
SHUT UP, BRAT.
GRMBL
YOU'VE GOT THE LOUDEST VOICE HERE.
GRMBL
Daion (Goddess of Wisdom) Miku Zeze

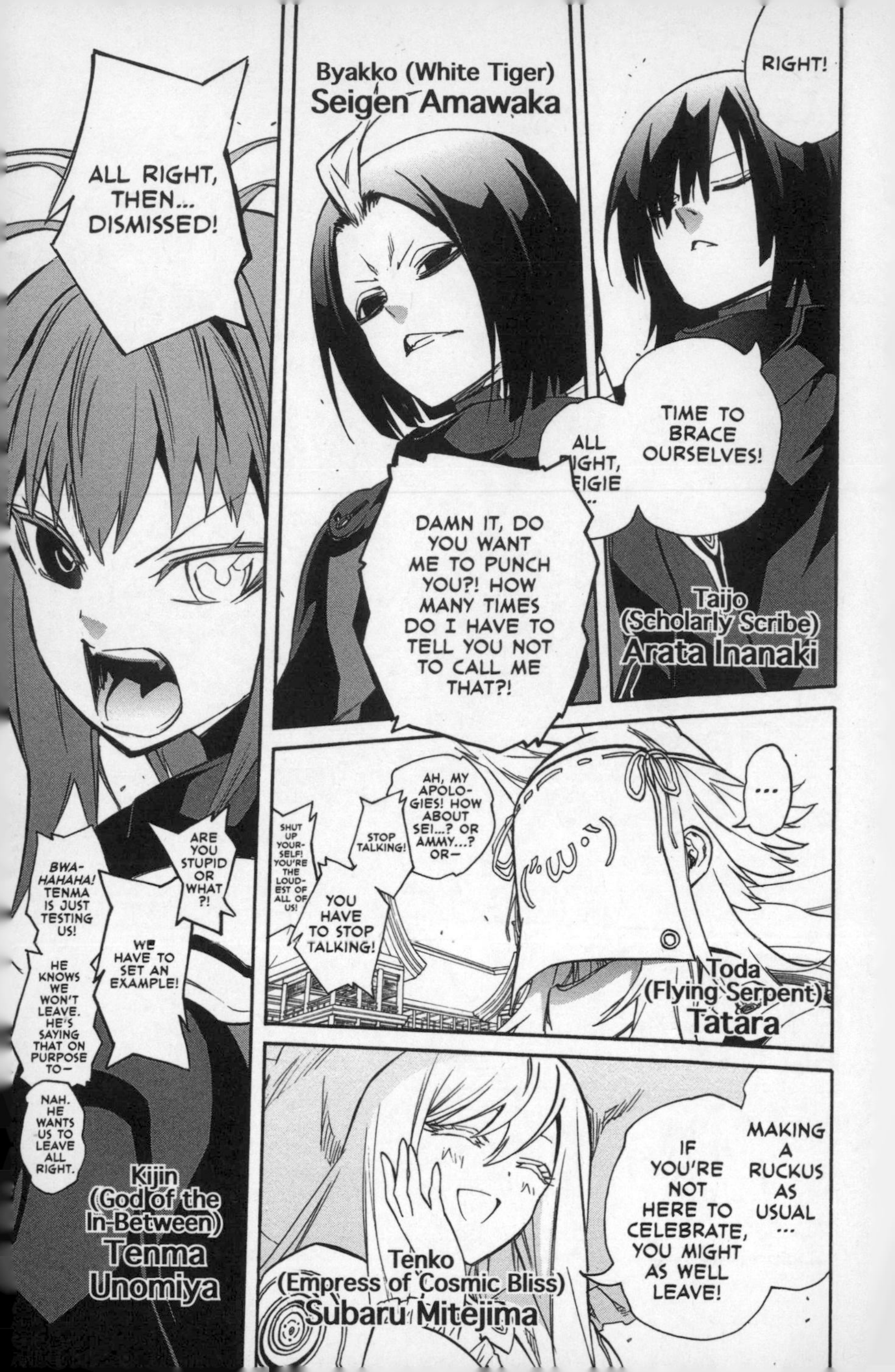
RIGHT!
TIME TO BRACE OURSELVES!
Taijo (Scholarly Scribe) Arata Inanaki
Byakko (White Tiger) Seigen Amawaka
ALL IGHT, EIGIE
DAMN IT, DO YOU WANT ME TO PUNCH YOU?! HOW MANY TIMES DO I HAVE TO TELL YOU NOT TO CALL ME THAT?!
...
AH, MY APOLOGIES! HOW ABOUT SEI...? OR AMMY...? OR—
STOP TALKING!
SHUT UP YOURSELF! YOU'RE THE LOUDEST OF ALL OF US!
YOU HAVE TO STOP TALKING!
Toda (Flying Serpent) Tatara
MAKING A RUCKUS AS USUAL...
IF YOU'RE NOT HERE TO CELEBRATE, YOU MIGHT AS WELL LEAVE!
Tenko (Empress of Cosmic Bliss) Subaru Mitejima
ALL RIGHT, THEN... DISMISSED!
ARE YOU STUPID OR WHAT?!
BWAHAHAHA! TENMA IS JUST TESTING US!
WE HAVE TO SET AN EXAMPLE!
HE KNOWS WE WON'T LEAVE. HE'S SAYING THAT ON PURPOSE TO—
NAH. HE WANTS US TO LEAVE ALL RIGHT.
Kijin (God of the In-Between) Tenma Unomiya

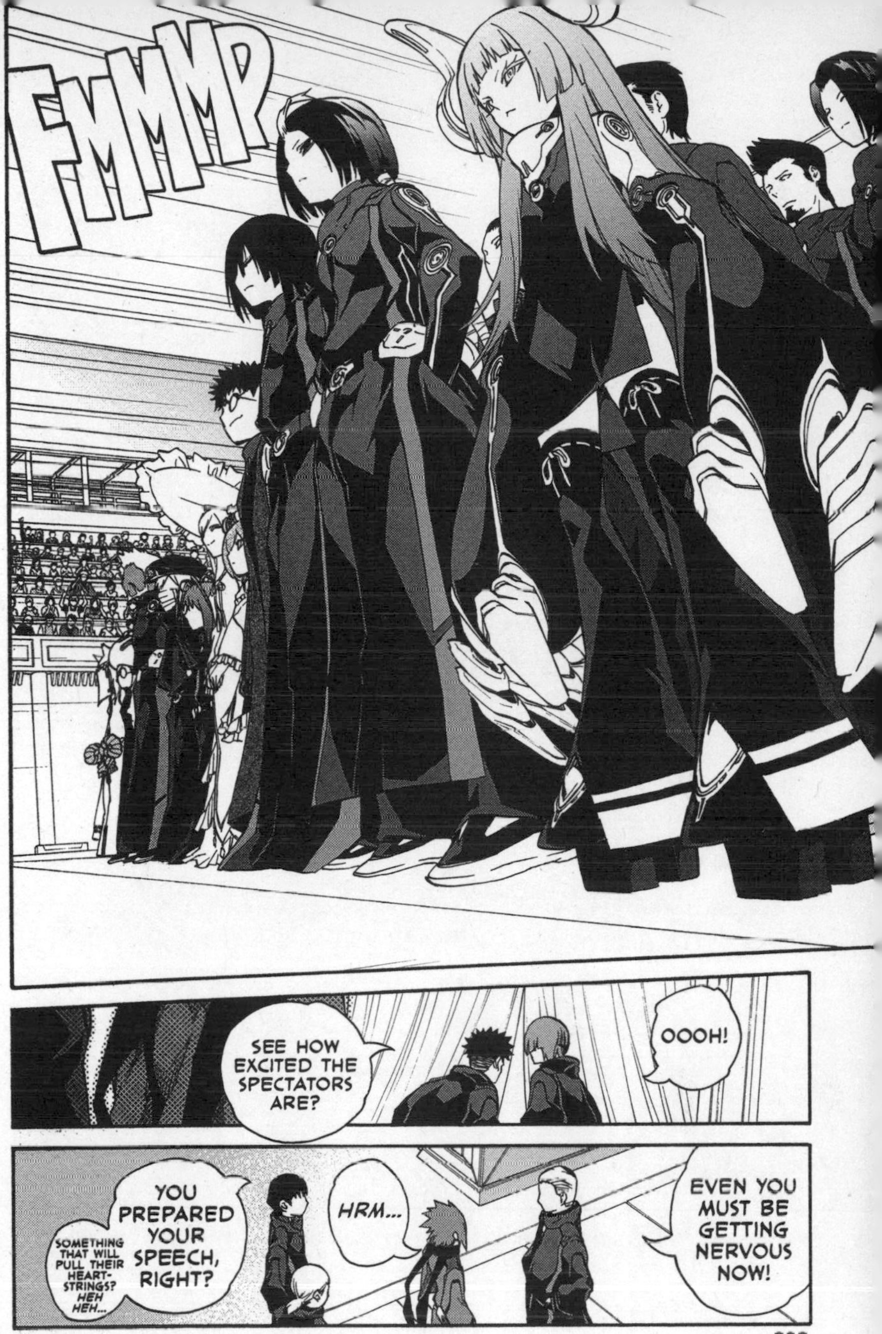
FMMMP
OOOH!
SEE HOW EXCITED THE SPECTATORS ARE?
EVEN YOU MUST BE GETTING NERVOUS NOW!
HRM...
YOU PREPARED YOUR SPEECH, RIGHT?
SOMETHING THAT WILL PULL THEIR HEART-STRINGS? HEH HEH...

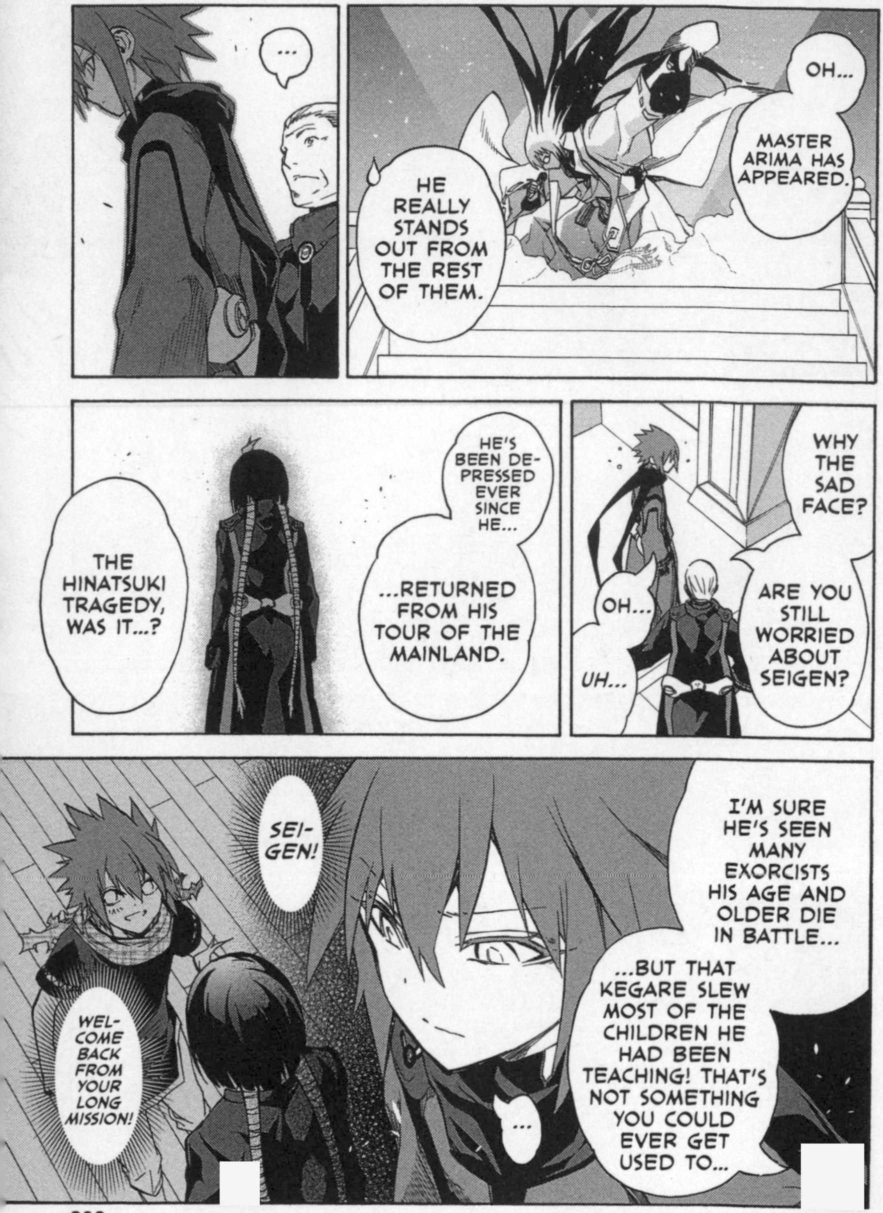
OH...
MASTER ARIMA HAS APPEARED.
HE REALLY STANDS OUT FROM THE REST OF THEM.
...
WHY THE SAD FACE?
ARE YOU STILL WORRIED ABOUT SEIGEN?
OH...
UH...
HE'S BEEN DE-PRESSED EVER SINCE HE...
...RETURNED FROM HIS TOUR OF THE MAINLAND.
THE HINATSUKI TRAGEDY, WAS IT...?
I'M SURE HE'S SEEN MANY EXORCISTS HIS AGE AND OLDER DIE IN BATTLE...
...BUT THAT KEGARE SLEW MOST OF THE CHILDREN HE HAD BEEN TEACHING! THAT'S NOT SOMETHING YOU COULD EVER GET USED TO...
SEI-GEN!
...
WEL-COME BACK FROM YOUR LONG MISSION!

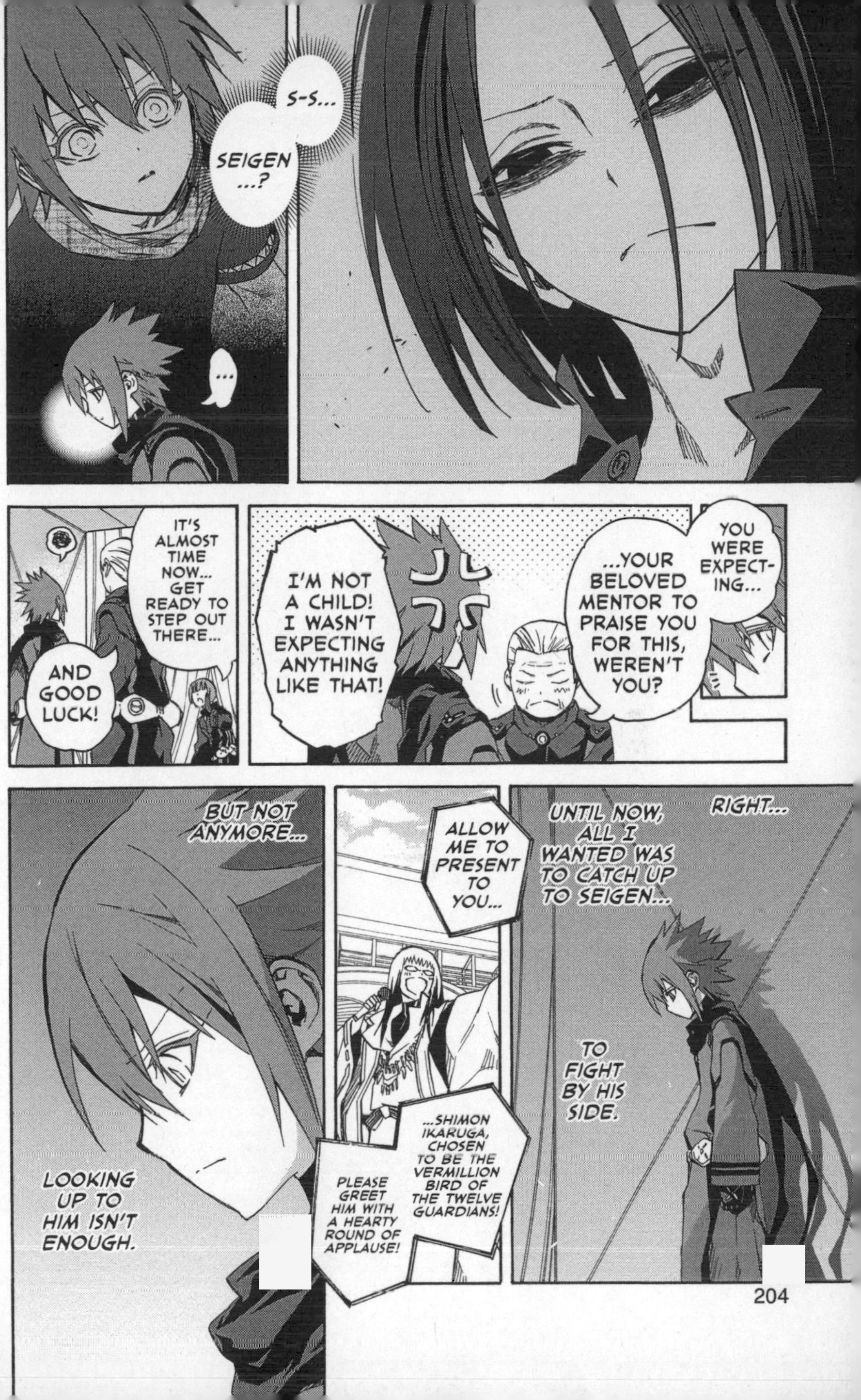
S-S...
SEIGEN ...?
...
YOU WERE EXPECTING...
...YOUR BELOVED MENTOR TO PRAISE YOU FOR THIS, WEREN'T YOU?
I'M NOT A CHILD! I WASN'T EXPECTING ANYTHING LIKE THAT!
IT'S ALMOST TIME NOW... GET READY TO STEP OUT THERE...
AND GOOD LUCK!
RIGHT...
UNTIL NOW, ALL I WANTED WAS TO CATCH UP TO SEIGEN...
TO FIGHT BY HIS SIDE.
ALLOW ME TO PRESENT TO YOU...
...SHIMON IKARUGA, CHOSEN TO BE THE VERMILLION BIRD OF THE TWELVE GUARDIANS!
PLEASE GREET HIM WITH A HEARTY ROUND OF APPLAUSE!
BUT NOT ANYMORE...
LOOKING UP TO HIM ISN'T ENOUGH.

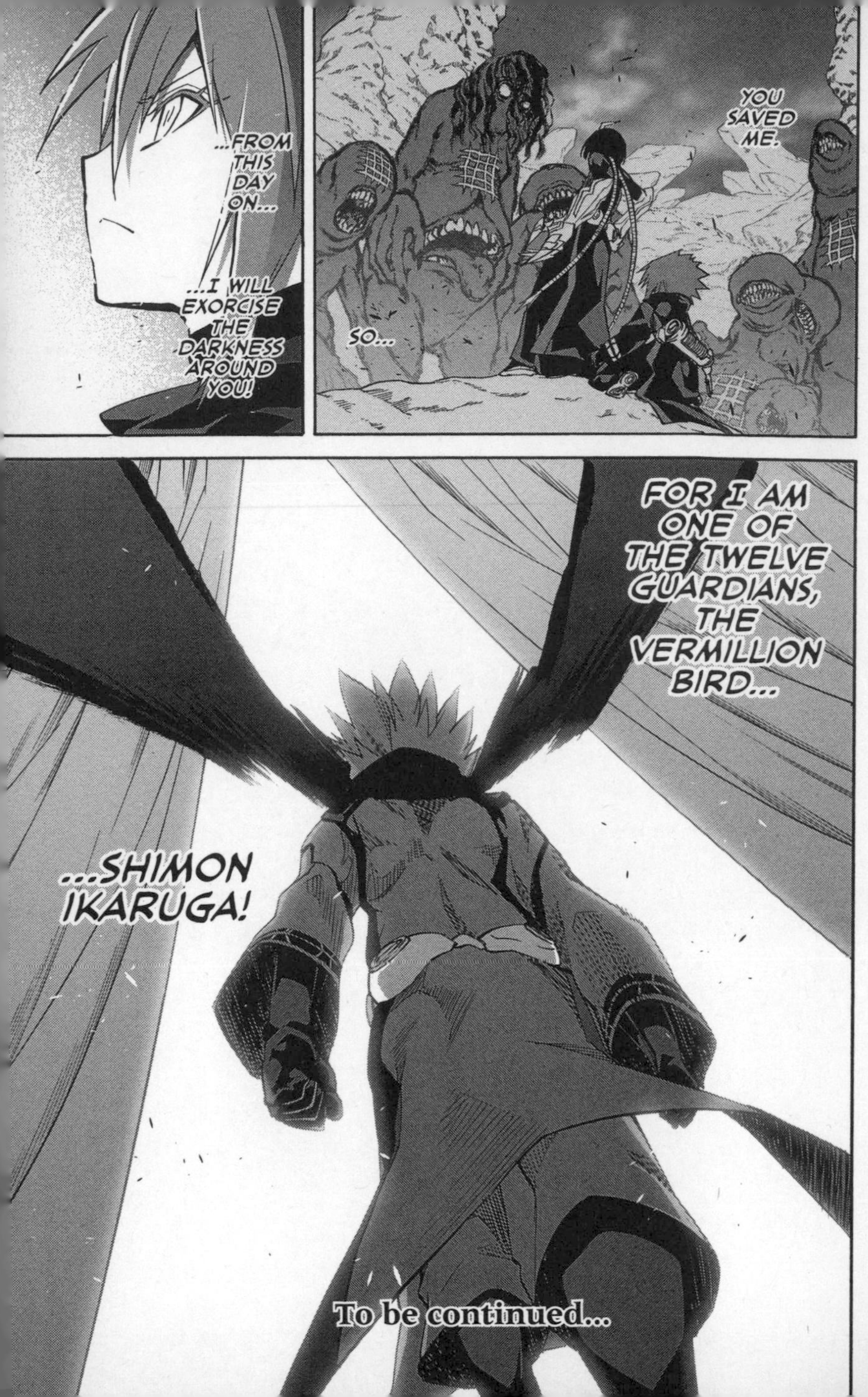
YOU SAVED ME.
SO...
...FROM THIS DAY ON...
...I WILL EXORCISE THE DARKNESS AROUND YOU!
FOR I AM ONE OF THE TWELVE GUARDIANS, THE VERMILLION BIRD...
...SHIMON IKARUGA!
To be continued...

TSUCHIMIKADO ISLAND TRAVELOGUE 1

KITSUNEKO

A mysterious animal whose only habitat is Tsuchimikado Island.

- They roam all over the island.
- Their cry sounds like "Meowack."

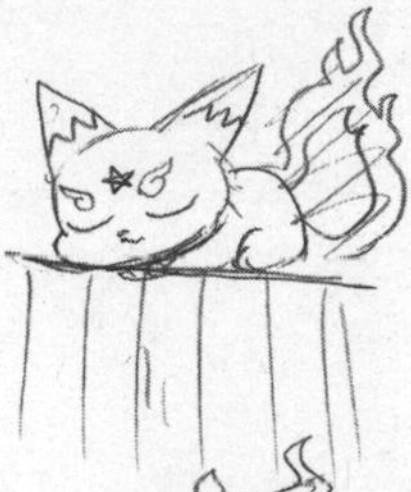

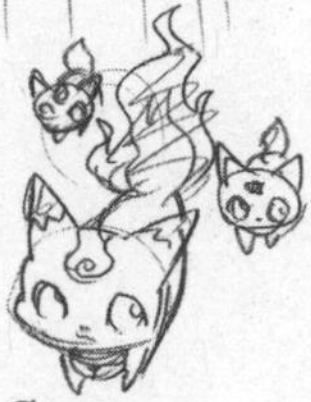

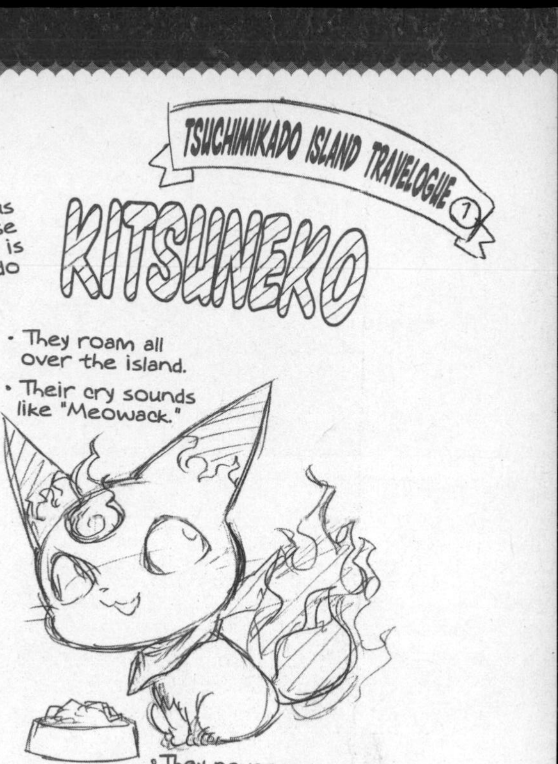

- They never eat cheap cat food.
- They are not a hybrid of a cat and a fox.

Tabby Calico: Its fur comes in a variety of colors.

- A huge Kitsuneko that seems to be the others' elder lives deep inside the woods. It is over ten feet in length, uses human speech and is thought to be over 500 years old. On the one day a month when the island's large shipment of supplies is delivered, it comes out of the mountains to buy a lot of mainland pop-star trinkets, then disappears back into the mountains.

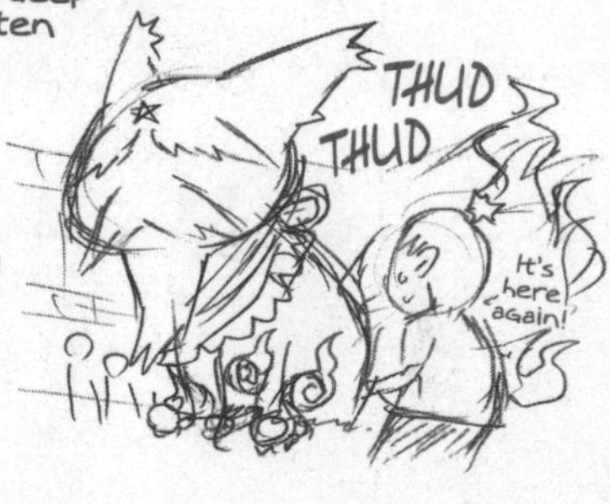
THUD
THUD
It's here again!

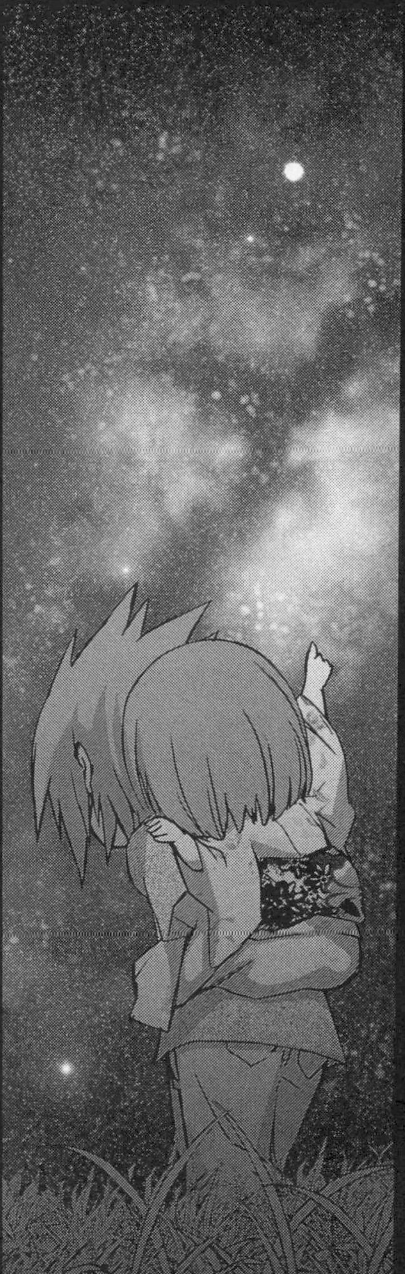

★Artwork★
Tetsuro Kakiuchi
Kosuke Ono
Takumi Kikuta
Tomohiro Fukuoka
koppy
Erubo Hijihara
Yoshiaki Sukeno

★Editor★
Junichi Tamada

★Graphic Novel Editor★
Hiroshi Ikishima

★Graphic Novel Design★
Tatsuo Ishino (Freiheit)

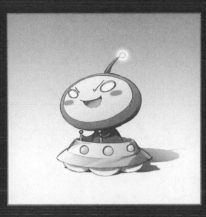

The concept of this series, which I discussed
with my editor before it started, was "battles and
romantic comedy." The romantic comedy part is
going to ramp up starting with this volume.

It was the same with *Good Luck Girl!*, my previous
series. I really enjoy working on a story that slowly
and steadily builds to a conclusion.

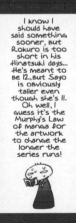

I know I
should have
said something
sooner, but
Rokuro is too
short in his
Hinatsuki days...
He's meant to
be 12, but Sayo
is obviously
taller even
though she's 11.
Oh well, I
guess it's the
Murphy's Law
of manga for
the artwork
to change the
longer the
series runs!

YOSHIAKI SUKENO was born July 23, 1981, in Wakayama, Japan.
He graduated from Kyoto Seika University, where he studied manga.
In 2006, he won the Tezuka Award for Best Newcomer Shonen Manga
Artist. In 2008, he began his previous work, the supernatural comedy
Binbougami ga!, which was adapted into the anime *Good Luck Girl!* in 2012

TWELVE GUARDIANS

(TWO YEARS BEFORE THIS VOLUME'S STORY BEGINS...)

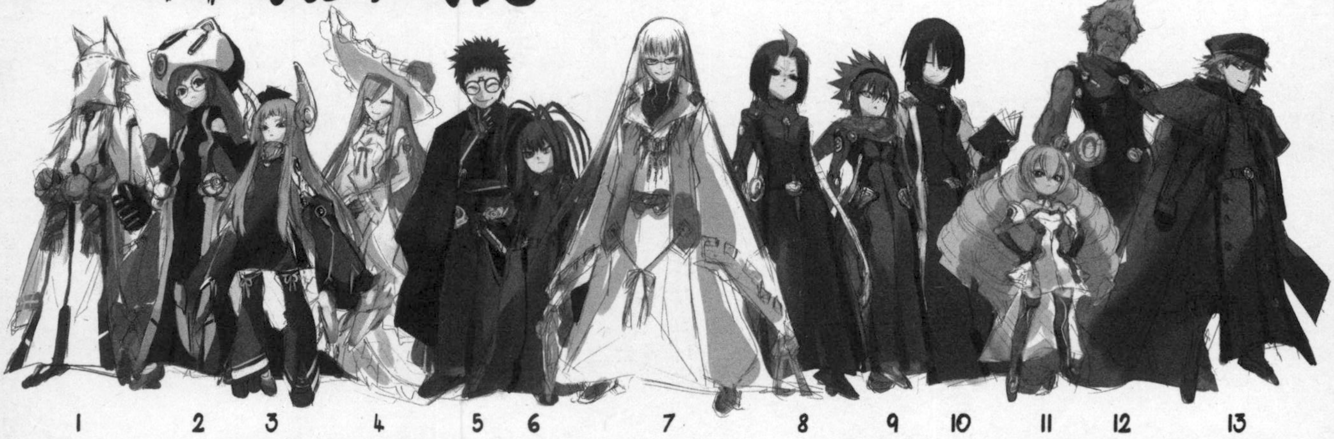
1
2
3
4
5
6
7
8
9
10
11
12
13

1. TODA (FLYING SERPENT): TATARA
2. RIKUGO (HARMONIOUS COSMOS): SAKURA SADA
3. TENKU (FORMLESS COSMOS): CORDELIA KASUKAMI
4. TENKO (EMPRESS OF COSMIC BLISS): SUBARU MITEJIMA
5. GENBU (BLACK TORTOISE): KENGO UJI
6. KIJIN (GOD OF THE IN-BETWEEN): TENMA UNOMIYA
7. CHIEF EXORCIST: ARIMA TSUCHIMIKADO
8. BYAKKO (WHITE TIGER): SEIGEN AMAWAKA
9. SUZAKU (VERMILLION BIRD): SHIMON IKARUGA
10. TAIJO (SCHOLARLY SCRIBE): ARATA INANAKI
11. DAION (GODDESS OF WISDOM): MIKU ZEZE
12. KOCHIN (GOLDEN SNAKE): NARUMI IOROI
13. SEIRYU (AZURE DRAGON): KANKURO MITOSAKA

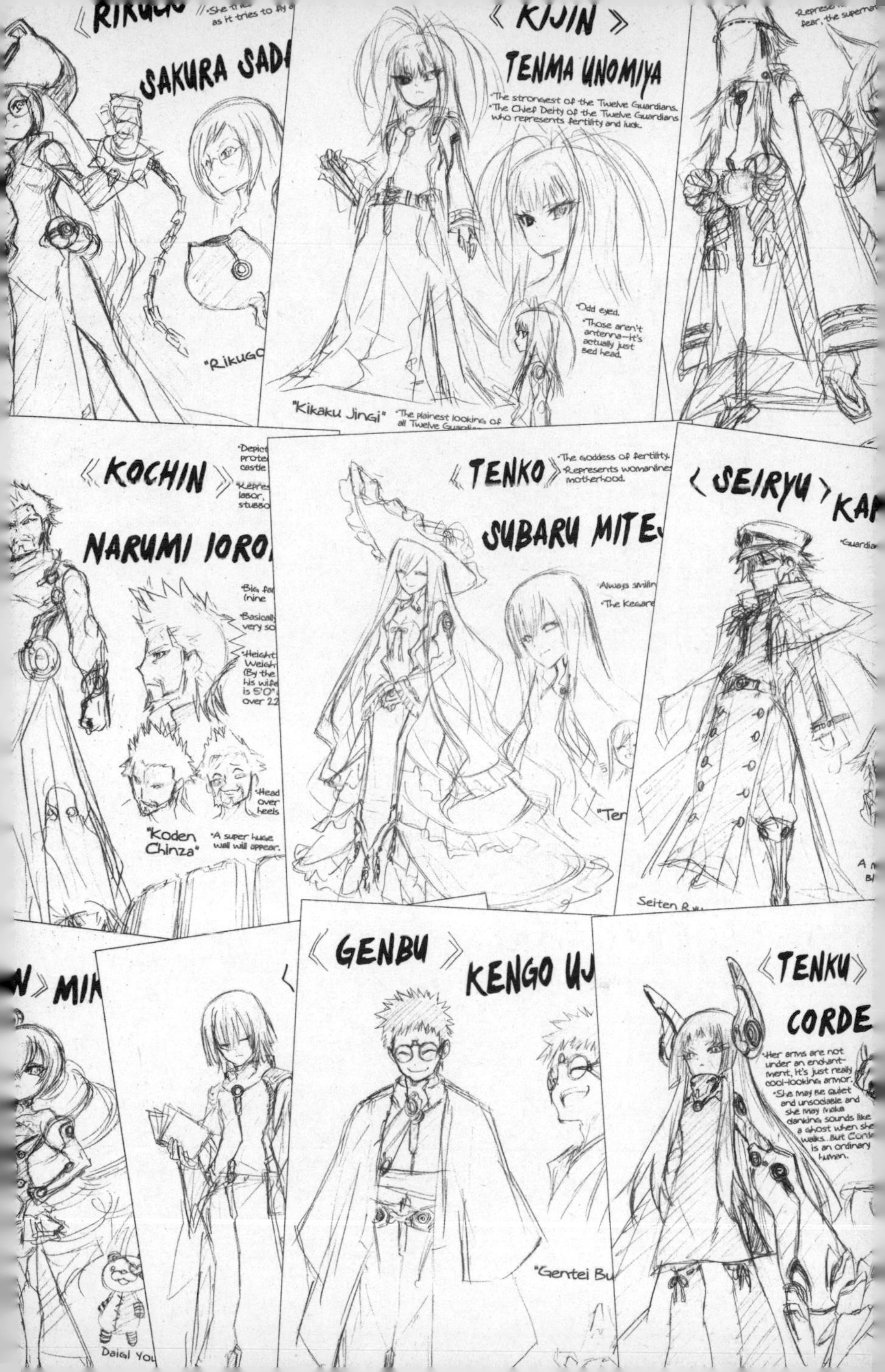

《KIJIN》
TENMA UNOMIYA
•The strongest of the Twelve Guardians.
•The Chief Deity of the Twelve Guardians who represents fertility and luck.
•Odd eyed.
•Those aren't antenna—it's actually just bed head.
"Kikaku Jingi"
•The plainest looking of all Twelve Guardi...
《RIKUGO
•She tri... as it tries to fly a...
SAKURA SADA
"Rikugo
《SEIRYU》 KA
•Guardia
Seiten R
A m
B
《TENKO》
•The goddess of fertility.
•Represents womanlines motherhood.
SUBARU MITE
•Always smilin
•The Kegare
"Ten
《KOCHIN》
NARUMI IORO
•Depict
prote
castle
•Repres
labor,
stubbo
•Big fa
(nine
•Basical
very so
•Height
Weigh
(By the
his wife
is 5'0"
over 22
•Head
over
heels
"Koden Chinza"
•A super huge wall will appear.
《TENKU》
CORDE
•Her arms are not under an enchantment, it's just really cool-looking armor.
•She may be quiet and unsociable and she may make clanking sounds like a ghost when she walks...But Corde is an ordinary human.
《GENBU》
KENGO UJ
"Gentei Bu
》MIK
Daigi You

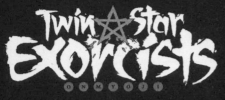

—SHONEN JUMP Manga Edition—

STORY & ART **Yoshiaki Sukeno**

TRANSLATION **Tetsuichiro Miyaki**
ENGLISH ADAPTATION **Bryant Turnage**
TOUCH-UP ART & LETTERING **Stephen Dutro**
DESIGN **Shawn Carrico**
EDITOR **Annette Roman**

SOUSEI NO ONMYOJI © 2013 by Yoshiaki Sukeno
All rights reserved.
First published in Japan in 2013 by SHUEISHA Inc., Tokyo.
English translation rights arranged by SHUEISHA Inc.

The stories, characters and incidents mentioned in this
publication are entirely fictional.

Printed in the U.S.A.

Published by VIZ Media, LLC
P.O. Box 77010
San Francisco, CA 94107

10 9 8 7 6 5 4 3 2 1
First printing, October 2016

www.viz.com

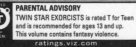

PARENTAL ADVISORY
TWIN STAR EXORCISTS is rated T for Teen
and is recommended for ages 13 and up.
This volume contains fantasy violence.
ratings.viz.com

www.shonenjump.com

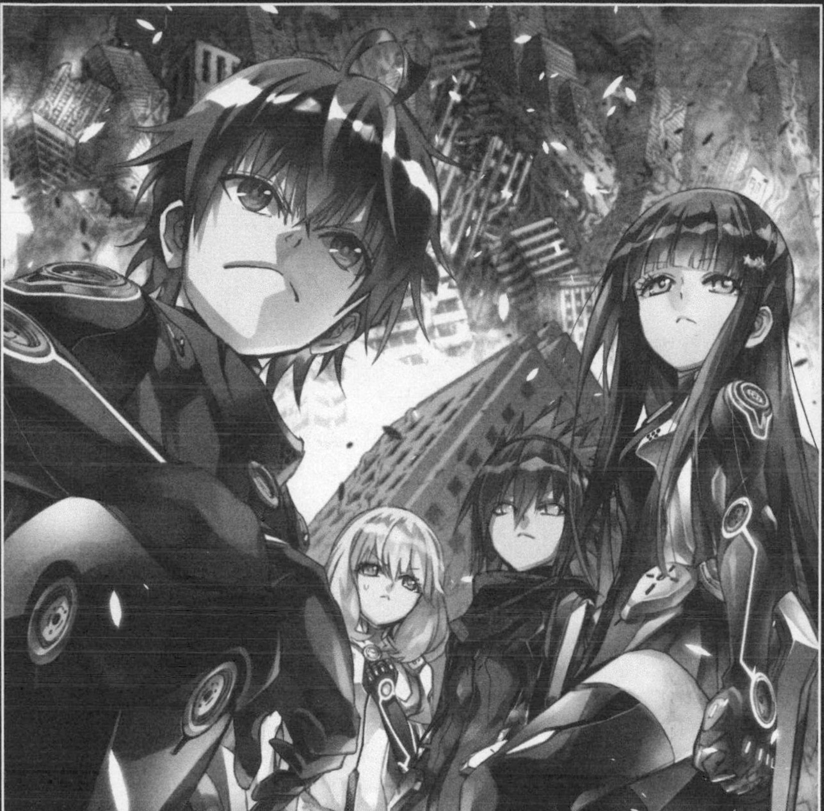
Rokuro's Spiritual Guardian appears to be someone it can't possibly be. Then, despite warnings, Guardian Shimon recruits the Twin Stars to help him rescue a young exorcist in training. But why does Seigen add his daughter, newbie exorcist Mayura, to their team...?
Volume 7 available January 2017!

Twin Star Exorcists

ONMYOJI

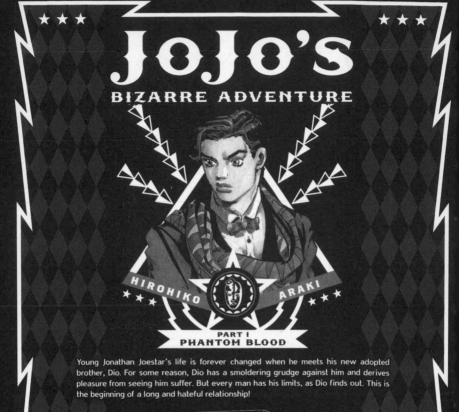
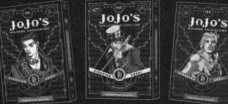
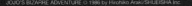

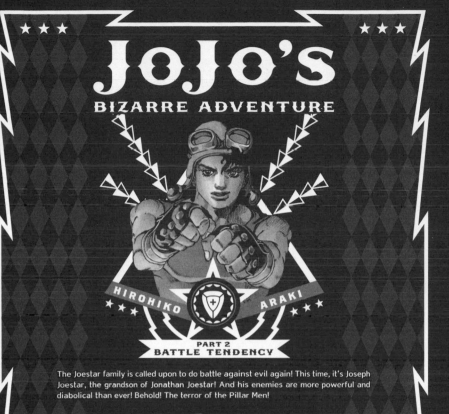
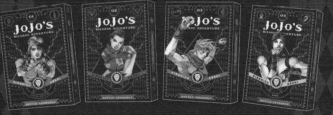

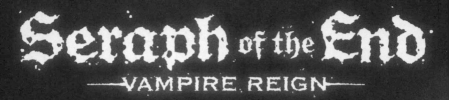
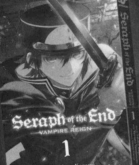

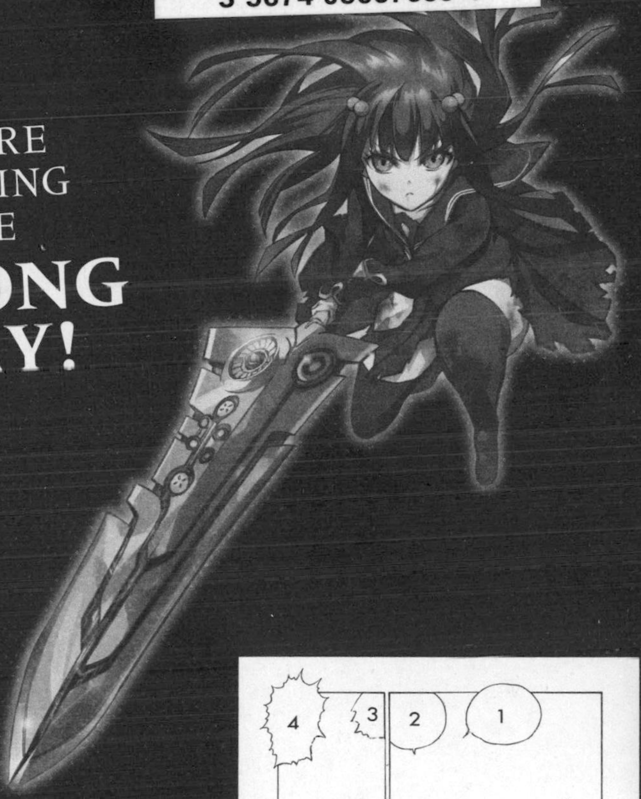

YOU'RE
READING
THE
**WRONG
WAY!**

Twin Star Exorcists reads from right to left, starting in the upper-right corner. Japanese is read from right to left, meaning that action, sound effects and word-balloon order are completely reversed from English order.

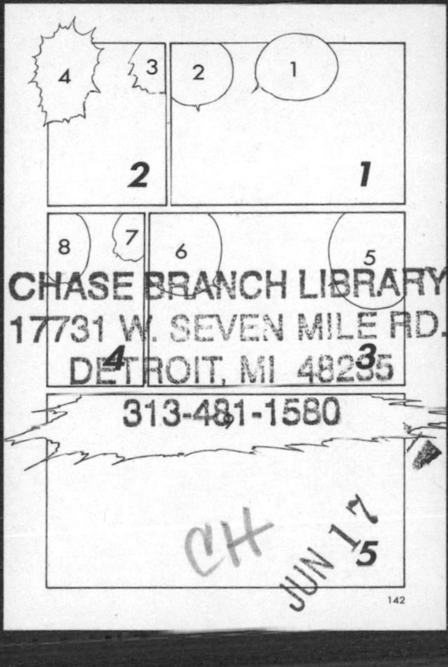
1
2
1
3
4
2
5
6
3
7
8
4
5
142